PARAMETRIC METHODS FOR BEGINNERS

This book introduces architectural applications of parametric methods in design, drawing direct connections between each phase of the architectural design process with relevant parametric approaches.

Readers will find applications of parametric methods with straightforward explanations of concepts, commands as well as applicable examples for each phase of the architectural design process. In addition to learning about the historical and conceptual background of parametric design, readers can use this book as a go-to source during their day-to-day design practice. Chapters are organized according to different phases of the architectural design process, such as site analysis, spatial organization, skin systems, and environmental performance analyses. Together, they deliver concepts, applications, and examples utilizing in-depth visual guides that explain commands, their outcomes, and their interrelationships. With over 350 images, this book includes examples from the author's own design studio and parametric design teaching in elective classes.

Based on the Rhinoceros and Grasshopper platforms, this book is an accessible, yet in-depth, resource for architecture students and early professionals who are considering integrating parametric applications into their design processes.

Umut Toker is Professor of Architecture in the College of Architecture and Environmental Design at California Polytechnic State University, San Luis Obispo. Umut received his PhD from North Carolina State University School of Architecture, College of Design. He holds both Bachelor of Architecture and Master of Urban Design degrees from Middle East Technical University in Ankara, Turkey. Umut's research and scholarship has been published in journals such as the *Journal of Architectural and Planning Research*, *Research Policy*, and *METU Journal of the Faculty of Architecture*. In 2012, his book on community design methods, *Making Community Design Work*, was published.

PARAMETRIC METHODS FOR BEGINNERS

ARCHITECTURE APPLICATIONS

Umut Toker

Routledge
Taylor & Francis Group
NEW YORK AND LONDON

Designed cover image: Umut Toker.

First published 2023
by Routledge
605 Third Avenue, New York, NY 10158

and by Routledge
4 Park Square, Milton Park, Abingdon, Oxon, OX14 4RN

Routledge is an imprint of the Taylor & Francis Group, an informa business

Library of Congress Cataloging-in-Publication Data
Names: Toker, Umut, author.
Title: Parametric methods for beginners: architecture applications/Umut Toker.
Description: New York: Routledge, 2023. | Includes bibliographical references. |
Identifiers: LCCN 2022031679 | ISBN 9781032136004 (hardback) |
ISBN 9781032136011 (paperback) | ISBN 9781003230052 (ebook)
Subjects: LCSH: Architectural design–Data processing. | Architecture–Mathematics. |
Parameter estimation. | Rhino (Computer file)
Classification: LCC NA2728 .T65 2023 | DDC 720.285–dc23/eng/20220720
LC record available at https://lccn.loc.gov/2022031679

ISBN: 978-1-032-13600-4 (hbk)
ISBN: 978-1-032-13601-1 (pbk)
ISBN: 978-1-003-23005-2 (ebk)

DOI: 10.4324/9781003230052

Typeset in Helvetica
by Deanta Global Publishing Services, Chennai, India

For Product Safety Concerns and Information please contact our EU representative:
GPSR@taylorandfrancis.com
Taylor & Francis Verlag GmbH, Kaufingerstraße 24, 80331 München, Germany.

DISCLAIMER

Every effort has been made to contact copyright-holders. Please advise the publisher of any errors or omissions, and these will be corrected in subsequent editions. During the development of this book, every effort has been shown to contact and acknowledge any individual who agreed to contribute any visual material for this book. To the publisher and the author's knowledge, no copyrighted images or text were included in the work without acknowledgment of their author(s). If informed, any omitted or erroneous acknowledgments will be updated and / or corrected by the publishers in later prints and / or editions of this book.

The publisher and author of this book have exhibited their strongest efforts in the development of this book. No warranties of any kind by the publisher, or by the author are offered, implied, or expressed with regards to the explanations, illustrations, or documentation included in this book. Neither the publisher nor the author accepts any liability for any damages, including, but not limited to lost profits, incidental and / or consequential damages related to the explanations, illustrations, or documentation included in this book.

Dedication

Dedicated to Mustafa Kemal Atatürk, the founder of the democratic and secular Republic of Turkey.

In Memoriam

In loving memory of my grandparents, Sıdıka Toker, Ömer Toker, Ulviye Türkan Usta, and Osman Usta. You are all dearly missed.

CONTENTS

Software and Plug-in Acknowledgments xv
Acknowledgments xvii

CHAPTER 01 Introduction to Parametric Design: Basics in Relation to Architectural Design Process Phases 1
1.1 What Is Parametric Design? 2
1.2 Developments in Design Thinking 4
1.2.1 Cognitive Models of Design Thinking 4
1.2.2 Computational Models of Digital Design Thinking: Computer-Aided Design and Digital Architectural Design 4
1.2.3 The New Wave of Digital Design: Parametric Models of Design 5
1.3 Basics of Parametric Interface, CAD Interface, and Parametric Relationships Using Rhinoceros and Grasshopper 6
1.3.1 Relationships between Geometry and Geometric Representations in Rhinoceros and Grasshopper 6
1.3.2 Basic Command Component Structure in Rhinoceros ... 7
1.3.3 Coordinated Interrelationships of Components in Grasshopper 8
1.4 Parametric Thinking, Parametric Methods, and the Architectural Design Process 9

CHAPTER 02 History and Conceptual Framework of Parametric Design in Architecture 10
2.1 Parametric Thinking: Before Computers and Digital Methods for Parametric Thinking 11
2.2 Parametric Design Following the Proliferation of Computers and Digital Applications 11
2.3 "Parametricism" and the Current Debate 13
2.3.1 The Parametricist Manifesto of 2008 13
2.3.2 Responses and Discussions Triggered by the Parametricist Manifesto 14
2.3.3 Parametricism 2.0 16
2.4 Parametric Design and Architectural Research 17
2.4.1 The Operationalization Challenge 17
2.4.2 Parametric Methods and Architectural Research 17
2.5 Parametric Design and Prospective Futures 18

CHAPTER 03 Site Analysis: Understanding the Site and Its Context Using Parametric Methods 20
3.1 Site Analysis: Methods 20
3.1.1 Site visits, observations, and archival methods 20
3.2 Elements of Site Analysis 21

3.2.1 Contextual Information, Rules, Regulations, and Physical Conditions in and around the Site 21
3.2.2 Environmental Information about the Site and Its Context 21
3.3 Parametric Methods for Site Analysis 22
3.3.1 Environment-Related Information That Can Be Analyzed Using Grasshopper 22
3.3.2 Accessing Local Climate Data 22
3.3.3 The Psychrometric Chart 24
3.3.4 Analyzing Solar Conditions 24
3.4 Site Conditions in Relation to Thermal Comfort 31
3.4.1 Mean Radiant Temperature and Outdoor Mean Radiant Temperature 32
3.4.2 Relative Humidity 32
3.4.3 Analyzing Wind 34
3.4.4 Bringing Thermal Comfort Information Together: Universal Thermal Climate Index 36
3.5 Site Conditions in Relation to Contextual Visual Connections 36
3.5.1 The Isovist 36
3.5.2 Visibility Percent Analysis 41
3.6 Site Conditions in Relation to Slope 41
3.6.1 Slope 41
3.6.2 Basic Even Subdivision of Surfaces 44
3.6.3 Visualizing a Site's Slope Condition 45
3.7 Using Site Analysis Findings to Inform Conceptual Development 47

CHAPTER 04 Conceptual and Preliminary Development: Formal Explorations and Iterations With Parametric Methods 48
4.1 Parametric Tools in Form Exploration for Conceptual and Preliminary Development 48
4.1.1 Parametrically Creating and Editing Irregular Shapes and Surfaces: NURBS Geometries 49
4.1.2 Parametrically Creating and Editing Irregular SubD Geometries: Meshes 56
4.2 Parametric Tools in Analyzing Contextual Relationships to Support Preliminary Development 63

CHAPTER 05 Spatial Organization and Visibility Analysis Using Parametric Methods 75
5.1 Visibility Analyses in Design Development 75
5.1.1 Basic Two-Dimensional Visibility Analysis for Interiors 75
5.1.2 Basic Interspatial Visibility Analysis Using Grasshopper's Native "Isovist" Component for Building Interiors 76
5.1.3 Representing Space and Movement in Visibility Analysis: The Minkowski Model 81
5.2 Spatial Organization Analysis in Design Development 83
5.2.1 Basic Definitions in Space Syntax Methods 83

CHAPTER 06 Skin Systems: Repetition, Subdividing Geometries, and Paneling Approaches ... 86
6.1 Surface Subdivision ... 87
6.1.1 Subdividing Complex Surfaces Creating Straight Edges for Simplified Subsurfaces ... 91
6.1.2 Subdividing Complex Surfaces with Commonly Utilized Plug-ins ... 92
6.2 Relationships with Daylight: Direct Sun Hours Analysis of Building Components ... 93
6.2.1 Direct Sun Hours Analysis of Building Components ... 93
6.2.2 Preliminary Interpretations of the Results of Direct Sun Hours Analysis: Designing Parametric Façade Screen Systems to Balance Direct Sun Hours ... 94
6.3 Other Repetition and Paneling Approaches to Subdividing Surfaces ... 109
6.4 Repetition and Paneling Approaches Subdividing Complex Geometries ... 114
6.5 Populating Complex Surfaces with Predesigned Units: Repeating Modular Units on Complex Surfaces ... 115
6.6 Populating Complex Surfaces with Predesigned Units: Repeating Modular Units on Complex Surfaces to Avoid Distortion ... 115
6.7 Conclusion ... 118
Note ... 118

CHAPTER 07 Evolutionary Applications: Using Parametric Applications to Generate, Analyze, and Select Design Iterations ... 119
7.1 Evolutionary Applications: Background ... 119
7.2 The Solution Process ... 120
7.2.1 Advantages and Disadvantages of Evolutionary Solvers ... 121
7.3 Single-Objective Optimization ... 122
7.4 Evolutionary Solvers in Architecture: Single Objective Optimization Examples ... 126
7.4.1 Identifying the Orientation of Workspaces to Minimize Direct Sun Access and Glare ... 126
7.4.2 Identifying the Building Orientation That Allows Maximum Access to Desired Views ... 128
7.4.3 Identifying the Highest Visibility Point for Multiple Storefronts for a Commercial Space ... 130
7.5 Multi-objective Optimization ... 131
7.5.1 Defining a Multi-objective Optimization Problem ... 132
7.5.2 The Optimization Procedure ... 133
7.5.3 Interpreting Findings ... 133
7.6 Evolutionary Solvers in Architecture: Multi-objective Optimization Examples ... 135
7.6.1 Optimizing Building Orientation to Minimize Energy Consumption ... 135
7.6.2 Optimizing Views and Square Footage to Increase Real Estate Value ... 140

CHAPTER 08 Parametric Methods for Introductory Environmental Performance Analyses ... 147
8.1 Architectural Design and Energy ... 147
8.1.1 Architecture 2030 ... 148
8.1.2 Energy Use Intensity ... 148
8.1.3 Surface Area to Volume Ratio ... 149
8.2 Parametric Methods for Analyzing Energy Use Implications ... 149
8.2.1 EUI: Basic Simulation Using Ladybug, Honeybee, and Honeybee Energy ... 149
8.2.2 EUI: Multiple Building Use Zone Simulation Using Ladybug, Honeybee, and Honeybee Energy ... 152
8.2.3 Looking into EUI With a Louver System ... 157
8.2.4 Surface Area to Volume Ratio (SA/V) as It Relates to EUI ... 158
8.3 Architectural Design and Daylight ... 160
8.3.1 Spatial Daylight Autonomy (SDA) ... 161
8.4 Parametric Methods for Analyzing Lighting and Energy Use Implications ... 161
8.4.1 Looking into SDA With a Louver System ... 163
8.5 Measuring Building Environmental Performance Using "Ladybug Tools": Observations ... 165

CHAPTER 09 Practical Matters: Parametric Methods and Digital Fabrication for Architectural Model Making ... 166
9.1 Cutting Operations and Parametric Methods in Architectural Modeling ... 168
9.1.1 Laser Cutting ... 168
9.1.2 Plasma Cutting ... 171
9.1.3 Waterjet Cutting ... 172
9.1.4 Time-Saving Model Building Strategies Using Parametric Methods with Cutting Operations in Mind ... 172
9.2 Additive Techniques: Three-Dimensional Printing ... 175
9.2.1 Fused Deposition Modeling 3D Printing Basics ... 178
9.2.2 FDM 3D Printing in the Architectural Design Process ... 180
9.3 Subtractive Techniques ... 180
9.3.1 Basic CNC Milling Steps ... 182
9.4 Mixing and Matching Methods and Materials: Digital Fabrication Techniques and Architectural Model Building Materials ... 184
9.4.1 Representing the Site ... 184
9.4.2 Representing the Structural System and Slabs ... 184
9.4.3 Representing Vertical Circulation Elements ... 185
9.4.4 Representing Façade Materials ... 185
9.4.5 Entourage ... 185
9.5 Possible Developments: Parametric Methods, Digital Fabrication, and the Future of Architectural Model Making ... 186

CHAPTER 10 Recontextualizing Parametric Methods in Architecture: Routes for Further Development ... 187

10.1 Contributions of Parametric Methods in the Architectural Design Process ... 187

10.1.1 Contributions to Development, Analysis, and Manipulation of Complex Geometries ... 188

10.1.2 Contributions by Bringing in Empirical Approaches and Methods into the Architectural Design Process ... 188

10.1.3 Decreasing the Number of Third-Party Software and Streamlining the Design Process ... 189

10.1.4 Time- and Effort-Saving Optimization Techniques in Design Decision-making: Evolutionary Solvers ... 189

10.1.5 Advances in Digital Fabrication Methods and Tools ... 190

10.2 Computer-Aided Design, Parametric Design, Digital Fabrication, and Emerging Concerns in Architectural Design ... 191

10.3 Parametric Futures ... 193

10.3.1 Stronger Connections Between Design Disciplines and Basic Science ... 193

10.3.2 Key Skills Remain Crucial ... 193

10.3.3 Architects and Designers Mastering Data Management ... 194

10.3.4 Looking into the Future ... 194

References ... 195

Index ... 198

SOFTWARE AND PLUG-IN ACKNOWLEDGMENTS

This text mentions the names of multiple software and plug-ins for explanation only. The names of these software and plug-ins may be registered trademarks or trademarks. These include the following:

Rhinoceros and Grasshopper are registered trademarks of Robert McNeel and Associates. The Paneling Tools plug-in for Rhinoceros and Grasshopper was developed by Rajaa Issa and McNeel Associates. The Galapagos evolutionary solver plug-in, which is a part of core Rhinoceros, was developed by David Rutten. The Octopus evolutionary solver plug-in was developed by Robert Vierlinger. The LunchBox plug-in was developed by Nathan Miller, CEO of Proving Ground. The Weaverbird plug-in was developed by Giulio Piacentino. Weaverbird is a trademark of Giulio Piacentino and/or respective suppliers.

Ladybug Tools was originally started by Mostapha Sadeghipour Roudsari, who was later joined by Chris Mackey for further development. As of the writing of this book, Ladybug Tools and their accompanying plug-ins and tools were being maintained by Mostapha Sadeghipour Roudsari, Chris Mackey, and a team of contributors. Ladybug Tools logo and Ladybug Tools are registered trademarks of Ladybug Tools LLC.

The digital studio site context models (displayed in Figures 3.2 to 3.5, 3.9, 3.13 to 3.15, 4.12 to 4.15, 6.5 to 6.9, 6.12, to 6.19, and 8.8) were developed by the author with his students' help for use by the entire studio. For some of these digital studio site context models, and for some digital site context models displayed in other figures, the website https://cadmapper.com and other data sources were consulted. The website https://cadmapper.com data files are distributed under the Open Database License. More information is available at https://www.openstreetmap.org/copyright.

ACKNOWLEDGMENTS

First and foremost, I am grateful for the presence of my beloved family for standing with me all these years and through the writing of this book. My parents, Nedret Toker and Mithat Toker, who are scientists, teachers, and avid followers of empirical and artful thinking, are behind everything I have ever accomplished in my life. My sister Dr. Mine Toker, my best friend forever, never failed me for a second in my life. A scientist, academic, and art lover herself, she has always inspired and supported me in every single endeavor in my life. Without my parents and my sister, I would be unable to start and sustain my career, let alone publish any academic works. Thank you to my dear family for supporting and teaching me about the power and value of knowledge. Furthermore, I would like to sincerely thank my spouse, Dr. Isinsu Baylam, for standing with me through the writing process of this book. She always believed in my efforts and supported me as a science and art lover herself.

I am grateful to my colleagues and my former students at Cal Poly SLO Architecture for reviewing and providing feedback for various chapters of this book. I also would like to thank all my students, who have taken my architectural design studios and parametric design elective classes over the years for their enthusiasm, feedback, support, and hard work.

Finally, anonymous peer reviewers invited by Routledge and my editor colleagues at Routledge have been very helpful throughout the development of this book with their feedback. Thank you, all.

May 2022
San Luis Obispo, California, USA

CHAPTER 01

INTRODUCTION TO PARAMETRIC DESIGN Basics in Relation to Architectural Design Process Phases

Whether you are a practicing architect, an architectural designer, or an architecture student, imagine receiving a new project proposal, a design problem, a program, a new site – a new challenge as a designer. The scenario you have in hand has all of the usual architectural challenges you are familiar with: programmatic challenges that emerge with the project description, site and environmental performance-related inputs, structure-related possibilities, along with new ideas on the physical expression of the building in relation to all of the other factors you have in mind. You can always employ the familiar design thinking and design methods to develop a design proposition; however, based on recent reviews of architectural literature and media you think that deploying parametric thinking and parametric methods may lead to a novel design proposition that responds to multiple inputs. You would like to experiment with this new approach, but you are not sure where to begin. In addition, the language and methods look so specific and technical that they feel intimidating as a designer. After all, you are an architect, an architecture student, a designer. How can one employ parametric design thinking and parametric methods in their architectural design processes without getting buried under a large pile of technical terms and a completely new language?

Parametric methods in architecture are an addition to the arsenal of architects' tools. ***Parametric thinking*** is different from pre-parametric ways of design thinking in various ways. Parametric thinking requires a nonlinear approach. Although we say the design process is nonlinear, its conceptualization is to a large extent linear. Although designers visit phases of the architectural design process in a nonlinear fashion, the conceptualization remains linear: we usually start with studying the program, then analyze the site, develop design concepts, develop the design, detail it, and prepare for presentation. We visit these phases numerous times back and forth throughout the design process.

Parametric thinking, however, requires knowledge beyond (on top of) this traditional knowledge of the architectural design process. When we employ parametric thinking and parametric methods in the architectural design process, we not only design the building as required by the program; we also need to consider the parametric workflow. When designing the parametric workflow, we need to design the sequence in which parametric methods will operate. This is commonly referred to as the ***script***, or, the ***definition***.

In addition to learning about parametric thinking and how to use parametric methods, parametric design in architecture also requires us to rediscover principles we learned in our physics, mathematics, geometry, and biology classes. Many parametric methods employ concepts and calculations from such basic sciences to help build them easily into the design process.

DOI: 10.4324/9781003230052-1

This constitutes the rationale behind writing this book. Parametric design in architecture requires the designer to learn a new language and elaborate their design ideas proficiently in that new language. Thus, it is intimidating. There are many good publications out there introducing teaching parametric methods in architecture, but they tend to be software oriented. That is, they introduce concepts and operations based on the structure of the software package they focus on. There are even more guides that can be found online – written, image based, or video tutorials demonstrating methods. However, these tend to be software oriented as well.

As architecture students, architects and designers, we know the architectural language best. So, we need a resource relating this new way of thinking and this new set of methods to our modes of thinking and understanding of the phases of designing, so that we can learn parametric thinking and parametric methods by relating them to our work, instead of memorizing commands and procedures. This is what this book is about. The objective here is to introduce parametric thinking and parametric methods to architecture students and professionals in an accessible language – the architect's language.

1.1 WHAT IS PARAMETRIC DESIGN?

Our familiar architectural design medium is paper based. Tracing paper, pencil, and eraser are our foundational tools in architectural design. Using these basic materials, we can achieve precision if we add tools such as a T-square, triangles, rulers, and a straight-edged drafting surface (Woodbury, 2010). All architects, architecture students and architectural designers use and treasure these tools, even though today computer-aided design (CAD) software has alleviated a good portion of the time spent in the architectural design process. So, what does CAD software do?

Becoming accessible to many designers and offices in the 1980s, computer-aided design software essentially imitated the conventional architectural design medium. Whether precise or not, they enabled architects to draw lines and curves and, if necessary, to delete (erase) and edit them. In doing so, they became incredibly time-saving tools. Using concepts such as blocks and layers, they made it easy to organize components of drawings, and enabled rapidly mass-editing of them. CAD software also increased the speed in which architects could develop perspective drawings, making it easy to view the design proposal from multiple angles, both inside and outside. Furthermore, CAD software made walk-through and walk-around animations easily developable by using financially accessible everyday computers. This brought an advanced experiential medium to the architectural design process, enhancing testing of design ideas, presentations, and communication with clients.

Nevertheless, architects' design thinking processes remained essentially the same while using CAD software. Using CAD software, we still mainly engage in exploration and draw as if we are using pencil and paper. We do so, using our knowledge of how to run the software: we use commands such as "line," "circle," "trim," "delete," "extend," etc. to replicate what we do on paper. ***Just like on paper, when we edit a part of the drawing, the remaining parts are not affected.*** For example, when we delete a line, the neighboring elements (lines, curves, points, etc.) are not affected. We just do the eraser's job using a keyboard and a mouse within the medium of the preferred CAD software.

This process changes in parametric design. First off, in parametric design there are two interfaces. The first interface, the ***parametric interface***, is for writing the "script" – the medium in which command components that direct the connected CAD software are located, arranged, and interconnected in a linear fashion. This medium interacts with the CAD software, which receives instructions from the ***parametric interface*** and visualizing geometry in the ***CAD interface***. In essence, the ***parametric interface*** is for writing the commands, and the ***CAD interface*** is for visualizing the geometries requested by the ***parametric interface*** (Figure 1.1).

The key difference of the parametric interface from the CAD interface is that, its command components interrelate to one another, and when one command component changes, interconnected other command components change as well. As a result, the visualization of geometry in the CAD interface changes. All of these operations happen real-time, so when the designer changes parameters of a command component – say, the scale factor of a scaling procedure – all command components that come after the scale component, ***and*** the visualization on the CAD interface, change and update accordingly.

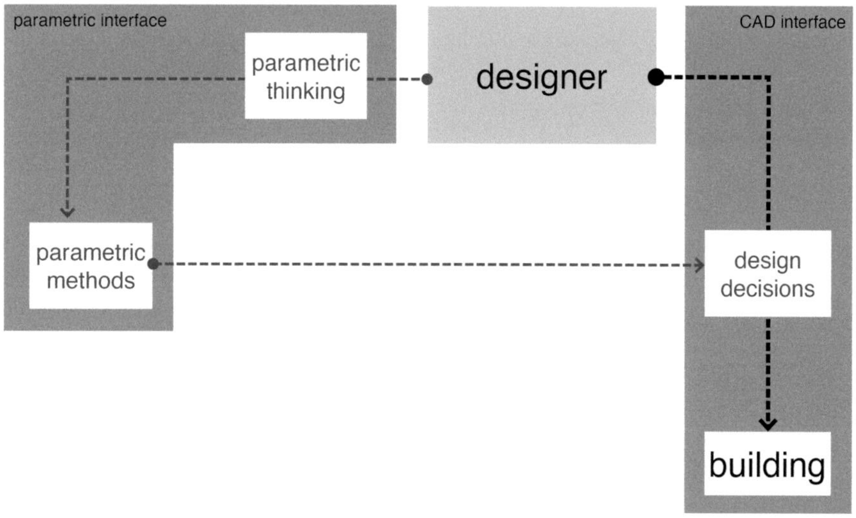

Figure 1.1 *Relationships among the designer, parametric thinking, parametric methods, design decisions, and the resulting building.*

This interrelated, coordinated change procedure makes parametric design different from earlier design approaches. Be it on paper or on CAD software, when we change or edit a geometry, the remaining geometries remain the same. In parametric design, however, one can make multiple changes and/or edits by altering the parameters of one command component. Robert Woodbury (2010) describes this parametric procedure as follows:

> ***Parametric modeling*** (also known as ***constraint modeling***) introduces a fundamental change: "marks," that is, ***parts of a design***, relate and change together in a coordinated way. No longer must designers simply add and erase. They now ***add, erase, relate*** and ***repair.*** (Woodbury, 2010: 11. All emphases in italics belong to R. Woodbury.)

Another aspect of parametric design in architecture is that it is usually deployed to address specific generative or performative design objectives for parts of the overall design proposition. The overall composition of a building can certainly be developed parametrically during the conceptual development process. Often, however, parts of the design are resolved using parametric design – such as resolving a façade system through form generation or performative objectives.

1.2 DEVELOPMENTS IN DESIGN THINKING

Now that we have an introductory description of parametric design, let us take a look into developments and differences in various modes of design thinking, so that we can locate parametric design in the larger universe of design thinking.

Researchers have long been studying the ways in which designers think and make design decisions. Usually referred to as "design studies" or "design research," this line of research focuses on peeling the layers of design processes and building explanations about how designers operate in various design media: paper-based, computer-aided, digital, parametric, etc.

In her 2017 article, Rivka Oxman reviews the developments in research into design thinking, and identifies three models of design thinking based on existing research: cognitive models of design thinking, computational models of digital design thinking, and parametric models of design. The author places parametric design thinking at the intersection of these three lines of thought. Indeed, once one becomes familiar with parametric design thinking, it becomes clear that parametric design thinking carries knowledge and design approaches from all three of these lines of thought. Let us take a look at the three lines of research that helped explain cognitive models of design thinking, computational models of digital design thinking, and parametric models of design.

1.2.1 Cognitive Models of Design Thinking

A prominent line of research in the area of design thinking emerged in the early 1980s, with the work of Nigel Cross (1982). Through observations of designers' behavior during the design process, this line of research developed a cognitive model of design thinking. This research-based model of design thinking proposes that in the design process, designers first take a design action and then reflect upon the outcomes of this action, evaluating the positive and negative characteristics of the design as it stands. They then develop modifications for the design based on this evaluation. These modifications result in refinements. Through multiple refinements, designers go through refinement cycles and reach a design proposition. Needless to say, in the 1980s, this line of research and its result, this cognitive model of design thinking, focused on the paper-based medium.

Another prominent line of research was developed by Schön (1983). Based on systematic observations of designers during the design process, Schön's cognitive model of design thinking proposes that designers, after making design decisions and reflecting upon them, make a new design move as a response to the outcomes of their reflection. Then, through naming and framing, designers bring in the influence of the context into the design process. Through continuous observation-based research, the model proposes that patterns of reasoning in designers' behavior can be identified. Like the work of Nigel Cross, this cognitive model of design thinking also focused on the paper-based medium.

1.2.2 Computational Models of Digital Design Thinking: Computer-Aided Design and Digital Architectural Design

With the proliferation of computer-aided design software, research on design thinking started to yield new findings about the design process. As discussed in the previous section, early CAD applications essentially imitated the paper-based medium. Nevertheless, they did bring in time-saving techniques as well as developments in design evaluation and representation, such as the rapid development of multiple three-dimensional (i.e., axonometric, perspective) views and animations. These developments clearly contributed to the reflective and evaluative phases of the design process.

Post 2000, three-dimensional form making and visualization capabilities of CAD software significantly increased. Besides rapid two and three-dimensional representation, many software packages started offering easy, rapid generation and editing of complex forms. In her 2007 article, Rivka Oxman differentiates Digital Architectural Design (DAD) from Computer-Aided Design (CAD) and proposes that while CAD was based on imitating paper-based processes, DAD focused on digital form making and the processes that lead to digital form.

In this article, Oxman (2007) proposed that architecture then faced new terrain in design thinking, and we went through a paradigm shift in the architectural design process. A new form of architectural knowledge emerged as the relationship between digital design and digital design models. Digital methodologies, at that point, enabled generative and performative processes that were not available in conventional paper-based methods. This started to affect the sequences of conventional design process phases. In that same article, Oxman discusses Gehry's Disney Concert Hall as an example of DAD and a display of departure from predefined formalism: it sets an example for the influences of digital design on conceptualization and formal response, while demonstrating the disappearance of hierarchy and the introduction of complex forms in digital architectural design.

This period of digital architectural design thinking displays a rejection of compositional strategies offered by modern and postmodern thinking, while designers' dependence on precedents and typologies are being replaced by generative and performance-based approaches in digital design (Oxman, 2007). Thus, the early 2000s witnessed the start of a paradigm shift in design thinking: while reflective processes as identified by cognitive models of design thinking continued in designers' minds, the medium of digital architectural design started to enable and encourage new modes of design thinking in form making through generative and performance-based approaches.

1.2.3 The New Wave of Digital Design: Parametric Models of Design

Looking into parametric design with the developments discussed in the previous section in mind, it becomes clear that many of the principles in design thinking exist within parametric design. Based on our earlier introductory definition of parametric design, then, in parametric design, exploration and editing/re-editing happen through associative relationships of geometry within the parametric interface. Cognitive design thinking phases such as exploration, design decision, reflection, and modification still exist in parametric design. However, due to its capacity of editing associative relationships, parametric design makes it possible to alter the sequence of events (Oxman, 2017). One can place parametric thinking and parametric methods within the larger universe of design thinking as a new way of thinking and a new set of tools that enable nonlinear information flow (Figure 1.2).

Oxman (2017) specifies two interrelated types of parametric modeling: generative and performative. In generative parametric modeling, the focus is on form generation through describing relationships between objects. The designer specifies the desired characteristics of the interrelationships, interdependencies, and transformations between objects using the parametric interface. Due to this interdependency between design elements, this process is nonhierarchical but form generation oriented. A simple example of generative parametric modeling could be the design of a modular façade system, where the scale of apertures on the modules gradually changes based on their location on the façade. Of course, the scale change parameters are defined by the designer using the parametric interface, and the outcomes are displayed on the CAD interface.

In performance-based parametric modeling, the focus is on performance simulations, using plug-ins and parametric components designed specifically to measure performance based

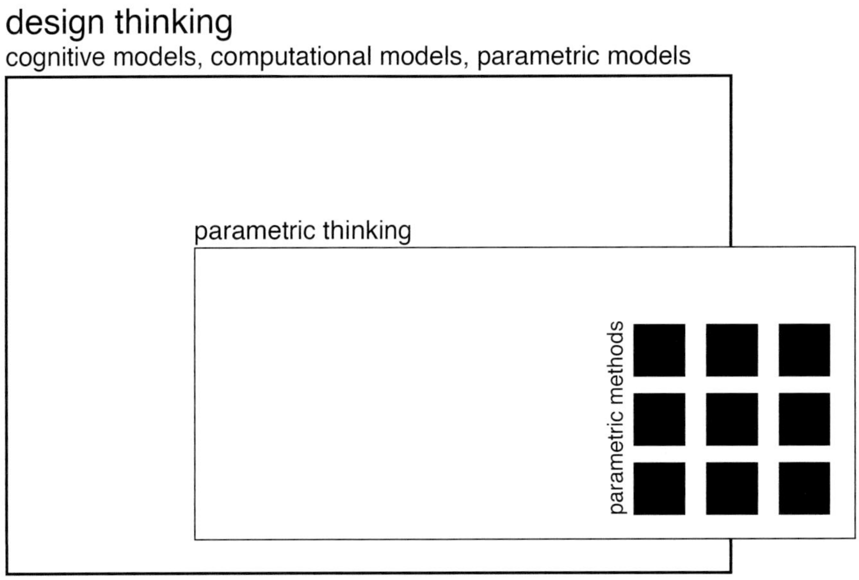

Figure 1.2 Parametric thinking and parametric methods in relation to the larger universe of design thinking.

outcomes on a given set of criteria. By observing the performance-based outcomes of design decisions and simultaneously editing parts of the design parametrically, the designer enhances performance. A simple example for performance-based parametric modeling could be to alter the scale of the apertures discussed earlier to minimize solar exposure on a south-facing façade. It is important to note here that generative parametric modeling and performance-based parametric modeling are not mutually exclusive: they often inform one another in support of informed decision-making.

1.3 BASICS OF PARAMETRIC INTERFACE, CAD INTERFACE, AND PARAMETRIC RELATIONSHIPS USING RHINOCEROS AND GRASSHOPPER

Having briefly introduced the definition, background, and basic principles of parametric design, it is time to illustrate the basic interface and command structure on software. There are various software packages available to designers. This book will illustrate software applications using Rhinoceros as the CAD software and Grasshopper as the parametric software. This selection was made due to the widespread use of these software in architecture schools, as well as by professionals beginning parametric design. Another factor is the fact that this software can operate on more than one operating systems. As discussed earlier, regardless of which software is used, the key in parametric design is to develop parametric thinking skills. Once parametric thinking develops and main parametric concepts are comprehended, designers can adapt to different CAD and parametric software packages.

The interface relationship between CAD and parametric software was conceptually introduced in Figure 1.1 using Rhinoceros and Grasshopper, this relationship is executed as illustrated in Figure 1.3. The designer uses one side of the screen to provide input into Grasshopper; the other side of the screen is used to view outcomes in Rhinoceros, which visualizes the geometric outcomes of Grasshopper commands.

1.3.1 Relationships between Geometry and Geometric Representations in Rhinoceros and Grasshopper

A key concept here is the difference between geometry created in Rhinoceros and Grasshopper. When a geometry such as a curve or surface is created in Rhinoceros, Grasshopper cannot recognize them. To introduce them into Grasshopper, the appropriate

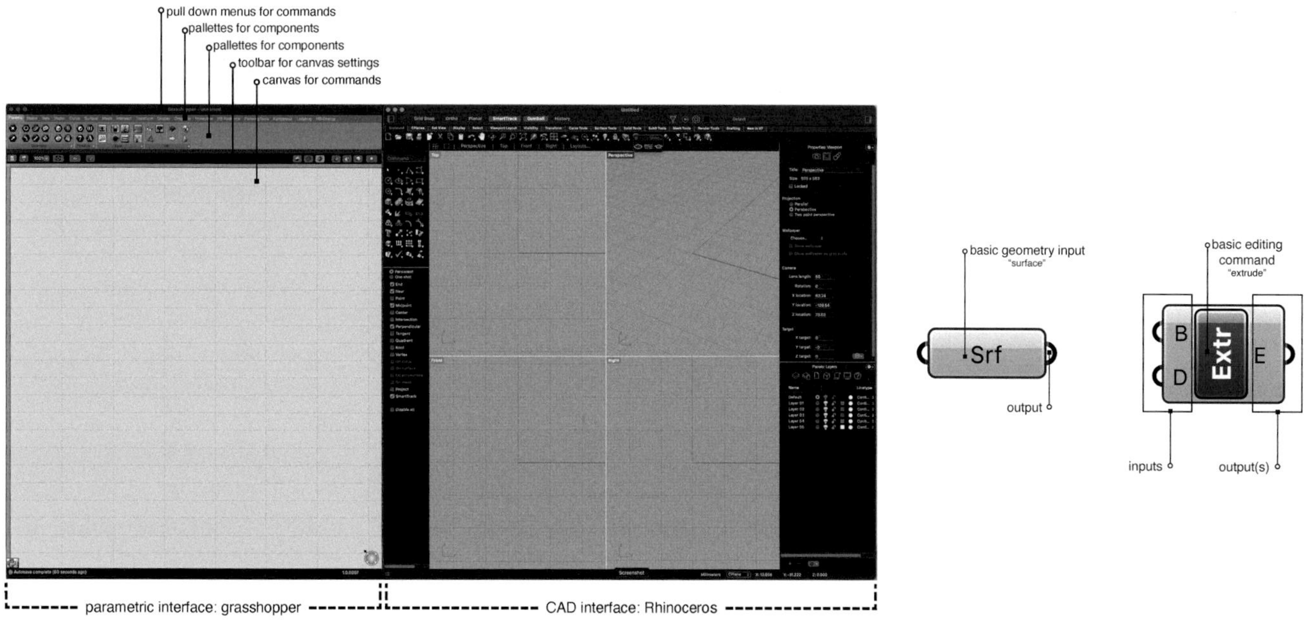

Figure 1.3 Left: Grasshopper/Rhinoceros interfaces. Right: "Surface," a basic geometry input, and "Extrude," a basic editing component. Note the data input and output connections on the basic editing component.

Grasshopper component needs to be brought onto the Grasshopper canvas (i.e., "curve," "surface," etc.). The user can right-click onto the Grasshopper component, and select "set one curve" or "set one surface" and then point at the vector-based geometry in Rhinoceros. As a result, Grasshopper recognizes and highlights the selected geometry.

A similar relationship exists between geometry created in Grasshopper and visualized in Rhinoceros. When a geometry is introduced in Grasshopper using a component (i.e., a sphere), it is visualized in Rhinoceros as a highlighted, semitransparent geometry. The user cannot manipulate this object using Rhinoceros commands, since it is a visualization, or a boundary representation (Brep) of the data provided to Grasshopper. All edits (i.e., sphere's center coordinates, its radius, etc.) can only be edited using the Grasshopper interface. To manipulate the geometry in Rhinoceros, the user needs to right-click on the Grasshopper component, and select "bake." The "bake" command converts the Grasshopper object from a visualization, or a Brep into a vector-based geometry in Rhinoceros.

1.3.2 Basic Command Component Structure in Rhinoceros

Figure 1.3 illustrates two basic Grasshopper command components: the "surface" component, on the left, is a basic geometry input. Basic geometry input components like "surface" can be connected to vector-based Rhinoceros geometry as discussed in Section 1.3.1. The "extrude" component on the right, however, is a basic editing component. Components like "extrude" require inputs on the left – in this case, B, being the base geometry to extrude, and D being the extrusion direction and magnitude. After the component processes the input data, the output data are provided on the right side of the component – in this case, E, being the output extruded geometry. The majority of Grasshopper components operate like this – input(s) on the left, component name in the middle on a black background, and output(s) on the right.

One important property of Grasshopper components is their capability of providing brief descriptions when the user floats their cursor over the component. When the user floats their cursor over input or output connections, brief information about the type of data that needs to be input or that will be output will be displayed. Similarly, when the user floats their cursor over the name of the component, brief information about how the component works is displayed. Components in Grasshopper can be selected from the component palettes or can be typed

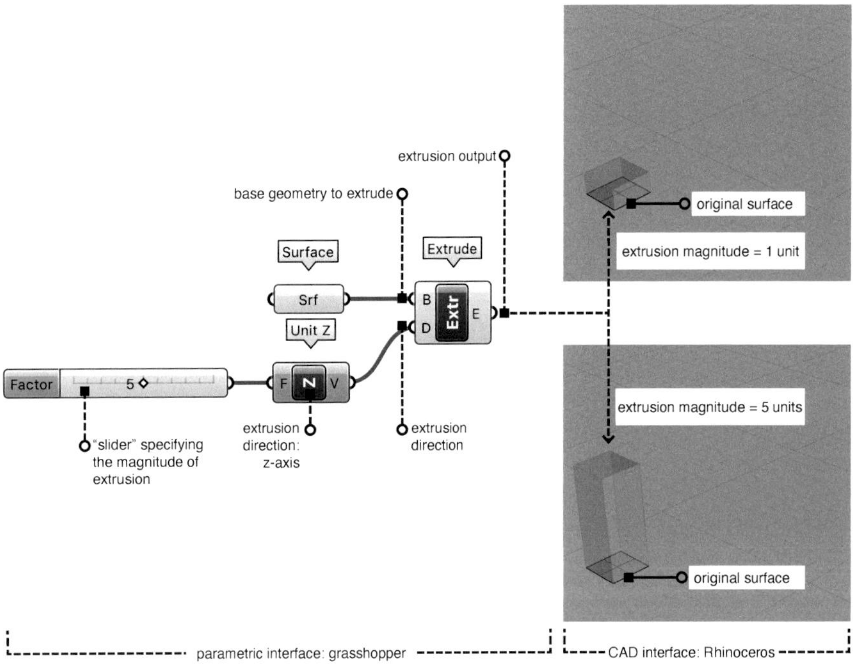

Figure 1.4 *Basic geometry editing and coordinated interrelationships of components in Grasshopper.*

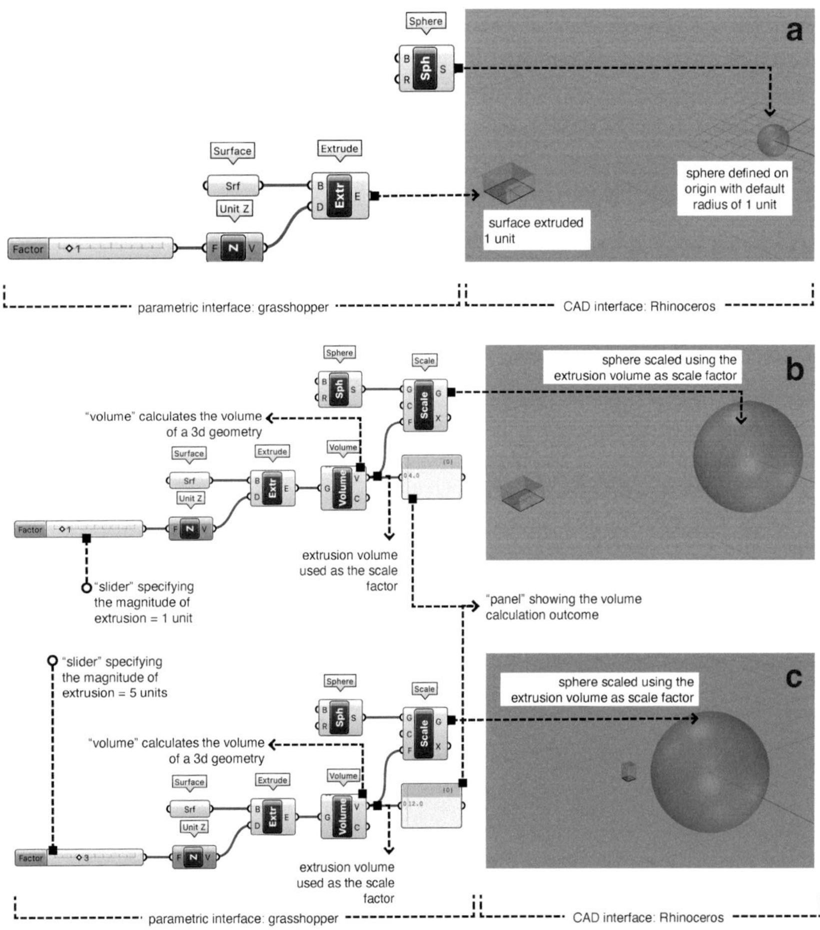

Figure 1.5 *(a) Sphere added into the script from Figure 1.4 using the "sphere" component; (b) Sphere scaled based on the volume magnitudes of the original extrusion; and (c) Sphere scaled based on the volume magnitudes of the original extrusion.*

onto the canvas after double-clicking anywhere on the canvas.

1.3.3 Coordinated Interrelationships of Components in Grasshopper

Since most Grasshopper components have input connections on the left and output connections on the right, script structure primarily moves from left to right. Figure 1.4 illustrates a basic example of this. The script starts with a square Rhinoceros surface introduced into Grasshopper. The extrude component is then provided with the surface to extrude, the Z-unit as the direction of extrusion, and an extrusion magnitude using a "slider." The slider is an adjustable component that provides numeric input into quantifiable operations. It can be set up to provide various minimum and maximum values, integers, and round numbers. The coordinated interrelationships between these components can be seen in Figure 1.4: when the slider is set to 1, the surface is extruded 1 unit; when it is set to another number (in this case, 5), the extrusion is edited real-time to that extrusion magnitude.

The coordinated interrelationships of components in Grasshopper can be extended into multiple processes and multiple geometries. This enables chain-linking multiple editing procedures. Figure 1.5 illustrates a basic example of this. In Figure 1.5a, a sphere is added into the script from Figure 1.4, using the "sphere" component. On the "space" component, the default base plane input is the "XY plane" with its center on the origin (0,0,0), and the default radius is a set to one unit. Therefore, although no input is provided to the "sphere" component, Rhinoceros still visualizes it with its center at the origin (0,0,0) and with a radius of one.

In Figures 1.5b and 1.5c, a "scale" component is connected to the sphere component. "F," the scale factor, requires a numeric input. In this example, using the "volume" component, the volume of the extruded rectangular prism is measured. The "V" output of the volume component, a numerical value, is then fed into the scale factor of the scale component. In Figure 1.5b, the sphere is scaled four times, since the volume of extrusion is four units. In Figure 1.5c, the sphere is scaled 12 times, since the volume of extrusion is 12 units. This example shows that by chain-linking multiple editing components, we can interrelate geometries. This example also shows that when multiple geometries are interconnected, we can control their properties at the same time by using a single data input – in this case, the slider that provides magnitude date to the initial extrusion.

1.4 PARAMETRIC THINKING, PARAMETRIC METHODS, AND THE ARCHITECTURAL DESIGN PROCESS

Parametric thinking and parametric methods can contribute to different phases of the architectural design process in different ways. This book is organized so that we can demonstrate how each of these phases can benefit from parametric design. Let us briefly discuss phases of the architectural design process.

Pressman (2012) identifies six phases in the architectural design process: problem definition, information gathering, analysis, synthesis leading to diagrammatic schemes, schematic design development, and soliciting and responding to critical feedback. Problem definition covers identification of expectations from the resulting building, such as functional requirements and performance. Information gathering refers to the process of collecting critical data that would inform the design process, such as site, climate, and context-related data. Analysis helps refine the collected data, build an understanding of the data, and clarification of design problems. In the synthesis phase, problem definition, collected data, and analysis findings inform studies on form and design response possibilities. During schematic design development, design ideas are further refined. Finally, reflecting and editing of the design proposal is informed by critical feedback, which can come from the client, fellow designers, as well as performance simulations and evaluations.

In a more recent publication, Makstutis (2018) defines the phases of the architectural design process as research, proposition, analysis, and revision. Research includes problem definition, collecting relevant information, and making sense of this information; proposition development refers to the development of design concepts and design responses; the analysis phase refers to the evaluation of the design proposal, which is followed by revisions and edits.

These two definitions of the architectural design process phases not only support one another, but their phases also have strong resemblance to elements of the cognitive and computational design thinking models we discussed earlier. In the process-related chapters of this book, we will follow a similar roadmap. In Chapter 3, we will discuss parametric methods that help the designer collect and understand data about a project site and its context. In Chapter 4, we will look into parametric methods and concepts that can enhance formal explorations as well as their relationships to site conditions and performance-related criteria. In Chapter 5, parametric methods and concepts about refining the design proposal will be introduced. Chapter 6 will introduce skin and façade system design using parametric methods. In Chapter 7, we will discuss evolutionary parametric applications and using parametric methods to create, analyze, and select design iterations. Chapter 8 will introduce performance-related simulations using parametric methods in order to enhance skin and façade system design. In Chapter 9, we will look into materializing parametric design decisions using digital fabrication techniques in architectural model making. In the last chapter of the book, we will engage in an informed discussion about routes for the future development of parametric thinking and methods in architecture. Before starting this endeavor, however, we will take a deeper look into the conceptual background and history of parametric design in architecture in Chapter 2.

CHAPTER 02

HISTORY AND CONCEPTUAL FRAMEWORK OF PARAMETRIC DESIGN IN ARCHITECTURE

We discussed an introductory definition of parametric design in architecture in Chapter 1 and reviewed the interconnected nature of its "elements." Before delving into parametric design's conceptual framework and history, let us investigate various definitions of parametric design by different authors to develop a stronger understanding.

Publications on parametric design methods for architects began appearing in articles and books mainly post-2000. For the purposes of this text, we will use the definition authored by Wassim Jabi in "Parametric Design for Architecture," published in 2013. In this publication, Jabi defines parametric design as:

> a process based on algorithmic thinking that enables the expression of parameters and rules that, together, define, encode, and clarify the relationship between design intent and design response. (Jabi, 2013: 196)

Jabi (2013) refers to "algorithmic" thinking in the definition of parametric design. Parametric design bears the question "what is an algorithm?" Although this term is a mathematical concept, since our focus is on parametric methods in architecture, let us look into a definition provided by Arturo Tedeschi (2014), an architect and computational designer:

> An algorithm is a procedure used to return a solution to a question – or to perform a particular task – through a finite list of basic and well-defined instructions. Algorithms follow the human aptitude to split a problem into a set of simple steps that can be easily computed, and although they are strongly associated with the computer, algorithms could be defined independently from programming languages. (Tedeschi, 2014: 22)

From these two definitions, we can already see that parametric algorithms entail the use of "parameters and rules," which help reduce a question or problem into a set of "basic and well-defined instructions." Parallel to our discussion in Chapter 1, these definitions indicate that parametric methods provide descriptions on how to form and evaluate geometry. In essence, parametric methods allow the designer to define the formation, geometry, and/or performance of a component or part. The parts of the composition that "affect" other geometries do so through functions and variables – they "describe" the steps that should follow each step taken to achieve a formal, geometric, or performative result.

In sum, parametric thinking, parametric design, and parametric methods involve step-by-step definitions and instructions to guide generation and evaluation of associative architectural elements that affect one another through changes – and ultimately affect the outcomes. Let us now delve into parametric architectural design behind the scenes based on these definitions, historical developments, and the contemporary debate.

DOI: 10.4324/9781003230052-2

2.1 PARAMETRIC THINKING: BEFORE COMPUTERS AND DIGITAL METHODS FOR PARAMETRIC THINKING

The main idea in parametric thinking is not using a computer, but really defining associative relationships among parts of the design. Considering that parametric design is a form of description and definition-based design decision-making, we can come to understand that parametric thinking and decision-making dates back to antiquity, and it has existed in a variety of forms in the Middle Ages (in Gothic architecture), late nineteenth century, and twentieth century (Carpo, 2016; Frazer, 2016; Burry, 2016).

Human beings have a long history of definition-based design. Both Vitruvius and Leon Batista Alberti wrote manuscripts that included procedural algorithms without visuals or images for architectural design, which defined proportional relationships among architectural elements. Similarly, in medieval and Gothic architecture, rules that defined proportional relationships existed, without prescribing form (Carpo, 2016). Frazer (2016) refers to Ada Lovelace's 1843 work for Charles Babbage's proposed analytical engine as an example of parametric work. Similarly, he suggests that architect Luigi Moretti's 1940s work on parametric equations, termed "architettura parametrica," provided foundations for today's parametric design and informed design of stadia.

Having extensively worked on deciphering Antoni Gaudi's architecture, Mark Burry (2016) indicates that Gaudi's work on gravity-affected form was indeed parametric. He also underlines that Frei Otto's twentieth-century explorations of gravity-affected architectural volumes were parametric in the sense that gravity-based descriptions informed architectural form.

Otto and Rasch (1995) reflect on the rationale behind this architecture in a publication for an exhibition in Villa Stuck in Munich, Germany, due to the award of the "1992 Deutscher Werkbund Bayern Prize" for their work:

> To solve today's problems, we need the new integrated architecture of the ecological surface of the earth's surface that is settled by man. Using the insights of all sciences the finding-form of this new, peaceful, self-settling system will be encouraged first of all by the fact that resistances are broken down. (Otto and Rasch, 1995: 14)

Burry (2016) also draws parallels between Theo Van Doesburg's 1924 manifesto (1970), "Towards a Plastic Architecture," and contemporary definitions of parametric architecture (i.e., Schumacher, 2008 and 2016) due to their approach that relied on rules and descriptions as opposed to prescribing form.

Since, like contemporary parametric architecture, these historical figures worked on classes of objects mathematically defined by generative rules, Burry refers to contemporary parametric design as "digital parametricism" (2016). Furthermore, he argues that Gaudi and Otto, working in different time periods, showed that parametric design methods, like digital parametricism, open the door to an extensive field of formal and performative architectural possibilities. Burry's argument emphasizes that, like its historical precedents, contemporary parametric design is not prescriptive and, with its procedural mechanisms, opens the door to an extensive field of formal and performative architectural explorations.

2.2 PARAMETRIC DESIGN FOLLOWING THE PROLIFERATION OF COMPUTERS AND DIGITAL APPLICATIONS

Having observed that contemporary parametric design methods derive from historical (non-computational) design thinking, let us take a deeper look at contemporary parametric design and computational methods. Clearly, with the contemporary digital hardware and software, contemporary parametric design offers extensive data processing and output power, which yields many advantages for contemporary architects. Nevertheless, looking back into historic developments, how have parametric approaches differentiated themselves from others without computing power?

The answer lies at paradigm shift moments where nonvisual, verbal, and mathematical formulas – generative algorithms – could be replaced by visual definitions and descriptions. Carpo (2016) points at the Renaissance as one of the historical paradigm shifts, where abstract generative formulas from antiquity and medieval eras were replaced by visual information in the form of printed pictures. This development was a starting point for human beings' capability for identical replication, which is very different from non-prescriptive descriptions and definitions.

Carpo (2016) further posits that the technical capabilities developed during and following the Industrial Revolution contributed to three-dimensional, identical replication – or mass production – since definitions and descriptions became visual, and with technology, mass replication became possible. According to Carpo (2016), contemporary parametric design (or in his terms, "digital parametricism"), just like the nonvisual descriptions of ancient/medieval/pre-Industrial Revolution times, produces variations based on abstract descriptions:

> This is what digital Parametricism stood up against at the close of the 20th century. And this is why it was and still is a revolution: because it produces variations, just like ancient parametricism, but uses machines, just like industrial modernity; and hence mass-produce variations, which neither antiquity nor modernity ever could. (Carpo, 2016: 29)

Visualizing the time period, design thinking method, and their outcomes helps make Carpo's timeline and arguments more easily understandable. Figure 2.1 illustrates an attempt to visually

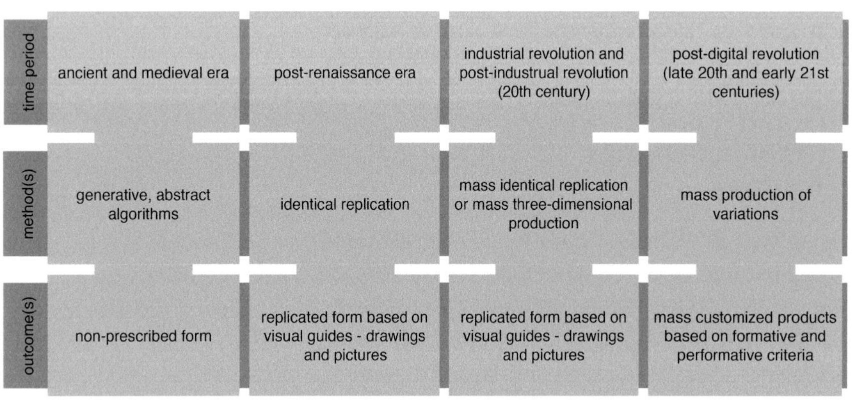

Figure 2.1 *The time periods in history, form and design generation methods, and their design outcomes, as described by Carpo (2016), Frazer (2016), and Burry (2016).*

summarize the series of events and their outcomes as described by Carpo (2016), Frazer (2016), and Burry (2016).

2.3 "PARAMETRICISM" AND THE CURRENT DEBATE

So far, we have discussed parametric thinking, its conceptual framework and history. Could this movement of design thinking and set of novel design methods define an "-ism" like the large historic movements defined by "-isms" in architecture?

2.3.1 The Parametricist Manifesto of 2008

During the 11th Architecture Biennale in Venice, Patrik Schumacher (then a principal at Zaha Hadid Architects), presented "Parametricism as Style – Parametricist Manifesto" (2008) at the "Dark Side Club," a critical "salon" for debates to take place about the Biennale's themes. In this manifesto, Schumacher argued that systematic, adaptive variation, continuous differentiation, and parametric dynamic figuration are concerns of design professionals at multiple scales: from the urban scale down to architecture, tectonic details, furniture design, and product design. The primary argument of the manifesto is to reequip design disciplines to respond to the social and economic dynamics of the "post-Fordist" society, or the era of "post-Fordism":

> Architecture finds itself at the mid-point of an ongoing cycle of innovative adaptation – retooling the discipline and adapting the architectural and urban environment to the socio-economic era of post-Fordism. The mass society that was characterized by a single, nearly universal consumption standard has evolved into the heterogenous society of the multitude. The key issues that avant-garde architecture and urbanism should be addressing can be summarized in the slogan: organizing and articulating the increased complexity of post-Fordist society. (Schumacher, 2008: 1)

At this point, it would make sense to look into the terms "Fordism" and "post-Fordism" and what the terms refer to. Henry Ford, the founder of Ford Automotive Company helped to popularize the term "Fordism." The main objective of Ford was to maximize time and cost-efficient production through moving assembly lines. Fast and efficient mass production helped decrease the prices of produced goods, triggering mass consumption. Production in this system was dependent on minimally skilled labor and, where appropriate, machinery (Becker and Weissenbacher, 2020).

Coined much more recently, the term "post-Fordism" refers to a new paradigm where communities rely increasingly on the role of new technologies for production within a networked global economy. Also referred to as the "knowledge-based economy" or the "network economy," this new paradigm emphasizes the importance of knowledge and technology (Amin, 1994). Its production is not limited to material goods: it also includes immaterial production such as intellectual property. Schumacher's 2008 manifesto, therefore, argues that parametric thinking and computational parametric methods equip design disciplines to respond to the social and economic outcomes of the knowledge-based economy.

In the "Parametricist Manifesto" (2008), Schumacher draws parallels between avant-garde movements in design and novel scientific agendas. He argues that avant-garde movements present new conceptual frameworks, objectives, methods, and values and proposes that a research program based on parametric paradigms is the best approach to characterize the contemporary architectural avant-garde. In the manifesto, the term "parametricism" is coined based on this program and is referred to as a "style."

To what extent avant-garde movements in design and novel scientific agendas have methodological similarities and to what extent "parametricism" can be defined as a "style" are discussions beyond the objectives of this introductory book. It is nevertheless clear that the manifesto successfully opens a variety of discussion topics for scholars in architecture, design, philosophy and history of science, and basic science. Let us now take a look into the responses and discussions triggered by the Parametricist Manifesto (2008).

2.3.2 Responses and Discussions Triggered by the Parametricist Manifesto

Following the release of the Parametricist Manifesto, a variety of intellectual debates were triggered. One of these debates took place in a 2013 conference entitled "The Politics of Parametricism: Digital Technologies and the Future(s) of Sociality" at the Roy and Edna Disney/Calarts Theater in the Disney Concert Hall located in downtown Los Angeles. Organized by Matthew Poole, a curatorial theorist, and Manual Shvartzberg, an architect and researcher, the conference featured panelists with international architectural theory and practice backgrounds. The debates focused on questions on social and political implications of recent developments in computational and parametric design. The organizers then curated a series of texts from the conference in an edited anthology (Poole and Shvartzberg, 2015). The anthology sheds light onto the responses and discussions triggered by the Parametricist Manifesto by several practitioners and researchers with architectural theory and practice backgrounds.

In their introductory chapter to the anthology, editors Poole and Shvartzberg (2015) point to the political connections of the parametricist agenda due to Schumacher's emphasis on connections with post-Fordist societal and economic agendas:

> Specifically, he ***(Schumacher)*** considers parametricism to be the "epochal style" of the "post-Fordist network society" that emerges after his so-called "transitional periods" of postmodernism and deconstructivism. In this teleological scheme of styles corresponding to the "great epochs" of Western civilization, parametricism is, according to Schumacher, poised to become the new hegemonic movement for the twenty-first century, replacing modernism as the new "International Style." He thus considers himself and his project – and others like it – to be the transformational avant-garde of the discipline that will usher in this epochal change. (Poole and Shvartzberg, 2015: 5)

Poole and Shvartzberg then underline the difference between the terms "parametrics" or "parametric design" and "parametricism", referring to Schumacher's 2008 manifesto:

> "Parametrics" or "parametric design," by contrast, is not necessarily associated with a style or a movement but refers to the adoption of a very broad series of techniques of computation in virtual modeling processes. (Poole and Shvartzberg, 2015: 5)

In the same anthology, one of the chapters was written by Ted Cruz, an architect as well as a researcher and professor at the University of California, San Diego. In the chapter titled "The Architecture of Neoliberalism," Cruz (2015) critically approaches certain aspects of the Parametricist Manifesto. Referring to Parametricism's alignment with the era of post-Fordism, Cruz argues that, as defined, parametricism stays indifferent to the outcomes of neoliberal politics and argues that it is these outcomes that need to be confronted: socioeconomic inequalities, unprecedented growth of slums around the world, urban conflicts, uneven urbanization, and increasing privatization of public resources and public spaces. Although he acknowledges that such complex problems are hard to confront through a single discipline such as architecture, Cruz also reminds the reader that the most striking avant-garde movements in design within the last 100 years have engaged persistent social and economic issues.

Characterizing the stance of the Parametricist Manifesto as a top-down, autonomous, and self-referential language, Cruz posits the question of which institution(s) can actually build future-looking buildings like those proposed by parametricism in the absence of progressive welfare states. In doing so, Cruz proposes that a more experimental architecture, one that can respond to contemporary socioeconomic inequalities, is needed:

> In fact, recent shifts in the last two decades, from linear thinking to systems thinking in science and many other fields, show a move from the type of silo-thinking that fields of specialization have perpetuated to a more complex ecology of inter-dependencies, embedding scientific and formal research into a more complex cultural context. The hope is that Parametricism in architecture could complicate itself by more comprehensively engaging the sort of systems thinking that is (seemingly) at the base of its generative formal processes. The problems of the contemporary city are systemic problems that need a deeper ecological thinking. (Cruz, 2015: 196)

Consequently, Cruz (2015) proposes "The Informal Algorithm Manifesto," in which he posits that bottom-up urban alterations could transform top-down institutional dynamics, and top-down resources could stretch to reach urban sites of marginalization and transform conventional understandings of infrastructure. The 15-point "Informal Algorithm Manifesto" introduces a series of proposed moves (Cruz, 2015).

Another chapter in the same volume, authored by Peggy Deamer (2015), then Assistant Dean and Professor of Architecture at Yale University, highlights a parametric design-related dichotomy in the profession of architecture. In the chapter titled "Parametric Schizophrenia," Deamer (2015) emphasizes the differences between:

> parametrics as form-driven scripting and parametrics as intelligence management – BIM (Building Information Modeling). (Deamer, 2015: 178)

In this chapter, Deamer (2015) describes two dichotomous worlds inside the world of architecture: the form-driven scripting world authored by "researchers, hipsters, and avant-gardists," and data-driven building information modeling world, authored by corporate employees, architectural/engineering/construction (AEC) professionals, and managers. In essence, she points to the world of data and parameter-based form explorations versus the data and parameter-based, performance-oriented world of building production. While the form-driven scripting world produces algorithmic systems, unfabricated seamless objects, and product icons, the data-driven building information modeling world produces functional systems, fabricated disjunctive objects, and process icons. Moreover, while the audience of form-driven scripting world is composed of students, generation Y, and products of social media, the audience of the data-driven building information modeling world is composed of practitioners, generation X, and products of network theory (Deamer, 2015).

It is not challenging to observe these two realms in schools of architecture as well as the profession. In many schools of architecture, one finds classes and design studios that have a highly exploratory nature where parametric methods are used for experimentations in form generation. Similarly, classes and design studios with a strong emphasis on building performance analysis keep their distance from exploratory form generation. Upon graduation, individuals with professional interests in either of these areas can find practices that focus on one of these two realms.

Referring to this dichotomy as "Parametricism's schizophrenia," Deamer responds by returning to psychoanalysis. Accordingly, the underlying logic of schizophrenia is the "desire of the ***other***," with the objective of being recognized by the "other." Within this framework, Deamer speculates that the "other" for both parametric worlds is modernism, with its emphasis on the development of abstract form while maximizing efficiency. Deamer underlines that despite the failure of the modern project in both areas, repeating redemption attempts continue, and speculatively concludes that formal parametrics embraces the formalism of modernism, while information modeling parametrics embraces modernism's attempts at efficiency (2015).

As a response to this parametric schizophrenia, Deamer proposes a deterritorialization of the architectural profession, where designers can oscillate between branding and entrepreneurialism and have access to affordable information sharing without being monitored. Consequently, the architectural outcome would benefit on multiple fronts:

> The architectural "object" would announce that its spectacle is not merely visual but spatial, that its intelligence was not merely economic but aesthetic, where "aesthetic" refers to the profound way in which spaces, materials, proportions, structure, stability, and light convey architecture's message. (Deamer, 2015: 185)

According to this proposal, the deterritorialized architectural profession architects' expertise would be valued in building procurement, fees would be based on the value created and long-term economic benefits for the client, and a more democratic urban ordering would depart from developer-driven systems (Deamer, 2015).

The responses to the Parametricist Manifesto are not limited to the ones introduced here. Many scholars, researchers, professionals, and designers approach the debate from multiple vantage points and disciplines. The responses of Cruz (2015) and Deamer (2015) illustrate the depth of the debate at multiple scales. While Cruz focuses on the relationship between parametric design and the larger social, economic, and political developments worldwide, Deamer starts with an analysis of the conflicts and dichotomies inside the profession. As one delves into the spectacular world of parametric design, it is important to keep such perspectives in mind, and not get lost among the artifacts of parametric form generation or performance analyses. Yet, the debate continues.

2.3.3 Parametricism 2.0

Following up on the debate about the Parametricist Manifesto, AD Magazine published its March/April issue in 2016 focusing on "Parametricism 2.0." Edited by Patrik Schumacher, this volume expands the debate on parametricism from the vantage points of multiple authors. In this volume, Schumacher acknowledges the criticisms parametricism received in previous years, and increases his emphasis on the social and technical functionalities of parametric design:

> While artistic and technological creativity, as well as esoteric internal design process orientation, must still play a part in creating the avant-garde character of Parametricism, this must now recede and give way to a focus on social performance if the movement is to mature, go mainstream, and be accepted as a serious contender for global best practice. (Schumacher, 2016: 10)

In this volume, multiple authors respond to parametricism with a social and functional agenda. For example, while Philippe Block introduces parametric design's contributions by drawing from historical knowledge about complex curved structures of Gothic Cathedrals, Philip Yuan demonstrates, under the title "Parametric Regionalism," that parametric design can relate to local cultural contexts with examples of his research and design in China.

In the same volume, Burry (2016) discusses the potential future developments in parametric design and speculates that the architect can act as the equivalent of a stage arts producer if parametric inputs are expanded into inputs including, but not limited to, social, political, economic, and behavioral parameters. He envisions that novel flexible design strategies may expand architects' repertoire of methods and tools and underscores that parameters from non-architectural fields need to be incorporated into architecture.

2.4 PARAMETRIC DESIGN AND ARCHITECTURAL RESEARCH

The developments starting with the second half of the twentieth century have changed the conventional relationship between humans and machines. In many fields, both analog and digital machines have moved beyond being mere tools and have become an integral part of human thinking and making – particularly design thinking and making. The fast-paced advancement of digital technologies and digital fabrication methods have accelerated this unified design and making process:

> In synthesizing material culture and technologies within the expanding relationship between the computer and architecture, this phenomenon defines a digital continuum from design to production, from form generation to fabrication design. This new continuity transcends the merely instrumental contributions of the man-machine relationship to praxis and has begun to evolve as a ***medium that supports a continuous logic of design thinking and making***. As such, the digital in architecture has begun to enable a set of symbiotic relationships ***between the formulation of design processes and developing technologies.*** (Oxman and Oxman, 2014: 1)

Now that the relationships among the designer, design tools, and design processes are becoming ever more fluid, it is time for human and natural variables and parameters to get in the picture through technology taking advantage of the advances offered by science, research, and technology.

The scientific community, including both social and natural sciences, has decades of experience in empirical research with clearly defined research methodologies, methods, and tools. Their findings and advances have been dependent on laboratory and field-based, real-world data. On the other hand, with some exceptions, architecture and other design disciplines have relied on intuitive responses, positions, arguments, and criticism in search of progress. Collaborations with the social sciences have proven productive, but this side of the architectural research community tends to withdraw from providing architectural responses to their research findings. Collaborations with the natural sciences have proven equally productive, but this side of the architectural research community tends to overlook the Vitruvian "delight" argument or focus heavily on performative issues. This duality is reminiscent of the "parametric schizophrenia" introduced by Deamer (2015), in a slightly different intellectual context with slightly different actors – but still within the realm of architecture.

2.4.1 The Operationalization Challenge

One of the largest challenges for empirical architectural research is the "operationalization challenge." Operationalization refers to how a variable can be measured. For example, a scientist in a laboratory may want to operationalize the unit expansion of a metal sample based on increasing context temperature. This measurement may be the expansion observed per unit temperature increase. In architecture, however, we are not as fortunate as a scientist in a laboratory. Many of the variables we are interested in cannot be operationalized quantitatively. We can indeed operationalize variables through methods borrowed from social sciences, most of them being qualitative approaches. Nevertheless, for many research endeavors, the operationalization challenge stays the same.

2.4.2 Parametric Methods and Architectural Research

The introduction of parametric design in architecture may constitute a historically fortunate moment in history that may allow us to operationalize some variables and bring them into endeavors in empirical architectural research. In Section 2.3, we reviewed some of the work of authors who have been encouraging the expansion of architectural parameters to variables. The algorithmic, relational, and systematic nature of parametric methods may allow just that: while experimenting with the spectacle of unusual geometries and geometric compositions, architects may be able to bring in empirical variables into the architectural design process through parametric methods.

A good example would be the design of a façade system with environmental performance and visual connections in mind. As is often the case, we may end up with a scenario where visual connections within a public space is a positive factor, while extensive solar exposure through the same façade may be undesirable. It is not uncommon to see analyses on both variables get conducted but are not interrelated sufficiently to influence design decisions due to the time-consuming nature of analyses through conventional and analog methods.

Parametric methods, on the other hand, offer just that: thanks to the power and efficiency of algorithm-based analyses and calculations, a single individual can efficiently evaluate visibility and solar exposure at the same time. By bringing in a parametrically designed louver system, and parametric environmental performance analysis tools, one can easily evaluate multiple parametric louver systems in relation to the visibility they allow and solar exposure they minimize.

One can therefore argue that parametric design can efficiently bring together measurements of variables that were historically challenging to relate to one another in the design proposal. At this point, it is possible to argue that even if for short-term practical objectives, moving beyond epistemological discussions and diving into a methodological debate may prove beneficial for architectural research. That said, one cannot undervalue the debate about parametric design at the ontological and epistemological levels. That debate needs to continue for the advancement of architecture with close connections to science, research, and technology. But for immediate architectural solutions and smaller architectural research projects, it is not too hard to argue for parametric interventions in the quest for efficiency and overcoming the operationalization challenges.

2.5 PARAMETRIC DESIGN AND PROSPECTIVE FUTURES

Some of the developments in parametric design, discussed in earlier sections, are already in progress. In the following chapters, we will engage in introductory discussions on such developments with examples of parametric applications.

Rapid developments in parametric methods have expanded form generation and analysis capabilities. Visibility and configurational analysis tools that we will discuss in Chapters 3, 4, and 5, for example, can easily bring social and behavioral data into the discussion. These data are of significant importance not only to designers, but also users and organizations in many settings, such as work environments, healthcare settings, and educational institutions.

Similarly, environmental and performance analysis tools, which we will discuss in Chapters 3, 6, and 8, are so rapidly developing that we can integrate them into design processes in more time and cost-efficient ways. Unlike past testing and analysis methods, parametric tools can easily integrate real-time performance evaluation into the design process with limited time consumption, further streamlining the design process.

Another rapidly developing set of tools include evolutionary solvers, which we discuss in Chapter 7 of this book. By incorporating social and environmental data into the equation, evolutionary solvers can support architects at various phases of the design process. The possibilities afforded by evolutionary solvers are extensive. They can help designers in multiple phases of the design process, from mass composition and orientation to interior spatial organization, creating and evaluating a multitude of design options with multiple variables.

Fast advancing digital fabrication and rapid prototyping tools, which we will discuss in Chapter 9, become more cost efficient by the day. Having easier and greater access to such modeling and prototyping tools will inevitably contribute to the productivity of the design process. Designers can now generate and quickly 3D-print multiple massing options in a relatively short amount of time. Similarly, scaled, or even real-life, one-to-one scale detailing options can be conveniently fabricated for testing.

Given their expanding capabilities, use in academia and practice, and inherent controversy, parametric design methods and digital fabrication tools will continue to be subjects of extensive discussion in upcoming years. Rapid developments in software and hardware will most likely contribute to, and affect the course and intensity of, the debate. Any designer interested in parametric methods will feel the need to keep up to date not only about the current state of the debate but also the latest developments in software. In this chapter, we discussed the current state of discussions on parametric design and their potential implications. In the following chapters, we will look into how these discussions, multiple parametric methods, and digital fabrication tools may contribute to the architectural design process.

CHAPTER 03

SITE ANALYSIS Understanding the Site and Its Context Using Parametric Methods

It is crucial for the designer to thoroughly know about the existing conditions of the project site and its context as the architectural design process starts. By learning about the existing conditions of the project site and its surroundings, the designer can carefully consider the potential relationships between the design proposal and its physical, environmental, and social context. Thus, the site analysis phase entails research and information search into the existing conditions in and around the project site: it yields an inventory of all conditions that would inform the design process, as well as the interactions among these conditions.

3.1 SITE ANALYSIS: METHODS

The site analysis phase in the architectural design process is essentially a series of research and information search tasks. While collecting site-related information, the designer uses multiple information (or data) collection methods. This information is then studied and interrelated, yielding results in the form of drawings, maps, and reports. As in any research and information search endeavor, using multiple methods and resorting to multiple sources of information increase the reliability of findings. Over the years, architects have developed, adopted, and used various site analysis methods.

3.1.1 Site visits, observations, and archival methods

Traditionally, designers have used a series of methods to collect information about the site and its context. Among these, site visits and observations have been the dominant methods: visiting the site in person and observing the conditions and recording this information in the form of notes, sketches, drawings, and photographs. In-person interviews and casual conversations with the population on and around the site constitute another set of valuable methods, which can yield crucial information that may not be observable in person or through the duration of the site visit. Archival research is another method that yields key information. Using this method, the designer visits information sources about the site, which can include a wide array of sources: city or county archives that may provide historic and social background information, city documents that include zoning information, maps and drawings, design guidelines, climate and environment-related information, and other rules and regulations that may inform or guide the design process.

Starting with the 1990s, digital resources made newer methods available. The expanding use of geographical information systems (GIS) prompted continuously increasing amounts of data collection and storage. In layers, this digital information source contains, but is not limited to, information on land uses, topography, urban infrastructure, transportation, and vegetation on and around a site. Based on the data resources made available by the relevant jurisdiction, the designer can access such data fairly easily. Many jurisdictions now make such data easily accessible to designers and researchers. The designer then uses a GIS software package to organize, sort, and make sense of the collected data about the site and its context. Such

 DOI: 10.4324/9781003230052-3

software packages make it possible to relate multiple sets of data to one another based on analysis criteria, build and work on queries to find answers, and visualize the results in terms of maps, 3D models, and reports. In this book, it is not our objective to discuss GIS analysis methods in depth. There are many valuable publications that introduce the logic and approach of GIS methods in existing literature (i.e., Steinberg and Steinberg, 2015; Bolstad, 2019).

Especially starting with the 2000s, increasing availability of freely accessible online information packages have also made new software and websites easy-to-access and important information sources for the designer. Using many of the online mapping and modeling platforms, the designer can now gain access to preliminary, basic information about a project site such as aerial photos and site plans.

In recent years, developing parametric methods started offering analytical tools, which have proven useful and time saving during the site analysis phase. Parametric Grasshopper plug-in packages such as Ladybug Tools, for example, provide tools for analyzing environmental data about the site, such as climate, solar access, and wind patterns, among others. One can also use local Grasshopper tools to analyze and visualize certain properties of the site, such as topography and views into and from a given site. Although not all site-related data can be analyzed using parametric methods, they help analyze and visualize various site-related information in a rapid and efficient manner. In addition to aggregate data, parametric methods also enable the designer to look into specific moments and conditions, providing in-depth information about the site.

The designer can develop a reliable set of site analysis findings mixing and matching these available tools and methods, given the background and the context of the project. Let us now look into the elements of site analysis: the types of information collected during the site analysis phase.

3.2 ELEMENTS OF SITE ANALYSIS

To relate and respond to the project context, the designer needs to be informed about its existing conditions: the site's social, cultural, and economic context; the rules and regulations of the jurisdiction; physical conditions in and around the site; and the site's environmental context.

3.2.1 Contextual Information, Rules, Regulations, and Physical Conditions in and around the Site

While information about the social, cultural, and economic context can be accessed through archival research (i.e., existing documents and reports) and in-person interviews and conversations with the local population, information on the rules and regulations of the jurisdiction can be accessed through existing plan documents and guidelines. This information includes location, size, site coordinates, zoning information (allowed building types), as well as physical guidance (i.e., design guidelines, setbacks, height limits, etc.) (White, 1983; Pressman, 2012).

In terms of physical conditions, it is important to identify existing building uses in context (i.e., commercial, residential, industrial, public, etc.); circulation access (i.e., public transportation, pedestrian, vehicle, and bicycle access); traffic conditions; and existing building heights (in number of floors and feet) around the site.

3.2.2 Environmental Information about the Site and Its Context

Most of the information types discussed so far can be accessed via in-person inquiry, observations, and archival research through existing documents. Parametric methods prove useful when we start to collect, analyze, and visualize environmental information.

Contemporary digital sources of information and parametric methods make it easy to access, analyze, and visualize location and climate-related information. Among these, sun trajectory, prevailing winds, precipitation, vegetation and humidity information, topography, and temperature patterns are information types that strongly inform the design process. Another important information type includes the views from and into the site based on the surrounding context (Pressman, 2012). Kwok and Grondzik (2011) further underline daylighting, passive solar heating, passive cooling, water/stormwater runoff, acoustics, and air quality as key architectural issues for environmentally conscious design propositions. Similarly, solar (insolation) resource data are required by more and more jurisdictions.

3.3 PARAMETRIC METHODS FOR SITE ANALYSIS

It is important to note that, based on the project's program and design objectives, site analysis can have stronger emphasis on certain information types. For example, for a commercial project in an urban site, visibility from a large percentage of the surrounding context can be an important concern. Similarly, for a project in a hot and humid context, site information related to passive cooling and ventilation can be on the forefront, prompting detailed analysis of solar access and local wind patterns. In this section, we will look into the types of information in site analysis for which parametric methods can be efficient and time saving for information collection, analysis, and visualization.

3.3.1 Environment-Related Information That Can Be Analyzed Using Grasshopper

Without being fluent in advanced computer programming, it would be very time-consuming and complicated for the everyday user to write Grasshopper definitions that conduct environment-related analysis using native components. Individuals and institutions specializing in such analyses develop and make available "plug-ins" as time and effort-saving tools. A "plug-in" refers to a smaller piece of software that operates under a larger, "parent" software package. There are many plug-ins that work under the Grasshopper framework. Once such plug-in we will discuss here is "Ladybug Tools," which was developed in 2013 (Sadeghipour and Pak, 2013). Since then, this set of tools has been consistently developing and evolving. As of the time this book was written, this set of tools was being maintained by Mostapha Sadeghipour Roudsari and Chris Mackey at Ladybug Tools LLC, who were also joined by a team of contributors. More information about Ladybug Tools is available at https://www.ladybug.tools (Ladybug Tools LLC, n.d.), and an extensive list of specific methods and components used by Ladybug Tools can be found at https://www.ladybug.tools/publication.html (Ladybug Tools LLC., Publications, n.d.).

Before we proceed into environment-related information that can be analyzed by using Grasshopper, it is important to note that software packages rapidly change and develop. In this book, we will demonstrate site analysis methods using Grasshopper's Ladybug Tools plug-in. However, as in any software package, the most important issue for the reader is to understand the concepts. It is only by understanding the main concepts that the reader can update themselves to use future versions of software. In the following pages, we will introduce how to access, analyze, and visualize information using Ladybug Tools under Grasshopper. This selection was made due to the common use of this plug-in in architecture schools and industry.

Using Ladybug Tools, it is possible to analyze local climate and geography-related site properties. This includes environmental comfort as it relates to temperatures, wind and solar access. Analyses of views into and from the site can also be conducted using a number of native Grasshopper components, Ladybug Tools, and other plug-ins. The first step in these analyses entails access to local climate data.

3.3.2 Accessing Local Climate Data

The first step in analysis is accessing the climate data for the site. Ladybug uses the EnergyPlus Weather data format as input (EPW format). EnergyPlus is an open-source whole building energy modeling engine developed by the US Department of Energy. Started in 1997, the EnergyPlus program has a number of public and private performers and partners (www.energyplus.net – retrieved March 2, 2021).

An EnergyPlus Weather File (EPW) is a file that carries weather data for a particular location for use in weather-related building performance analysis and simulation. Weather data in the EPW format is publicly available for more than 2000 locations around the world. Ladybug can help one select EPW data for one of these locations visually through a world map. When the "EPWMap" component is introduced to the Grasshopper canvas and its "epw_map" component is activated by setting a toggle controller to "true," a world map with highlighted locations is presented. In this example, one of the three locations closest to San Francisco was selected, and the URL address of that location's EPW data was copied.

One can then paste this URL address into a Grasshopper panel and connect it to the "Download EPW" component of Ladybug, which downloads the data from that source. The data then needs to be imported into Grasshopper using the "ImportEPW" component. ImportEPW is an intermediary component that translates the data available on the EPW file into readable elements. It yields information on various weather conditions for the selected location, such as relative humidity, wind direction, etc. (Figure 3.1). Once climate data is imported, Ladybug offers a variety of components to analyze and visualize it.

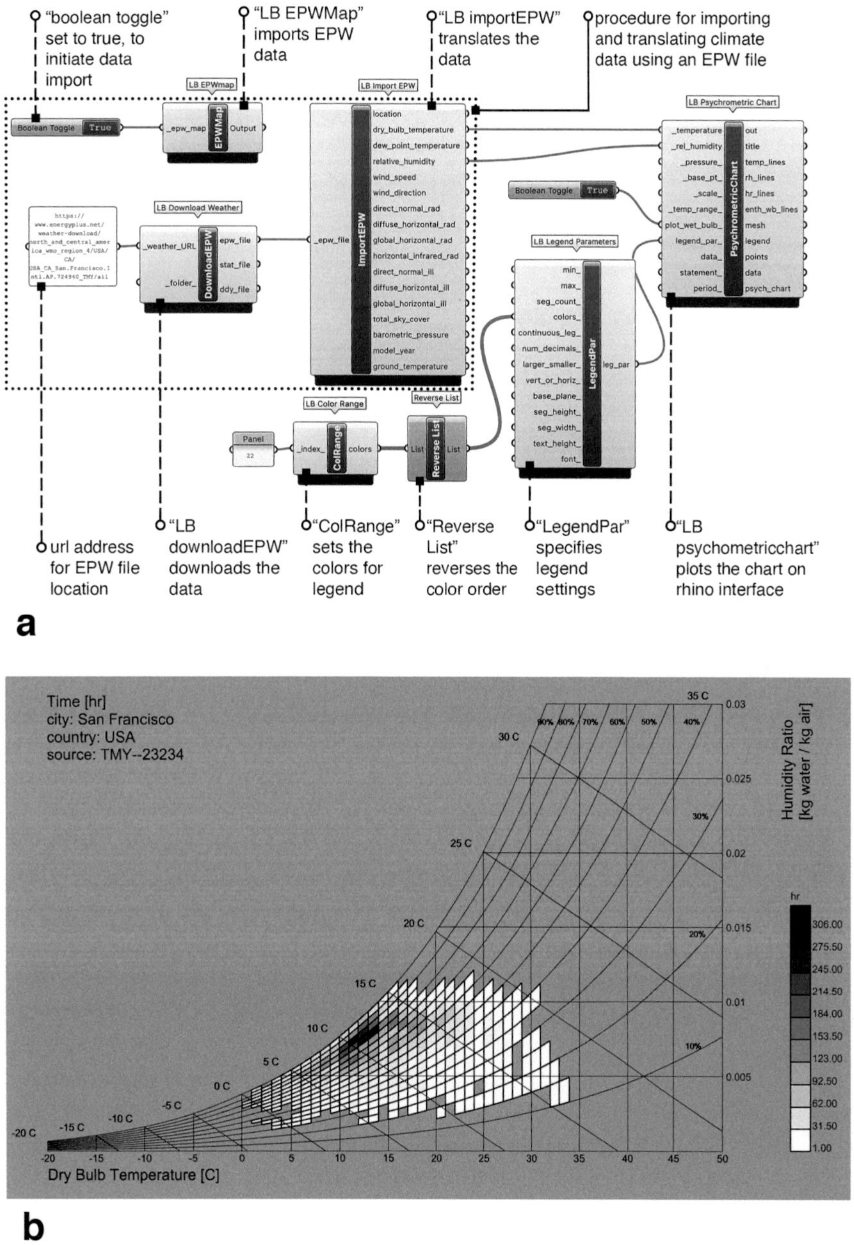

Figure 3.1 *(a) Importing and translating climate data using an EPW file and plotting the "psychrometric chart" using Grasshopper and Ladybug; (b) the "psychrometric chart" for San Francisco, plotted using Ladybug and Grasshopper.*

3.3.3 The Psychrometric Chart

Two key factors contributing to our comfort are the temperature and humidity in the environment. Based on its location, a given site has changing patterns of temperature and humidity throughout the year. In environmental comfort analysis, what we commonly refer to as "temperature" on a day-to-day basis is the "dry bulb temperature." The reason behind the term "dry bulb" is the fact that it is measured by a thermometer not affected by the moisture in the air. The two common measurement units for dry bulb temperature are Celsius (C°) and Fahrenheit (F°).

In environmental comfort analysis, what we commonly refer to as "humidity," or "moisture" in the air, is measured as "relative humidity." "Relative humidity" is a measure of water vapor in the air, in relation to the temperature of the air. It is the ratio of actual water vapor in the air as compared to the total amount of water vapor that can exist at the air's current temperature. In a given location, cooler air yields higher relative humidity, and warmer air yields lower relative humidity.

In 1963, Victor Olgyay introduced a method for analyzing climate patterns through the seasons based on location (Olgyay, 1963). Using this method, dry bulb temperature and relative humidity patterns for a given location can be plotted on a chart for each month throughout the year. Using the psychrometric chart, one can start identifying future climate-related needs based on our comfort level expectations. Charts for various locations are available from many resources. When one is using Rhinoceros and Grasshopper in their design processes, it can prove time saving to utilize the same software package to analyze and visualize environmental data. Let us take a look at how we can plot a psychrometric chart using Ladybug in Grasshopper.

Using the EPW data imported and translated in Section 3.2.2, plotting a psychrometric chart is simple. First, we introduce the "LB Psychrometric Chart" on the Grasshopper canvas. Then, connecting the relative humidity and dry bulb temperature outputs from the "Import EPW" component to the same inputs on the LB Psychrometric Chart, the psychrometric chart is plotted on the Rhinoceros screen (Figure 3.1b). The "plot_wet_bulb" Boolean input controls whether or not wet bulb temperature is plotted.

Finally, the "LB LegendPar" component edits the legend's parameters for number of hours. In this example, instead of the default Ladybug colors, to achieve a white-to-black legend, the "LB ColRange" component is used. When one floats the mouse over the "index" input of this component, a pop-up shows a various color composition options window from 0 to 25. Number 22 is selected for "black to white," and Grasshopper's "reverse list" component is used to reverse the legend from white to black, with white color indicating smaller number of hours, and darkening shades of gray indicating higher numbers of hours for the respective values of dry bulb temperature and humidity ratio. The resulting list of values, fed into the "LB LegendParameters" component, yields a grayscale legend.

The resulting psychrometric chart indicates that through a high number of hours in San Francisco, dry bulb temperature remains between 10°C and 15°C, and humidity ratio remains between 0.005 kg water/kg air and 0.01 kg water/kg air. Note that the portion of the Grasshopper definition marked as the "procedure for importing and translating climate data using an EPW file" is the basic starting procedure for environmental analysis using Ladybug and will be replicated in the following analyses (Figure 3.1a).

3.3.4 Analyzing Solar Conditions

The sun is an enormous input for human life. It is a gigantic source of energy influencing all facets of life. Based on our location on the face of the earth, sunlight has a lot of implications for architectural design: daylighting, heating, cooling, etc. Therefore, the sun also influences our patterns of energy use. This is especially important in architecture, given the current developments in global warming and increasing energy consumption. Consequently, analyzing solar conditions is a crucial aspect of site analysis. Analyzing solar conditions yields many implications for the design process and proposition – especially if we want to minimize energy use and maximize the passive solar advantages of the sun.

Parametric methods have proven useful and time efficient when analyzing solar geometry. The sun path, its location at specific times and dates in a year, direct sun exposure patterns, shadow patterns, and more can be studied with ease given the current state of parametric methods and the abundance of data we can access in the digital era.

3.3.4.1 Sun Path

We conceptualize the relationship of the sun to the earth through an imaginary "sky dome" on which the sun "moves" throughout the year. Although it is our earth that revolves around the sun, for practical reasons the imaginary solar dome and the sun's "movement" on this dome help calculations on how much solar exposure a given site will have through time (Lechner, 2015).

An early step in site analysis is constructing a plot of the sun path through the year and on specific times and dates. Through this analysis, one can better understand the relationships between the sun's rays and the given site. We will demonstrate the plot of a sun path using a fictitious "site" (an existing parcel) in an urban area in San Francisco, CA (Figure 3.2a). Ladybug's "LB Sunpath" component uses the same procedure of importing and translating climate data using an EPW file – as discussed in Section 3.2.3. By connecting the "location" output of the "ImportEPW" component to the "location" input of the "LB SunPath" component (Figure 3.2b), one can plot a basic sun path specific to the coordinates of the given site (Figures 3.2c). The plotted sun path can be centered around the site by connecting the centroid of the site to the "pt" input of the "LB SunPath" component, and can be scaled by specifying a scale factor (Figure 3.2a). One can also alter the sun path to cover the entire year using the "LB AnalysisPeriod" component. In the example shown in Figure 3.2d, the analysis period is set to an entire year, with a start day of 1, start month of January (1), start hour of midnight (0), and an end day of 31, end month of December (12), and an end hour of midnight (23). The resulting sun path shown in Figure 3.2b shows 8760 point locations for the sun, one for each hour of the year. On these Ladybug components, the term "hoy" refers to an hour of year, hoy(s) making the term plural for multiple hours.

Sun's location can also be analyzed and visualized at specific dates and times using Ladybug's "LB Calculate HOY" component. This component simply calculates individual dates and times to be fed into the "hoys" input of the "SunPath" component, replacing the "LB AnalysisPeriod" component illustrated in Figure 3.2b. In the example in Figure 3.3, the sun path is plotted, and the location of the sun at 9:00 am (09:00), 12:00 pm (12:00), and 3:00 pm (15:00) is visualized for Spring equinox (March 21), Summer solstice (June 21), Fall equinox (September 21), and Winter solstice (December 21).

3.3.4.2 Direct Sun Hours and Shadows Analysis

The amount of sunlight received by various parts of the site has important implications on the design proposition, as well as its location and orientation on the site. To make informed decisions, we can conduct direct sun hours and shadows analysis, exploring the hours of sun exposure and shadows a site receives. Using the same Grasshopper definition for the "sun path for all hours of the year" from Figure 3.2b, we can analyze the total number of hours our fictitious site in San Francisco will receive throughout the year. In the example illustrated in Figure 3.4a, the "LB SunPath" component from Figure 3.2b is connected to the "LB DirectSunHours" component using the sun vectors ("_vectors") input. The site's surface is connected to "_geometry," referring to the geometry to be analyzed. The "opaque geometry"

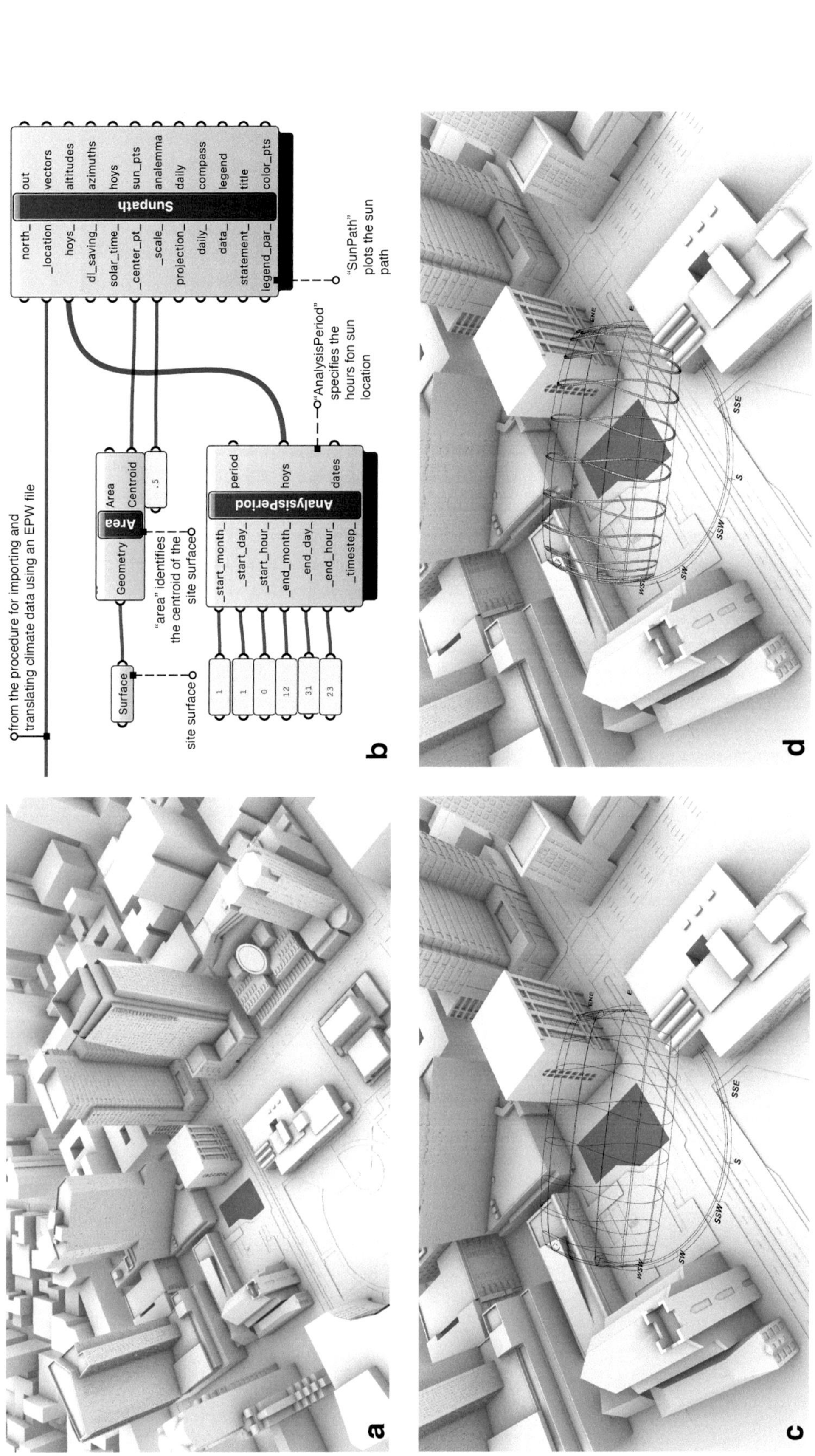

Figure 3.2 (a) The fictitious site in San Francisco, CA; (b) the Grasshopper definition plotting the sun path; (c) the basic sun path plotted; (d) sun path plotted for all hours of the year.

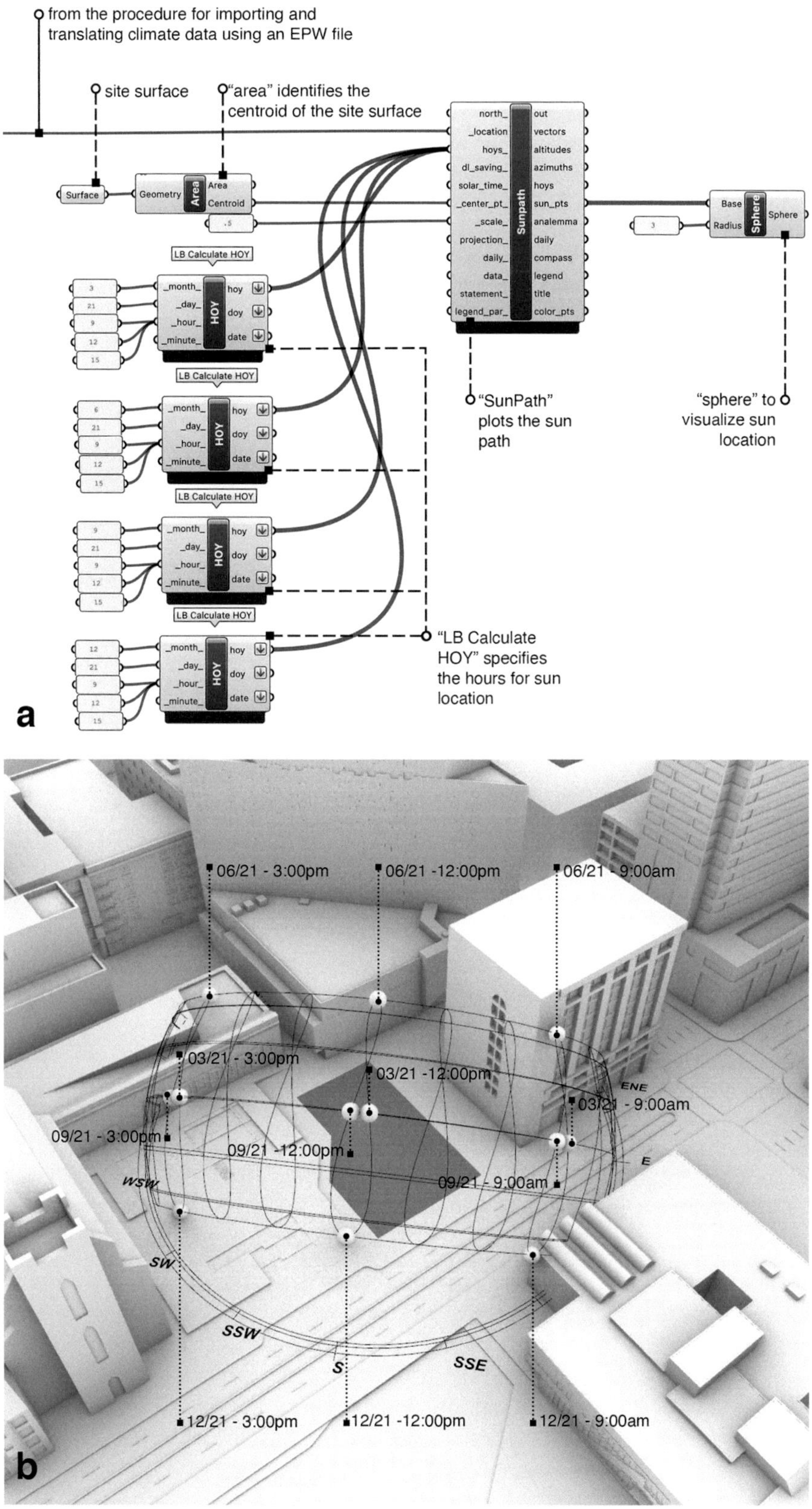

Figure 3.3 *(a) The Grasshopper definition for identifying and visualizing sun location and specific dates and times; (b) location of the sun at 9:00 am (09:00), 12:00 pm (12:00), and 3:00 pm (15:00) is visualized for Spring equinox (March 21), Summer solstice (June 21), Fall equinox (September 21), and Winter solstice (December 21).*

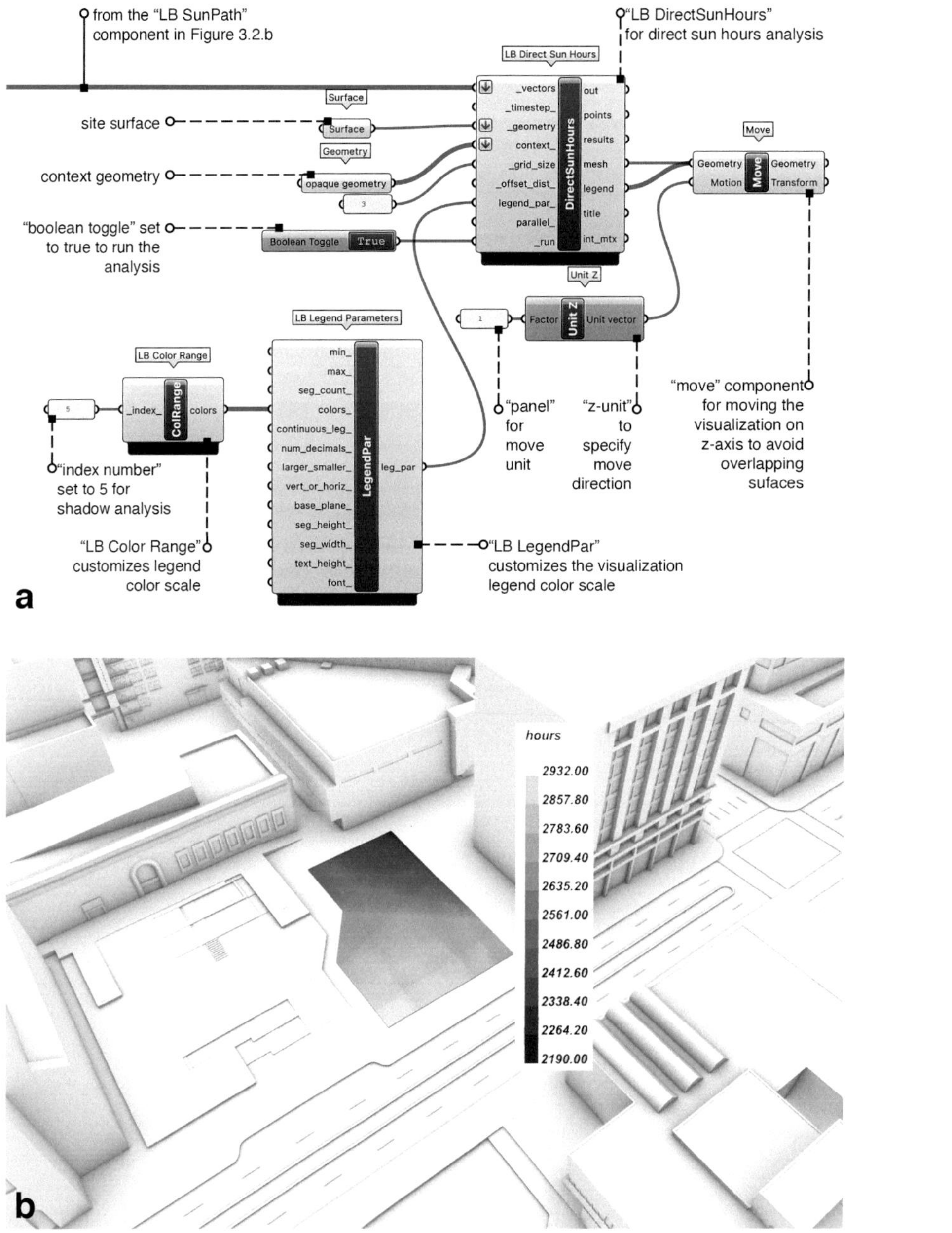

Figure 3.4 *(a) The Grasshopper definition for analyzing and visualizing direct sun hours for the sample site; (b) visualization of direct sun hours for the sample site.*

includes all the geometry of the buildings surrounding the site surface. The "_grid_size" input specifies the size of the grid for analyzing the site surface, which was set to 3 feet by 3 feet in this example. Using this grid, Ladybug analyzes each square, and assigns each square the number of hours it is exposed to sun through 8760 hours of the year based on the sun path. When the analysis is run by setting a Boolean toggle to "true," the site is color-coded based on the number of hours each square is exposed to sun. The "LB DirectSunHours" component color codes the site's sun hours using the default Ladybug color scale.

Ladybug's color scales can be customized according to the analysis type conducted, using the "LB Color Range" component. The component offers 25 different color scales for various analysis types to customize the legends on their visualizations (i.e., 4 for view analysis, 5 for shadow analysis, 6 for glare analysis, etc.). Although not required, such customizations can help the legibility of the visualization. Using Grasshopper's "move" component, the resulting color-coded mesh and legend was moved one unit above the site's surface to avoid overlapping surfaces. The visualization in Figure 3.4b shows that the northern part of the site receives lower number of direct sun hours (a minimum of 2,190 hours of the year's 8,760 hours) due to the tall buildings around the site, while the southern part of the site receives a gradually increasing number of direct sun hours (a maximum of 2,932 hours of the year's 8,760 hours).

3.3.4.3 Solar Irradiance and Illuminance

Based on our day-to-day experience, we intuitively know that sun rays' access to a surface or space means a raise in temperature. This means that that surface or space is receiving solar energy. **Solar irradiance** refers to the amount of solar energy that arrives at a surface. It is measured per unit area of the surface receiving sun rays. Therefore, solar irradiance is measured in terms of the amount of unit solar energy per unit area of surface. A typical measurement unit for solar irradiance is watts per square meters (W/m2). Solar irradiance is usually measured through a period of time, depending on the objectives of the analysis. **Illuminance**, on the other hand, refers to solar radiation in the region of the solar spectrum which is visible to us – i.e., our eyes respond to it. It is measured as the number of lumens falling on unit surface (i.e., square foot). Illuminance is measured in lux, and is dependent on direct solar irradiance. Solar irradiance and illuminance are important variables for a site, since they influence the amount of energy we need to use for heating, cooling, and illuminating the spaces on it (Lechner, 2015).

We can analyze and visualize the illuminance of a site surface through the year by using Ladybug's "LB Directional Solar Irradiance" component (Figure 3.5). This component collects location information, hourly direct normal illuminance, hourly diffuse horizontal radiation from the "procedure for importing and translating climate data using an EPW file" introduced in Figure 3.1. The component has a ground reflectance setting, which can be set to various values between 0 and 1 based on the context. In this example, since our sample site is in San Francisco, the value 0.18 was selected for "urban." Ground reflectance values can be viewed by floating the mouse over the "_ground_ref_" input. The "anisotropic" input requires a Boolean toggle to specify isotropic or anisotropic sky settings. An "isotropic" sky setting refers to a sky model whose properties are the same value in all directions. An "anisotropic" sky setting, on the other hand, refers to a sky model that takes variations in the sky into account (Loutzenhiser, Manz, Felsmann, et al., 2007). Finally, based on the slope and orientation of the site, surface azimuth and surface altitude values can be specified. In this example, the default azimuth of 180 (irradiance evaluated with azimuth set to south) and altitude of 90 (site surface facing straight up) were used.

In Figure 3.5, illuminance values on the sample site (throughout the year) are visualized based on the site's direct total solar irradiance. The "LB Direct Solar Irradiance" also calculates direct, diffuse, and reflected irradiance values. Figure 3.5b illustrates that highest illuminance values occur between 6:00am and 6:00pm throughout the year, with more even and higher illuminance values spreading into further hours of the day in summer months.

Incident Radiation. Incident radiation refers to the amount of solar radiation that reaches a surface. It is measured as the amount of solar energy received per unit area of the surface under analysis. A typical unit of measurement, therefore, is kilowatt-hour per square meter (kWh/m2). While surfaces parallel to the ground plane (facing the sky) receive the highest amounts of incident radiation, sloped surfaces receive varying levels of incident radiation based on their orientation and the objects around them. Incident radiation measurements can be very informative in decision-making on orientation and form, especially if design objectives include making use of solar energy.

To illustrate the possible variations in incident radiation on different surfaces, a rectangular prism was placed on our sample site, mimicking a building. The prism has a "roof," and

a

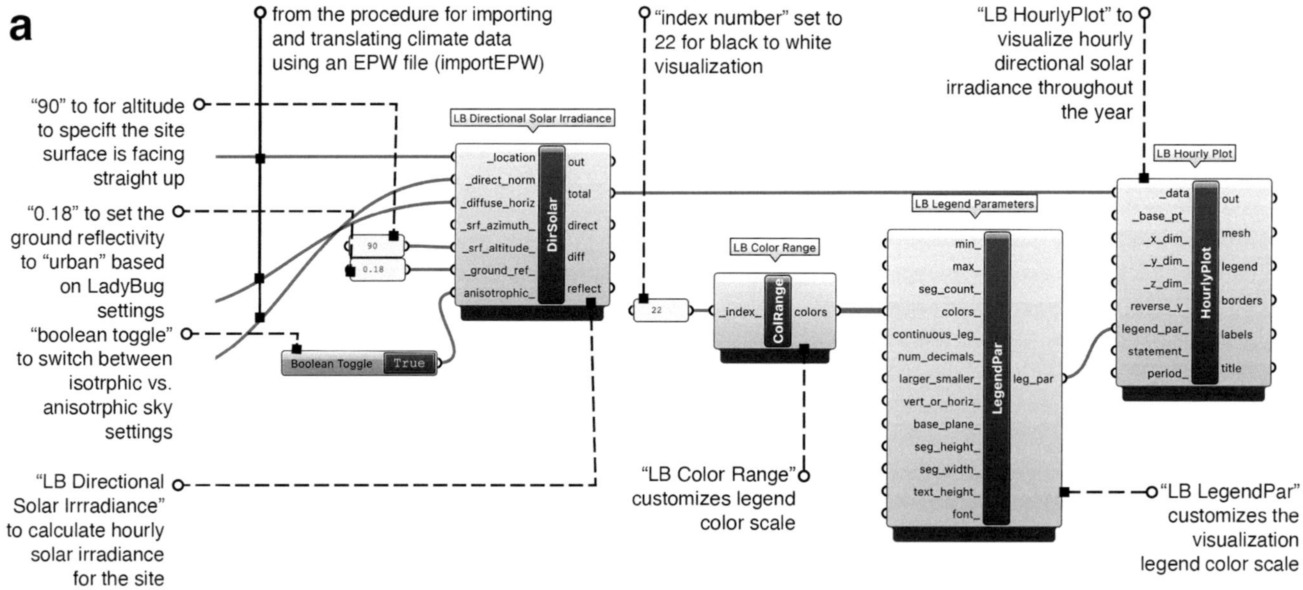

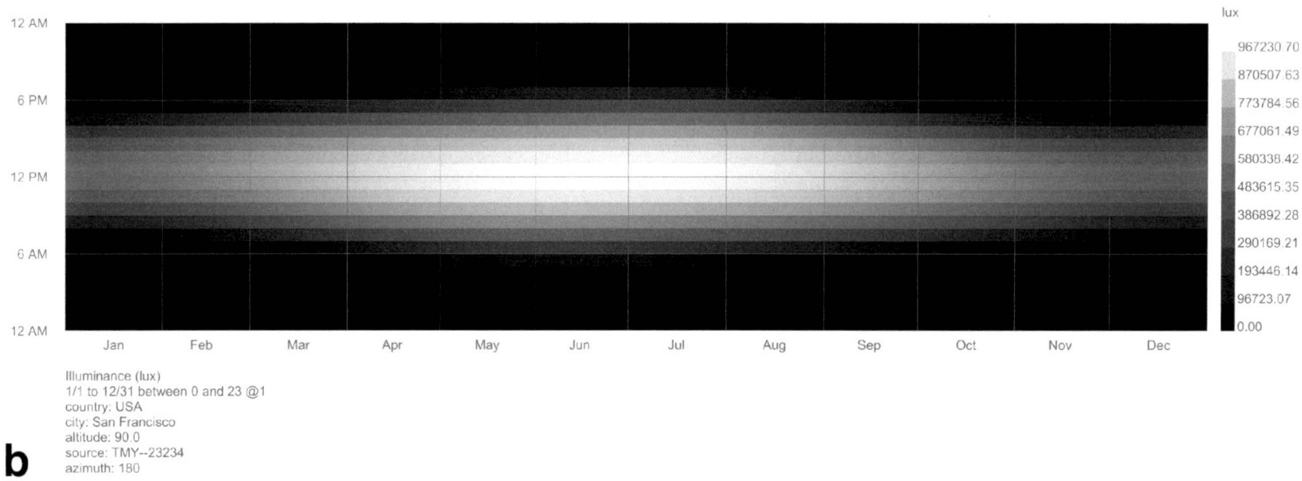

b

Figure 3.5 (a) Analyzing the illuminance of a site surface through the year by using Ladybug's "LB Directional Solar Irradiance" component; (b) illuminance values on the sample site (throughout the year) visualized based on the site's direct total solar irradiance.

has southwest, southeast, northwest, and northeast surfaces. Figure 3.6b illustrates the Grasshopper definition used for calculating incident radiation values on these surfaces. Ladybug's "LB Incident Radiation" component was used for analysis. The component requires a "sky matrix," which was created using Ladybug's "LB Cumulative Sky Matrix" component. This component creates a matrix subdivision of the sky dome, and yields solar radiation values for each cell on this matrix, based on the location, diffuse radiation, and direct radiation data from the EPW file. For the "LB Incident Radiation" component, the rectangular prism was identified as the input geometry to be analyzed, and the buildings surrounding our sample site were identified as the context geometry. Figure 3.6c and d illustrate the analysis results when the "LB Incident Radiation" component is run by setting the "run" input to "true" using a Boolean toggle.

In this analysis, the analysis period was set to an entire year. One can see that the southwest and southeast faces of the prism receive higher levels of incident radiation, and these values change on different parts of the surfaces. For example, incident radiation decreases when analysis points are closer to the ground. The northeast and northwest faces of the prism

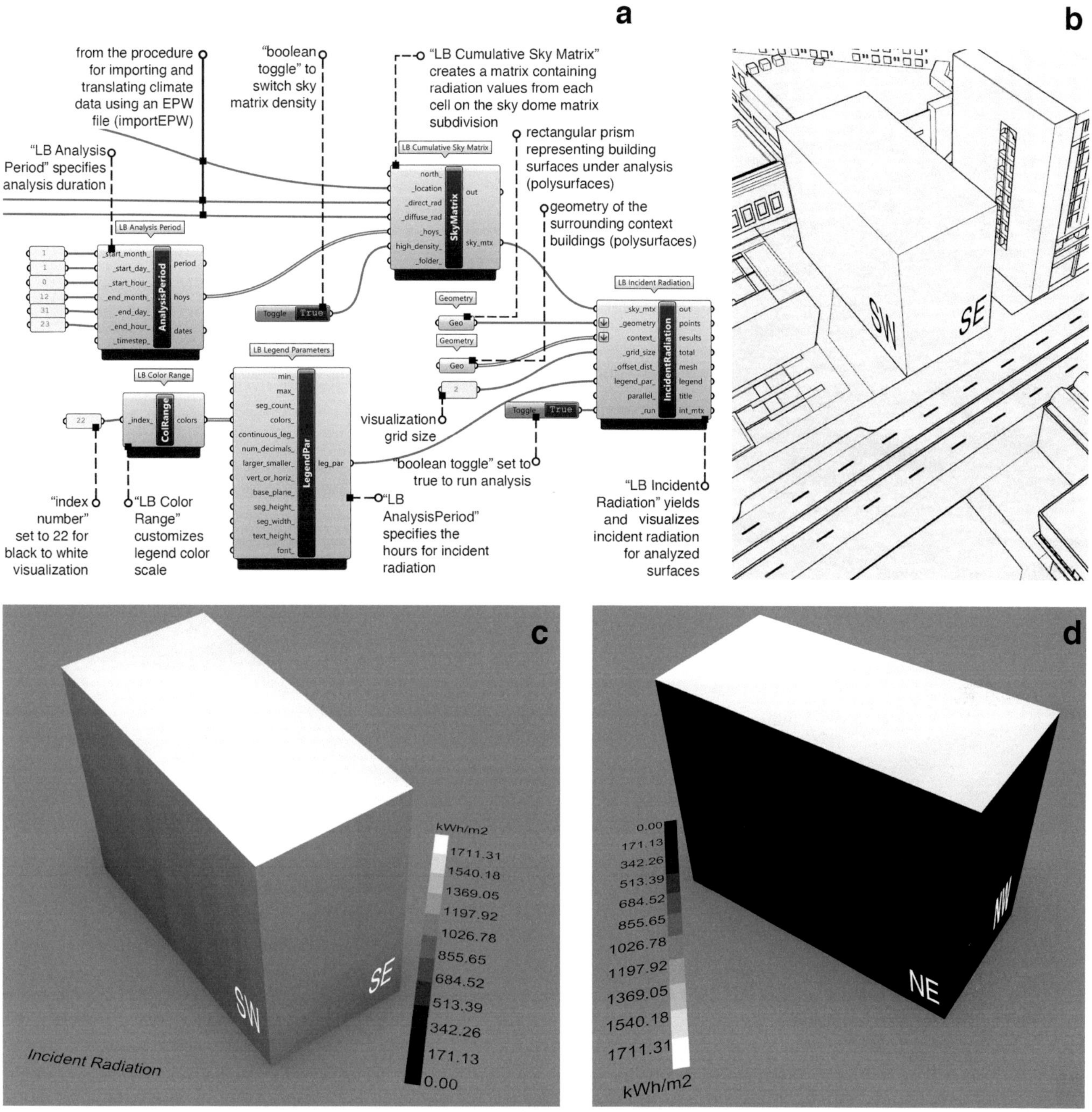

Figure 3.6 (a) The Grasshopper definition used to analyze the incident radiation levels on the sample prism; (b) the prism and its orientation analyzed; (c) incident radiation levels on the "roof," southwest and southeast faces; (d) incident radiation levels on the "roof," northwest, and northeast faces.

receive much lower levels of incident radiation, both because of their orientation and the surrounding buildings. Finally, the "roof" of the prism receives the highest levels of incident radiation, indicating that this surface may be a good place to install solar panels. Findings like these, during the site analysis phase, can influence decisions such as orientation, form, and composition in the early phases of the design process.

3.4 SITE CONDITIONS IN RELATION TO THERMAL COMFORT

Solar conditions also have important implications for human comfort. We experience the effects of temperature differences between our body and the environment through radiant heat exchange. **Radiation** is defined as heat transfer between two objects that are not in contact, and not separated by another object, through electromagnetic radiation (Kwok and Grondzik, 2011). As a result, variables such as air temperature and relative humidity around us, as well as personal factors such as personal metabolism and clothing, affect our thermal comfort. Thus, it would be reasonable to look into environmental variables, such as air temperature and relative humidity, during site analysis. Although both of these variables require complex and sophisticated calculations, parametric methods prove time and effort-saving in their analysis. Being able to calculate mean radiant temperature and relative humidity also makes it possible to calculate certain thermal comfort indices, which will be discussed in the following section.

3.4.1 Mean Radiant Temperature and Outdoor Mean Radiant Temperature

Mean radiant temperature is one of the factors that influence human comfort. It is defined as the average temperature of surfaces that surround a given point in relation to human comfort (Palmer and Chapman, 2000). When the point is outside, mean radiant temperature is influenced by solar radiation, being referred to as outdoor mean radiant temperature (OMRT). Personal factors such as body posture, height, and exposure to sun also affect the outdoor mean radiant temperature. During the site analysis phase, learning about OMRTs can be informative about how various dates and times will feel when one is outside on the project site.

Ladybug's "LB Outdoor Solar MRT" component can plot OMRT values for a location for selected periods of time. The component collects location, surface temperature, and solar radiation information from the EPW file. To provide input about personal factors such as body posture, height, and exposure to sun, Ladybug offers two components. The "LB Solar Body Parameters" component provides input on various body conditions. The "LB Human to Sky Relation" component, on the other hand, provides data on exposure to sunlight. In the example illustrated in Figure 3.7, OMRT values for our sample site are plotted for the entire year (Figure 3.7b) and for the month of June (Figure 3.7c) as two examples. In addition to location, surface temperature and solar radiation information from the "LB Import EPW" component, the "LB Outdoor Solar MRT" is provided with the default body posture information. The sample human height is set to 6 feet. The output from the "LB Outdoor Solar MRT" is then visualized using the "LB Hourly Plot" component, which is customized for analysis period using the "LB Analysis Period" component. The resulting plots show that OMRT values increase in summer months as well as around noon.

3.4.2 Relative Humidity

Another factor influencing human comfort is relative humidity. A measure of water vapor in the air, relative humidity refers to the percentage of water vapor that is present in the air, compared to the maximum amount of water vapor that could exist (dew point) (NOAA's National Weather Service; July 2021). During site analysis, analyzing the relative humidity conditions on the site can be informative about how various dates and times will feel when one is outside.

Ladybug's "LB Relative Humidity from Dew Point" component provides a straightforward method to analyze relative humidity for a selected period of time. In Figure 3.8, the Grasshopper definition used to analyze relative humidity conditions on our sample site for the month of June (Figure 3.8a), and the resulting plot (Figure 3.8b) are illustrated. The "LB Relative Humidity from Dew Point" component uses dry bulb temperature and dew point temperature data from the EPW file. As in previously discussed plots, the resulting relative humidity values are then visualized for the month of June using the "LB Hourly Plot" component.

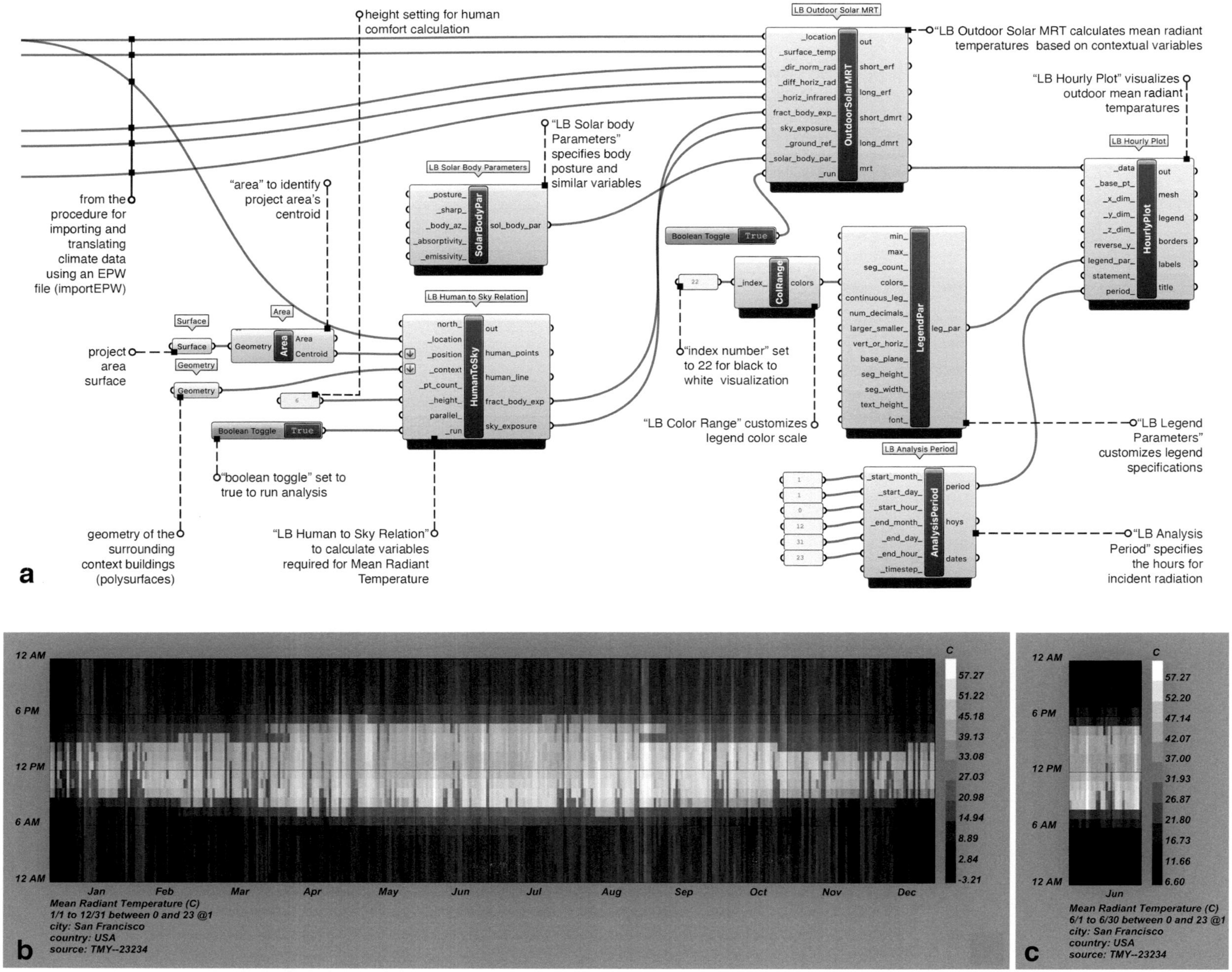

Figure 3.7 *(a) The Grasshopper definition used for plotting the sample site's outdoor mean radiant temperature (OMRT); (b) results of the analysis for the entire year; results of the analysis for June.*

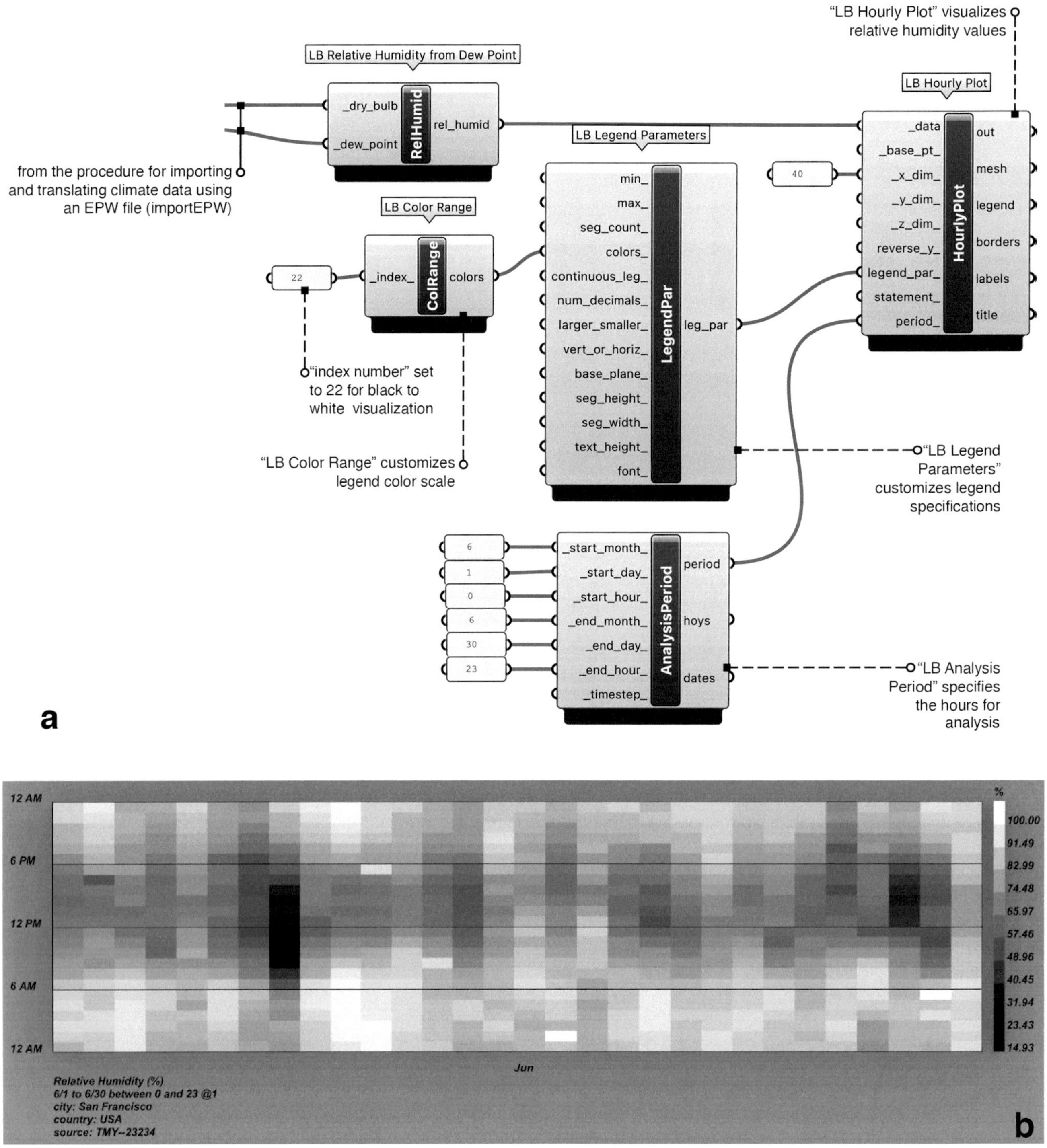

Figure 3.8 (a) The Grasshopper definition used for plotting the sample site's relative humidity values (b) results of the analysis for June.

3.4.3 Analyzing Wind

Another key variable in site analysis is wind. Wind can significantly impact indoor and outdoor comfort. While it can be advantageous for passive cooling in hot humid and hot arid climates, it can also prove disadvantageous in multiple climates. Wind speed and direction can make outdoor spaces uncomfortable, while making indoors and/or outdoors hard to keep comfortable. The key variables about wind for a given site are its speed and directional patterns. By analyzing these features, one can make informed decisions about orientation of outdoor spaces, aperture locations, passive cooling, and so on.

A common method of analyzing and visualizing wind conditions about a given site entails plotting a wind rose. A wind rose is essentially a circular visualization of wind patterns, displaying wind directions and speed for a given site for a selected period of time. Using Ladybug's "WindRose" component, we can analyze and visualize wind patterns for selected periods of time on our sample site in San Francisco. The analysis process starts with the procedure for importing and translating local climate using an EPW file, as introduced in Section 3.2.2.

In Figure 3.9, the construction of a wind rose for the sample site in San Francisco is illustrated. Starting with the procedure for importing and translating local climate using an EPW file, Ladybug's "LB WindRose" component is provided with the local wind speed and direction information. To specify the location of the wind rose, the site's centroid is provided to the component by using the "area" component yielding the centroid of the site surface. Ladybug's "LB WindRose" component then plots a wind rose around the site's centroid, visualizing wind speeds and directions.

An analysis period was not specified; therefore, the figure illustrates a yearly pattern in Figure 3.9. Based on the visualization, one can observe that the predominant wind direction and speed throughout the year is from west – northwest direction for our sample site. West and northwest directions follow the predominant wind pattern with their direction and speed data.

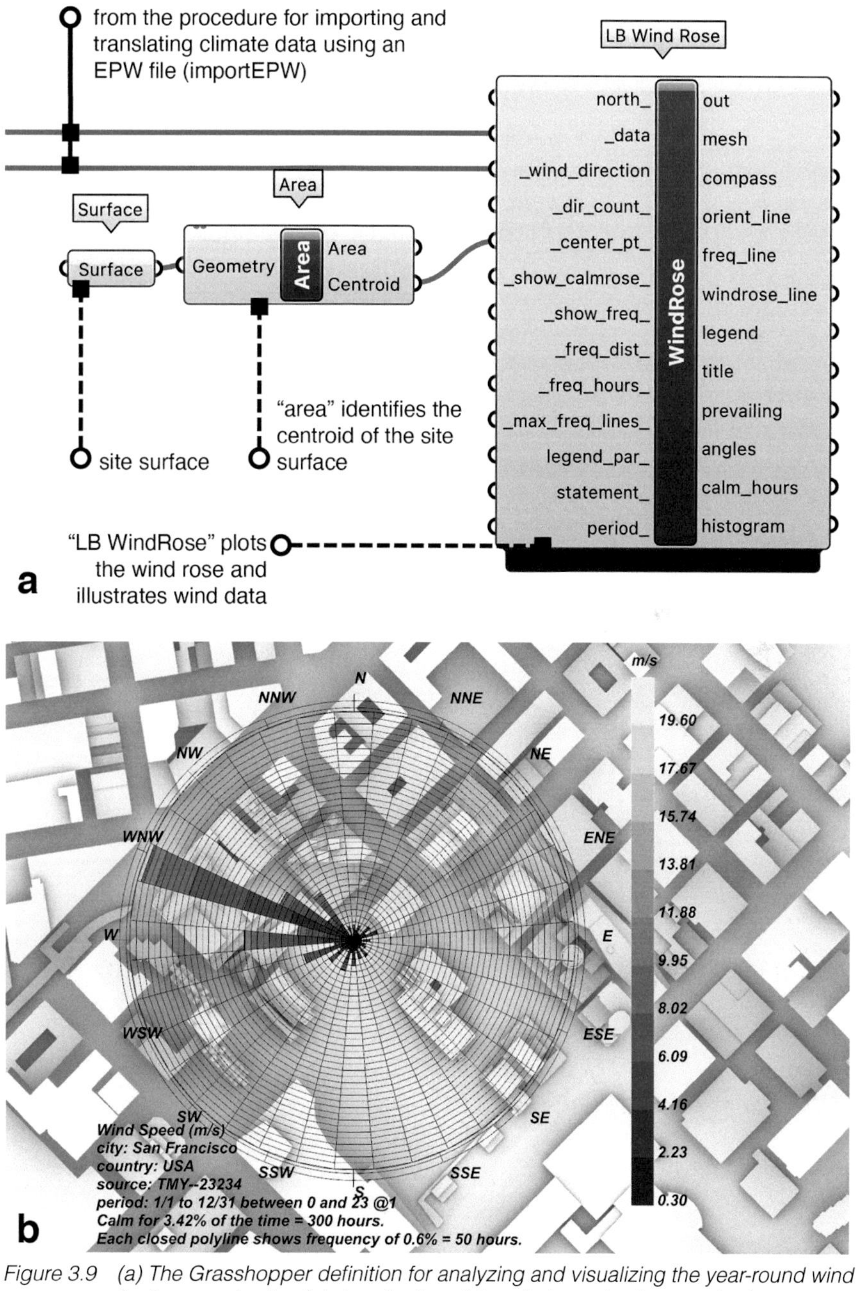

Figure 3.9 (a) The Grasshopper definition for analyzing and visualizing the year-round wind rose for the sample site; (b) visualization of the wind rose for the sample site.

3.4.4 Bringing Thermal Comfort Information Together: Universal Thermal Climate Index

Another way to describe human comfort is to use thermal comfort indices. Thermal comfort indices help identify the way humans experience the environment, specifically atmospheric conditions. One of these indices is the Universal Thermal Climate Index (UTCI). UTCI's calculations are based on air temperature, relative humidity, wind speed, and mean radiant temperature. UTCI categorizes human thermal experience – thermal stress – under the following headings: extreme heat stress (temperatures higher than +46°C), very strong heat stress (temperatures between +38°C and +46°C), strong heat stress (temperatures between +32°C and +38°C), moderate heat stress (temperatures between +26°C and +32°C), no thermal stress (temperatures between +9°C and +26°C), slight cold stress (temperatures between +9°C and 0°C), moderate cold stress (temperatures between 0°C and −13°C), strong cold stress (temperatures between −13°C and −27°C), very strong cold stress (temperatures between −27°C and −40°C), and extreme cold stress (temperatures below −40°C) (European Climate and Health Observatory, July 2021). Since the UTCI considers multiple factors in describing human comfort, it is a clear indicator of a site's thermal conditions throughout the year.

Ladybug's "LB UTCI Comfort" component uses dry bulb temperature, mean radiant temperature, relative humidity, and wind velocity data to calculate UTCI values (Figure 3.10b). Mean radiant temperature data are provided by the "LB Outdoor Solar MRT" component, through the procedure described in the outdoor mean radiant temperature section (Figure 3.7). "LB UTCI Comfort" component generates four types of outputs. The "UTCI" output provides the main UTCI values (Figure 3.10b).

The "comfort," "condition," and "category" outputs categorize the UTCI data into various scales of thermal comfort. The "comfort" output categorizes the data into "comfortable" and uncomfortable" thermal conditions (Figure 3.11a). The "condition" output categorizes the data into "hot," "neutral," and "cold" thermal conditions (Figure 3.11b). Finally, the "category" output categorizes the data into 11 thermal stress categories (Figure 3.11c). The examples introduced in Figures 3.10 and 3.11 covered an entire year's period. Each of the rectangular cells in the visualizations represent one hour of the respective date and time. Based on these visualizations, one can interpret that San Francisco's climate yields mainly moderate thermal conditions.

3.5 SITE CONDITIONS IN RELATION TO CONTEXTUAL VISUAL CONNECTIONS

Views to and from the site constitute an important part of site analysis. There may be views around the site to avoid or emphasize based on design objectives. Visual connections between a building, its spaces, and desirable urban and/or natural spaces are influential on human preferences of space occupancy. Based on the program of the project, the design proposal may need to have high or low visibility from the surroundings. Analyzing views, therefore, may be influential on design decisions.

While visibility and its influences on human behavior and perceptions have been studied quantitatively and qualitatively over the past few decades, parametric software and methods, especially during the last decade, have enabled more complex analysis of spatial visibility using higher resolutions.

3.5.1 The Isovist

A key metric that enables quantitative visibility analysis is termed the "isovist." The term "isovist" refers to the total set of all points that can be seen from a selected vantage point in a spatial configuration. Specifically, for any vantage point in a spatial configuration (i.e., vantage point x), all points visible from a given vantage point x constitute a set of points in that spatial configuration. This set of points visible from a given vantage point is referred to as an "isovist":

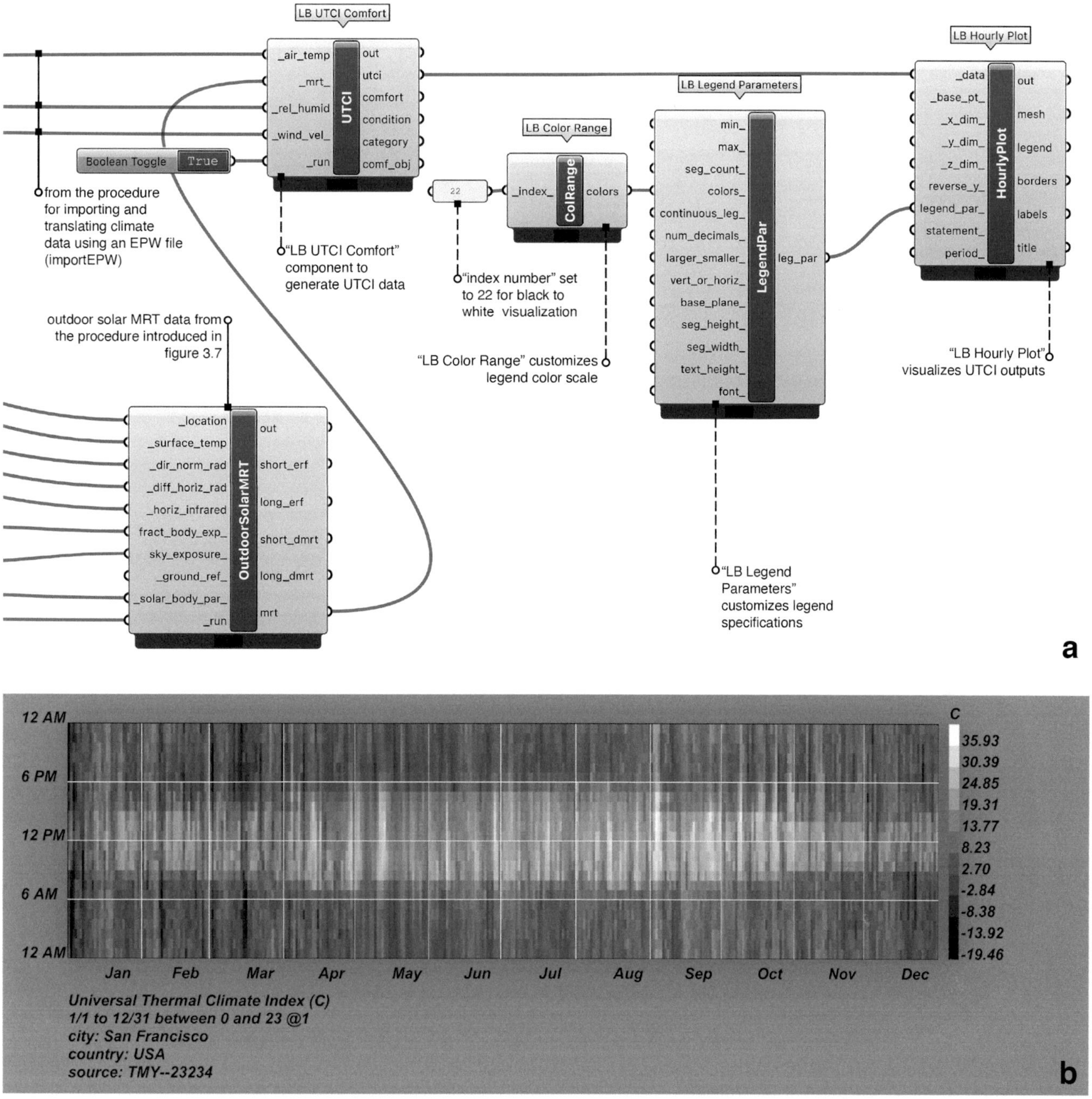

Figure 3.10 (a) The Grasshopper definition used for calculating UTCI values; (b) UTCI values (Celsius) for the sample site in San Francisco.

$$Vx = \{v \in D: v \text{ is visible from } x\} \text{ (Benedikt, 1979: 49)}$$

Benedikt (1979) defines the area of an isovist for a vantage point x as "Ax = A(Vx)," which refers to the area of how much space can be seen from vantage point x.

An isovist for a given vantage point ***x*** in space can easily be drawn manually by taking the vantage point as the start point of lines that extend to infinity, and stop whenever they hit an object, such as a building or wall. If this process is repeated for a high number of times (i.e., every 10 degrees) in all directions (i.e., 360 degrees), and the endpoints of the lines are connected, what results is an isovist for the given vantage point.

Figure 3.12 illustrates the manual development of an isovist for our sample urban site's centroid. First, the site's centroid is identified, and lines of sight are extended every 10 degrees

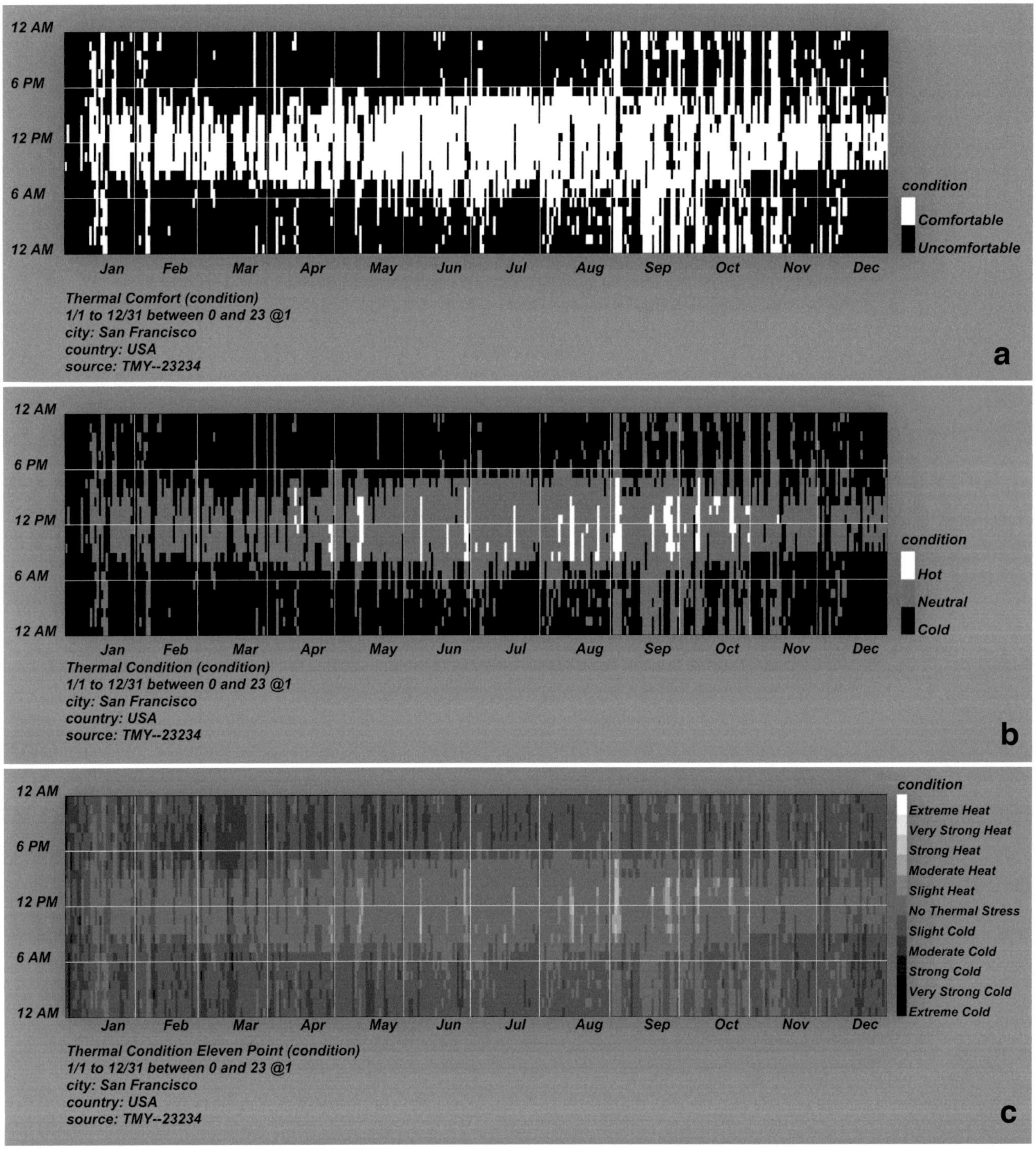

Figure 3.11 UTCI visualizations using three outputs: (a) "comfort" output categorizes the data into "comfortable" and uncomfortable" thermal conditions; (b) "condition" output categorizes the data into "hot," "neutral," and "cold" thermal conditions; and (c) "category" output categorizes the data into 11 thermal stress categories.

with a radius of 400 feet, where each line stops when it hits an obstacle (in this case, neighboring buildings) (Figure 3.12a). Then, additional lines of sight are drawn through those corners of all obstacles that are visible from the vantage point. Like the original lines of sight, the lines through visible corners of obstacles stop at the next possible obstacle (Figure 3.12b). When the endpoints of all lines of sight are connected as a polyline, the isovist for the centroid of our sample site is plotted (Figure 3.12c). Figure 3.12d shows the isovist along with all lines of sight drawn.

Plotting and visualizing isovists have become much more time efficient thanks to parametric methods. Grasshopper provides a native "IsoVist" component for parametrically developing isovists. The Ladybug plug-in also provides components that can develop isovists, as well as components that can conduct visibility analysis, by simultaneously developing isovists for multiple points in space and then visualizing all points' isovist areas through color-coding, as if they are pixels.

To illustrate isovist analysis using parametric methods, let us first analyze our sample urban site's visibility in San Francisco by developing the isovist of a vantage point on the site. Figure 3.13a illustrates the Grasshopper definition used for this analysis. First, the site surface's centroid is identified using the "area" component, and the centroid is then moved in the z direction for 5.5 feet to emulate an eye-level vantage point. The centroid is then connected to the "plane" input of the "IsoVist" component. The "count" input specifies the number of lines that will be drawn starting with the vantage point, and the "radius" specifies the limit at which each line will stop of they don't hit an obstacle. In this example, the radius was set to 1000 feet. The higher the number of lines drawn, the more precise the isovist calculation gets. The buildings around the site are then introduced to the "obstacles" input. The "points" output of the component provides coordinates for the endpoint of each line. When these points are connected using the "Polyline" component and turning on the Boolean toggle for "closed" on, the closed polyline of the vantage point's isovist is drawn. For visualization purposes, the closed polygon is then used to define a

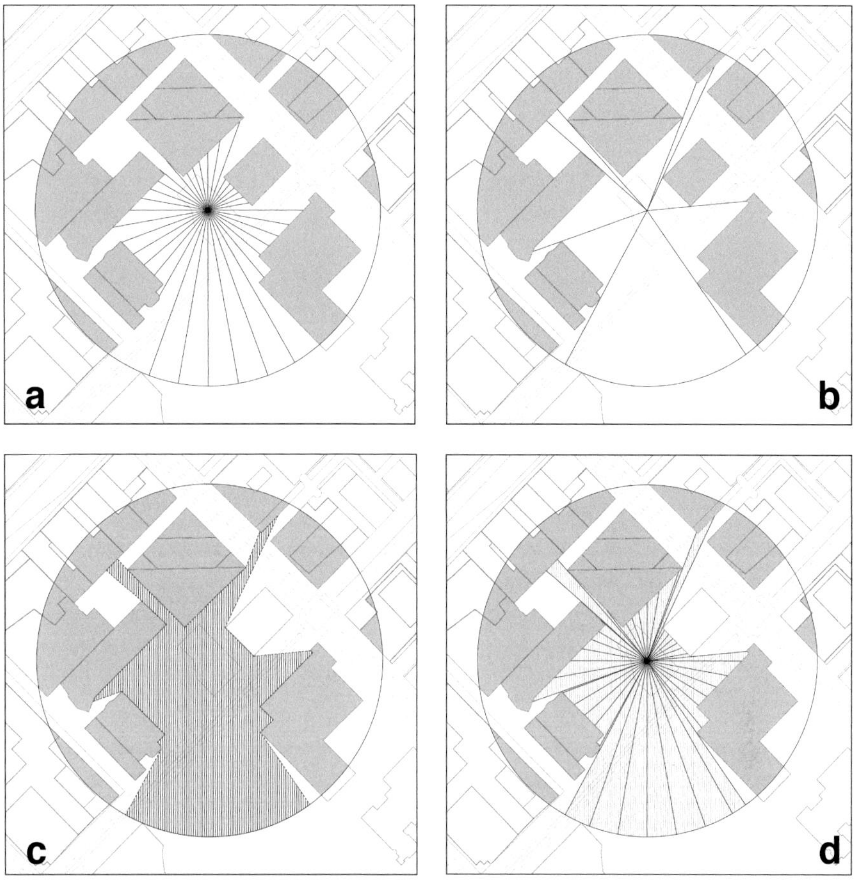

Figure 3.12 *Manual development of an isovist for the centroid of the sample site in San Francisco using a 400-feet radius. (a) Lines of sight drawn from the site's centroid in all directions every 10 degrees; (b) lines of sight drawn through those corners of all obstacles that are visible from the vantage point; (c) the resulting isovist; (d) the isovist and all lines of sight together.*

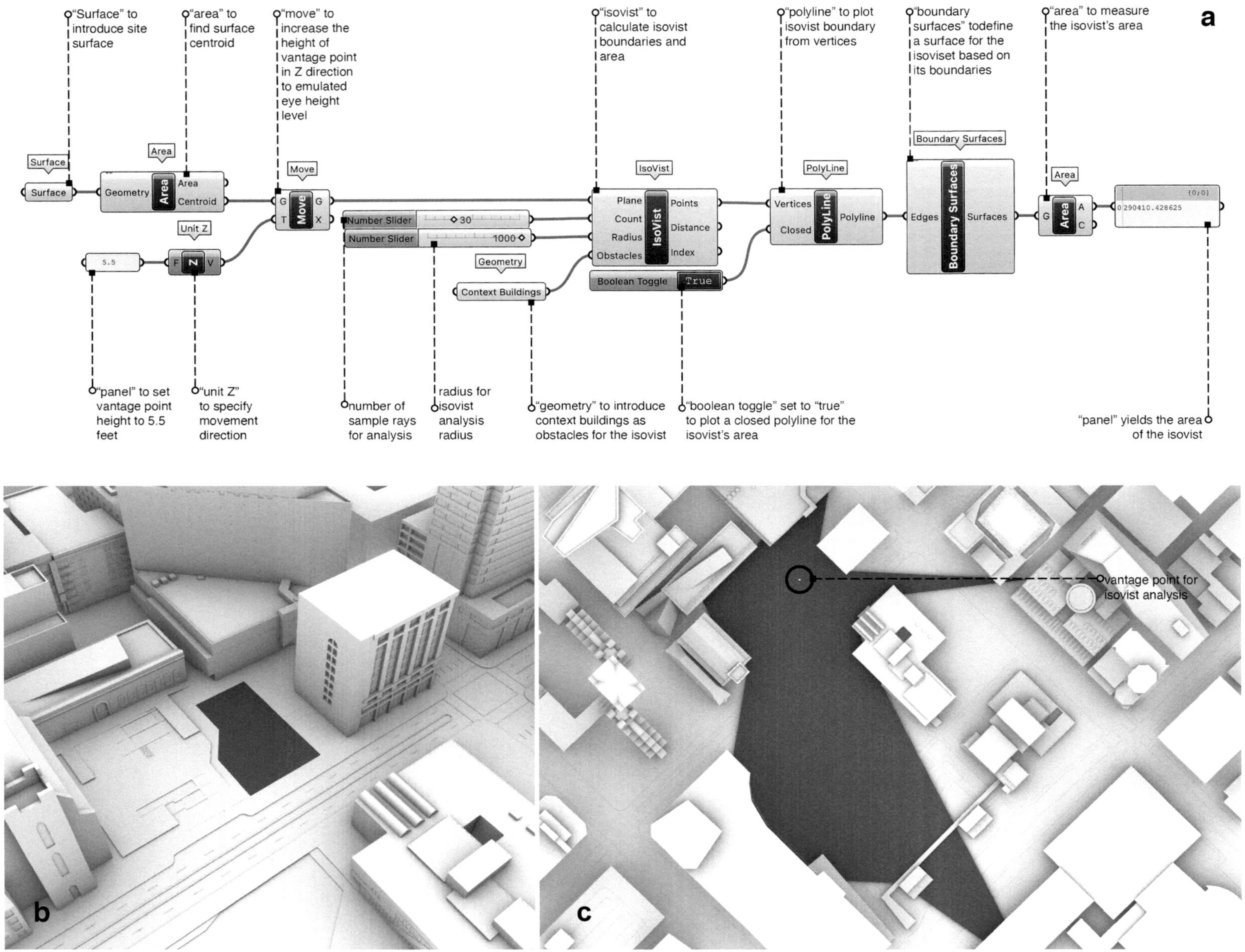

Figure 3.13 (a) The Grasshopper definition used to develop the isovist for the sample site's centroid at 5.5 feet height; (b) the isovist of our sample site's centroid in top view.

surface by using the "Boundary Surfaces" component (Figure 3.13b). Finally, the area of the isovist is calculated using the "area" component.

A similar definition can be used to develop a multi-isovist analysis of a site. Let us imagine that the southern portion of our sample urban site is being considered for commercial uses, for which high visibility is a desirable feature. In Figure 3.14, 24 sample vantage points are created 5.5 feet over the target site using Grasshopper's "Planar Grid" component. The distance between points on X and Y directions is set to 10 feet, therefore a 6 × 4 grid, 24 vantage points, are sufficient to cover the target site (Figure 3.14a). Rotating the vantage points to cover the surface of the site, the same procedure described for Figure 3.13 is followed. The resulting 24 isovists are visualized and the isovist areas are calculated. To get a cumulative isovist area for the target site, isovist surfaces can be joined, and the resulting polygon's area can be calculated to compare with alternative sites (Figure 3.14c).

3.5.2 Visibility Percent Analysis

It is also possible to conduct a comparative visibility analysis for multiple vantage points. While this can be done using native components analyzing a grid of vantage points superimposed on the site, a variety of plug-ins also offer time-saving components to conduct visibility analysis. The commonly used Ladybug plug-in introduced earlier in this chapter provides a "LB View Percent" component for visibility analysis.

Figure 3.15 illustrates a sample visibility analysis for our sample urban site in San Francisco. The site surface to be analyzed and the buildings in context are introduced to "_geometry" and "context_" inputs, respectively. The "view type" input offers five different analysis types to be selected using a number slider. In this example, view type 1 refers to the approximate human peripheral vision, where visibility is measured with a 60-degree vision cone (30 degrees above and below the horizontal eye line). The grid size was set to two feet, placing a vantage point grid of 2 feet by 2 feet on the site. Finally, the offset distance was set to move vantage points 6 feet above the site (Figure 3.15a). When the "_run" input is set to true using a Boolean toggle, the component yields a color-coded plot of visibility values in percentage (Figure 3.15c). The plot shows that visibility on and from the site gradually increases as vantage points get closer to the street. Such findings can be influential on design decisions in relation to the visibility requirements of program elements.

3.6 SITE CONDITIONS IN RELATION TO SLOPE

Getting a solid understanding of the slopes on a site is the last site analysis aspect we will discuss using parametric methods in this chapter. Analyzing a site's slopes using parametric methods requires knowledge of how slope is calculated. In addition, since a sloped site's surface is essentially a complex surface, and since project sites rarely have a single slope, slope analysis using Grasshopper also requires knowledge of complex surface subdivision. Let us first take a look into how slope of a surface is calculated.

3.6.1 Slope

Given a sloped surface's cross section, the slope of the surface is measured by dividing the site's (vertical) rise by its (horizontal) run. For example, if there is 10 feet of level change between two sides of a site, and the distance between those two sides is 100 feet, the slope equals 0.1. Slope is commonly reported as percentage slope, which is the slope value multiplied by 100. Therefore, a site that has a slope value of 0.1 has a percentage slope of 10 (percentage slope = 10%). Figure 3.16 illustrates a sloped surface, its cross section and its slope calculation.

It is rare that a project site has a single slope value. The earth's terrain is a complex surface composed of hills and dips, yielding different slope values at different portions of land. In

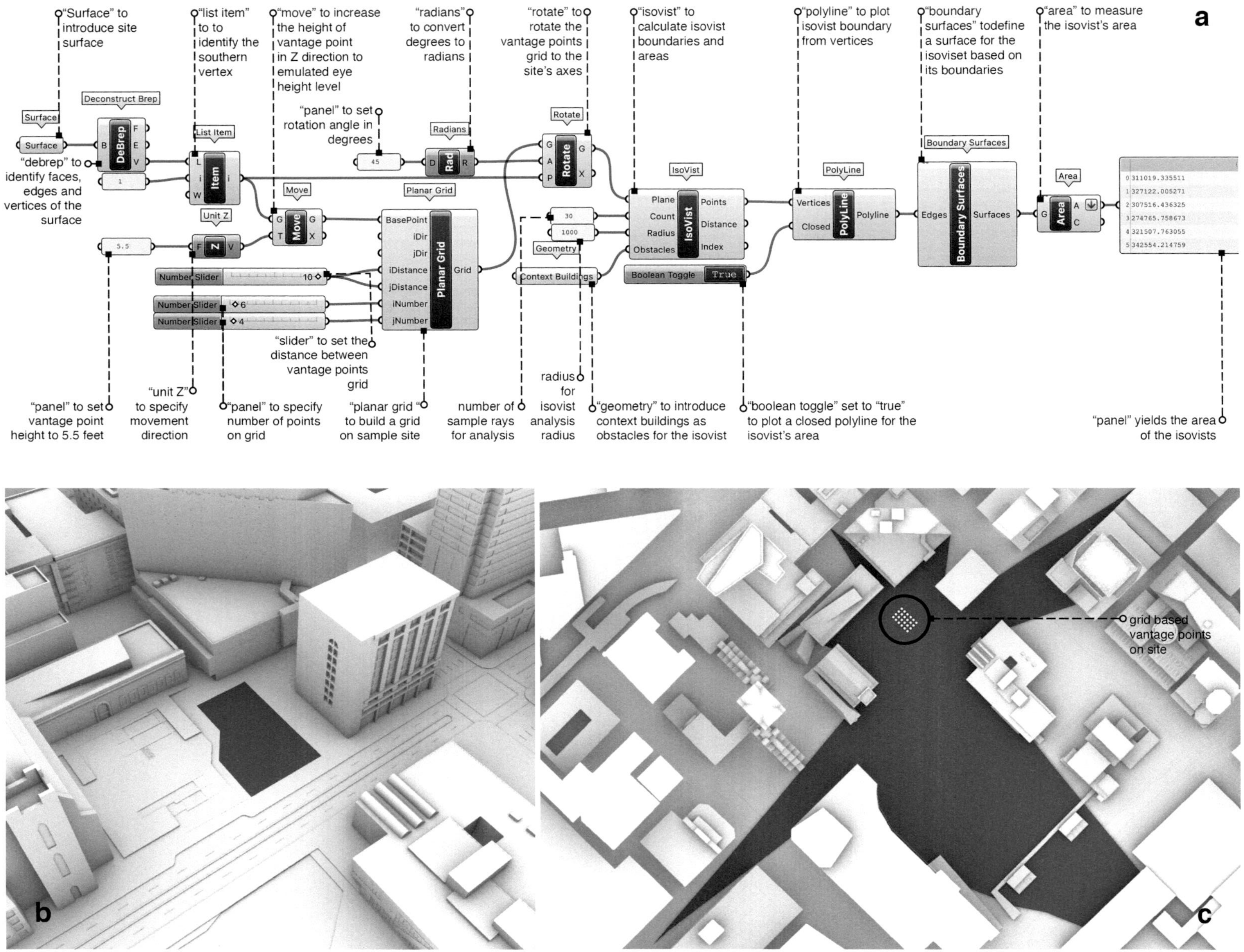

Figure 3.14 (a) The Grasshopper definition used for isovist analysis with multiple vantage points; (b) the target site; and (c) resulting isovists developed for the 24 vantage points created.

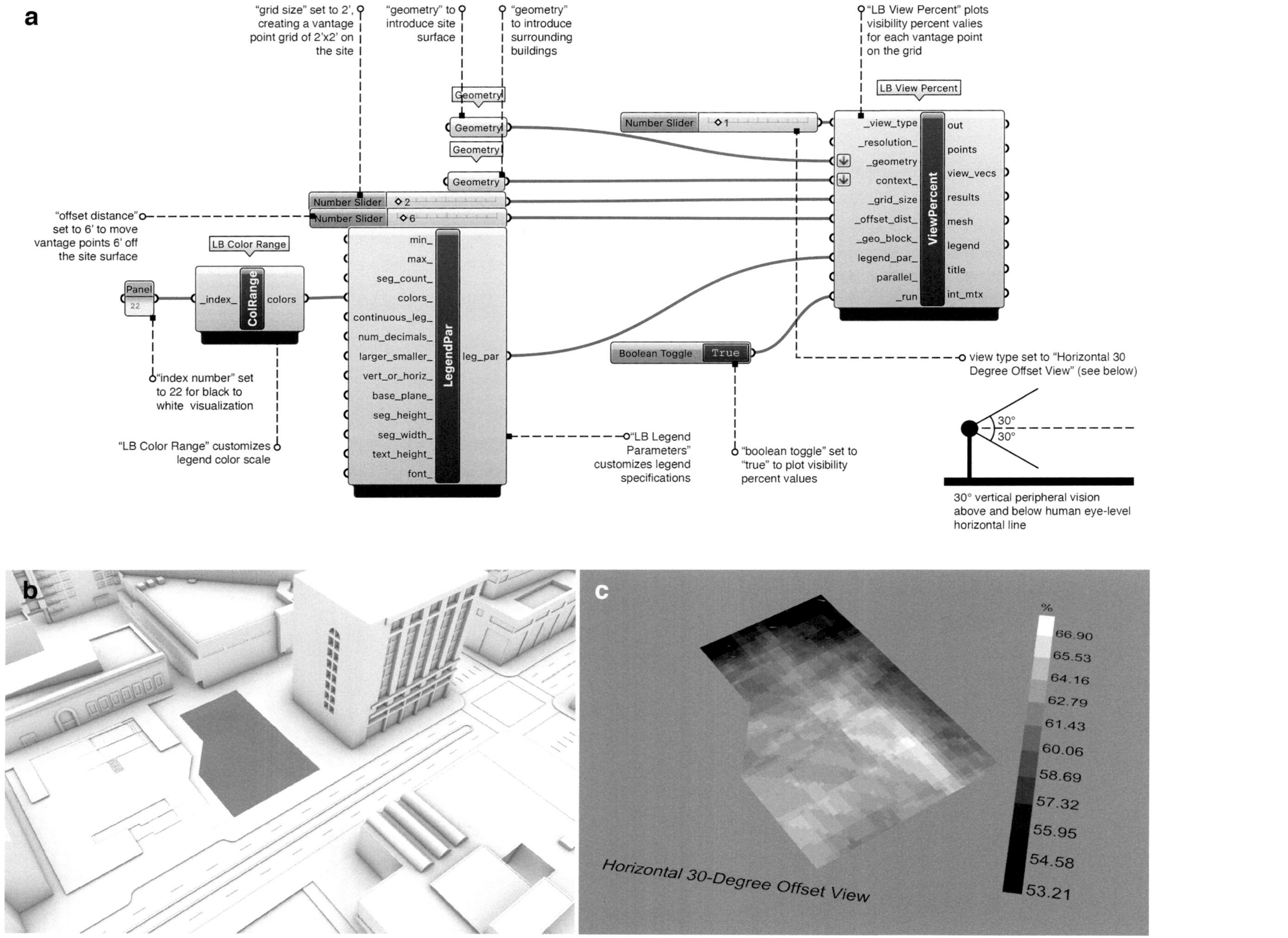

Figure 3.15 (a) The Grasshopper definition used for visibility percent analysis; (b) the sample urban site in San Francisco; (c) resulting plot from visibility percent analysis for the sample site.

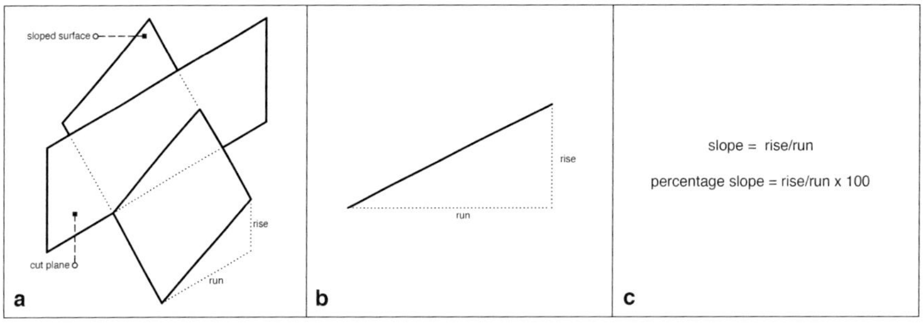

Figure 3.16 (a) A sample sloped surface; (b) the surface's cross section; (c) the surface's slope.

order to conduct a thorough slope analysis, it is common to subdivide the site into a number of its subdivisions and analyze the slope of each subdivision. This way one can make decisions about which portions of the site are more suitable for various uses. For example, a portion of the site may have a very steep slope, making it less suitable for a building, but more suitable for another use, such as landscape feature. Color-coding the site based on its slope values is a common method for visualizing slope conditions on the site. Color-coding is often done by subdividing the site using a grid, and then color-coding each square on the grid based on its slope value. To undertake this task, we will first discuss basic even subdivision of complex surfaces using Grasshopper.

3.6.2 Basic Even Subdivision of Surfaces

Systematic subdivision of surfaces is based on the Cartesian coordinate system – a system which all computer-aided design software relies on to define points, lines, surfaces, and volumes. A Cartesian coordinate system defines every point in space by associating it to a set of three numbers. These three numbers refer to three axes, non-coplanar X, Y, and Z axes that all intersect at one point: the origin, which is identified with the coordinates "0, 0, 0" (Korn and Korn, 2000).

A surface is a two-dimensional geometry. Consequently, it can be divided in two directions. In parametric modeling, these dimensions are commonly referred to as U and V directions on the surface's coordinate system. This system is akin to the Cartesian coordinate system's X and Y coordinates in two dimensions. The U and V axes refer to the axes of the target object's coordinate system, which in this case is a surface.

The sample curved surface in Figure 3.17 can be subdivided evenly using Grasshopper's "Isotrim" component. This component subdivides a surface in U and V directions. To do the subdivision, "Isotrim" needs subdivision of a "two-dimensional domain" in two directions. A "domain" is a set of two numbers between a minimum value and a maximum value. A single-dimensional domain only has a U dimension, such as a minimum of 0 and a maximum of 10. A two-dimensional domain has U and V dimensions, each of which have their own minimum and maximum values. For example, the U dimension of a two-dimensional domain can have a minimum value of 0 and a maximum of 10, while its V dimension can have a minimum value of 10 and a maximum of 20. A three-dimensional domain has U, V, and W dimensions akin to the X, Y, and Z dimensions on the Cartesian coordinate system, and each of these dimensions can have minimum and maximum values independent of each other.

Figure 3.17 illustrates a two-dimensional curved surface introduced into the Grasshopper interface. When the surface is introduced into Grasshopper and connected to the "Surface" input of the "Isotrim" component, one notices that a "Domain" input is required to complete the subdivision. Since this is a two-dimensional surface, a two-dimensional domain can be defined by using the "Divide Domain 2" component. The surface defines the two-dimensional domain when it is connected to the "I (domain)" entry of the Isotrim component. The U and V

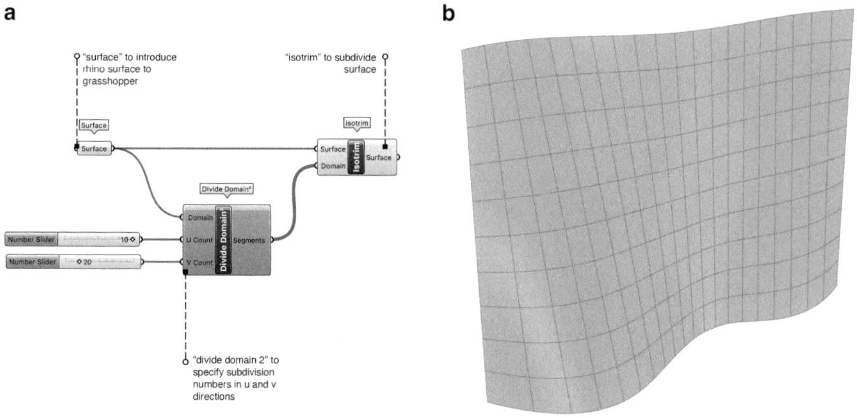

Figure 3.17 Basic curved surface subdivision using the Isotrim and Divide Domain2 components. (a) The Parametric subdivision operation; (b) resulting subdivided surface.

values can then be specified using Grasshopper panels or sliders set to integer values. By connecting the divided domain to the "D (domain)" input of the Isotrim component, one can subdivide the surface evenly on U and V axes with different U and V values. In Figure 3.17, the surface subdivided into 10 on U axis, and 20 on V axis is illustrated. Such subdivisions set the foundation for many parametric operations. In this section, we will subdivide a site's complex surface. However, similar subdivisions are also used in other phases of the architectural design process, such as skin systems, paneling systems, and modular applications.

3.6.3 Visualizing a Site's Slope Condition

Let us now look into how we can use the information on slope and parametric complex surface subdivision to visualize a new sample site's slope condition. The sample urban site we have been referring to for examples so far is flat; therefore, in this section we will refer to a sloped site with a complex terrain.

Figure 3.18 illustrates the procedure for color-coding the sample site based on its slope conditions. As shown in Figure 3.18b and c, the sample site's surface is complex, and it has varying slopes across the terrain. The Grasshopper definition used for visualizing the varying slopes on the site starts by subdividing the site's surface using the "divide domain 2" and "isotrim" components into 100 subdivisions on the site's U and V directions, which gives us 10,000 surfaces to analyze for slope. Since each subdivision has a different slope, and we have many subdivisions to analyze, a time efficient method to calculate slope is to find each subdivision's normal vector. Since the normal vectors are perpendicular to each subdivision, it is possible to measure their slope degrees by measuring the angle between the normal vectors and the Z-axis.

In the definition introduced in Figure 3.18a, normal vectors for subdivisions are identified by first using the "area" component to identify each subdivision's centroid, and second, using the "evaluate surface" component, which yields normal vectors. The intermediate component in this process is the "surface closest point" component, which identifies those 'u, v' points that correspond to the location of centroids on each subdivision. The resulting normal vectors and Z-axis are then connected to the "angle" component, which yields angle measurements in radians. The angle between each normal vector and Z-axis is equal to the angle between each subdivision's surface and XY plane. Using the "degrees" component, the angles are converted to degrees.

Four components are then used to translate the slope degree values to grayscale values. First, minimum and maximum slope degree values are specified using the "bounds" component

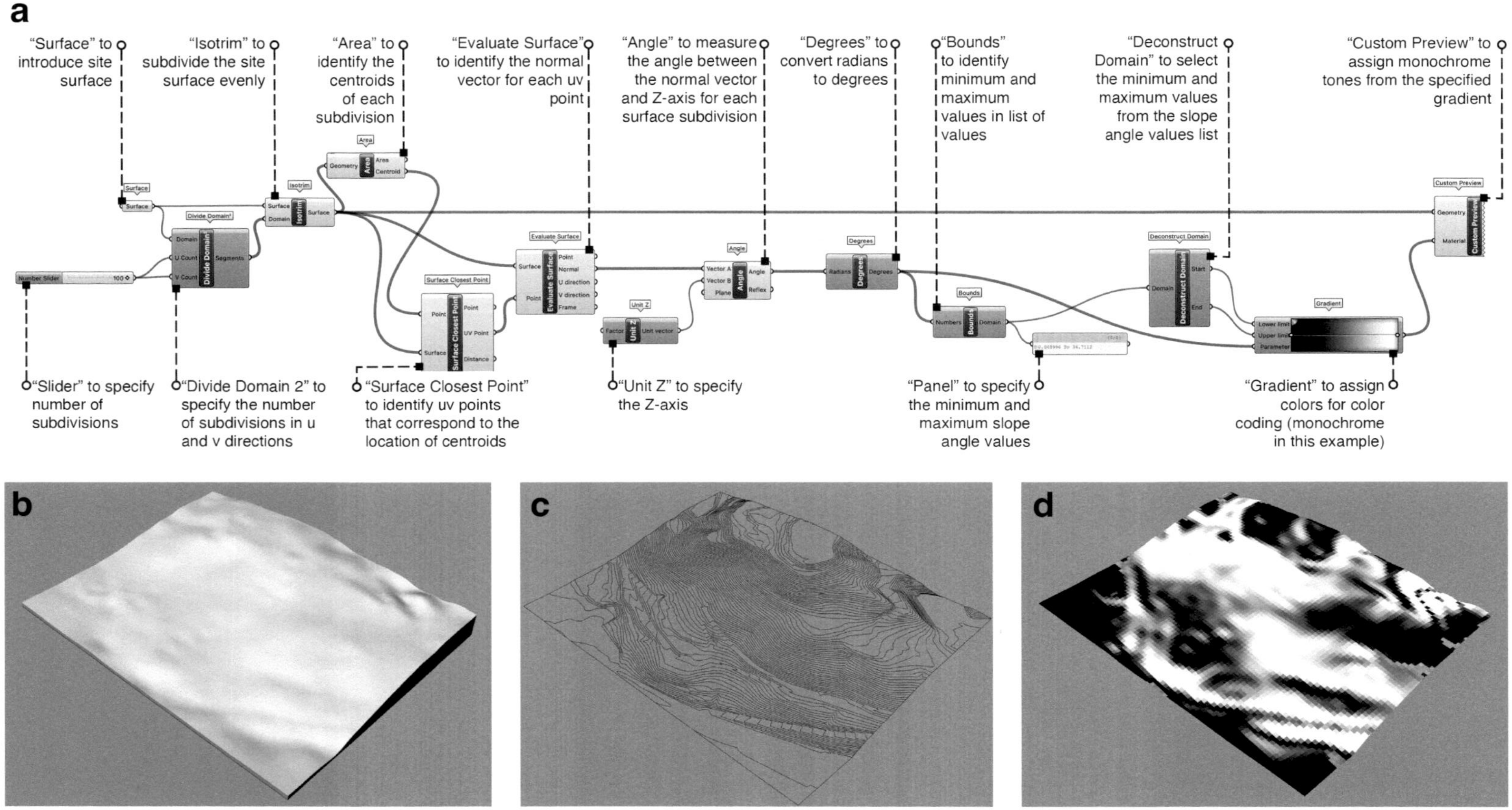

Figure 3.18 *(a) Grasshopper definition used to color-code site terrain based on slope analysis; (b) 3D model of the sample site; (c) contours of the sample site; (d) sample site subdivisions monochrome coded based on slope degree of site surface subdivisions.*

and then separated using the "deconstruct domain" component. These values correspond to the lowest value and the highest value. For the "gradient" component, the slope degree of each subdivision (the output of the "degrees" component) constitutes the "parameter" input, while the lowest and highest values constitute the "lower limit" and "higher limit" inputs. Once these inputs are provided, the "gradient" component assigns monochrome values for each slope degree value. The resulting monochrome values are then visualized using the "custom preview" component, which yields the monochrome-coded surface once it is baked into Rhinoceros environment (Figure 3.18d). The monochrome values displayed in the Rhinoceros environment provide a comparative visualization of slopes: the brighter the tone, the higher the slope of a subdivision.

3.7 USING SITE ANALYSIS FINDINGS TO INFORM CONCEPTUAL DEVELOPMENT

It is common practice to develop visual guides that bring together site analysis findings, so that informed conceptual development decisions can be made. This usually entails the development of information boards, presentations, and reports. In this chapter, we discussed an overview of site analysis and how parametric tools can contribute to the analysis. As discussed earlier, parametric methods cannot support all aspects of site analysis but can contribute to the analysis of certain types of data, particularly quantitative information. In the following chapter, we will look into the use of parametric methods in conceptual development.

CHAPTER 04

CONCEPTUAL AND PRELIMINARY DEVELOPMENT Formal Explorations and Iterations With Parametric Methods

All architectural design processes are based on an architectural concept. The architectural concept drives the designer's response to the architectural problem, program, and its context. As the rationale behind the designer's strategies, the architectural concept influences all aspects of the project from initial mass composition moves to spatial organization, material selection, and detailing. Essentially, the architectural concept defines the reason for the existence of the project:

> "Concept" derives from the Latin ***conceptum***, meaning "something conceived." The term should not be viewed as purely an abstract headline, though, but as something more universal: it is the reason for being of any object, entity, or product created by human endeavor and thought. (Tait, 2020)

An architectural concept is built on a conceptual framework that can be influenced by many factors based on the architectural problem and its context. These factors constitute sources of inspiration. Sources of inspiration for an architectural concept and its framework are many: technology, nature, human well-being, social equity, diversity, local vernacular, environmental consciousness, daydreaming, local social and environmental context, local history, politics, and so on; and their various combinations all constitute potential sources of inspiration.

Following the designer's formation of a conceptual framework, decisions on preliminary form, mass composition, and contextual relationships are made. At this stage, we as designers already have a myriad of methods and tools at our disposal. Parametric methods can especially contribute to decision-making through time-saving and novel ways of form exploration and analyzing contextual relationships to support conceptual and preliminary development. In this chapter, we will look into how parametric methods can contribute to the design process in the conceptual and preliminary development phase.

4.1 PARAMETRIC TOOLS IN FORM EXPLORATION FOR CONCEPTUAL AND PRELIMINARY DEVELOPMENT

Conceptual and preliminary development in the architectural design process often comes with a series of form explorations. The development of an architectural concept requires visual explorations in mass composition, form development in relation to the set of ideas, and inspiration sources supporting the conceptual and preliminary framework. Sketching, drawing, collage development, 3D analog modeling, and digital modeling all contribute to this process. For 3D analog modeling, materials include, but are not limited to, paper products

 DOI: 10.4324/9781003230052-4

and sculptable products such as clay. For 3D digital modeling, a variety of computer-aided design (CAD) software packages have been available for years. Parametric methods bring yet another set of materials and techniques to the conceptual and preliminary development phase in the architectural design process. In this section we will discuss parametric methods that can help with form exploration, starting with simple commands and moving toward more complex commands.

4.1.1 Parametrically Creating and Editing Irregular Shapes and Surfaces: NURBS Geometries

Non-Uniform Rational B-Splines (NURBS) are essentially mathematical representations of two- or three-dimensional geometries that are used to describe various shapes. Therefore, NURBS provide a high level of accuracy in geometric representation and can be edited by selecting and moving control points. Let us look into parametrically creating and editing irregular NURBS geometries.

Loft. Conventional CAD software offers many commands that enable the creation and editing of irregular shapes and surfaces. Among these, "lofting" two or more curves to create irregular surfaces is a common technique using Rhinoceros. Parametric techniques bring flexibility to this process, enabling fast, real-time form editing and evaluation.

Let us consider the development of a parabolically inspired shell. Conventionally, one can create and interpolate a number of points to create parabolic curves, and then loft the curves to create the shell. Parametric methods enable real-time form exploration in developing the shell through real-time editing of the source points' locations. Figure 4.1a illustrates the Grasshopper definition used for such an exploration. First, nine points created in Rhinoceros are introduced to Grasshopper using nine different "point" components. The intent is to create interpolated curves using each row of three points. Before interpolation, the middle point of each row is moved in the Z direction, using the "move," "unit Z," and "slider" components. Once the middle points are moved off of the XY plane on the Z-axis, points are interpolated using the "interpolate curve" component. Since the middle point of each row of points is moveable parametrically, the upcoming lofted surface now becomes parametric.

The last two steps in the process involve the "loft" and "loft options" components. First, the three interpolated curves are lofted to create an irregular surface depending on the parametric curves created. Then, loft properties are specified using the "loft options" component. The result is a surface dependent on the parametric interpolated curves. By moving the Z-axis location of the middle points on each row of points, one can rapidly create and evaluate many iterations. Figure 4.1b and 4.1c illustrate two options, and the vertically moveable points enable parametric editing of the parabolically inspired shell (Figure 4.1).

Sweep 1. "Sweep" is an efficient and time-saving command in Rhinoceros, which is commonly used in many types of exploration. The command provides two options: "sweep 1" and "sweep 2." Both commands also exist in Grasshopper, making it possible to conduct sweep operations parametrically. Let us look into the development of a parabolically inspired shell using the "sweep 1" component.

In this case, the same points are being used from the "loft" example, except the middle point of the middle row. Therefore, a total of eight points are used to construct the shell. Using the "move" component, the middle points of the rows and columns are moved on X and Z axes and the points are used to interpolate boundary curves. The "sweep 1" component requires two "section" curves, and one "rail" curve to guide the formation of the shell. When two "section" curves are fed into the "section" input, and the "rail" curve is fed into the "rail" input of the "sweep 1" component, the output is the desired shell surface, which comes in "boundary representation" (Brep) format (Figure 4.2).

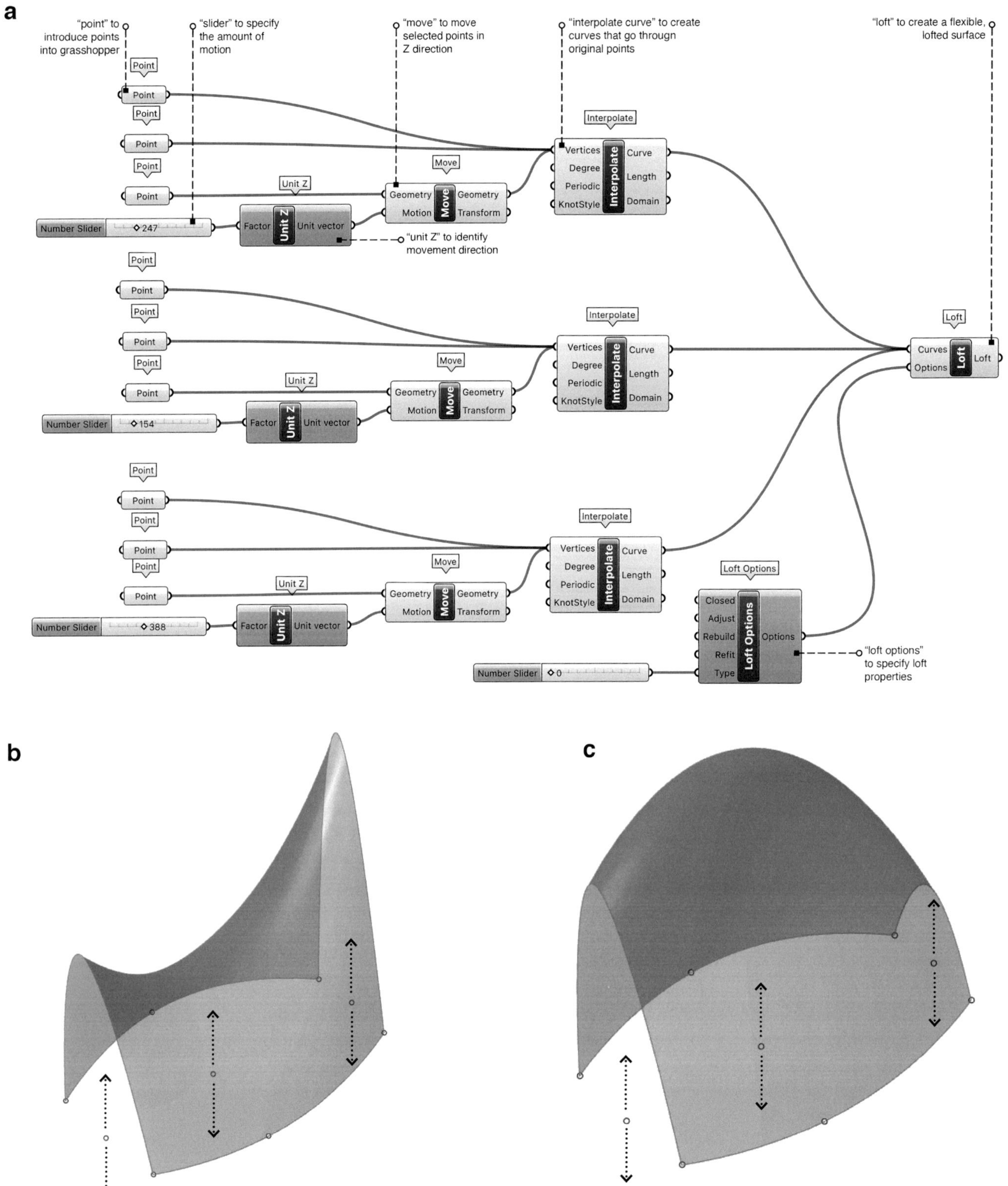

Figure 4.1 (a) The Grasshopper definition used to create a parametric, parabolically inspired shell; (b) and (c) two versions of the parabolically inspired shell created by altering the Z-axis location of the middle point of each row of points.

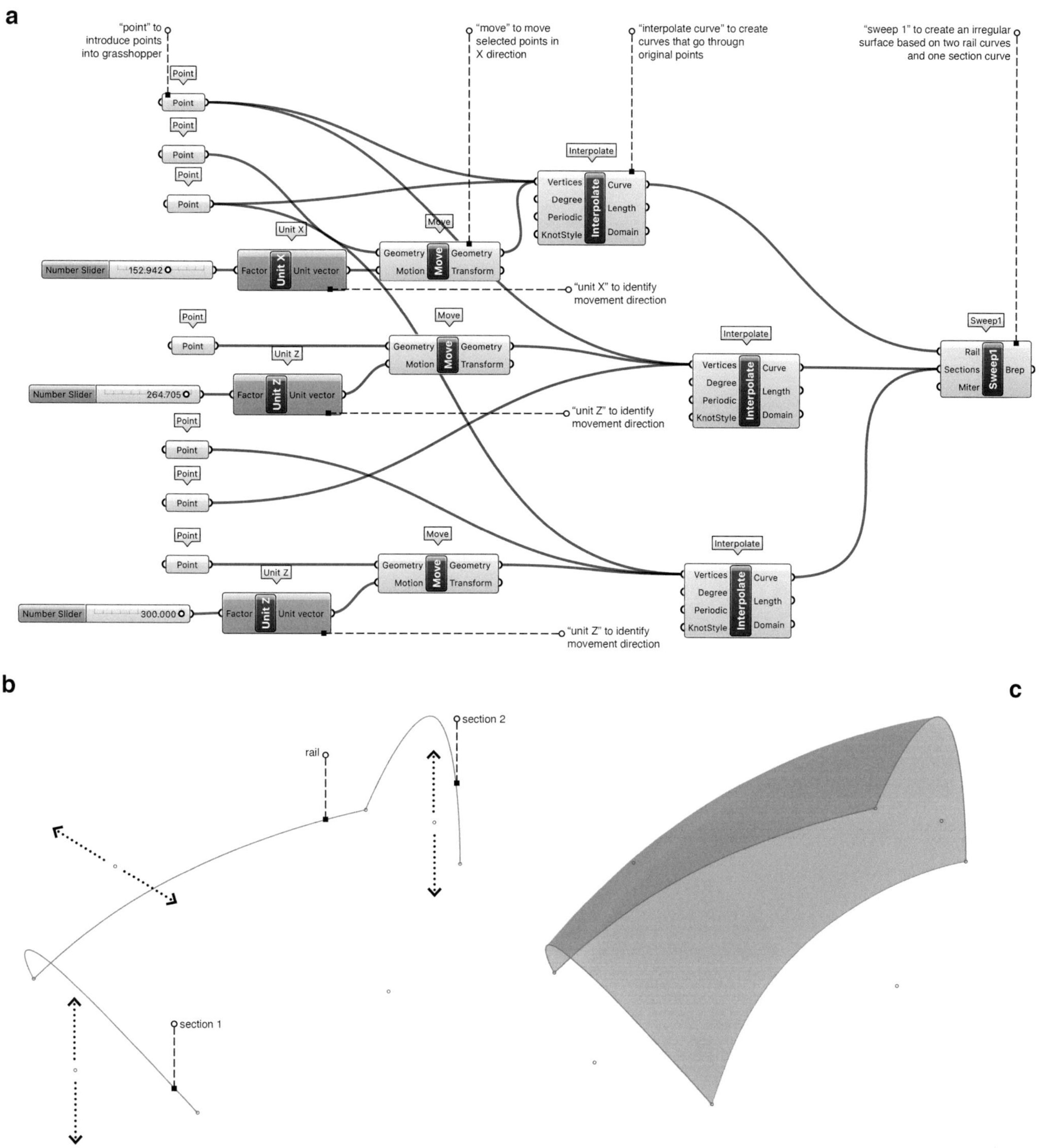

Figure 4.2 *(a) The Grasshopper definition used to create a parametric, parabolically inspired shell using the "sweep 1" component; (b) the parametric "section" and "rail" curves guiding the shell's formation; and (c) the resulting parametrically editable shell built using the "sweep 1" component.*

Sweep 2. The "sweep 2" command in Rhinoceros as well as its equivalent in Grasshopper uses two "section" and two "rail" curves to guide the formation of the shell. In this example, using the same set of points from the "sweep 1" example, two "rail" and two "section" curves are created. The "sweep 2" component yields the desired shell in Brep format when these interpolated curves are fed into the "rail 1," "rail 2," and "sections" inputs (Figure 4.3).

Surface from points. Another option for parametric form exploration is to create a set of points, whose locations can be parametrically altered, and create a surface based on the

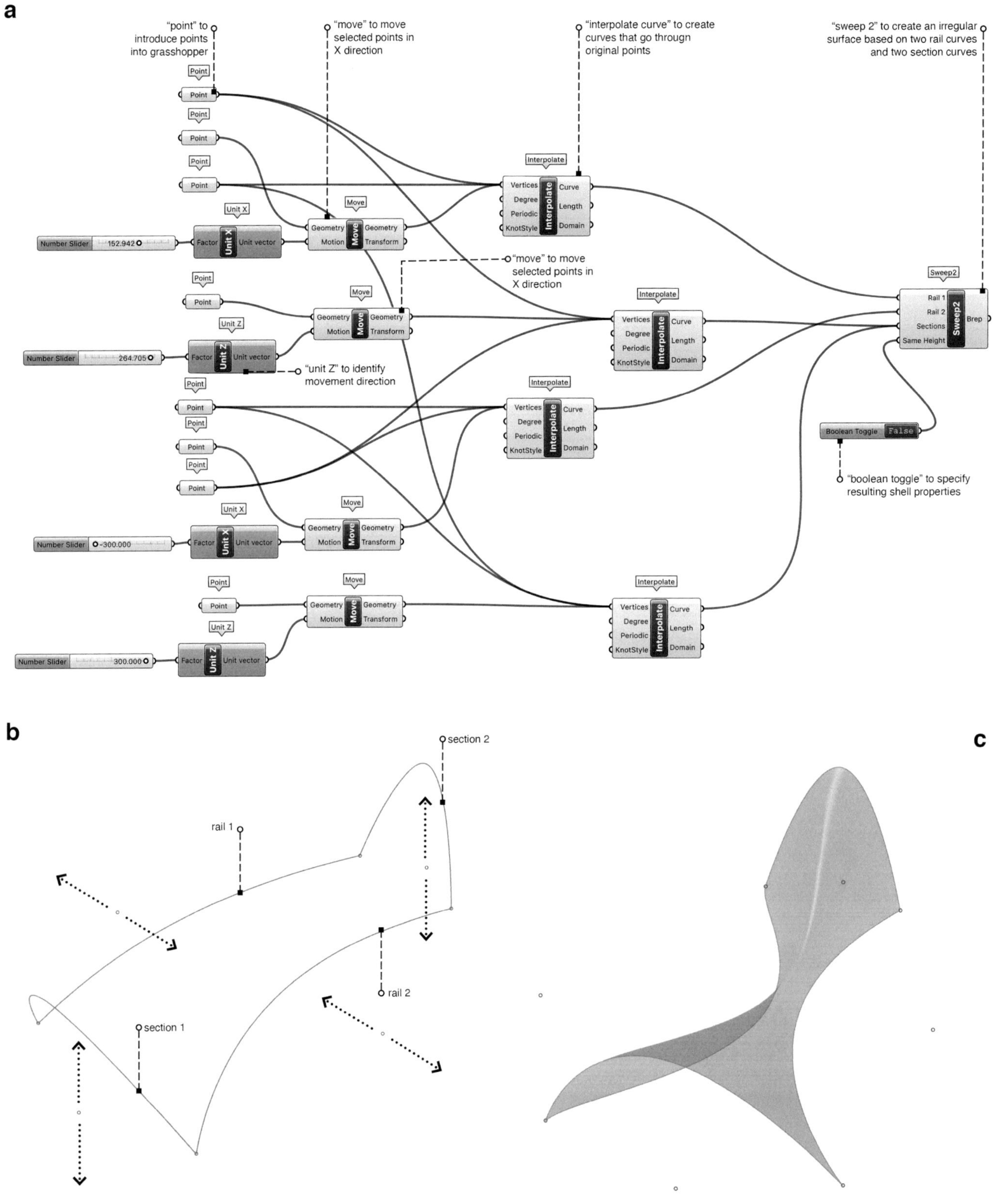

Figure 4.3 *(a) The Grasshopper definition used to create a parametric, parabolically inspired shell using the "sweep 2" component; (b) the parametric "section" and "rail" curves guiding the shell's formation; and (c) the resulting parametrically editable shell built using the "sweep 2" component.*

locations of those points. This option can be helpful in exploring façade and roof forms as well as terrains. Parametrically altering the location of points can be achieved in several ways. In this example, mathematical equations are used to alter the points' locations through the "graph mapper" component, which provides a visual interface for the user.

The exploration starts with two "construct point" components to create two surface grids: one for creating a curved surface, and the other one flat – to create a flat-based, curved roof mass. For both X and Y coordinates of the two grids, the "series" component is used to create 20 points on both axes with 10-unit distance from one another. This yields two 20 × 20 point grids. The Z-coordinates of one of the grids' points is left at the default 0. For the Z-coordinate alteration of points in the top grid, the "graph mapper" component is introduced. To select the graph types, one can right-click on the "graph mapper" component and select a graph type. In this case, the "parabola" and "sinc" graph types were selected to affect the top surface as two different ways. To address the number of gaps between points, the "range" component is introduced. The domain for the range is left at the default 0 to 1. However, the number of steps (number of gaps between points) is set to one less than the total number of points on each axis using the "subtraction" component. To exaggerate the effects of the "sine" equation, its output is multiplied with a large number using the "multiplication" component. Then, the outputs of both graph mappers are multiplied with one another to introduce a combined effect on the Z-coordinates of the points on the top grid. The output set of numbers is fed into the Z-coordinate input of the "construct point" component for the top grid. Now that two grids are ready – one flat and one curved – two surfaces can be created.

The outputs of both grids are fed into the "surface from grid" component, and one flat and one curved surface is created. To connect the two surfaces using side surfaces, both surfaces are deconstructed using the "DeBrep" component and their edges are selected using the "list item" component. Using the "loft" component to connect the edges, the side surfaces are created. Finally, the "face" of the two original surfaces are joint with the side surfaces using the "Brep join" component. The output now can be baked into a closed polysurface with a flat bottom and curved top. One can continue to explore the form of the top surface by editing the graphs, changing graph types, or altering the point locations using the sliders introduced (Figure 4.4). This Grasshopper definition can also be applied to generating curved geometries for building façades when applied on a vertically organized grid.

Repeating Data. In cases where form exploration is about rhythm in irregular shapes, Grasshopper's "repeat data" component may help support the process. In this example (Figure 4.5), a base ellipse is introduced to Grasshopper using the "curve" component. The ellipse's centroid is identified using the "area" component and is identified as the rotation center, while the ellipse is rotated using the "rotate 3D" component. Rotation angles ranging between 0 and 30 radians in 5-radian increments are then merged using a "merge" component, and these data are repeated using the "repeat data" component. A total of 13 rotations are specified. The rotated ellipses are then copied on the Z-axis using the "move" and "series" components. The movement amount is identified as 15 units. Finally, the copied and rotated curves are lofted using the "loft" component, yielding an irregularly shaped mass with a consistent rhythm. The "panel" shown in Figure 4.5 illustrates how the "repeat data" component processes the data. Although seven values are provided as input, the "length" of 13 steps yields 13 outputs, repeating the same data items 13 times.

Gradual Rotation. Another technique in form exploration could be to experiment with gradually rotating repeating geometries. In this example, a base rectilinear geometry is introduced into Grasshopper using the "curve" button. This geometry is copied vertically on the Z-axis ten times with 12-unit increments. To achieve gradual rotation, a few simple steps are involved. A maximum rotation of 45 degrees is targeted. To identify gradual rotation amounts, the "subtraction" component is used to subtract one from the total number of curves, to get the

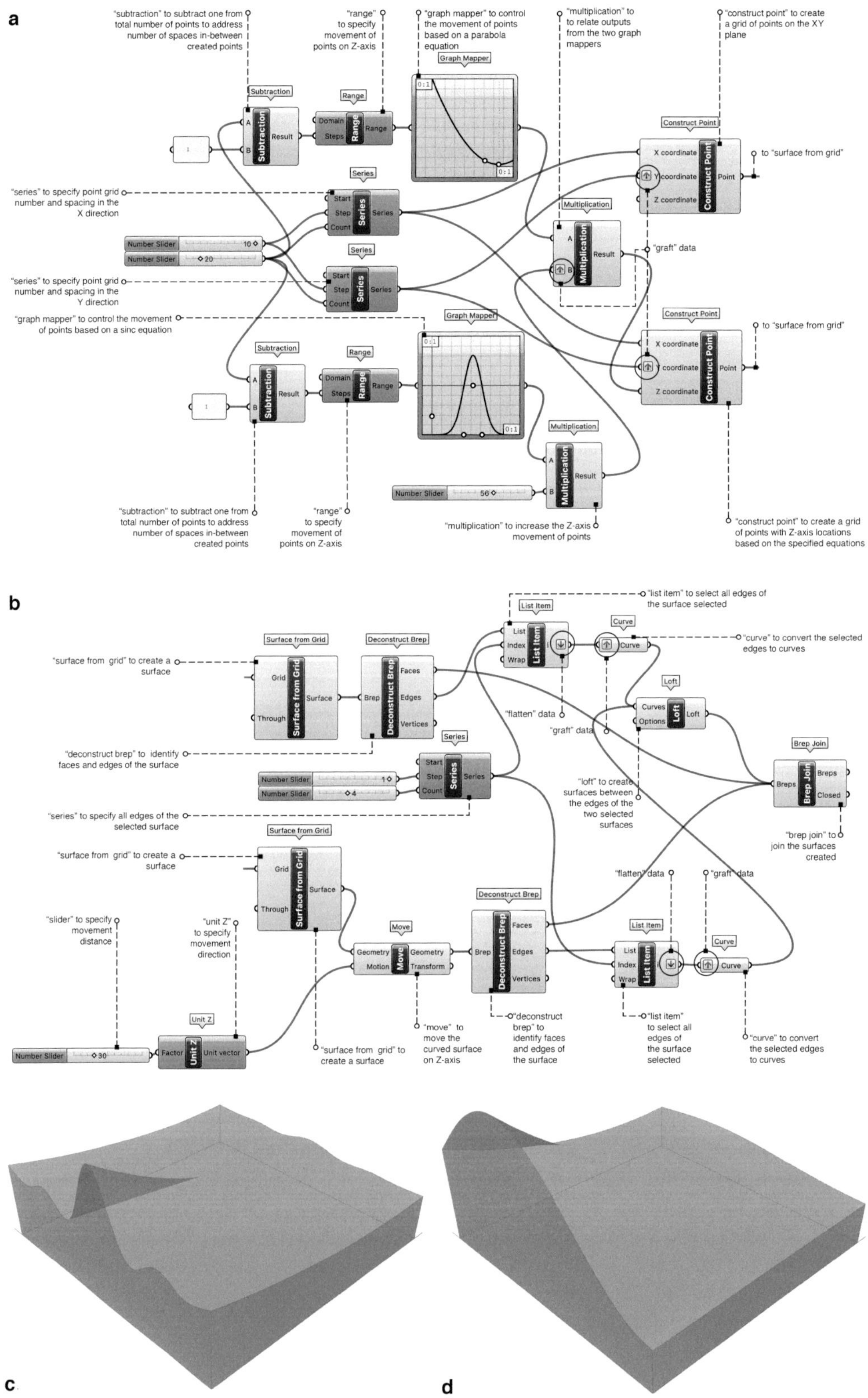

Figure 4.4 (a) The Grasshopper definition used for constructing two grids of points; (b) the Grasshopper definition used for constructing and joining two surfaces; (c) the resulting mass; and (d) an iteration of the mass created using the same Grasshopper definition but replacing the "sinc" graph with a "sine" graph.

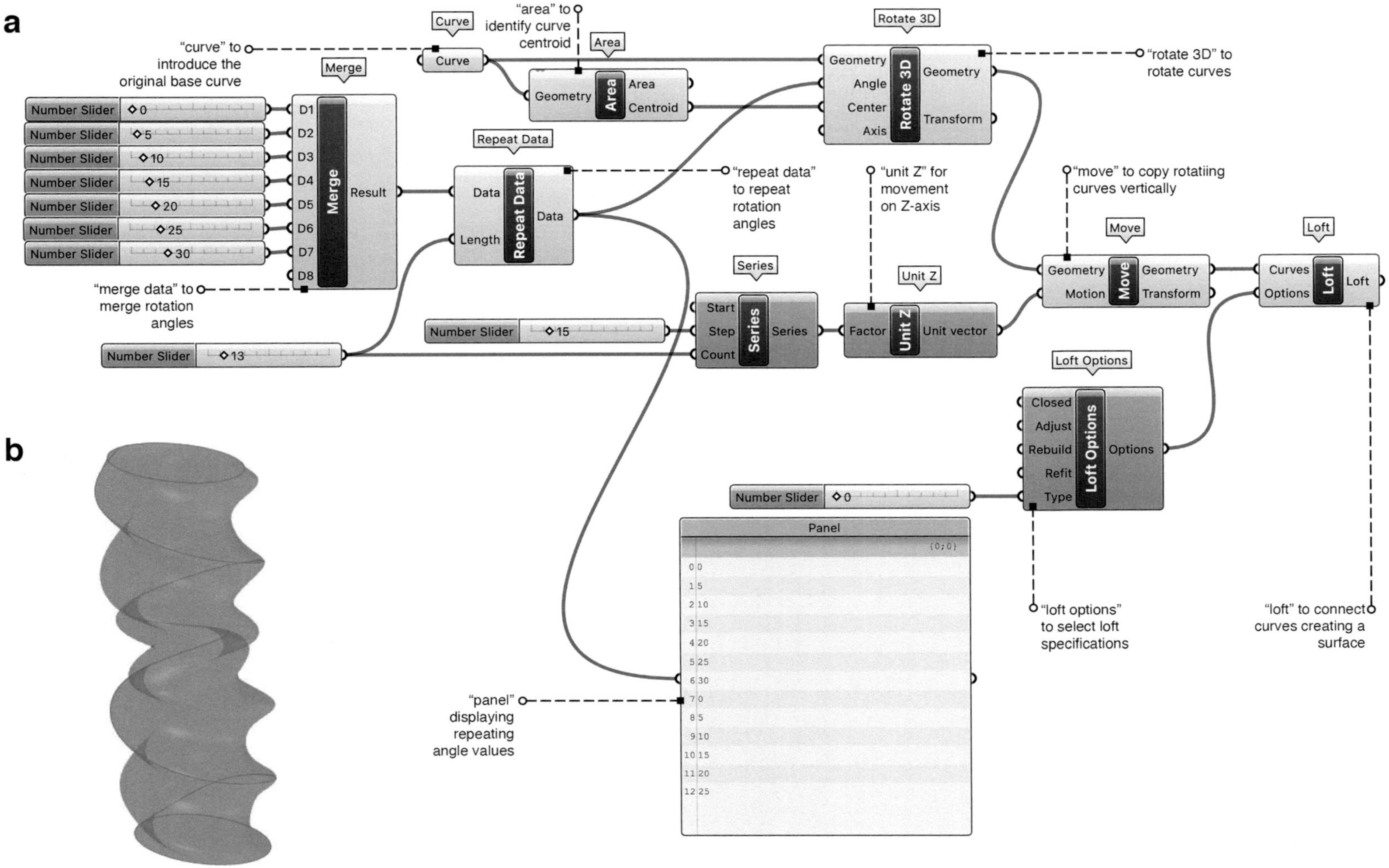

Figure 4.5 (a) The Grasshopper definition used for the sample data repetition procedure; and (b) the resulting irregular form.

number of steps between curves. The 45-degree total rotation is then divided into the number of steps using the "division" component, and the result is converted into radians to specify and lower the rotation value for each step (Since the rotate 3D component treats numerical angle data in radians).

A "series" component is used to specify the steps and total count of rotations for the curves that were copied on the Z-axis. The output data are fed into the "angle" input of a Rotate 3D component, which is used to generate gradual rotation steps for the vertically copied curves around their centroids, which were identified using the "area" component. Finally, the rotated curves are lofted using a "loft" component. Such explorations can also be used with more specific geometries by making minor changes. For example, instead of a base curve, a more complex geometry (i.e., a 3D digital model of a proposed building's single floor) can be introduced as a boundary representation (a "Brep") (Figure 4.6).

Such explorations can also be related to performance-related and other criteria using evolutionary solvers. By specifying desired criteria, such as visibility or solar exposure, evolutionary solvers can evaluate form exploration alternatives and yield formal compositions that meet the specified criteria. We will look into evolutionary solvers, single criterion, and multiple criteria optimization processes in Chapter 7.

4.1.2 Parametrically Creating and Editing Irregular SubD Geometries: Meshes

Unlike NURBS – geometries which rely on mathematical functions – Subdivision Surface Modeling (SubD)-based geometries, such as meshes, are composed of multiple, neighboring polygons. Also unlike NURBS, meshes do not provide smooth, continuous surfaces. However, since they are composed of multiple polygons, meshes that contain a high number of polygons are perceived as smooth surfaces. Mesh geometries can achieve high levels of smoothness through iterative algorithmic subdivisions and can be especially useful for highly complex geometries. Individual mesh polygons are composed of a face, edges, and vertices (Tedeschi, 2014).

Although there are three main methods of creating meshes in Grasshopper, a very common method for architects is the creation of a mesh geometry through a NURBS-to-mesh conversion. Due to their precision and ease of control, NURBS tend to be the most accessible and preferable geometries for many architects. Nevertheless, by converting NURBS into a mesh, architects can develop alternative approaches to creating and editing complex geometries. There are two types of mesh geometry definitions: quadrangular meshes, defined by polygons subdivided in U and V directions, therefore four-edged polygons; and triangular meshes, defined by three-edged polygons (Tedeschi, 2014).

Converting NURBS Geometries to Mesh Geometries. Grasshopper offers various components for converting NURBS geometries to mesh geometries. The "Mesh" component available under the "Param" tab provides the most basic conversion: it redefines a NURBS surface as a mesh. The "Mesh Surface" component available under the "Mesh" tab, on the other hand, redefines NURBS geometries as mesh geometries by specifying subdivisions in U and V directions. The "Equalize" input on the "Mesh Surface" component specifies whether the subdivisions should be in equal increments or follow the original geometry for subdivision increments (Figure 4.7). The "Simple Mesh" component available under the "Mesh" tab can convert more complex NURBS geometries such as polysurfaces and solids defined as Breps (boundary representations) into meshes using the simplest geometric definition. Finally, the "Mesh Brep" component available under the same tab can convert complex NURBS geometries defined as Breps into a mesh, but can provide control over the output mesh through the "Settings (Custom)" component.

Since for many architects and designers building NURBS geometries provides time-saving strategies, in this chapter we will rely primarily on mesh geometry development through

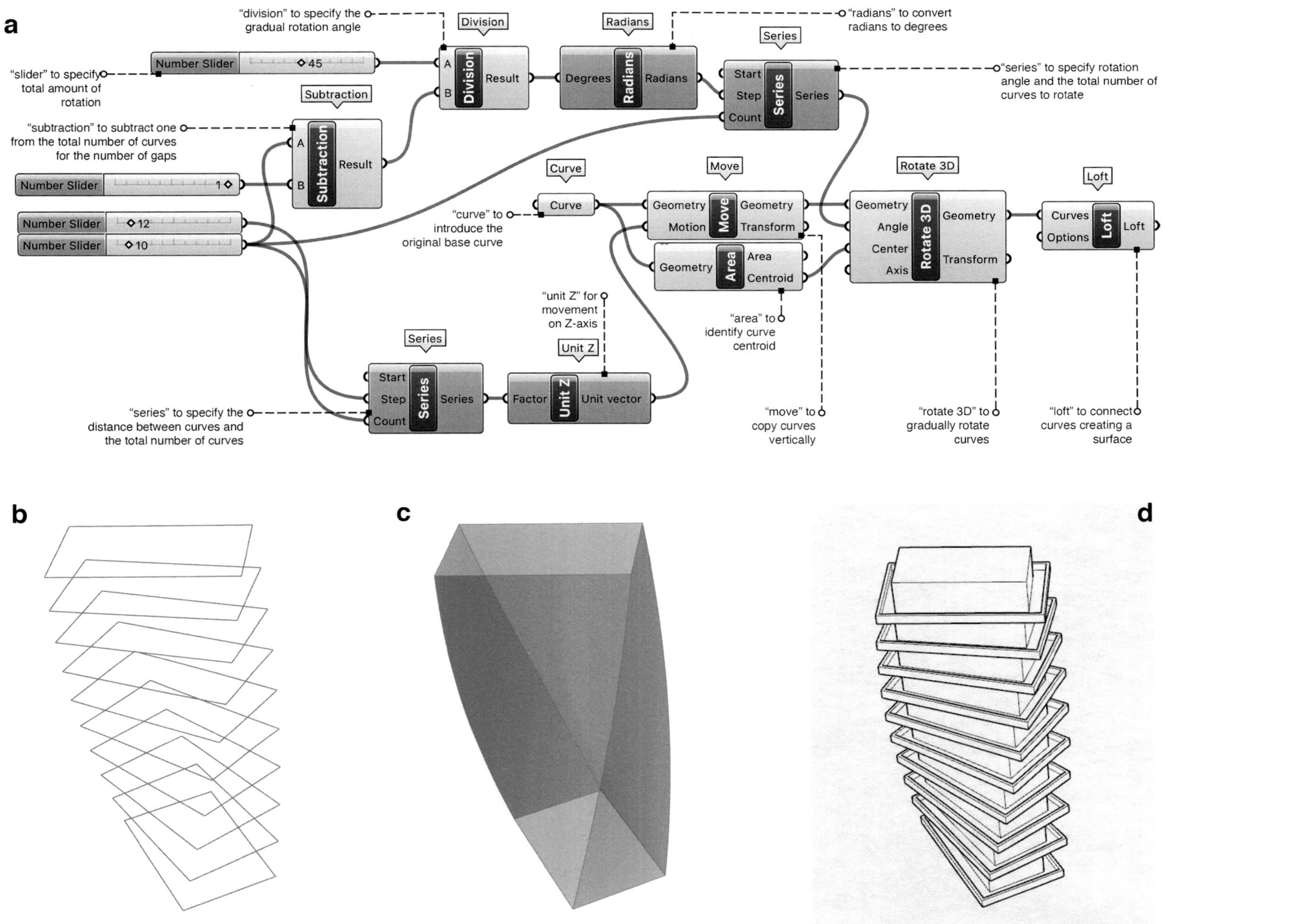

Figure 4.6 *(a) The Grasshopper definition developed for a sample experimentation with gradual rotation of curves; (b) gradually rotated curves; (c) the lofted mass; and (d) the same gradual rotation operation introducing a sample building floor as a Brep.*

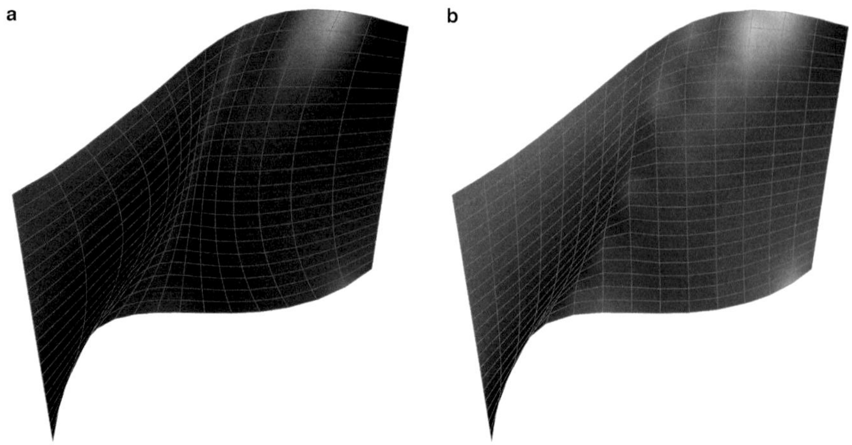

Figure 4.7 Two meshes developed using the "Mesh Surface" component: (a) equalize is set to "true"; and (b) equalize is set to "false."

conversion from NURBS geometries. However, Grasshopper also offers components that can help designers build mesh geometries from scratch.

Subdivision of Mesh Geometries. While a number of Grasshopper plug-ins are available for creating and editing mesh geometries, Weaverbird remains to be the most widely used mesh editing plug-in. Designed by Giulio Piacentino, an architect and educator, the plug-in can be downloaded online free of charge. The plug-in provides tools for editing mesh geometries through subdivision, as well as tools for defining basic geometries in mesh format.

Weaverbird offers a number of components that can apply various methods of mesh surface subdivision. The primary advantage of mesh surface subdivision is that the process yields smooth, continuous mesh surfaces (Tedeschi, 2014). Each subdivision method uses an algorithm that specifies the way mesh surfaces will be subdivided. Each component has a number of settings entries which provide modifications to the original algorithm. All subdivision algorithms have a "level" input, which controls a limited number of subsurface subdivisions. Some components also offer a Boolean toggle operated (true or false) "smooth naked edges" option. A "naked edge" is the edge of a surface, polysurface, or mesh surface that does not neighbor the edge of another surface. A smooth naked edge contributes to the smoothness of the target geometry's edges. Weaverbird provides eight components that offer eight different subdivision algorithms. Based on their location from top to bottom on the Weaverbird toolbar, these components are: Catmull-Clark Subdivision, Constant Quads Split Subdivision, Inner Polygons Subdivision, Loop subdivision, Midedge Subdivision, Sierpinski Triangles Subdivision, Split Polygons Subdivision, and Split Triangles Subdivision.

Subdividing and Iteratively Editing Quadrangular Meshes: The Catmull-Clark Subdivision Algorithm. One of the commonly used components for mesh geometry subdivision is the "Catmull-Clark Subdivision" component. It is capable of subdividing mesh geometries into quadrangular meshes. Introduced in 1978, the Catmull-Clark Subdivision Algorithm adds new vertices for the faces of a mesh geometry to smooth a rigid surface (Catmull and Clark, 1978; Tedeschi, 2014).

Let us take an introductory look into mesh surface subdivision with the Catmull-Clark Subdivision Component. In this example, a curved NURBS surface is developed by lofting three curves in Rhinoceros, which is introduced to Grasshopper using the basic "Surface" component. It is converted into a mesh surface using the "Mesh Surface" component with eight U and V direction subdivisions. A "Boolean Toggle" component is used to control equal subdivisions on U and V directions versus the subdivisions following the original geometry. Once the conversion to the quadrangular mesh surface is completed by the "Catmull-Clark Subdivision" component, the "subdivision level" and "smooth naked edges" settings are adjusted. Figure 4.8 illustrates the six possible outputs using the "Catmull-Clark Subdivision" component through the three "subdivision level" options (1, 2, and 3) and the two "smooth naked edges" options (true or false).

Another approach to developing and subdividing mesh geometries is to use the "Mesh Brep" component accompanied by the "Settings (Custom)" component. Using this approach, it is possible to specify the mesh settings through the "Settings (Custom)" component instead of specifying U and V subdivisions. Using this approach, a sharp version to the target object can be modeled using NURBS geometries in Rhinoceros, and be subdivided into a smooth, continuous mesh through the "Catmull-Clark Subdivision." Figure 4.9 illustrates an example of such an exploration.

In this example, a relatively complex NURBS geometry that may be a sculptural entity for a public building is modeled using standard Rhinoceros Boolean operations. The geometry is converted into an open polysurface by joining its parts in Rhinoceros and then introduced into Grasshopper as a Brep (Figure 4.9a and 4.9b). Unlike the previous example, the NURBS geometry is converted into a mesh using the "Mesh Brep" component. The "settings" input of the "Mesh Brep" component can be controlled using the "Settings" component. The resulting mesh geometry is then subdivided using the "Catmull-Clark Subdivision" component. At this point, the subdivision levels and "smooth naked edges" settings can be altered as in the previous example. The resulting subdivided, smooth, and continuous mesh geometry that has no thickness is illustrated in Figure 4.9c.

As we will discuss in Chapter 9, to be able to build a 3D physical model of a geometry like this example using additive digital fabrication methods, the geometry needs to be defined as a "closed" (watertight) NURBS or mesh geometry that has thickness. As illustrated in Figure 4.9a, the Weaverbird plug-in for Grasshopper offers a "mesh thicken" component that can develop a closed mesh with a defined thickness value. Figure 4.9d illustrates the mesh geometry thickened into a closed mesh using this component. Finally, when this geometry is "baked," it can be accessed and fabricated three-dimensionally as a closed mesh through the Rhinoceros interface (Figure 4.9e).

Altering Multi-part Mesh Subdivisions Using U, V Subdivisions and the Catmull-Clark Algorithm. The two examples introduced so far illustrated the use of the Catmull-Clark algorithm with a relatively simple geometry and a more complex, multi-part mesh developed using the "Mesh Brep" component. Using the "Mesh Surface" component and the Catmull-Clark algorithm together can afford a higher degree of control over the resulting mesh surface. In this section, we will introduce the process using a relatively simple set of geometries to illustrate how the combination of the two components can help control the mesh geometry.

Since the Catmull-Clark algorithm outputs quadrangular mesh subdivisions, the numbers of subdivisions in U and V directions become important when subdividing combined multi-part meshes. When two or more mesh surfaces are combined, the Catmull-Clark algorithm works when the number of U and V directions are set such that the subdivision edges from different surfaces meet at the vertices and not on an edge. Tedeschi (2014) refers to an end-to-edge perpendicular relationship as a "T-node," where the end vertex of a mesh surface's edge falls on another mesh surface's edge. To avoid this and maintain continuous smooth mesh output surfaces, it is important to avoid T-nodes (Tedeschi, 2014). T-nodes can be avoided through consistency in the number of subdivisions in U and V directions on multiple adjacent parts.

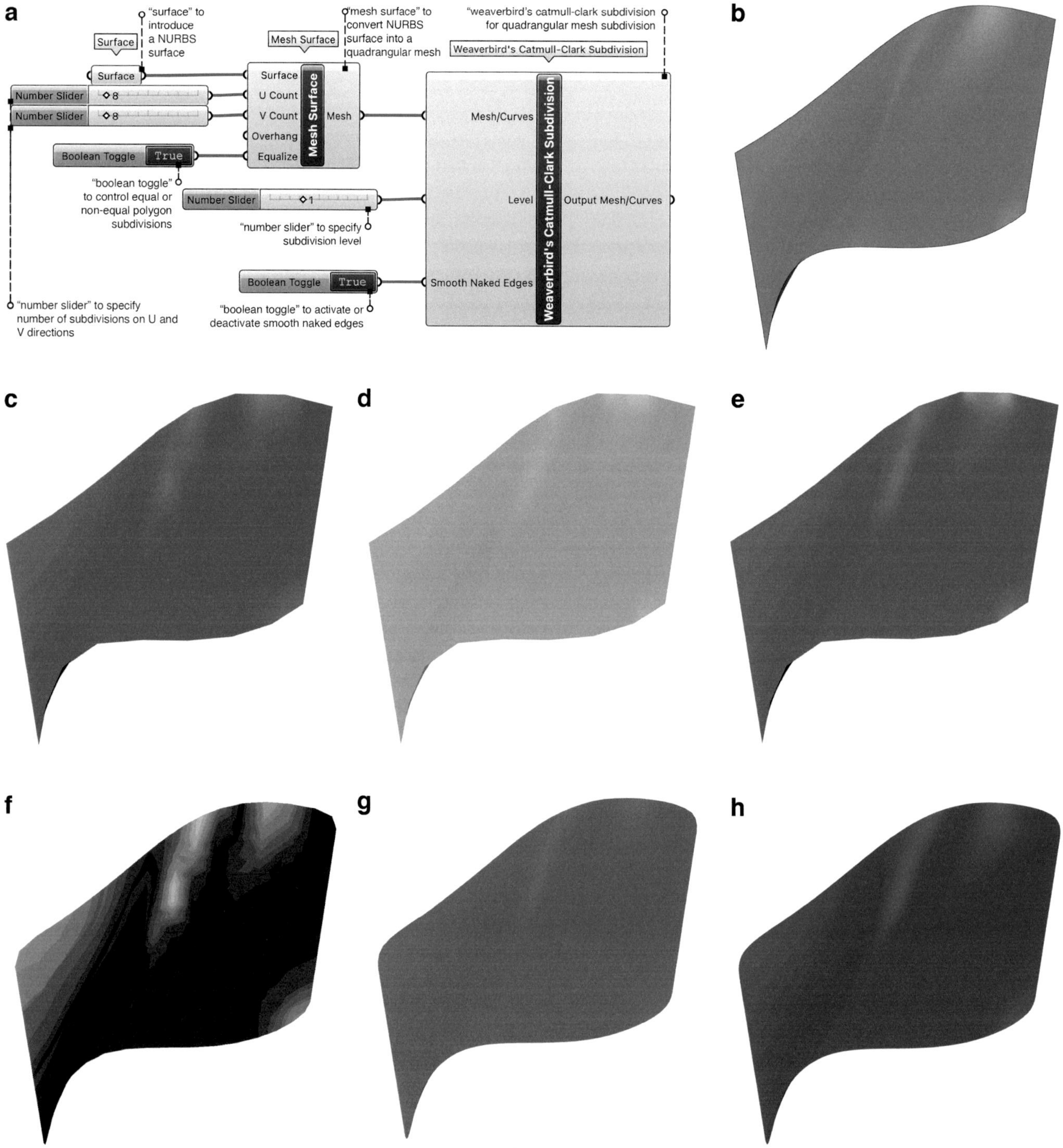

Figure 4.8 *(a) The Grasshopper definition used applies Catmull-Clark Subdivision on the mesh developed from the original irregular NURBS surface; (b) the mesh developed from the original surface; (c) subdivision level = 1, smooth naked edges = false; (d) subdivision level = 2, smooth naked edges = false; (e) subdivision level = 3, smooth naked edges = false; (f) subdivision level = 1, smooth naked edges = true; (g) subdivision level = 2, smooth naked edges = true; (h) subdivision level = 3, smooth naked edges = true.*

Let us illustrate the use of U, V subdivisions and the Catmull-Clark algorithm in a process of subdividing and softening using simple geometries. This process can easily be introduced in early mass composition studies. In this example, a rectangular geometry and its center is used to generate four closed triangular polylines in Rhinoceros. The four polylines are then offset such that the outcome of each offset yields a closed triangular polyline smaller than its original (Figure 4.10b). The offset closed polylines are then moved in the Z direction and

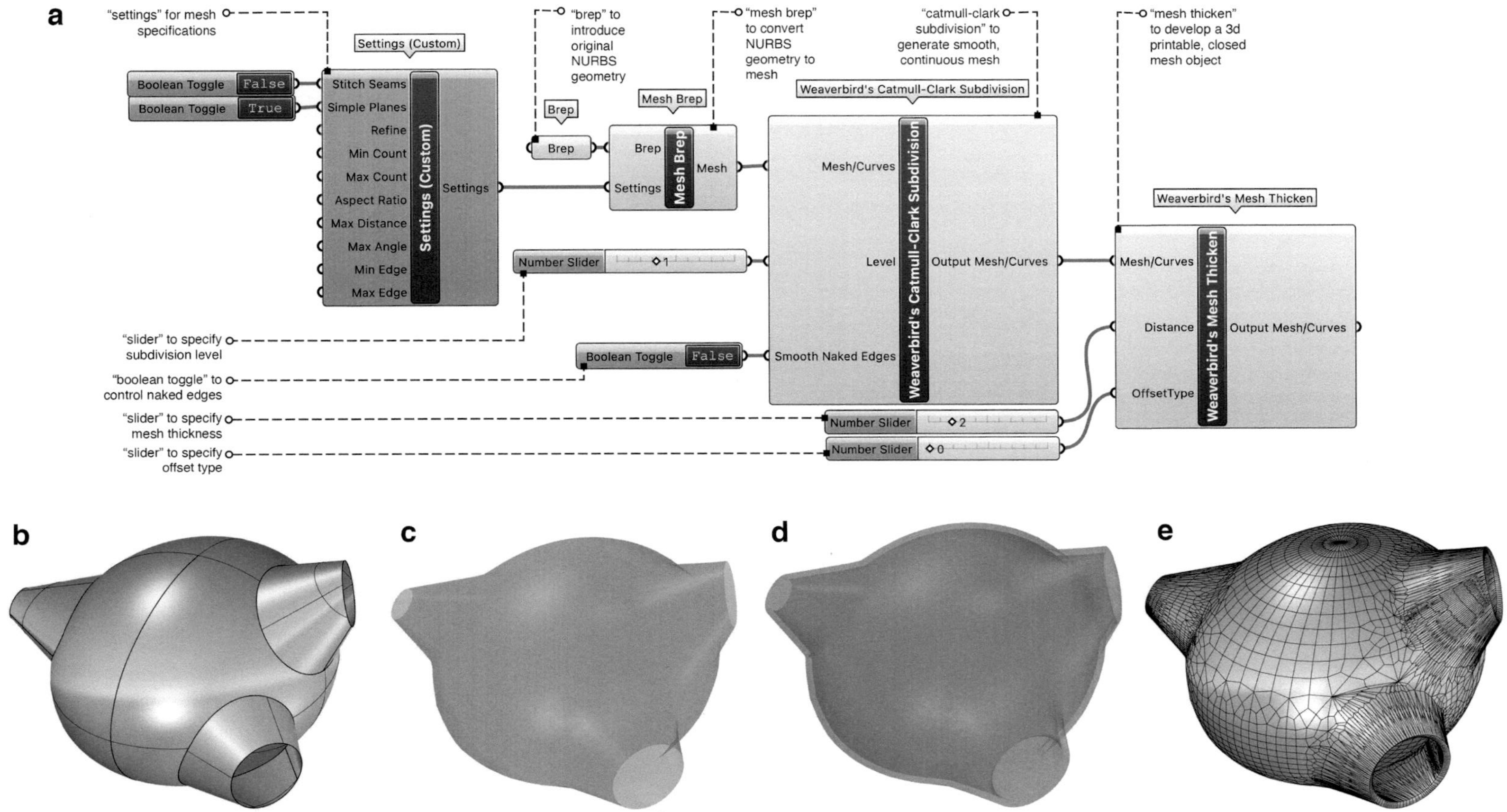

Figure 4.9 *(a) The Grasshopper definition developed to convert the original NURBS geometry into a mesh, subdivide it, and convert it into a closed mesh with thickness; (b) the original NURBS geometry in Rhinoceros interface; (c) the subdivided smooth and continuous mesh geometry in Grasshopper interface; (d) the closed mesh with thickness developed in Grasshopper interface; and (e) the resulting closed mesh baked into the Rhinoceros interface.*

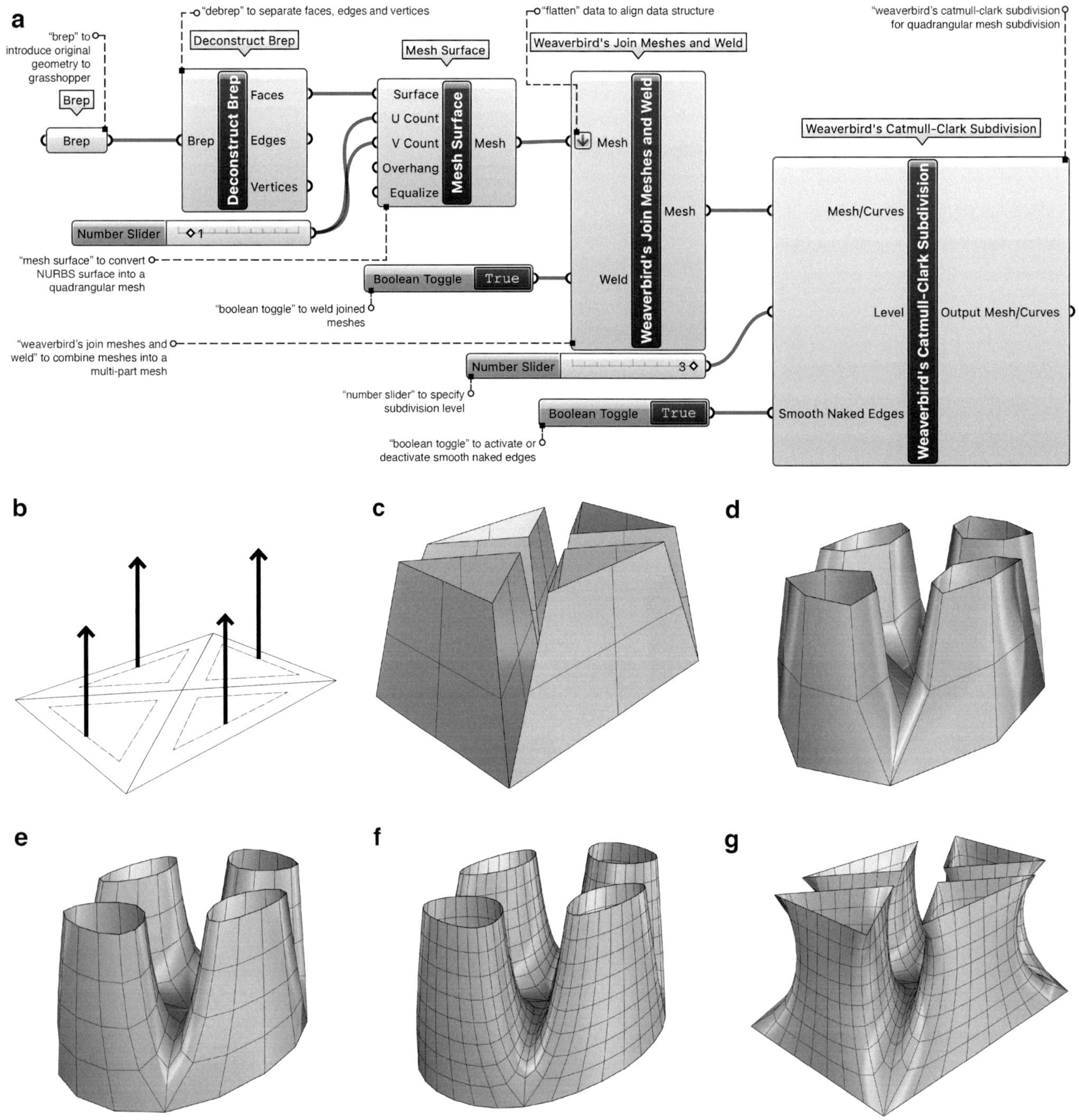

Figure 4.10 *The Grasshopper definition used to edit the NURBS object's mesh version using the Catmull-Clark algorithm; (b) total eight closed polylines, including the four offset versions prior to vertical movement; (c) the resulting polysurfaces following the loft operation in Rhinoceros; (d) joined and welded meshes subdivided using the Catmull-Clark algorithm (level = 1, smooth naked edges = true); (e) joined and welded meshes subdivided using the Catmull-Clark algorithm (level = 2, smooth naked edges = true); (f) joined and welded meshes subdivided using the Catmull-Clark algorithm (level = 3, smooth naked edges = true); and (g) joined and welded meshes subdivided using the Catmull-Clark algorithm (level = 3, smooth naked edges = false).*

the original and the offset curves are lofted in Rhinoceros, yielding four open polysurfaces (Figure 4.10c).

From this point on, the geometry is edited using Grasshopper. First, the lofted NURBS geometry is introduced into Grasshopper using the "Brep" component, selecting the "set multiple Breps" option. Using the "Deconstruct Brep" component, the geometry is separated into its faces, edges, and vertices. The resulting faces are then converted into meshes using the

"Mesh Surface" component. In doing so, the U and V subdivision numbers are set to equal values so that T-nodes can be avoided in the resulting meshes. The resulting mesh surfaces are then joined and welded together using the "Weaverbird's Join Meshes and Weld" component, where the mesh input is flattened to adjust data structure, and the "weld" option is set to "true." The mesh geometry is now ready for subdivision using the Catmull-Clark algorithm (Figure 4.10a).

The joined and welded mesh geometry is then fed into the "Weaverbird's Catmull-Clark Subdivision" component. Figure 4.10 illustrates the outcomes of this procedure: with "smooth naked edges" set to "true." Figure 4.10d shows subdivision level 1, Figure 4.10e shows subdivision level 2, and Figure 4.10f shows subdivision level 3. Figure 4.10g shows a level-3 subdivision with none of the naked edges smoothed.

Subdividing and Iteratively Editing Triangular Meshes: The Loop Subdivision Algorithm. The Loop algorithm edits triangular meshes. Developed by Charles Loop, the algorithm works by adding a vertex to the midpoint of each edge of triangular surfaces (Tedeschi, 2014). Let us investigate how triangular meshes and the Loop algorithm work by using the example we used to demonstrate quadrangular meshes and the Catmull-Clark algorithm (Figure 4.11).

In this example, the same geometry from Figure 4.10 is generated in Rhinoceros and introduced into Grasshopper as multiple Breps. The Breps are then deconstructed and connected to Weaverbird's "Delaunay Mesh" component for conversion into a triangular mesh. The resulting triangular mesh is then edited using Weaverbird's Loops subdivision, with various levels of subdivision (from 1 to 3) and various modes of naked edge smoothing (0 = fixed, 1 = smooth, and 2 = corner fixed).

Observations on the Use of Mesh Geometries in Architectural Design. SubD-based mesh geometries afford smooth geometric transitions especially for complex and high-resolution irregular, amorphous surfaces, and geometries. The amount of user control over these geometries tends to be limited to the components offered by Grasshopper and plug-ins like Weaverbird. Therefore, one can argue that ***currently*** these tools may be more relevant in areas such as industrial design and visual arts, such as three-dimensional character animation-based media. From this point of view, NURBS geometries continue to constitute a priority for designers in areas such as architecture and urban design. Nevertheless, SubD geometries seem to be making their way into more mainstream applications. For example, as of version 7, Rhinoceros software started to offer commands and tools for creating and editing SubD geometries using its native user interface. It is not unrealistic to expect developments like this to spread, develop, and become available in other software packages. Furthermore, tools and commands like this will most likely become more user friendly. Therefore, SubD techniques may be more available, user friendly, and intuitive for a wide range of designers in the near future.

4.2 PARAMETRIC TOOLS IN ANALYZING CONTEXTUAL RELATIONSHIPS TO SUPPORT PRELIMINARY DEVELOPMENT

In addition to form exploration during conceptual development, parametric methods can prove useful in preliminary decision-making in relation to local context and project program. In this section, we will look into some parametric tools using NURBS geometries in analyzing contextual relationships to support preliminary development.

Multi-point Isovist Analysis for Potential Retail Location. Grasshopper's native "isovist" component is a good example as a potential tool for identifying the location of particular programmatic elements based on their visibility. Visibility analysis can be conducted to maximize visual connections for program elements such as retail, eateries, etc. Similar analyses can

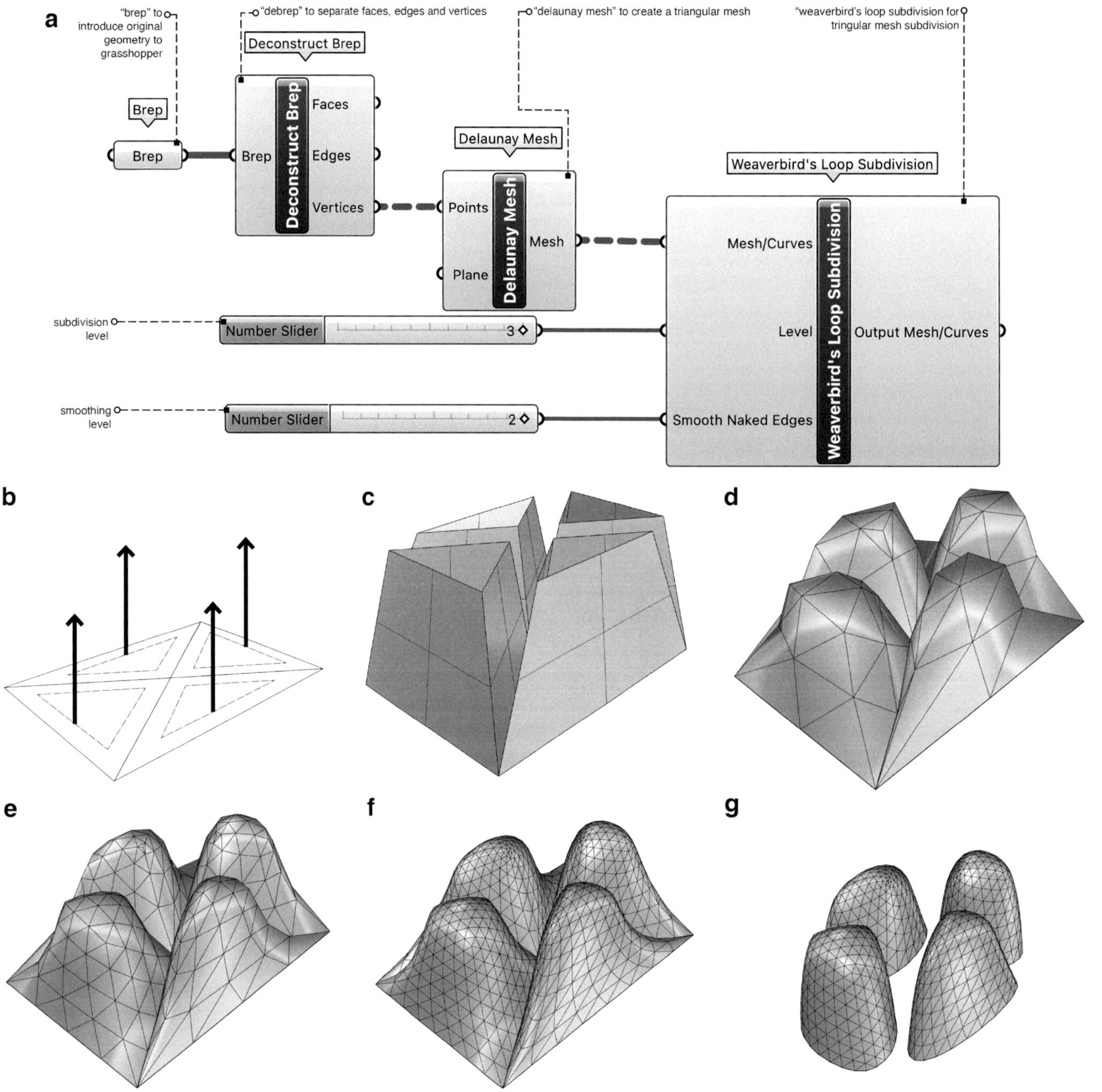

Figure 4.11 The Grasshopper definition used to convert a NURBS object's (Brep) mesh version using the Loop algorithm; (b) total eight closed polylines, including the four offset versions prior to vertical movement; (c) the polysurfaces following the loft operation converted into a triangular mesh using Delaunay triangulation; (d) meshes subdivided using the Loop algorithm (level = 1, smooth naked edges mode = 0); (e) meshes subdivided using the Loop algorithm (level = 2, smooth naked edges mode = 1); (f) meshes subdivided using the Loop algorithm (level = 3, smooth naked edges mode = 3); and (g) meshes subdivided using the Loop algorithm (level = 3, smooth naked edges mode = 2).

also be conducted to minimize visibility for programmatic elements that require privacy, such as residential functions. In this example, we will investigate a multi-point isovist analysis to identify the location with maximum visibility for a retail space in a proposed building.

Figure 4.12 illustrates a fictitious project site with an irregular geometry (Figure 4.12a) and a proposed building mass (Figure 4.12b). In this scenario, there are three potential locations for a retail space, each with their own, approximately same-sized storefronts: storefront 1, storefront 2, and storefront 3.

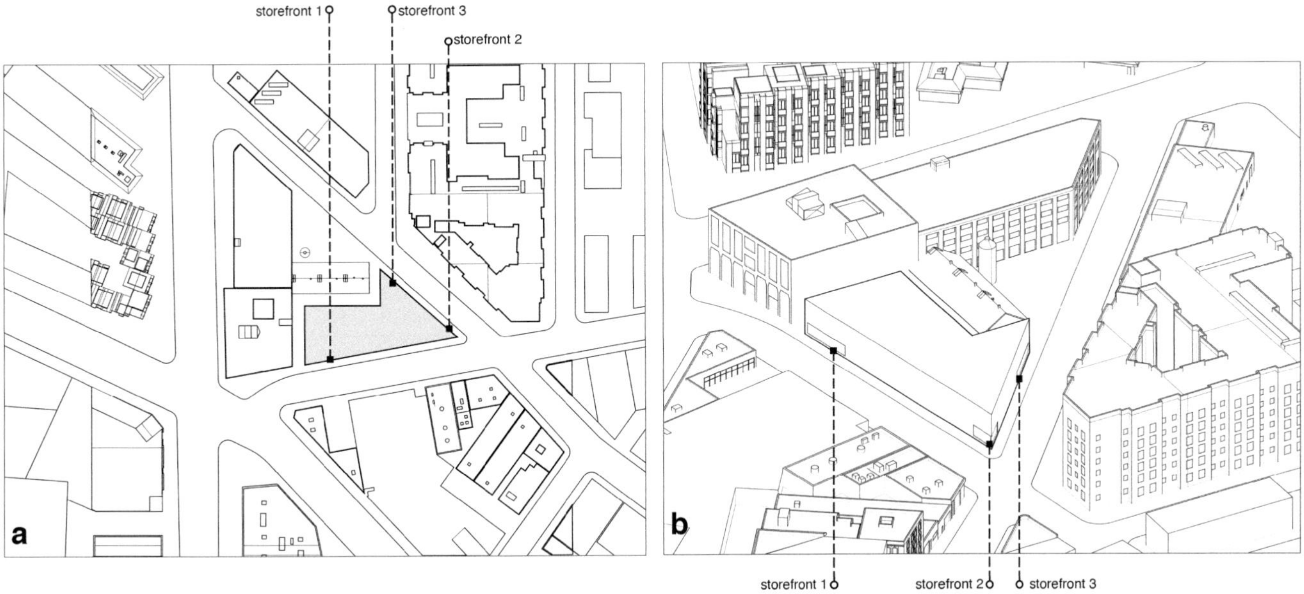

Figure 4.12 (a) Fictitious project site with an irregular geometry; (b) the proposed building mass. Both figures illustrate the locations of storefront 1, 2, and 3.

Assuming that maximum visibility provided at a storefront will facilitate highest business activity, the objective is to find the storefront that has the highest visibility from the street based on its centroid or centroids. For this reason, the objective in this analysis is to find the storefront option that provides the highest visibility. In Figure 4.13, storefront 1 is analyzed. The surface of storefront 1 is introduced into Grasshopper using the "surface" component, and its centroid is identified using the "area" component. The buildings surrounding the proposed building mass are introduced to Grasshopper as multiple geometries using the "geometry" component. Both geometries are then fed into the "isovist" component, setting the number of isovist points to 100, and the isovist radius to 1320 feet.

In urban design, a quarter-mile distance is identified as a comfortably walkable distance for most humans. This distance equals 1320 feet; therefore, the isovist radius is set to 1320 feet, assuming that within this isovist area most pedestrians can get a glimpse of the storefront's centroid. When the isovist for storefront 1 is plotted, its vertices are connected with a closed polyline, and the area of this polyline is identified using the "area" component. Meanwhile, the command "boundary surfaces" is used to three-dimensionally visualize the isovist. The results indicate that the area of the isovist for the centroid of storefront 1 is 99,803 sq. ft. Figure 4.13b illustrates storefront 1's isovist visualized with a highlighted polyline.

Unlike storefront 1, storefront 2 has two faces since it goes around the corner of the site. In this scenario, isovists of the two sides of the storefront are plotted and joined using the "solid union" component (Figure 4.14a). The initial steps for analyzing the isovists for the centroids of the two sides of the storefront both replicate the process used to calculate the isovist area for storefront 1. The findings indicate that the total isovist area for the two portions of storefront 2, based on their centroids, is 267,831 sq. ft. This value is significantly larger than the centroid isovist value of storefront 1, indicating that people within the identified area of storefront 2 isovist will have direct visual access to storefront 2 (Figure 4.14b).

Similar to the analysis illustrated in Figure 4.13, for storefront 3, an individual vantage point analysis and visualization is conducted to highlight the isovist for the centroid of single-piece storefront 3. Figure 4.15a illustrates the Grasshopper definition used to calculate the isovist for storefront 3, and Figure 4.15b illustrates storefront 3's isovist visualized with a polyline (Figure 4.15b). The findings indicate that the total isovist area for storefront 3, based on its

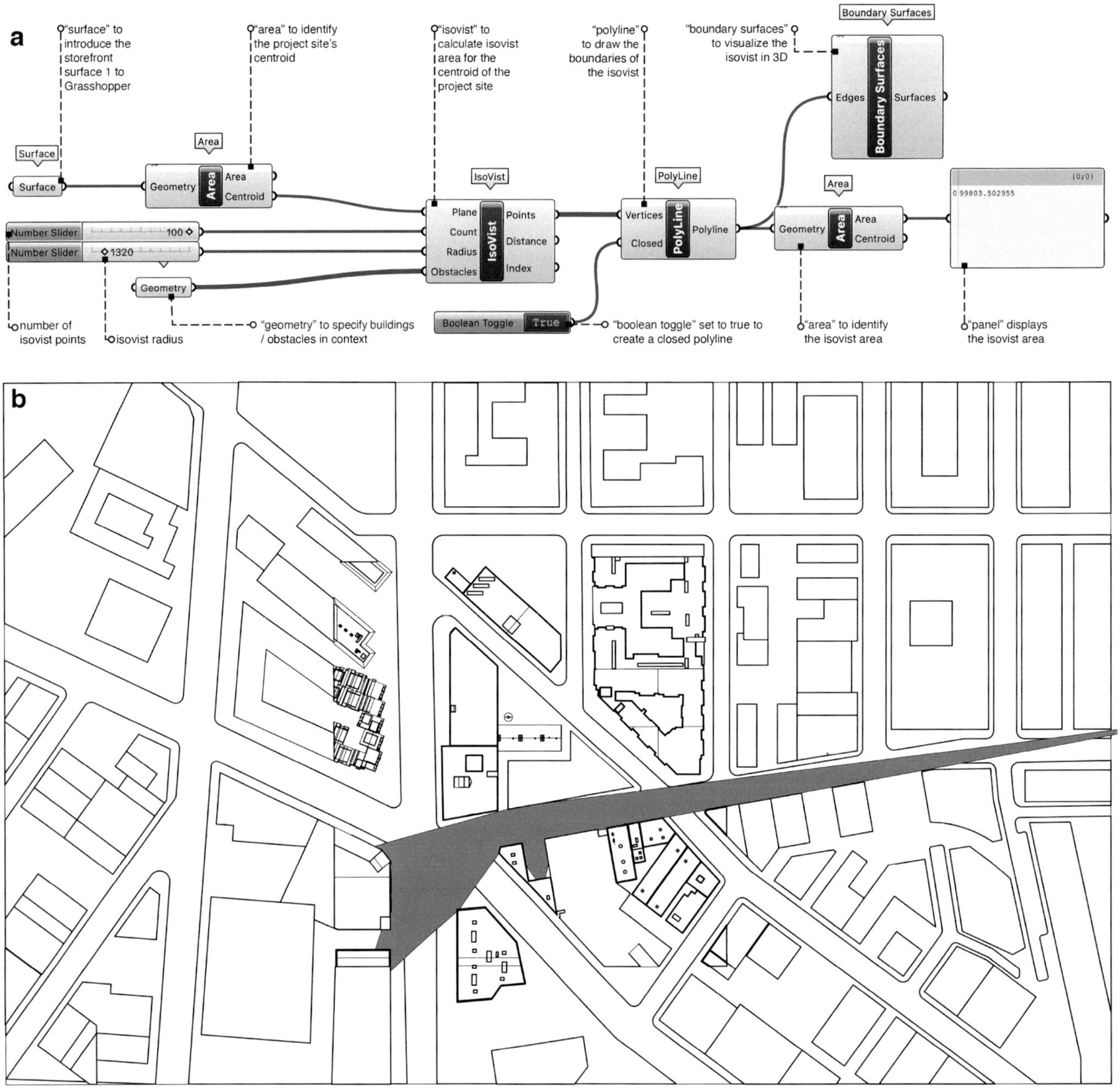

Figure 4.13 (a) Grasshopper definition used to identify the storefront 1's isovist based on its centroid within the given context; (b) storefront 1's isovist visualized with a polyline.

centroid, is 267,014 sq. ft. – while having the highest isovist area, a value very close to storefront 2 with its two storefront faces.

This example illustrates the importance of using empirical findings in decision-making – as opposed to intuition-based decision-making – for measurable variables. Clearly, decision-making based on individual variables cannot support creative ***and*** rational decision-making at the same time. Nevertheless, examples in Figures 4.13, 4.14, and 4.15 clearly indicate that if visibility is a very important variable, the quantitative isovist area analysis indicates that storefront options 2 and 3 are not very different from one another. On the other hand, simply based on intuition one could assume or expect that the storefront with two façades (storefront 2) would have a significantly higher level of visibility compared to the two other options. This analysis indicates that quick measurements conducted using parametric methods can be efficient in saving analysis time and helping decision-making.

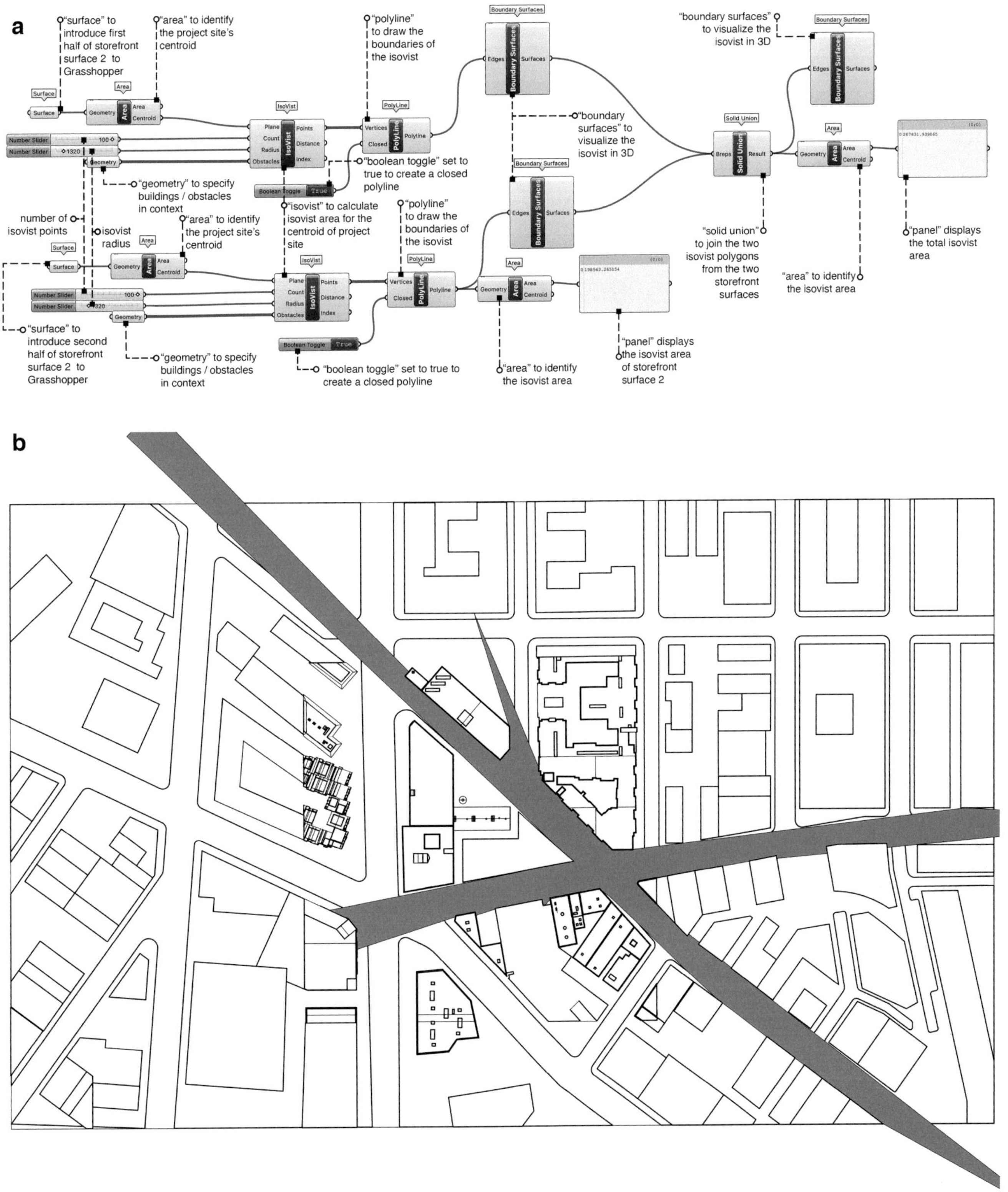

Figure 4.14 (a) The Grasshopper component used to identify and join the centroid-based isovists for the two-part storefront 2; and (b) storefront 2's isovists visualized with a polyline.

View Percent Analysis for a Potential Commercial Building Location on a Given Site. As we discussed in Chapter 3, Ladybug tools and the Ladybug plug-in prove useful in view and visibility percent analysis in site analysis and preliminary decision-making. In this example, we will investigate view percent analysis for four mass composition possibilities on an urban

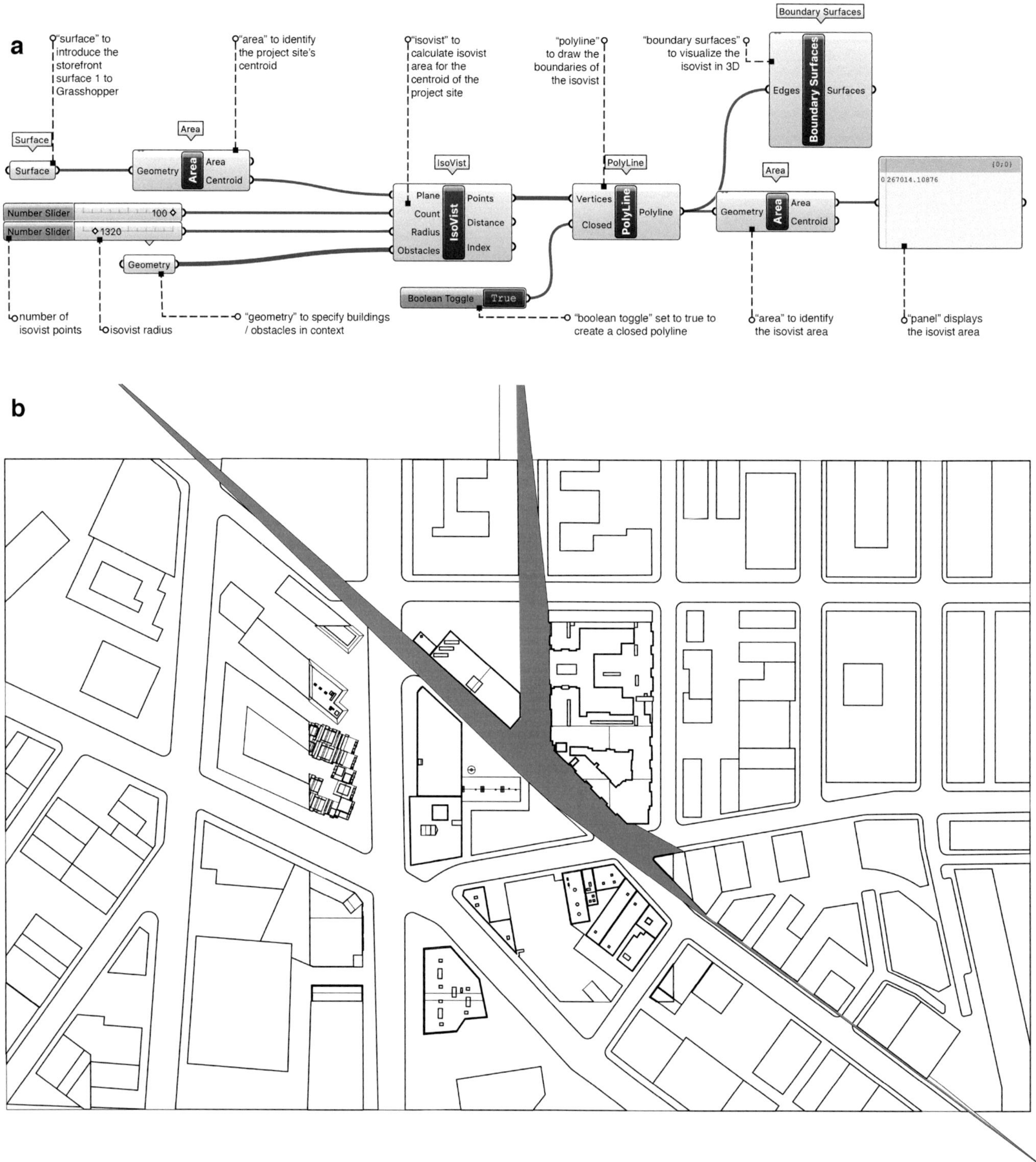

Figure 4.15 (a) Grasshopper definition used to identify the storefront 3's isovist based on its centroid within the given context; (b) storefront 3's isovist visualized with a polyline.

site in a high-density urban environment within a fictitious scenario. Figure 4.16 illustrates the urban site in the high-density urban environment from (a) a high elevation, and (b) from a lower vantage point. All fictitious mass composition possibilities have the same footprint areas; however, the composition and height for each possibility varies. With the assumption that this proposal would eventually be used for commercial purposes, visibility of the mass composition options from the human eye level on the street becomes critical. Therefore, the

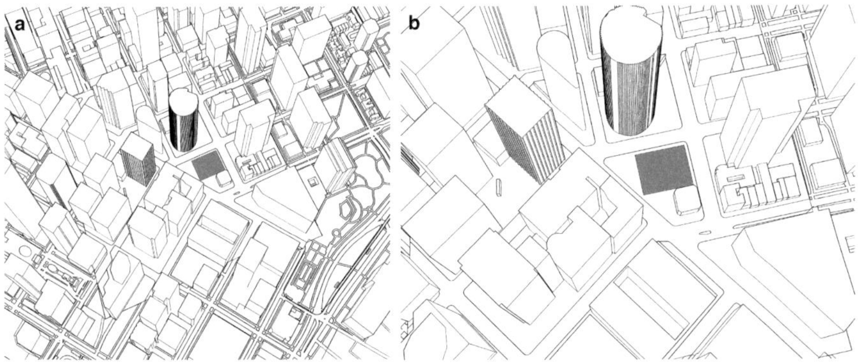

Figure 4.16 *The commercial urban site in a high-density urban environment under investigation for view percent analysis, from (a) a high elevation, and (b) from a lower vantage point for four different mass composition possibilities.*

objective is to investigate view percent access to four different mass composition possibilities from the human eye level on the street.

The "LB View Percent" component provided by the LadyBug (LB View Percent) plug-in for Grasshopper evaluates the percent view from an input geometry to the surrounding context based on its context. The "LB View Percent" component requires two sets of geometries – one set for the proposed mass composition, and one set for the contextual objects (i.e., buildings and trees) that constitute obstacles to visual connections. In this example, four mass composition possibilities were individually connected to the "geometry" input of the "LB View Percent" component on four different Grasshopper definitions.

In this scenario, the "_view_type" input is set to "1," which is identified as the horizontal 30-degree offset view by the plug-in. This analysis yields the percentage of the 360-degree horizontal view from a given vantage point. Since humans' peripheral vision is approximately limited to a 60-degree horizontal cone parallel to the ground plane from a given vantage point, the "_view_type" input is set to "1" for an analysis based on the horizontal 30-degree offset view. The analysis grid size is set to a 5-foot grid, and the "_geo_block" input is set to "true" using a Boolean toggle, so that the inner surfaces of the geometry that is analyzed can block the visibility for outer surfaces of the analyzed geometry. Finally, the "_run" input is set to "true" using a "Boolean toggle," allowing the component to run the view percent analysis (Figure 4.17a).

The "LB View Percent" component yields view percent analysis findings for each 5' × 5' grid cell identified in the Grasshopper definition. The findings are presented under the "results" output, where a numerical view percent value for each grid cell is made available. Since findings are presented from each grid cell on all surfaces of the given geometry, it is important to make sense of the output data (findings) for comparison purposes. One of the indicators for comparison purposes is the maximum and minimum view percent values. A mean view percent value for grid elements, while helpful, has the potential for a neutralizing effect for view percent values. Therefore, to identify the mass composition possibility with grid elements that provide the highest view percent percentage, the Grasshopper definition is set up such that, (a) first, the resulting list of values is organized into ascending order using the "sort list" component, (b) the "keys" output of the "sort list" component is reversed to reorganize the output into descending order, (c) the top 10% of the findings are selected using the "list item" and "series" components, and (d) the arithmetic mean of the top 10% of findings is identified using the "average" component.

Using the Grasshopper definition presented in Figure 4.17a, four mass composition geometry possibilities were analyzed – as illustrated in Figure 4.17b, c, d, and e. Each of the four

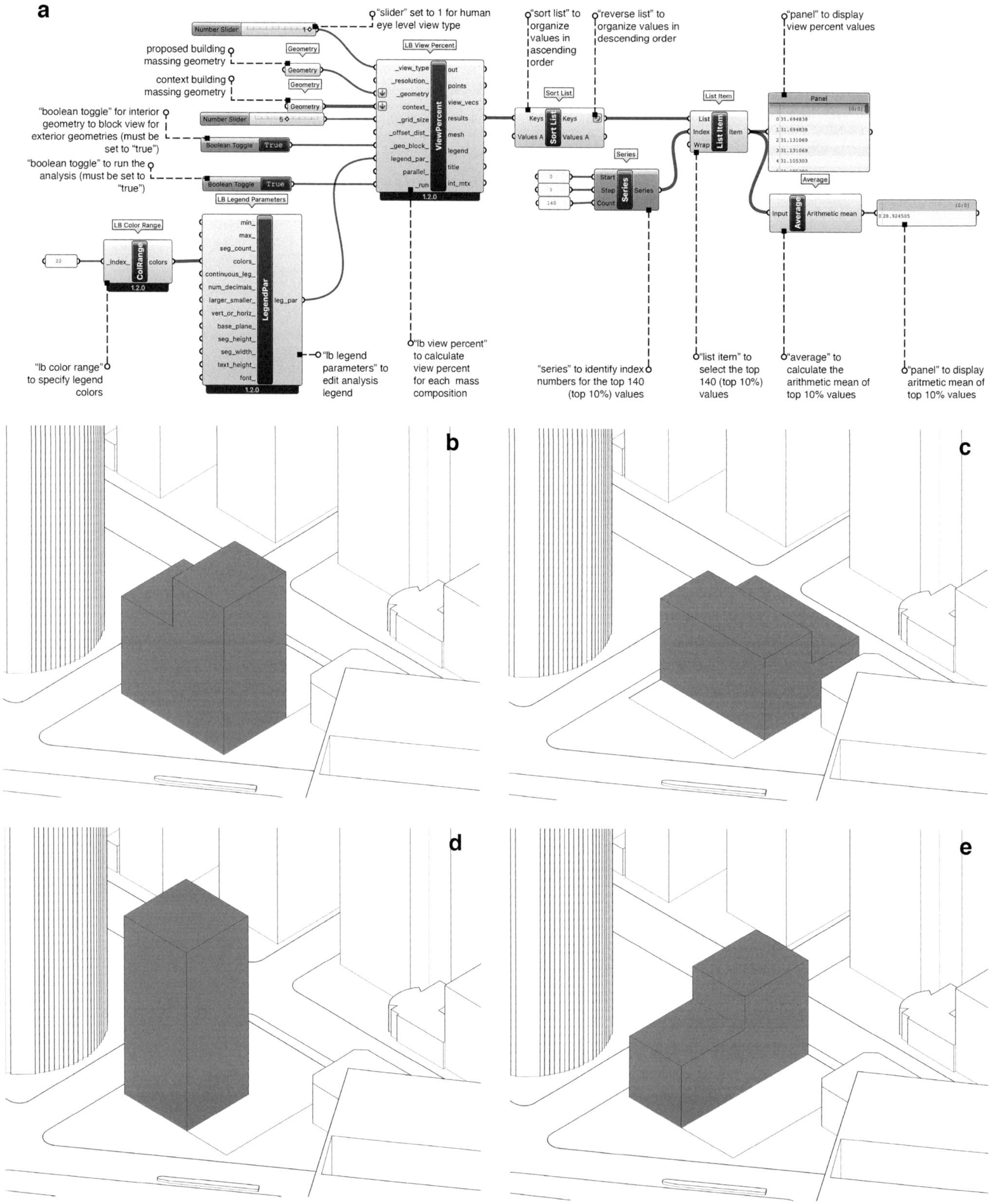

Figure 4.17 (a) The Grasshopper definition used to analyze four different mass composition geometries based on view percent to the context; (b) mass composition geometry 1; (c) mass composition geometry 2; (d) mass composition geometry 3; and (e) mass composition geometry 4.

Table 4.1 Maximum and minimum mass composition heights, their respective minimum view percent, maximum view percentage, and average view percentage of the top 10% grid cells for the four mass composition geometry possibilities.

Mass composition geometry options	*Maximum building height (ft.)*	*Minimum building height (ft.)*	*Maximum view percent*	*Minimum view percent*	*Average view percentage of top 10% grid cells for the mass composition geometry*
1	180	120	31.70%	27.44%	28.93%
2	100	60	29.93%	27.43%	28.25%
3	220	0	31.69%	27.59%	29.24%
4	120	80	30.49%	28.08%	29.03%

possibilities, with the same footprint area but with varying height and mass compositions, were fed into the same Grasshopper definition as the geometry for analysis. The analysis with four alternative mass compositions yields a variety of view percent results based on the four input compositions. Table 4.1 illustrates maximum and minimum mass composition heights, their respective minimum view percent, maximum view percentage, and average view percentage of the top 10% grid cells for the four mass composition geometry possibilities (Table 4.1).

This analysis indicates that although option 3 is the tallest option, because of its form and location on the site, it provides the highest maximum view percent and average view percentage of top 10% grid cells. Although the view percent measurements are close, this finding does show that at the human eye level on the sidewalk, option 3 provides the highest visibility. When considered with other design considerations, one can factor this finding into decisions about mass composition.

View Percent Analysis for a Potential Hotel Building Location Considering Three Potential Sites. When considering visibility during preliminary project development, the view percent analysis component ("LBViewPercent") provided by the Ladybug plug-in can prove useful. In this example, we will analyze and cross compare three different massing and location options for a potential hotel building close to a fictitious waterfront. Since rooms with a waterfront or ocean view are traditionally more profitable in tourism, our assumption will be that the location and massing option that has the highest waterfront/ocean visibility is the most desirable solution. Once the most desirable option is identified, the spatial organization of the building can be resolved such that a maximum number of hotel rooms are on the desirable location and massing option's waterfront façade.

To conduct this analysis, initially, a semi-circular surface was developed by extruding an arc – the geometry representing the desirable waterfront and ocean views. This geometry was introduced to Grasshopper using a "geometry" component, and target viewpoints were generated using Ladybug's "LB Generate Point Grid" component on a 40 ft × 40 ft grid introduced through a "slider." The waterfront facing façade of each of the three options were introduced into Grasshopper as individual surfaces using the "geometry" component. Similarly, the buildings in the surrounding context of each option were introduced to Grasshopper through the "geometry" component, by selecting "set multiple geometries" and selecting context building masses in closed polysurface format. Finally, the analysis grid size for each option's waterfront façade is set to 10 ft × 10 ft, using a "slider" and setting the "run" input of Ladybug's "LB Visibility Percent" component to "true" using a Boolean toggle (Figure 4.18b and c).

As illustrated in Figure 4.18b and c, this analysis yields the percentage of visibility access to the desirable view geometry from the analyzed façade for a 10 ft × 10 ft grid, and the results can be viewed using a "panel" component. Unlike the previous examples in this chapter, in this example, the three considered façade options are located on three alternative site locations. Therefore, significant differences among findings are possible. Since mean (average) of

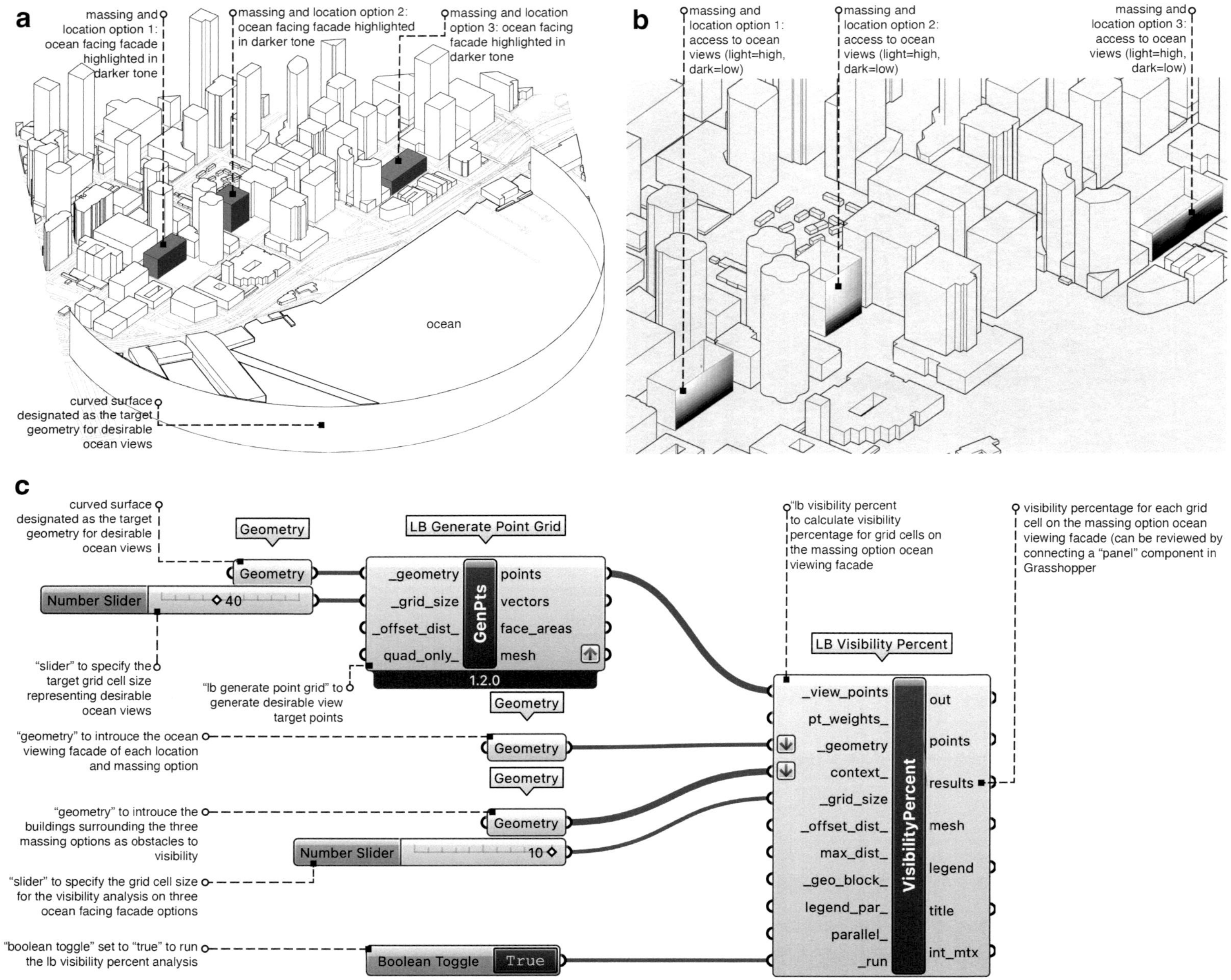

Figure 4.18 *(a) Three different massing and location options for a potential hotel building close to a fictitious waterfront; (b) the visibility percent findings of each façade grid cells visualized using a black and white scheme (lighter tones indicate higher visibility); and (c) the Grasshopper definition constructed to calculate the visibility percent values for the three massing and location options using the Ladybug plug-in's "LBViewPercent" component.*

multiple values tend to neutralize significant, extreme values by bulking them into an average value, from a statistical point of view it will make more sense to investigate median visibility and standard deviation values.

All three of the proposed options in this example have an approximate total area of 198,000 square feet. Option 1 features an approximate footprint of 22,000 square feet, while option 2 features an approximate footprint of 27,000 square feet, and option 3 features an approximate footprint of 43,000 square feet. Consequently, option 1, with the smallest approximate footprint has a proposed number of nine floors; option 2, with a slightly larger footprint has a proposed number of seven floors, and option 3, with the largest footprint has a proposed number of five floors. At this point, let us take a look into the definition of the terms "median" and "standard deviation" in statistics, since these values can help us get a clearer understanding of the findings compared to findings based on a "mean" (average) value calculation (Table 4.2).

In a given numerical data set (such as a list of values from Grasshopper), ***median*** is defined as the value that constitutes the middle value in between the top half and the lower half of the list of numbers. As an example, let us imagine a set "A" which contains 5 numbers, and depict it as:

$$A = \{2, 3, 8, 12, 100\}.$$

In this set, the median value would be 8, since it is the value that separates the upper half and lower half of the list of numbers. The advantage of looking into the median value in a set is that, unlike mean, median is not affected by an extremely high or extremely low values that may be in the set. If we were to simply look into the mean (average) value, we would find that the mean value in this example is 25 – a result heavily affected by the one extremely high value of 100. However, most of the values in this set are between 1 and 15; therefore, in this case the median value provides a clearer understanding of the data (Agresti and Finlay, 2000).

Once the median of a set of numerical values is identified, one can also get a better understanding of the data by looking at its standard deviation. In a given numerical data set, standard deviation is the amount of deviation of values from the average (mean) value. The smaller the standard deviation, the closer the values are to the average (mean) value. This indicates that the data set is more stable, and most values in the data set are close to the mean value, making the mean a more reliable indicator. If the standard deviation is a high value, it is likely that more values in the data set are far different from the average (mean) value, indicating that the average (mean) value may be skewed by an extremely high or low value in the data set (Agresti and Finlay, 2000).

Many pieces in existing literature provide formulas for calculating mean, median, and standard deviation values along with explanations behind the rationale of these calculations such

Table 4.2 Approximate footprint square footage, approximate total square footage, proposed number of floors, median visibility (%), visibility standard deviation (%), and minimum and maximum analysis grid cell visibility (%) for the three location and massing options under analysis.

	Approximate footprint (sq. ft.)	*Proposed number of floors*	*Approximate total sq. ft.*	*Median visibility (%)*	*Mean visibility (%)*	*Visibility standard deviation (%)*	*Minimum grid cell visibility value (%)*	*Maximum grid cell visibility value (%)*
Location and massing option 1	22,000	9	198,000	60.07	53.47	25.06	4.95	89.39
Location and massing option 2	27,000	7	198,000	46.22	39.77	14.88	2.52	54.95
Location and massing option 3	43,000	5	198,000	23.74	32.67	23.35	7.28	79.86

as the key book on statistical methods for behavioral sciences by Agresti and Finlay (2000). In this book, our focus is on parametric methods in architectural design; therefore, we will not go into the details of these calculations. Nevertheless, the author highly recommends architecture students and architects to get a basic understanding of quantitative data analysis in order to get a good sense of numerical findings.

By looking at the median value and standard deviation values of a set of numbers, we can get an understanding of the data without having to observe the effects of extremely high or extremely low values. In this example, location and massing option 1 has the highest median value, and with its standard deviation of 25.06%, we can see that the minimum visibility of a grid cell on the façade is 4.95%. Location and massing option 3, on the other hand, has a median visibility value of 23.74%, and with its standard deviation of 23.35%, the minimum visibility of grid cells on the façade can be as low as 7.28%. These values clearly indicate that location and massing option 1 will provide the highest visual access to the rooms facing the waterfront. Option 1 is followed by options 2 and 3 (Table 4.2). Since all options provide the same square footage when access to ocean views is considered, location and massing option 1 proves more advantageous for a hotel. Clearly, access to ocean views will constitute only one of the factors to consider in decision-making. However, in early project development, conducting a parametric analysis like this example will help with the evaluation of alternatives.

Additional Approaches Evaluating Alternatives in Early Project Development. When multiple factors need to be considered in the early project development phase, the extensive amount of data generated using parametric methods can be overwhelming for the designer and accompanying decision-makers. At this point, optimization techniques using evolutionary solvers prove helpful. By taking one or multiple factors into account, evolutionary solvers can evaluate large data sets and help the designer and accompanying decision-makers. We will delve into the rationale and use of such solvers in Chapter 7.

CHAPTER 05

SPATIAL ORGANIZATION AND VISIBILITY ANALYSIS USING PARAMETRIC METHODS

Following conceptual and preliminary design development, a common move in the architectural design process is to start thinking about spatial organization. During this phase, beyond programmatic considerations such as adjacencies among programmatic elements, organizational and atmospheric considerations enter the picture. When organizational decisions are considered, the interrelationships between programmatic elements are crucial. For example, in a public building, spaces with a need for high privacy may need to be kept a few spaces away from major circulation routes. Similarly, in many settings, various concerns about visibility, whether they are related to maximizing visibility for more visual access or minimizing visibility for privacy or security may require analysis. Another variable that may be considered during organizing program elements is walking distance. A number of factors such as the required interface frequencies between individuals occupying different program elements may trigger analyses of walking distances among program elements during the design process.

Since parametric methods operate using quantitative data, they can fulfill a supportive role when architects and designers are in the process of design decision-making. Clearly, when making decisions about any spatial organization, the program and the social, economic, environmental context, and the target building's use(s) are major factors in decision-making – not only about spatial organization, visibility, and walking distances but also the spatial atmosphere of each proposed space. In this chapter, we will discuss parametric methods that can assist with the design process through analyses of two and three-dimensional visibility, spatial organization, and walking distances.

5.1 VISIBILITY ANALYSES IN DESIGN DEVELOPMENT

We introduced visibility analysis and the concept of isovists in Chapters 3 and 4. The two and three-dimensional visibility analyses introduced in those chapters were conducted in urban scale. In this section, we will discuss conducting various methods of visibility analysis inside buildings.

5.1.1 Basic Two-Dimensional Visibility Analysis for Interiors

When perceptual and behavioral influences are considered, visual connections among spaces inside a building are crucial. Research has shown that visual connections between spaces can influence behavior, such as social and work-related interactions, in work environments (Toker, 2006; Toker and Gray, 2008) as well as a variety of other spatial settings (Turner, Doxa, O'Sullivan, et al., 2001).

Visual connections between a building, its spaces, and desirable urban and/or natural spaces are also influential on human preferences of space occupancy. Interspatial and contextual connections have been studied in architectural and urban contexts, yielding results about the influential nature of visibility on human behavior and perception (Benedikt, 1979; Turner, Doxa, O'Sullivan, et al., 2001). While visibility and its influences on human behavior and perceptions have been quantitatively and qualitatively studied over the past few decades, especially in the last decade, parametric software and methods have enabled more complex analysis of spatial visibility using higher resolutions.

Inside a building, a mean isovist value can be calculated for each space based on its visual connections to the other spaces. Both parametric and non-parametric software make this calculation usually by first superimposing a high-resolution grid on the space's floor plan (i.e., floor surface), calculating the isovist values for each grid, and taking the mean value of the isovists on this grid (Benedikt, 1979). The resolution of this grid can be adjusted based on the accuracy preferred. In Chapter 3, we looked into conducting such analyses using Grasshopper's native "isovist" component as well as the tools provided by the Ladybug plug-in for Grasshopper. Let us discuss how these tools can be used to analyze interspatial visibility inside buildings.

5.1.2 Basic Interspatial Visibility Analysis Using Grasshopper's Native "Isovist" Component for Building Interiors

Figure 5.1a introduces the floor plan of a one-bedroom, two-bathroom, single-level fictitious house designed by the author. All spaces are accessible by a single door, and an interior aperture visually connects the home office and kitchen and dining spaces. Figure 5.1b illustrates the same floor plan ready for interior visibility analysis: all doors have been removed (assuming all doors are open during analysis) and exterior glazing is assumed opaque to focus on interspatial visibility. The only interior glazing frame has been omitted for visibility analysis to depict an interior transparent surface. All walls and glazing surfaces are introduced to Grasshopper as "obstacles" for isovist analysis.

In this example, we will take the centroid of each individual space as a vantage point for its isovist analysis. To define clear boundaries, we will define each rectilinear space as one space. Figure 5.2a illustrates the rectilinear spaces defined for isovist analysis, and Figure 5.2b illustrates the centroid for each space.

Figure 5.3a shows the Grasshopper definition developed for interspatial visibility analysis for this fictitious house. The rectilinear spaces are first introduced to Grasshopper as multiple geometries using a "geometry" component. Their centroids are then identified using Grasshopper's "area" component, which constitutes the vantage points for isovist analysis. These points are then identified as the location for the "plane" entry of the native Grasshopper IsoVist component. The number of isovist points is set to 1000 for precision, and analysis radius is set to 80 feet to make sure all spaces are included in analysis for each vantage point.

All walls and exterior glazing surfaces are introduced to Grasshopper using a "geometry" component as visual obstacles, so we can focus on interior interspatial visibility. The resulting isovist points are then joined with lines using the "polyline" component and setting its Boolean "closed" setting to "true" to achieve closed polylines. At the end of this process, we get access to an isovist for each vantage point. Figure 5.3b illustrates the isovist geometry for each space in the house taking its centroid as the vantage point.

The Grasshopper definition then moves each isovist on the Z-axis using the "series," "Unit Z," and "Move" components. In doing so, we move the first isovist (space 0) to 12 feet, and then each isovist up in Z direction for 34 feet. There is nothing specific about these values since the objective was to simply move isovists in Z direction until all isovists can be visible without overlapping in isometric view. Figure 5.4a illustrates the isovist geometry for each space three-dimensionally in an exploded isometric format. When we overlay all isovists in plan format by

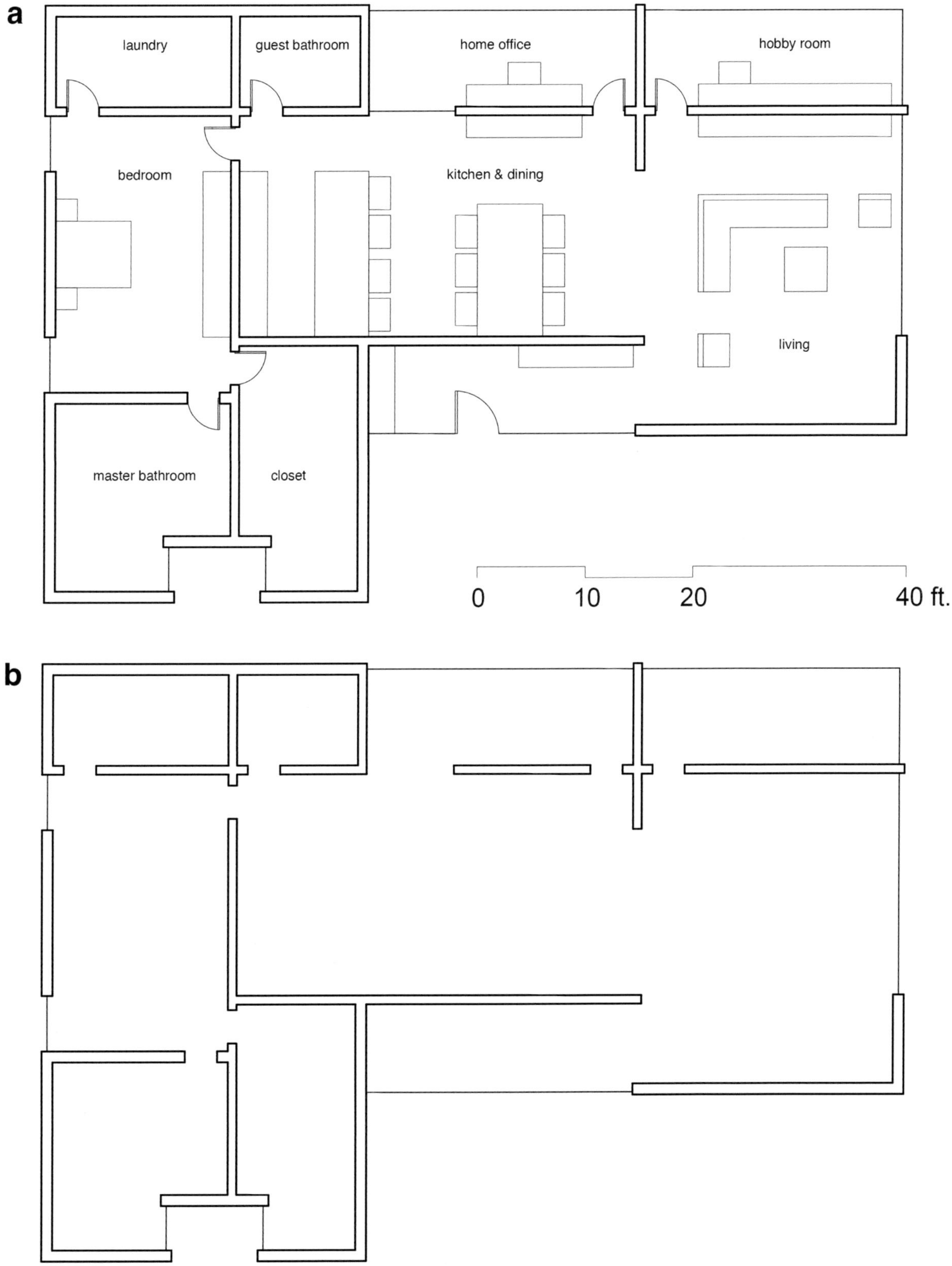

Figure 5.1 *(a) Floor plan of the single-level fictitious house designed by the author and (b) all house doors and interior glazing hidden, making the floor plan available for interior-only visibility analysis with the assumption that all doors have been removed and exterior glazing is opaque. The only interior glazing frame has been omitted for visibility analysis to depict an interior transparent surface. All walls and glazing surfaces are introduced to Grasshopper as "obstacles" for isovist analyses.*

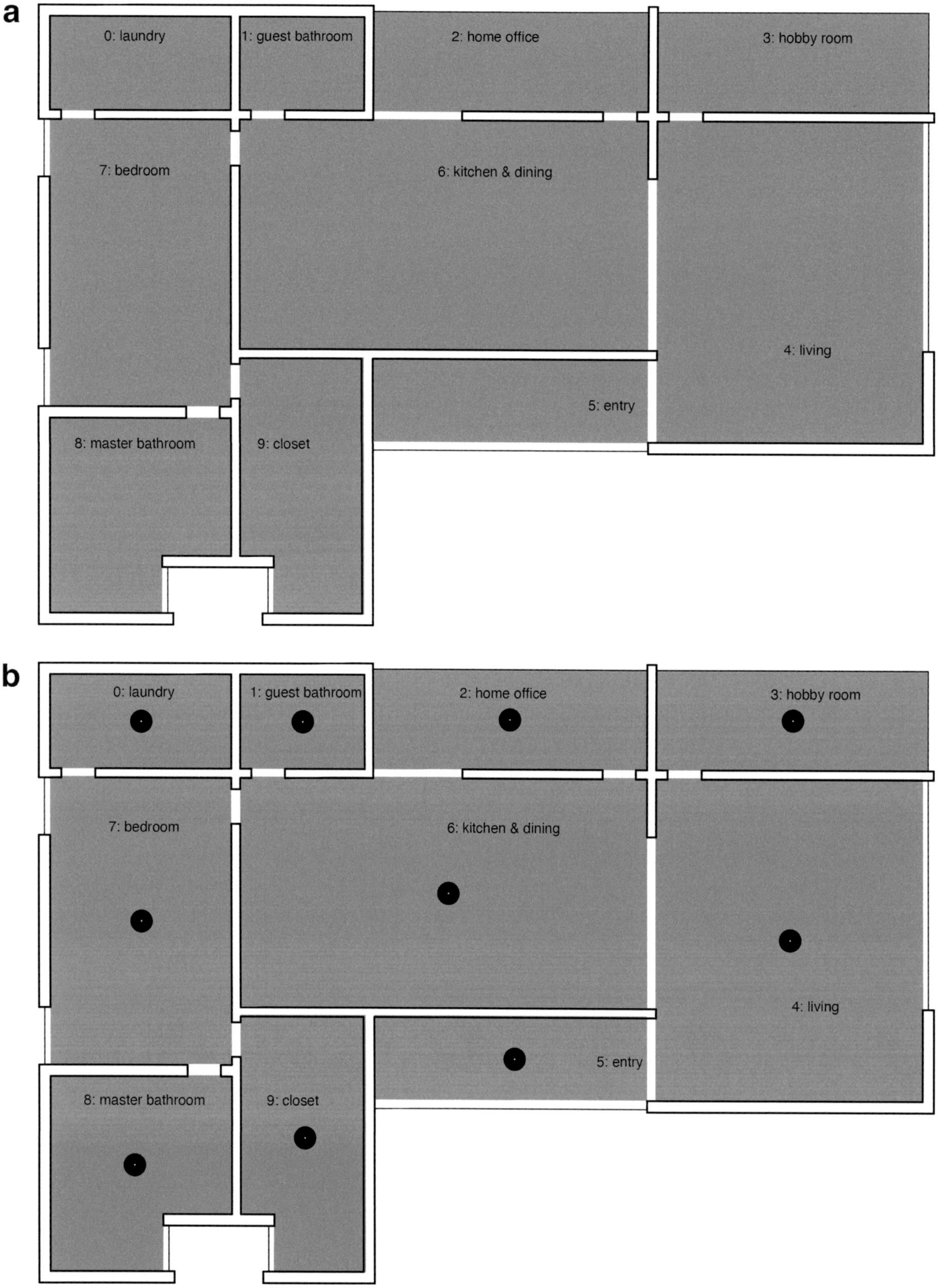

Figure 5.2 *(a) Floor plan of the single-level fictitious house designed by the author with programmatic intent labeled for each rectilinear space and (b) the centroids of each space identified using Grasshopper's "area" component for visibility analysis using Grasshopper's isovist component.*

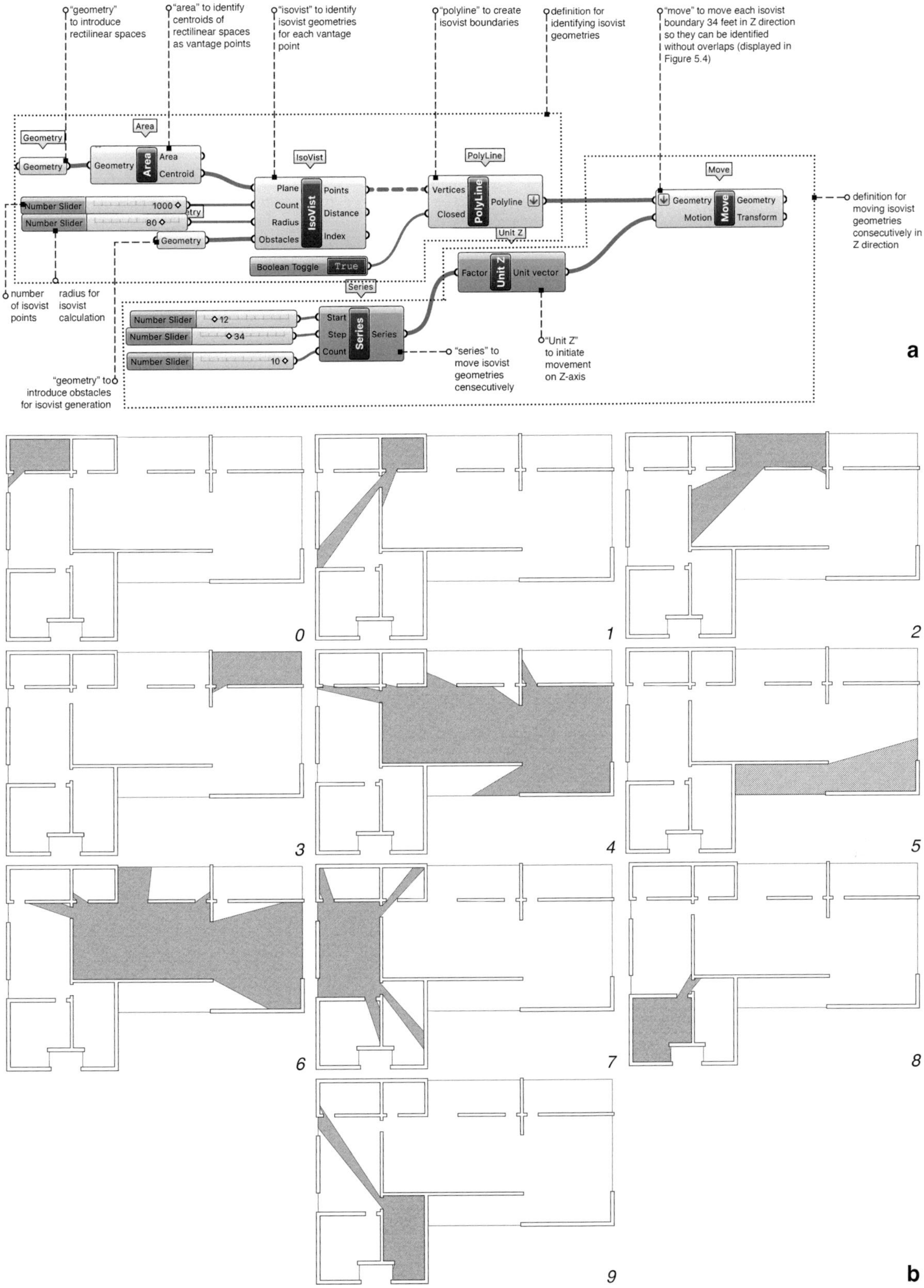

Figure 5.3 *(a) The Grasshopper definition developed to identify isovists for each space in the house and (b) the isovist geometry for each space in the house taking its centroid as the vantage point.*

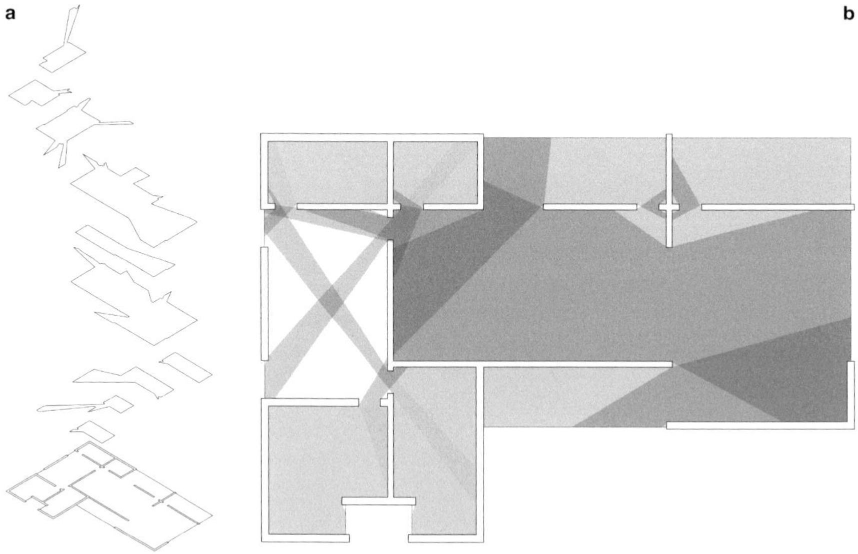

Figure 5.4 *(a) The isovist geometry for each space illustrated three-dimensionally in an exploded isometric format and (b) all isovists overlaid in plan format by assigning them a black hue with 15% opacity. Overlapping isovists are indicators of higher visibility in that area. The darker an area gets, the higher its visibility is.*

Table 5.1 Comparative isovist analysis for the fictitious house introduced: the programmatic intent, square footage, and total isovist area of each space; the isovist area outside of each original space; and the Ratio of Isovist Area Outside of each Original Space to the Original Space's Floor Area (based on the original space's centroid as the vantage point).

Space No.	*Programmatic Intent*	*Space Floor Area (sq. ft.)*	*Total Isovist Area (sq. ft.)*	*Isovist Area Outside the Original Space (sq. ft.)*	*Ratio of Isovist Area Outside the Original Space to Original Space's Floor Area (sq. ft.) (based on the original space's centroid as the vantage point)*
0	Laundry	132.84	140.69	7.85	0.06
1	Guest bathroom	91.84	185.80	93.96	1.02
2	Home office	214.02	375.89	161.87	0.76
3	Hobby room	209.67	212.80	3.13	0.02
4	Living	660.8	1519.73	858.93	1.30
5	Entry	182.88	450.21	267.33	1.46
6	Kitchen and dining	748.0	1420.36	672.36	0.90
7	Bedroom	405.0	524.20	119.20	0.29
8	Master bathroom	244.4	261.17	16.77	0.07
9	Closet	229.2	303	73.80	0.32

assigning them a black hue with 15% opacity, we start observing the overlaps among isovists (Figure 5.4b). Darker areas on the floor plan indicate higher visibility due to overlapping visibility areas. In this example, we can clearly see that the entry, living room, and kitchen and dining spaces are high visibility spaces, while the bedroom is a low visibility space, which is a positive indicator for higher privacy in many cultures and contexts.

The Grasshopper definition developed for isovist analysis also yields numeric values on the square footage of visibility from each vantage point. Intuitively, we can guess that most of each isovist's square footage would be limited to the boundaries of the original space (i.e., the space's floor area square footage). By subtracting each space's floor area square footage from its isovist's square footage, we can identify the square footage of the space visible from each space's centroid vantage point. For a comparative analysis, we can also look into the ratio of isovist area outside the original space to the original space's floor area. Table 5.1

demonstrates that the entry and living spaces not only have high visibility values but also have high values for the isovist area outside the original space. The kitchen and dining space similarly has a high visibility value, and a high value for the isovist area outside the original space.

5.1.3 Representing Space and Movement in Visibility Analysis: The Minkowski Model

Another simple but efficient method of representing visibility changes on a horizontal plane is to develop a "Minkowski model." This model represents visibility by illustrating isovists of multiple vantage points (on a given path on the horizontal plane) vertically as they change with movement. In other words, as a person moves horizontally on a path, their changing isovists are represented through isovist geometries stacked vertically according to time (Benedikt, 1979).

We can demonstrate this representation technique on the fictitious house we have been analyzing in the previous sections. Figure 5.5a shows the floor plan of the house with the movement path of an individual

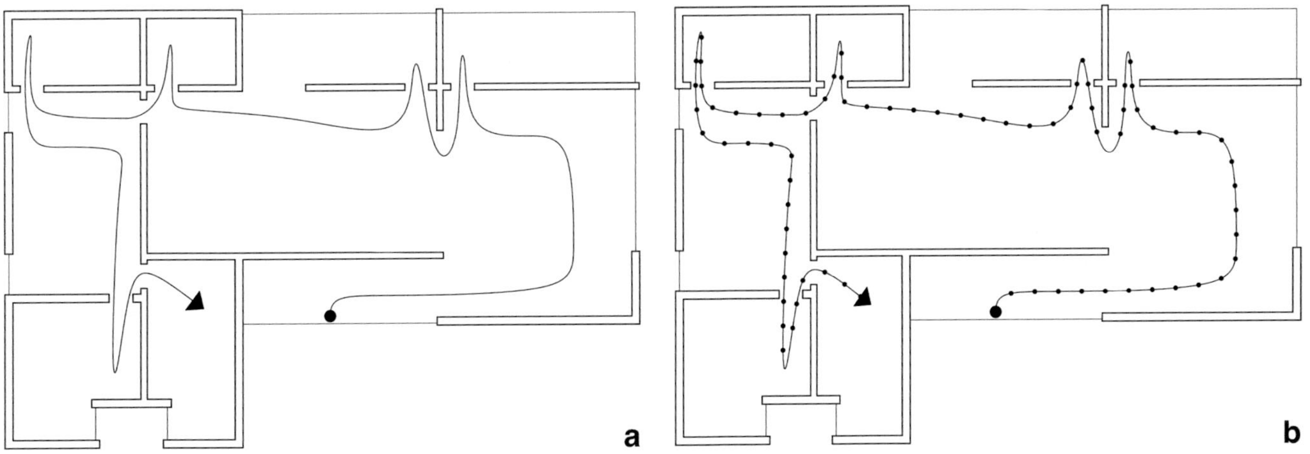

Figure 5.5 *(a) Floor plan of the fictitious house introduced in Section 5.1.1 with a given movement path starting at the entry of the house and ending in the closet space for the bedroom and (b) the same movement path subdivided into 3-foot increments to identify the location of vantage points during movement.*

starting at the entry of the house and ending in the closet space for the bedroom. The path is divided into 3-foot increments, and each node represents one vantage point for an isovist (Figure 5.5b).

Figure 5.6a illustrates the Grasshopper definition used to develop a Minkowski model for this house along the given movement path. Initially, the movement path is introduced into Grasshopper using a "curve" component, which is divided into three-foot increments by using a "divide distance" component. Similar to the examples in previous sections, the number of isovist points is set to 1000, isovist radius is set to 80 feet, and all walls and exterior glazing are introduced to the "isovist" component as obstacles. The "points" output of the "divide distance" component is used to provide the desired vantage points to the "isovist" component.

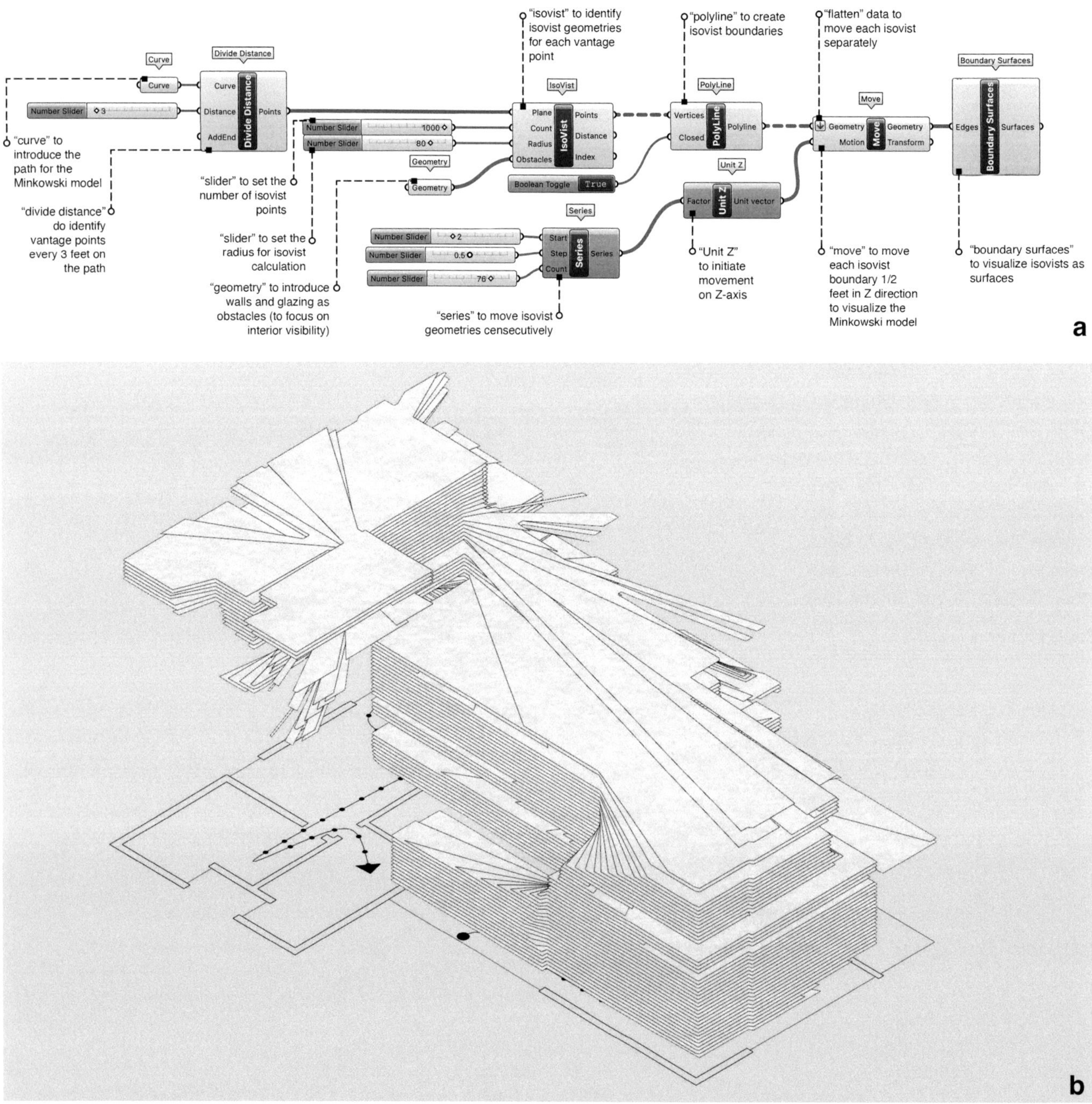

Figure 5.6 (a) The Grasshopper definition used to develop a Minkowski model for the fictitious house using the path introduced in Figure 5.5 and (b) the Minkowski model along the path with vantage points located at three-foot increments.

The resulting isovists are then vertically moved to start at 2 feet from the original floor plan and to be located vertically 1/2 foot from each other, yielding a Minkowski model for this path in the fictitious house (Figure 5.6b). For visual clarity, the "boundary surfaces" component is used to eliminate overlapping lines of isovists.

5.2 SPATIAL ORGANIZATION ANALYSIS IN DESIGN DEVELOPMENT

Since parametric methods in architecture primarily operate on quantitative data, the number of variables that can be utilized in design development are limited. So far, we have investigated various definitions of visibility since visibility as a variable easily lends itself to quantitative measurement and analysis. Besides visibility, metric interspatial distances can be used in analysis and development due to their quantitative nature.

How about spatial organization? Can we conduct a quantitative analysis of proposed spatial organization schemes using a quantitative method, which may lend itself to parametric methods? A commonly used spatial analysis method that can quantify spatial interrelationships was developed at University College London's Bartlett School of Architecture starting in the 1980s. Termed the "space syntax method," this spatial analysis approach was developed based on graph theory in the field of mathematics.

Developed by Professors Bill Hillier and Julianne Hansen, the space syntax method analyzes all adjacencies and connections among all spaces within a system of spaces, such as a building (Hillier and Hanson, 1984; Hillier, 1996). Over years of theory-building and research using the space syntax method, Professors Hillier and Hansen and their colleagues presented findings on how spatial variables operationalized (measured) using the space syntax method can relate to social and behavioral patterns of human beings (Hillier and Hanson, 1984; Penn, Desyllas, and Vaughan, 1999; Hillier and Penn, 1991).

Years of research using space syntax methods have illustrated many patterns of relationships between space and human social and behavioral patterns. Our objective in this book is to discuss parametric methods for architectural design processes, therefore we will not go into the details of space syntax methods. Nevertheless, due to the quantitative nature of space syntax methods, a number of space syntax-based plug-ins for Grasshopper have been developed over the years. In this section, we will introduce the basics of graph theory and space syntax methods, so that readers interested in both space syntax methods and parametric methods have a foundation-level understanding of how parametric techniques can be adopted to conduct space syntax analysis to inform design development.

5.2.1 Basic Definitions in Space Syntax Methods

Let us revisit the floor plan of the fictitious house introduced in Section 5.1.1. To start with a space syntax analysis of this floor plan, we first need to divide the floor plan's spaces into the fewest number of "convex" spaces (i.e., spaces whose plan width to length ratio is closest to 1). Even though four solid walls may not exist to define a space on the floor plan, spaces with a plan width to length ratio close to 1 can be considered "convex" spaces. In Section 5.1.1, we referred to such spaces as rectilinear spaces (Figure 5.7a).

The method then represents each "convex" space with a circle and each connection between each pair of spaces with a line. The lines at this point represent doorways connecting spaces or, in the absence of doors, the linear threshold that needs to be crossed to move from one space to another (i.e., in this example, from the entry space to the living space). The set of circles and lines is then organized to start at a point (in this case, the exterior of the house). The starting point is commonly referred to as the "carrier" in space syntax literature. Lines represent each "step" of passing a threshold from one space to the next (Figure 5.7b). When this set of lines and circles are divorced from the original floor plan and organized as a graph

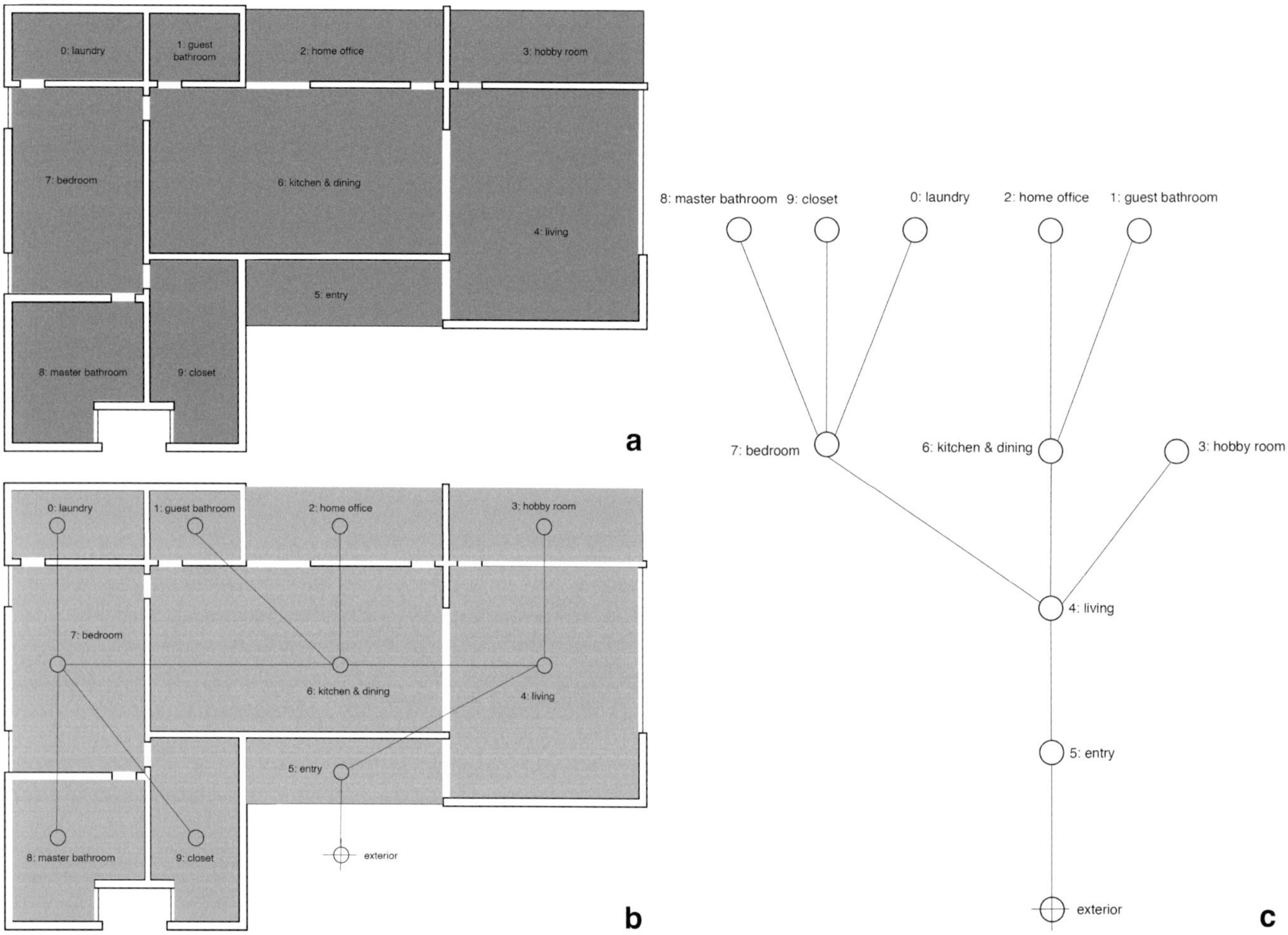

Figure 5.7 (a) The "convex" spaces of the fictitious house introduced in Section 5.1.1; (b) spaces and thresholds being represented with circles and lines; and (c) the justified permeability graph of the house.

representing all spaces, thresholds, and connections that start with the entry, a "justified permeability graph" is formed (Figure 5.7c) (Hillier and Hanson, 1984).

The "justified permeability graph" is important in space syntax methods since it represents non-metric and non-geometric relationships on the floor plan. In other words, instead of looking into walking distances or a spaces' geometry, we can focus on the interrelationships among all spaces in a system of spaces. In this way, spatial organizations that may not have similar metric distance or geometric similarities can still be compared based on their thresholds, connections, and their connection(s) to the starting point, the "carrier."

Based on this graph, each space is given a "point depth" value, which is equivalent to the number of thresholds one needs to pass through to reach the target space. By developing a series of algorithms on this foundation over the years, space syntax researchers have developed a quantitative measure of configurational accessibility for each space in a system of spaces: its "integration" value. Described in simple terms, the integration value of a space in a system of spaces is an indicator of how accessible that space is based on the number of thresholds to reach it from all other spaces in the system.

Since this threshold-based accessibility is a quantitative value by nature, space syntax researchers have been able to investigate the correlations between space syntax variables and patterns of social and behavioral occurrences in daily life. For example, in a workspace setting, higher integration values for a space may mean more possibilities for chance encounters, which may be an advantage for creative industries. The same space, however, may be less advantageous for a work organization that has a strong focus on concentrated work, therefore with a smaller need for impromptu chat among employees.

In recent years, various researchers and programmers from around the world have developed Grasshopper plug-ins that can analyze various spatial properties using the space syntax method. Many of these plug-ins can be downloaded for free from the website https://www.food4rhino.com. Each plug-in author provides their individual licensing requirements along with the plug-in files necessary. Readers interested in the space syntax method and its applications using parametric methods can explore these options.

CHAPTER 06

SKIN SYSTEMS Repetition, Subdividing Geometries, and Paneling Approaches

As discussed in Chapter 3, parametric methods can be used to analyze a site prior to the design process, yielding information on environmental properties of the site, including solar access potential, prevailing winds, and psychrometric data such as temperature and humidity. During the design process, these data are frequently referred to and revisited, as the building's enclosure and aperture design strategies are identified to optimize a solution for the specific location.

Using parametric methods can contribute to a building's physical expression and environmental performance through enclosure and aperture system design – the "skin system." Environmental performance criteria directly relate to the skin system design of a building: daylighting and solar exposure. Using parametric methods, designers can rapidly change a building's enclosure and aperture design strategies and measure the performance of multiple design iterations to maximize daylighting, reduce glare, and optimize natural ventilation, as well as to minimize energy use through reducing the necessity for active heating and cooling systems.

The use of parametric methods in skin system design is not limited to positively influencing a building's environmental performance. Design decisions about skin systems also directly influence the visibility relationships between a building's interiors and exteriors, as well as the overall physical expression of the building. Through use of parametric methods in aperture design, designers can empirically influence the visual connections between the building and its immediate and, in some cases, wider context.

Before Chapter 8, which will introduce parametric tools for environmental performance analysis, this chapter will introduce the basic principles and techniques of architectural applications of parametric methods in skin system design in relation to environmental comfort and relationship to the context and views. The fast and efficient capabilities of parametric design software in iteration generation and analysis largely relate to skin system design through surface subdivision techniques. Through surface subdivision, designers can rapidly generate and evaluate high numbers of surfaces and apertures.

In Chapter 3, we discussed basic even subdivision of surfaces. In Section 6.1, we will look into uneven surface subdivision using parametric techniques. We will discuss subdivision techniques using Grasshopper's basic command structure as well as using widely used plug-ins. Section 6.2 will discuss using parametric methods to increase influence on the direct sun hours of the building, through interventions on aperture system design using image samplers and remapping data. In Section 6.3, we will introduce alternative approaches to skin system interventions using control geometries. In Section 6.4, we will look into interventions into

 DOI: 10.4324/9781003230052-6

the physical expression of a building through repeating modular units on complex surfaces. Section 6.5 will introduce methods for populating complex skin system surfaces with predesigned units, such as repeating modular units.

6.1 SURFACE SUBDIVISION

Surface subdivision is a common method for controlling aperture properties such as size, shape, and operability. Since ancient times, humans have subdivided the façades of their buildings, which allows for creating apertures to provide views and allow light in, while still accommodating structural elements that help support the slab(s) and roof of their structures (Figure 6.1a). Following the Industrial Revolution and the advent of mass production techniques, developing façades independent of the structural system became possible. Modern architecture's development around the globe brought applications of curtain walls independent of the structural system (Figure 6.1b) (Murray, 2009). The idea of surface subdivision continues to be common. Due to several reasons such as material and building element limitations, search for rhythm, and environmental performance such as daylighting and ventilation, designers have continued to subdivide structure-independent façades. In contemporary architecture, the use of curtain walls, and façade screen systems for protecting large apertures and glass surfaces from unwanted environmental factors have become prominent for façade subdivision strategies – especially parametric strategies (Figure 6.1c). In this section, we will look into uneven subdivision of irregular surfaces.

Common curtain wall applications essentially create apertures by subdividing façade surfaces (Figure 6.1d). Parametric applications' capability of processing high quantities of data in a short amount of time makes them especially efficient in subdividing complex surfaces, making them powerful tools for designing skin systems with complex geometries. Using control geometries, bitmap images, or data remapping, parametric methods also enable varying the scale of apertures based on variables (i.e., solar exposure and orientation) instead of repeating aperture modules. Such applications will be discussed in the following sections of this book. In this section, we will introduce the basics of surface subdivision.

Common curtain wall strategies rely on offsetting surface edges on both directions of a surface, by the desired size and rhythm of apertures and modules. The desired size and rhythm of apertures and modules vary based on design intentions such as lighting, ventilation and heating. Modules or sets of modules are usually based on even or repeating subdivisions. Parametric methods enable subdivision of complex geometries evenly or unevenly.

Uneven Subdivision of Irregular Surfaces. While in many surface subdivisions even modules are preferred, given the complexity of contemporary form explorations and advanced performance analysis techniques in architecture, uneven subdivisions have become more common. For example, changing subdivision dimensions or scale based on environmental factors or aesthetic preference have become more common in recent years. Such variations can be achieved through a variety of methods using parametric applications. In this section, the main principles and an introductory method of uneven surface subdivision will be discussed. In the following chapters, we will introduce additional methods, along with approaches to responses to a variety of criteria.

There are multiple parametric methods that can generate varying numerical data by altering an existing set of data – such as using the "Graph Mapper" component, using bitmap images with the "Image Sampler" component and data remapping using the remap numbers component. Using control geometries is another common approach in parametric methods. This section will demonstrate the use of the Graph Mapper component for altering evenly divided numbers into a set of uneven numbers using mathematical functions through the Graph Mapper component.

Figure 6.1 (a) The former San Francisco Federal Building, San Francisco, California, USA (1936), designed by Arthur Brown, Jr.; (b1) the original Bauhaus Building, Dessau, Germany (1926) designed by Walter Gropius; (b2) curtain wall on front façade of the original Bauhaus Building; (c1) Emerson College Los Angeles Center, Los Angeles, California, USA (2014), designed by Morphosis Architects; (c2) parametric subdivision and façade application on Emerson College Los Angeles Center; (d) common curtain wall application: Construction Innovations Center, California Polytechnic State University San Luis Obispo, California, USA. Photographs by the author.

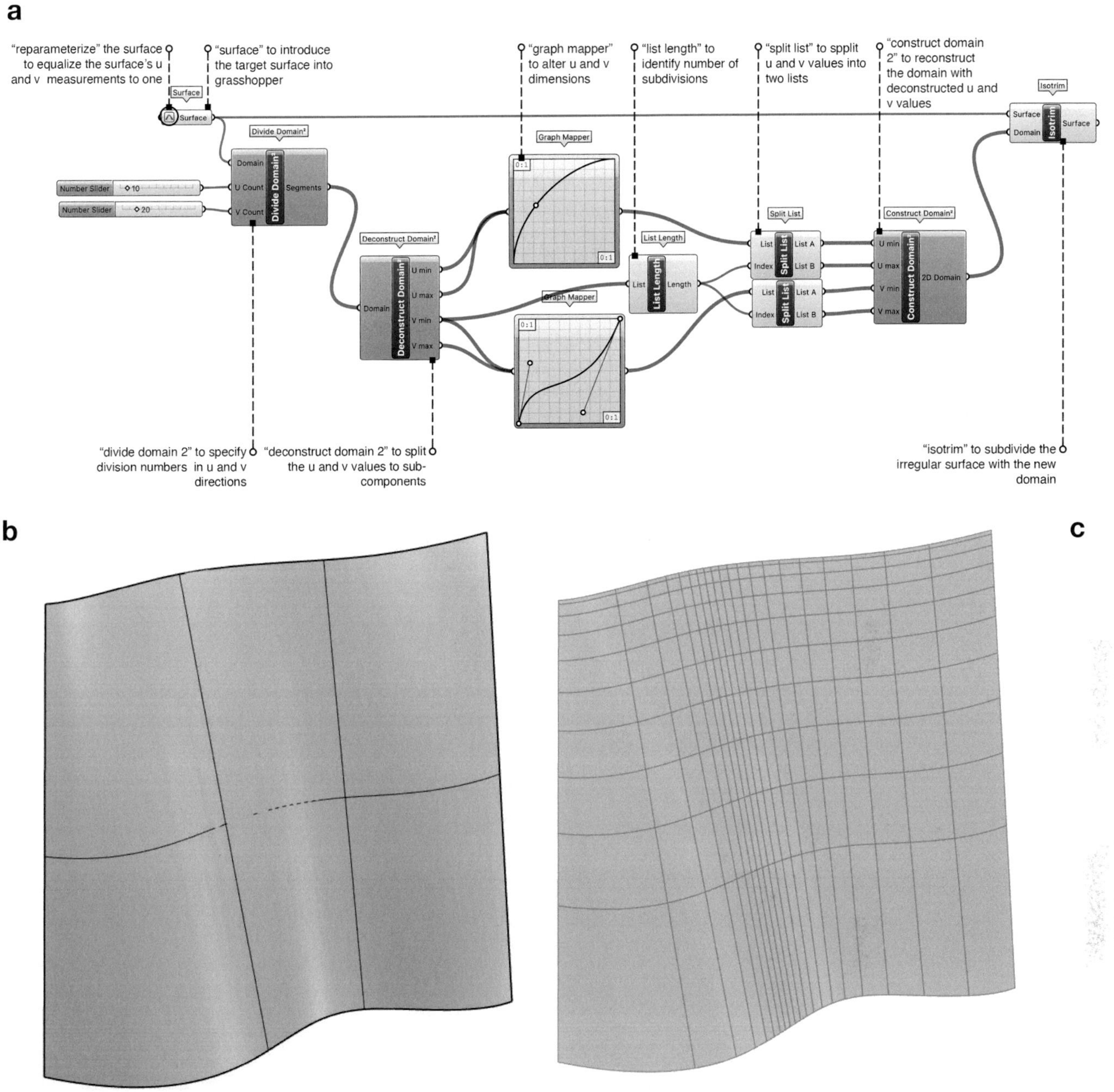

Figure 6.2 Uneven curved surface subdivision using the Isotrim, Divide Domain², Deconstruct Domain², and Graph Mapper components. (a) The Grasshopper definition developed for subdivision; (b) the sample uneven curved surface; and (c) the resulting uneven surface subdivision.

The Mathematical Function, Its Domain, and Range. We discussed the Graph Mapper component of Grasshopper in Chapter 4. The graph mapper allows us to generate data sets based on mathematical functions. In order to get a better understanding of the graph mapper, at this point, a basic introduction to mathematical functions will be appropriate.

Mathematical functions describe relationships between quantitative (i.e., numerical) variables, where one variable quantity is dependent on the other variable quantity's value (Thomas, Hass, Heil, et al., 2018). To verbally exemplify a function, one can think about the floor area of a room: given a constant ceiling height, if one increases the floor are of the room, the room's volume also increases. In this verbal description, the volume of the room (a variable quantity) is dependent on the floor area of the room (value of the other variable quantity). In mathematics, a function like this is represented with:

$$y = f(x)$$

(Thomas, Hass, Heil, et al., 2018)

In this function, y, the room's volume would be dependent on x (making it the "dependent variable"), the room's floor area (making it the "independent variable"). To customize the example, one can say:

$$V_r = f(A_r)$$

where V_r is the room volume and A_r is the room floor area. As one can imagine, a function has input and output values. In the $V_r = f(A_r)$ example, the room floor area becomes the input value, and the room volume becomes the output value.

In a mathematical function, the set of all possible input values is referred to as the "domain" of the function. The set of all possible output values is referred to as the "range" of the function (Thomas, Hass, Heil, et al., 2018). In the $V_r = f(A_r)$ example, all possible floor area values constitute the domain of the function, while all possible room volume values constitute the range of the function.

The definition of "domain" can now be revisited. Earlier, we described domain as "a set of two numbers between a minimum value and a maximum value." Having introduced mathematical functions, once can now see that the domain for the $V_r = f(A_r)$ is a set of available numbers for the room floor area with a minimum and maximum. Likewise, for $V_r = f(A_r)$, the range is a set of all possible output values of the volume.

Graph Mapper and Mathematical Functions. Having introduced the mathematical function, its domain, and range, it is time to take a closer look into the Graph Mapper component of Grasshopper. The Graph Mapper component provides the user with a tool to visually alter a variety of mathematical functions, making it possible to generate a set of numbers (the range) by altering original set(s) of numbers (the domain). One can also "deconstruct" and "reconstruct" a two-dimensional domain by way of using these components, thereby achieving a guide for an uneven subdivision of surfaces. The Graph Mapper component in Grasshopper provides a number of predefined functions, such as the parabolic curve, linear relationship, and the sine curve. Customized functions can also be integrated into the Graph Mapper. Once the component is introduced into Grasshopper, one can set the graph type by right-clicking on it. Input data can then be edited based on the selected function. The following example illustrates this by using two different functions through Graph Mapper.

The "Divide Domain^2" component introduced earlier yields even subdivisions on U and V axes. In an attempt to visually create and control uneven subdivisions on both axes, one can "deconstruct" the values created by the Divide Domain^2 component. The "Deconstruct Domain^2" (DeDom2Num) component of Grasshopper can take a U/V domain and "deconstruct" into U0 and U1 lists (lower and upper limits of the domain in U axis), and V0 and V1 lists (lower and upper limits of the domain in V axis), exporting 200 values for each list. In the example used in Section 6.1, 200 and 800 values are created consecutively ($10 \times 20 = 200$ values from the Divide Domain^2 component, and $200 \times 4 = 800$ values created by the DeDom2Num component). The newly created U0, U1, V0, and V1 domains can now be altered by using Graph Mapper component and associated mathematical functions.

The example in Figure 6.2 illustrates the altering of the U0 and U1 domains using a conical function, while altering the V0 and V1 domains using Bezier function. One can see that the combined domain inputs into the two graph mappers yield a total of 400 values each (200

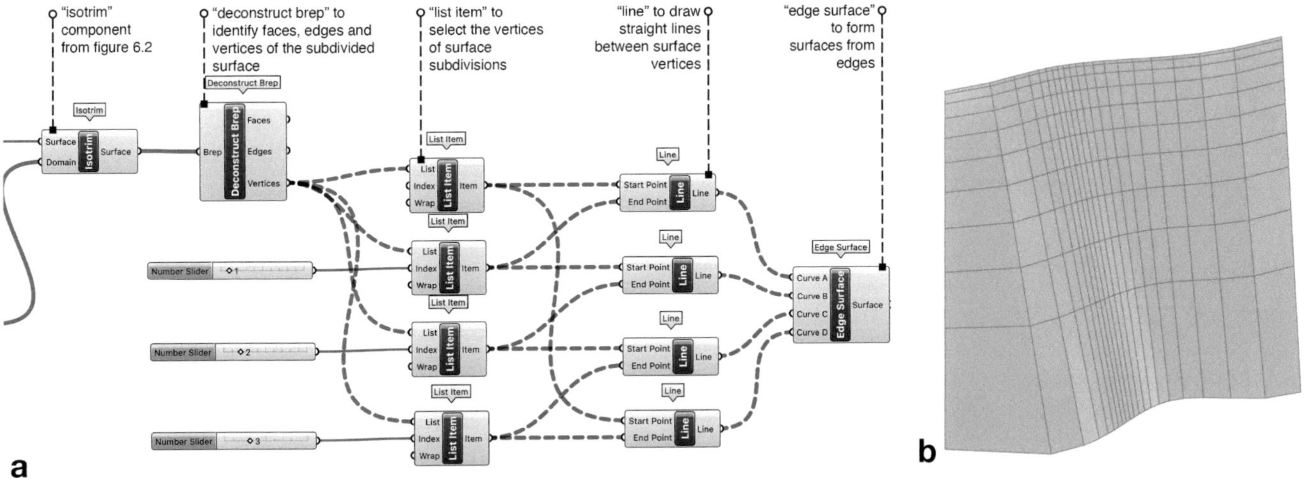

Figure 6.3 Straight edge framework of the curved surface from Figure 6.2a, achieved using Deconstruct Brep, List Item, and Line components. The surfaces were reconstructed using the Edge Surface component. (a) The Grasshopper definition developed for surface reconstruction using the Edge Surface component; and (b) the resulting subdivided surface.

from each domain). The target for these new values, altered by the graph mappers, is the "Construct Domain^2" component, which will yield the new dataset for the uneven subdivision.

The original Divide Domain^2 component yielded a total of 200 values, therefore, the target "Construct Domain^2" component must yield 200 values to reconstruct the altered domain. To achieve this, the graph mapper outputs, 400 values each, are divided in this example into lists of 200 by using the "split list" component, which takes the division index number from the "list length" component connected to one of the domain outputs from the Deconstruct Domain^2 component. This split operation splits the two lists of 400 values from the Graph Mapper components into two lists of 200 values, which are then connected to the U0, U1, V0, and V1 inputs of the "Construct Domain^2" component. Now, the "Construct Domain^2" component yields 200 values, which have been altered by the parametric altering process, allowing the uneven subdivisions to be visually controlled by moving the control points of the two graph mappers used.

Finally, a critical operation included in this process is the "reparameterization" of the original surface, shown in Figure 6.2a.The Graph Mapper component requires a domain from 0 to 1. However, in regular architectural operations, the dimensions of the original surface's dimensions will be different than "1" unit – i.e., 1 meter, 1 foot, etc. The command "reparameterize" on a Grasshopper component converts the original dimensions to an equivalent of one unit, therefore converting the domain to the required 0 to 1 unit. A Grasshopper component input or output can be "reparameterized" by right-clicking on one of the component's input or output links and selecting the "reparameterize" option.

6.1.1 Subdividing Complex Surfaces Creating Straight Edges for Simplified Subsurfaces

In Chapter 4, we introduced basic even surface subdivision. More recently, in the previous section, we introduced uneven surface subdivision, along with the introduction of the function, domain, and range. In this section, we will introduce a number of basic operations in relation to surface subdivision before we look into their architectural applications in Section 6.2.

When curved surfaces are subdivided as described earlier, resulting contours are curved as well. Considering that this may have construction implications, one may want to straighten those contours. If one were to straighten the contours of the example in Figure 6.2, the first necessary step would be to identify the endpoints of the existing contours, so that the endpoints can be connected with lines.

Following the subdivision of the surface in Figure 6.2a, the combinations of multiple surfaces emerge. In Grasshopper, individual or combinations of surfaces, whether two or three-dimensional, are referred to as "Boundary Representations" (Breps). A Brep is composed of faces, edges, and vertices.[1] In order to identify and operate on these elements, the Brep needs to be "deconstructed." The "Deconstruct Brep" (DeBrep) component, identifies the faces, edges, and vertices of a Brep.

In Figure 6.3, the operation starts with deconstructing the Brep from Figure 6.2. As can be seen in the panel, a total of 200 faces are identified, each of which have four edges and four vertices. The panels in Figure 6.3 also show that the vertices and edges are listed with numbers. For example, a face has four vertices that are listed as "0, 1, 2, 3." This is because Grasshopper starts listing items starting with zero. To select one of these vertices, one needs to use the "List Item" component and specify the target item's "index number" (0, 1, 2, or 3) on the list.

To connect the vertices of the faces with straight lines, the vertices need to be identified individually, and lines need to be drawn between them. Figure 6.3 shows the selection of four vertices using four List Item components, and four panels identify the index numbers 0, 1, 2, and 3. The following operation in Figure 6.3 shows that lines are drawn from vertices 0 to 1, 1 to 2, 2 to 3, and 3 to 0, yielding a straight-line version of the contours from Figure 6.2. The last step in Figure 6.3 shows that if desired, one can generate surfaces using four edges, with the "edge surface" component, which defines a surface defined by four edges.

The series of operations demonstrated in Section 6.1 so far allow simplification of complex curved surfaces using native Grasshopper components. The straight-line version of the sub-surface framework can be used for creating construction oriented, simplified geometry frameworks to support façade systems with complex geometries. In the following section, similar procedures will be illustrated using commonly used Grasshopper plug-ins.

6.1.2 Subdividing Complex Surfaces with Commonly Utilized Plug-ins

The LunchBox plug-in, developed by Nathan Miller, dates back to 2012 (Vukorep and Kotov, 2021). The plug-in can subdivide complex surfaces easily and yield several patterns such as regular rectangular panels, as well as more complex panels such as diagrids and hexagon cells. The plug-in also provides users with tools to generate complex structural systems from surfaces and curves, such as space truss applications.

Another commonly used plug-in is Paneling Tools for Rhinoceros and Grasshopper, by Rajaa Issa and McNeel Associates, which dates back to 2018. It provides the user with the capability to develop grids, as well as two-dimensional and three-dimensional panels on simple and complex surfaces. Figure 6.4 illustrates the use of Lunchbox and Paneling Tools at the introductory level.

One can complete even subdivisions of simple and complex surfaces using LunchBox Plug-in's surface subdivision components. As illustrated in the example in Figure 6.4a, simply introducing a surface into Grasshopper and connecting its "surface" component to one of LunchBox's surface subdivision components achieves the subdivision. One can also specify the number of u and v subdivisions though the use of panels and sliders.

The "Paneling Tools" plug-in, created by Rajaa Issa and McNeel Associates, can also subdivide surfaces in Rhinoceros and Grasshopper through a variety of components. In the example introduced in Figure 6.4b, the surface introduced to Grasshopper using the "Surface" component is subdivided by generating a grid with even subdivisions on the surface. To achieve this, the "PtsSrfDist" component is used, which enables the user to specify subdivision divisions in U and V directions. This component yields a grid of points on the source surface, which can be used by the user to generate lines, surfaces, and more complex modules.

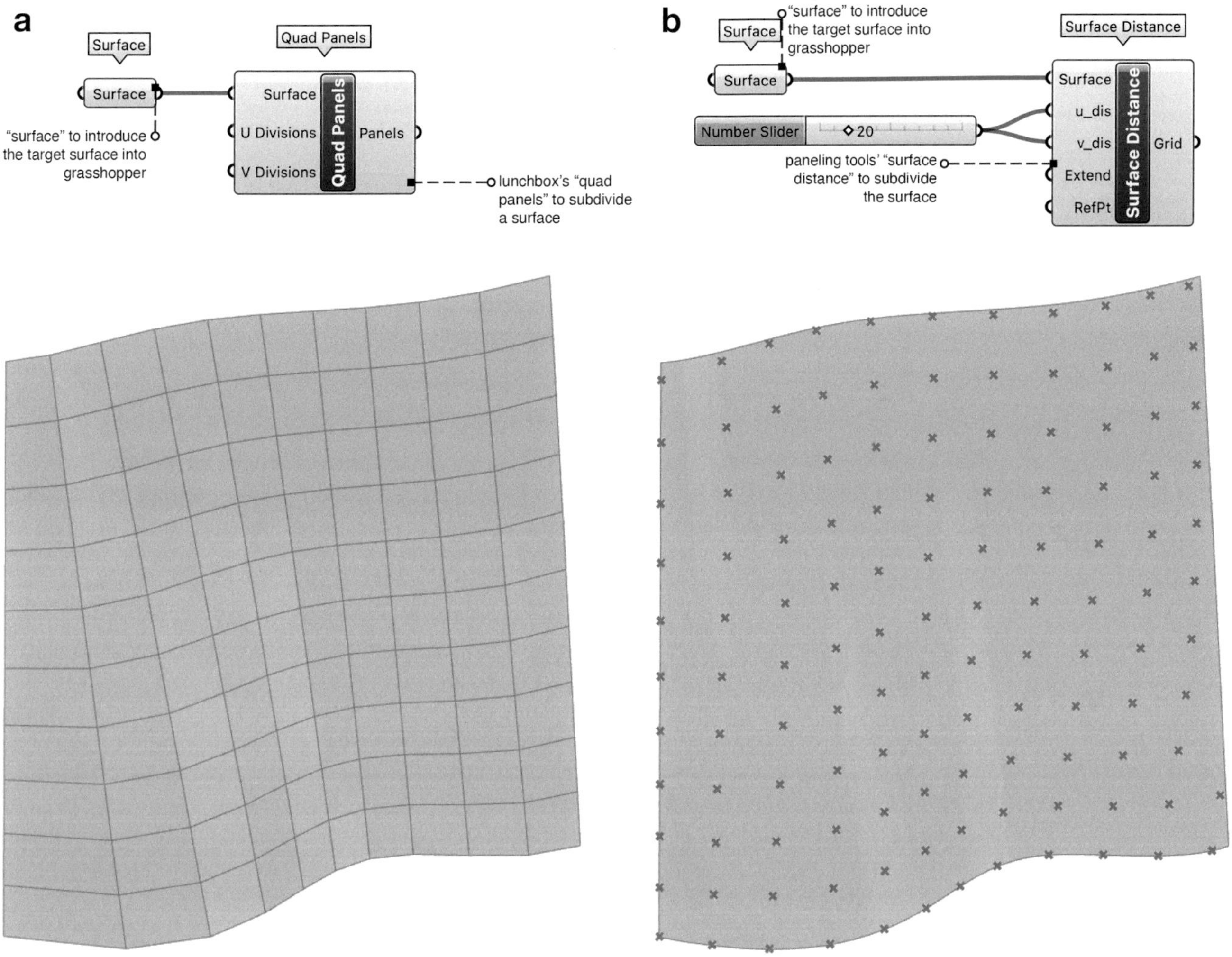

Figure 6.4 Basic surface subdivision (a) using the LunchBox Plug-in; and (b) using the Paneling Tools Plug-in.

6.2 RELATIONSHIPS WITH DAYLIGHT: DIRECT SUN HOURS ANALYSIS OF BUILDING COMPONENTS

We relate ourselves to a locale and time through our relationships with the natural environment. Daylight is one of the crucial environmental phenomena that influences our connection with our built and natural environment (Guzowski, 2018). While it is desirable to have access to daylight in our buildings, too much daylight may cause comfort issues. Additionally, unwanted heat gain due to solar exposure may increase peak loads and negatively impact a building's mechanical cooling loads.

Parametric applications in the architectural design process can be effective and/or supportive in the development of passive response systems to increase human comfort and decrease energy consumption through controlling a building's relationships with the sun. The objective of Section 6.2 is to introduce various parametric techniques in the analysis and design of façade elements toward such strategies.

6.2.1 Direct Sun Hours Analysis of Building Components

Following conceptual design development, programmatic studies, mass composition development, and aperture development often influence one another. At this phase it is important to make informed decisions about apertures' direct sun hours (i.e., number of hours of direct exposure to solar rays in a given period of time) as well as views into and from the surrounding context. The location of the site (i.e., its latitude and longitude), surrounding buildings, as well as its orientation affect an aperture's direct sun hours, yielding significant implications on a building's use of energy for heating, ventilation, and air conditioning. Depending on the programmatic intent of the building, issues such as overexposure and glare may be considered as well.

Let's take a sample urban site, such as the one illustrated in Figure 6.5b. It is surrounded by buildings of various heights, as well as a park to the south and southeast. Let us imagine that a sample public building with a large aperture facing the neighboring urban plaza is being analyzed. The large aperture would be facing southwest with a limited number of buildings blocking the sun, likely causing excessive direct sun exposure, increasing cooling loads, which are especially problematic on this face of a building (Figure 6.5b). The proposed aperture's direct sun hours can be analyzed for various periods of time using Ladybug's "Direct Sun Hours" component (Figure 6.5a).

We introduced Ladybug's "Direct Sun Hours" component in Chapter 3, Section 3.3.4. For conducting most analyses using Ladybug, we need to import and translate climate data using EnergyPlus Weather (EPW) data. Once the data is imported and translated using the "ImportEPW" component, the sun path for the project site can be constructed using the "Sunpath" component.

For the aperture's direct sun hours analysis, Ladybug's "Direct Sun Hours" component is used. To indicate the surface to be analyzed, the Rhinoceros surface of the aperture is introduced to Grasshopper as a "geometry" and connected to the "geometry" input of the "Direct Sun Hours" component. Similarly, the surrounding buildings as well as the non-aperture portions of the sample building is introduced to Grasshopper using a "geometry" component and setting "multiple geometries." This component is connected to the "context" input of the Direct Sun Hours" component. Here it is important to consider defining the context buildings in Rhinoceros as closed polysurfaces, so that the processing time and processing power needed for analysis can be reduced. Finally, the "grid size" refers to the number of subdivisions of the surface that will be analyzed. In this example, a 1' × 1' grid was set for analysis, using a slider set to 1.

In order to use the sun data from the sun path diagram, the "vectors" output of the "Sunpath" component is connected to the "vectors" input of the "Direct Sun Hours" component. The "vectors" here indicate the vectors for the direction of sunlight for each analysis period. Finally, the component is "run" by connecting a toggle button to the "run" input of the Direct Sun Hours component and setting it to "true.

The results of the analysis indicate that much of the aperture is exposed to sunlight for over 750 hours of the year, while the southwest side of the aperture is minimally protected from exposure by the sample building's own neighboring mass. The effect of the three-foot inset of the aperture can also be clearly observed on the top side of the aperture, gradient-coded with a high density of darker cells who do not have much direct sun hours. Figure 6.5 illustrates the parametric direct sun hours analysis operation, the sample building analyzed, and its outcome in the form of the color-coded aperture analyzed, accompanied by a legend specifying the number of yearly direct sun hours indicated by gradient-coding.

6.2.2 Preliminary Interpretations of the Results of Direct Sun Hours Analysis: Designing Parametric Façade Screen Systems to Balance Direct Sun Hours

The direct sun hours analysis introduced in Section 6.2.1 provides valuable information on how the sample building's large-scale aperture would be impacted by direct sun hours. A south-facing large aperture, such as the one discussed in Section 6.2.1, can be protected

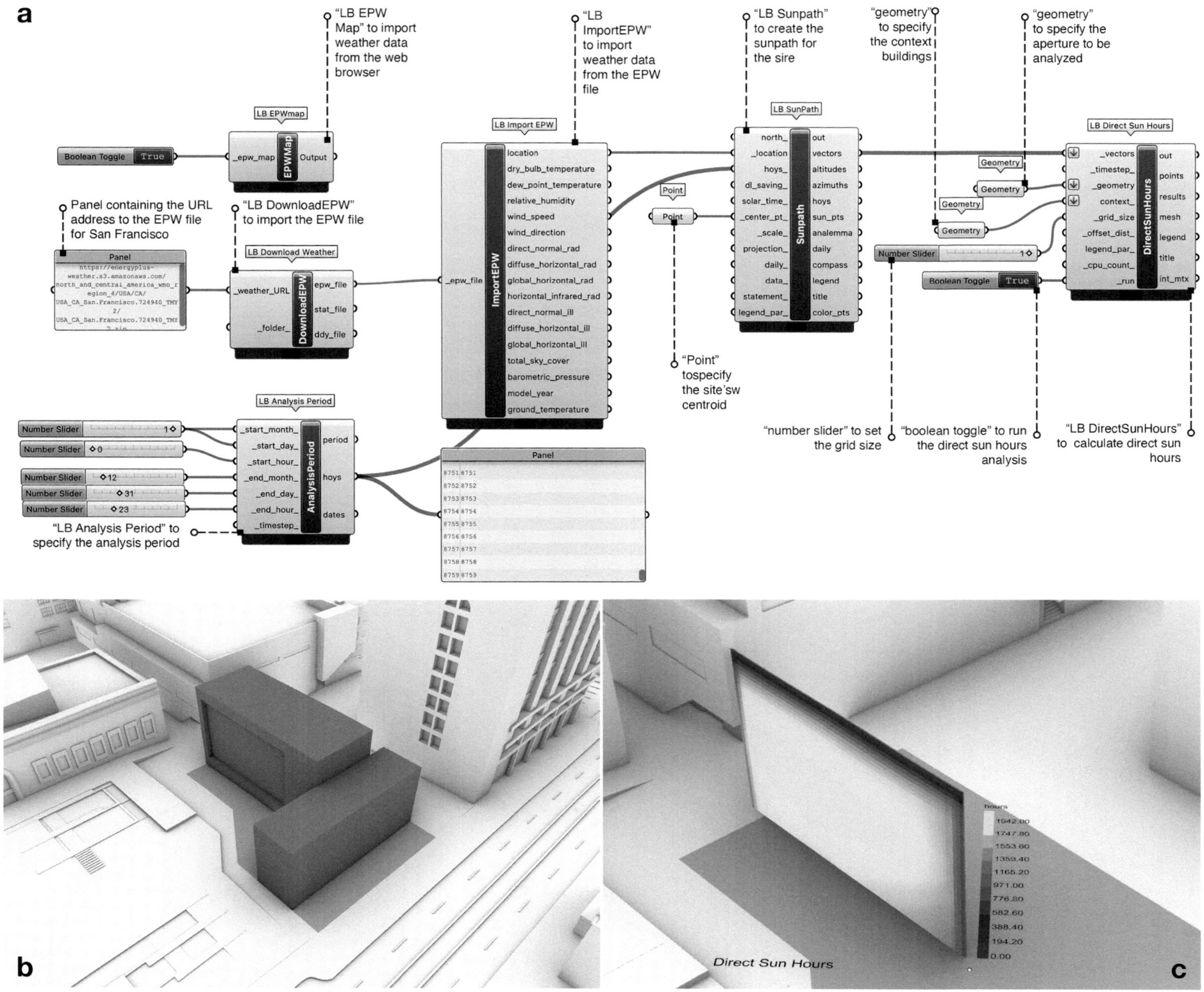

Figure 6.5 (a) The parametric annual direct sun hours analysis operation; (b) the sample building analyzed; and (c) analysis outcome in the form of the gradient-coded aperture, accompanied with a legend specifying the number of yearly direct sun hours indicated by gradient-coding. The digital 3D model of the site was collaboratively developed by the author and members of his Fall 2020 studio.

conventionally with horizontal louvers. Figure 6.6 illustrates that annual direct sun hours of the same aperture from Figure 6.5 can be reduced with a number of three feet deep horizontal louvers. Although the excessive depth of such louvers may be questioned, our intent here is to use exaggerated building elements to demonstrate the results of parametric analysis.

The impact of a southern exposure can also be reduced using parametric methods in various ways. For example, using the computing power and efficiency of parametric modeling, customized perforated screen systems can be designed for the specific location, building and aperture. In this section, four different approaches to the design of a parametric perforated screen system custom for the sample site, building and the aperture analyzed in Section 6.2.1.

Approach 1: Using a Line as Control Geometry

Since the aperture discussed in Section 6.2.1 is subject to increasing direct sun hours toward the bottom, we can respond by designing a perforated screen system where perforations get gradually larger beginning from the bottom of the screen to its top. This way, the screen can decrease exposure for the overexposed portions of the aperture and allow more exposure to the underexposed portions of the aperture.

For the purposes of this example, we will develop a perforated screen system with circular apertures with gradually changing radii. While the circular perforations can follow a variety of patterns, in this example a grid pattern will be introduced. As a first step, in Rhinoceros, a rectangular surface is created in front of the aperture, which is three feet larger than the original aperture in all four sides. Representing the screen that is under development, this surface is placed three feet off of the façade of the building.

Since the perforations will be organized on a grid pattern, a grid subdivision is created using the Divide Domain2 and "Isotrim" components introduced in Section 6.1. Then, to specify the center points of the circular perforations that will be created, the centroid of each of the subsurfaces is identified using the "Area" component. The circular perforations can now be created. For this, Grasshopper's "Circle with a Center" (Circle CNR) component is used. The Circle CNR component in Grasshopper has three inputs: C (center), N (normal vector), and R (radius). Since circles will be created around each centroid, the C output of the Area component can be directly connected to the C input of the "Circle CNR" component.

The normal vector of a surface or curve at a given point is defined as the vector that is perpendicular to the tangent of the surface or curve at that particular point (Thomas, Hass, Heil,

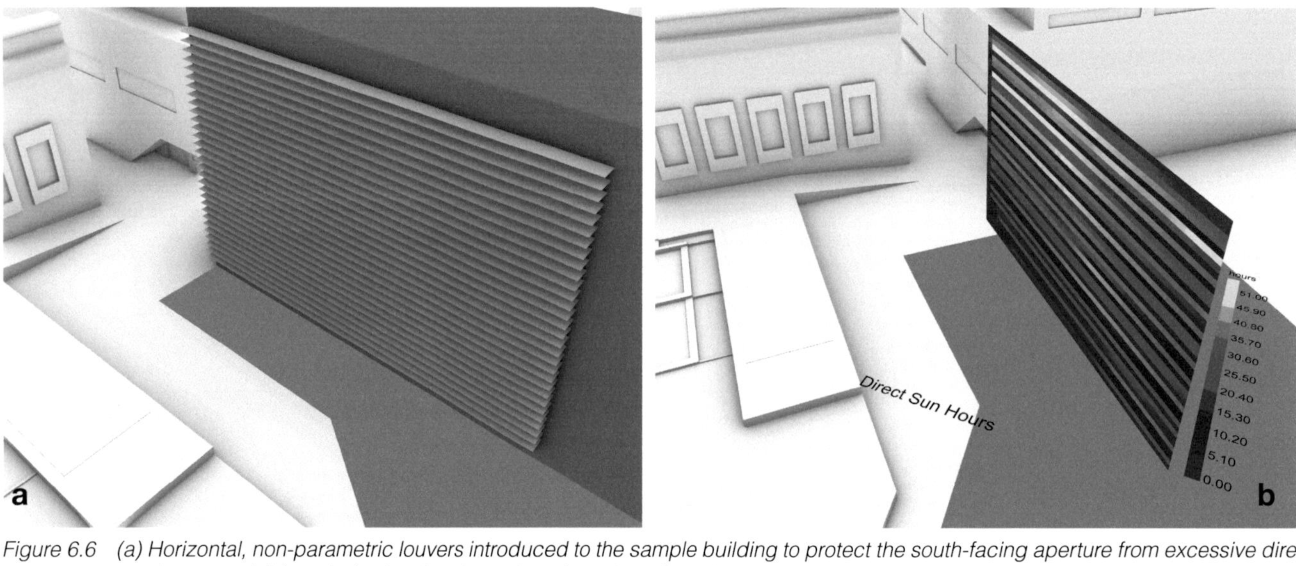

Figure 6.6 (a) Horizontal, non-parametric louvers introduced to the sample building to protect the south-facing aperture from excessive direct sun hours; and (b) analysis showing the reduced number of sun hours by the louvers.

et al., 2018). In this case, the normal vector of the screen surface needs to be identified at each centroid point so that a circle can be created around each centroid with its normal vector perpendicular to the screen – in other words, a circle on the *surface of the screen* instead of a circle parallel to the ground plane.

In Grasshopper, the "Evaluate Surface" (EvalSrf) component can analyze a given surface and identify its normal vectors at any specified point. It has two inputs, S, the surface to be evaluated, and uv, the uv point on the surface where the surface will be evaluated. This means that uv points on the screen need to be identified for the EvalSrf component. To identify those uv points on the screen, one needs to identify the points corresponding to each of the centroids identified using the "Area" component.

Grasshopper's "Surface Closest Point" (SrfCP) can identify uv points on a surface, which are closest to a given set of points, associating the given points and their closest counterparts on the surface. The "SrfCP" component has two inputs, P being the set of points to be associated with the surface, and S being the surface itself. Since the objective is to create a circle around each subsurface centroid, the centroids from the "Area" component are connected to the P input, and the subsurfaces from the Isotrim component are connected to the S input. The resulting uv points (uvP output of the SrfCP component) can now be connected to the uv input of the EvalSrf component. Once the subsurfaces from the Isotrim component are connected to the S input of the EvalSrf component, the N output yields the coordinates of each of the uv points on the screen.

Now that the centers and normal vectors are identified for each circle, it is time to identify the radius of each circle based on its distance from the bottom of the screen. The objective is to make the circles so that their radii get gradually larger as their distance from the bottom of the screen increases. Therefore, distance related data need to be connected to the "R" input of the Circle CNR component. The "Dist" (Distance) component in Grasshopper measures the distance between two points or two sets of points. Since the distance between the circles' center points and the bottom of the screen is needed, those points at the bottom of the screen closest to each circle center point need to be identified. To identify those points, the "Curve Closest Point" (CrvCP) component is used. The "CrvCP" component has two inputs, P being the point(s), and C being the target curve. The C output of the Area component, which correspond with the centers of circles constitute the "P" input of the "CrvCP" component. Using a "curve" (CRV) component, the bottom edge of the screen is introduced to Grasshopper as a curve, which becomes the "c" input for the "CrvCP" component. The P output now yields the coordinates for the second set of points on the bottom edge of the surface, which constitute the second set of points for the Distance component. When the two sets of points are connected to the A and B inputs of the "Distance" component, the output D provides a distance value for each point based on its distance from the bottom of the screen.

This "Distance" output could be directly used as the radii values for the circles, however since the distances are in feet and are large numbers, they will cause the circles to be excessively large and intersect with one another. Therefore, a "Division" component is added as an intermediary, and the values are divided with a scale factor. In this case, the Division output is connected to the R input of the CircleCNR component, and a slider is added to the Division input to visually decide on the division factor, picking a value that eliminates any intersection.

Now that a grid of circles whose radii gradually increase based on their distance from the bottom of the screen is generated, the screen can be split to achieve the desired perforations using the "Surface Split" (SrfSplit) component. The original screen surface is connected to the S (surface) input, and the circles from the Circle are connected to the C (curves) input of the "SrfSplit" component. The split yields a list of surfaces including the screen and the split circles on it. Using the "List Item" component, surface number 0, which is the original surface split, can be selected as the perforated screen with the desired pattern. Figure 6.7 illustrates the operation described above and the resulting perforated screen.

When the annual direct sun hours analysis discussed in Section 6.2.1 is repeated with the parametric screen introduced in Approach 1, one can observe its effects. For this, the newly introduced screen was simply added to the "context" geometry of the script shown in Figure 6.7a. The results of the analysis show that the total number of direct sun hours have decreased, and a more balanced direct sun hours distribution on the aperture can be observed (Figure 6.7).

Approach 2: Using Number Remapping and Control Geometries

Once the underlying rationale of paneling and control geometries are clear, it becomes easier to develop alternative approaches for parametric screen development. In Approach 1, the scale of the circular perforations was controlled using a division factor, which enabled visual control using a slider to avoid intersection of the circular perforations.

The scale of the circular perforations in such a scenario can also be controlled more precisely using the "Remap Numbers" (ReMap) component. This component has three inputs: V (the original values), S (the source domain), and T (the target domain). The component takes the original values from a list and, based on the original domain of the values, redistributes the values proportionally into a different domain specified by the designer.

In this approach, only the "division factor" portion of the script in Approach 1 is altered. The distance values between the centroids of subsurfaces and the bottom line of the screen are fed into the "V" input of the "ReMap" component. Using the "Bounds" (Bnd) component, the original domain of the distance values is created, and connected to the "S" (source domain) input. Finally, using the "construct domain" (Dom) component, a new target domain is created. When the output R, remapped number values, are connected to the scale factor of the "Scale" component, the outcome is a proportionally scaled set of circular perforations (Figure 6.8). This operation creates a similar screen pattern to the one introduced in Figure 6.7, although using a numerical domain.

The size of circular perforations can also be controlled using the "Minimum" (Min) and "Maximum" (Max) components of Grasshopper. The Min component compares a list of numbers with a given number and yields only the numbers smaller than or equal to the given number. This means that any value larger than the given number will be replaced with the given number. Using the Min component, the script limits the radii so that all values larger than 0.3 is replaced with a radius of 0.3.

When the annual direct sun hours analysis discussed in Section 6.3.1 is repeated with the parametric screen introduced in Approach 2, the results are very similar to those of Approach 1, since Approach 2 introduced additional ways to control the perforation radii (Figure 6.8). The following two approaches to parametric screen design will introduce more customizable solutions.

Approach 3: Using the Image Sampler

The first two parametric screen design approaches approximated a response that attempted to balance direct sun hours. The reducing effects created by the two approaches were illustrated by repeating the direct sun hours analysis after the screens were placed in front of the aperture. Using additional Grasshopper components, parametric screens that provide a more customized response can be developed. In Approach 3, we will use the Image Sampler component of Grasshopper to design a perforated screen that is customized for the specific location and orientation of the sample building.

Ladybug's "Sun Hours" component yields a color-coded mesh, where colors represent the number of direct sun hours across a surface for a given analysis period. This information can

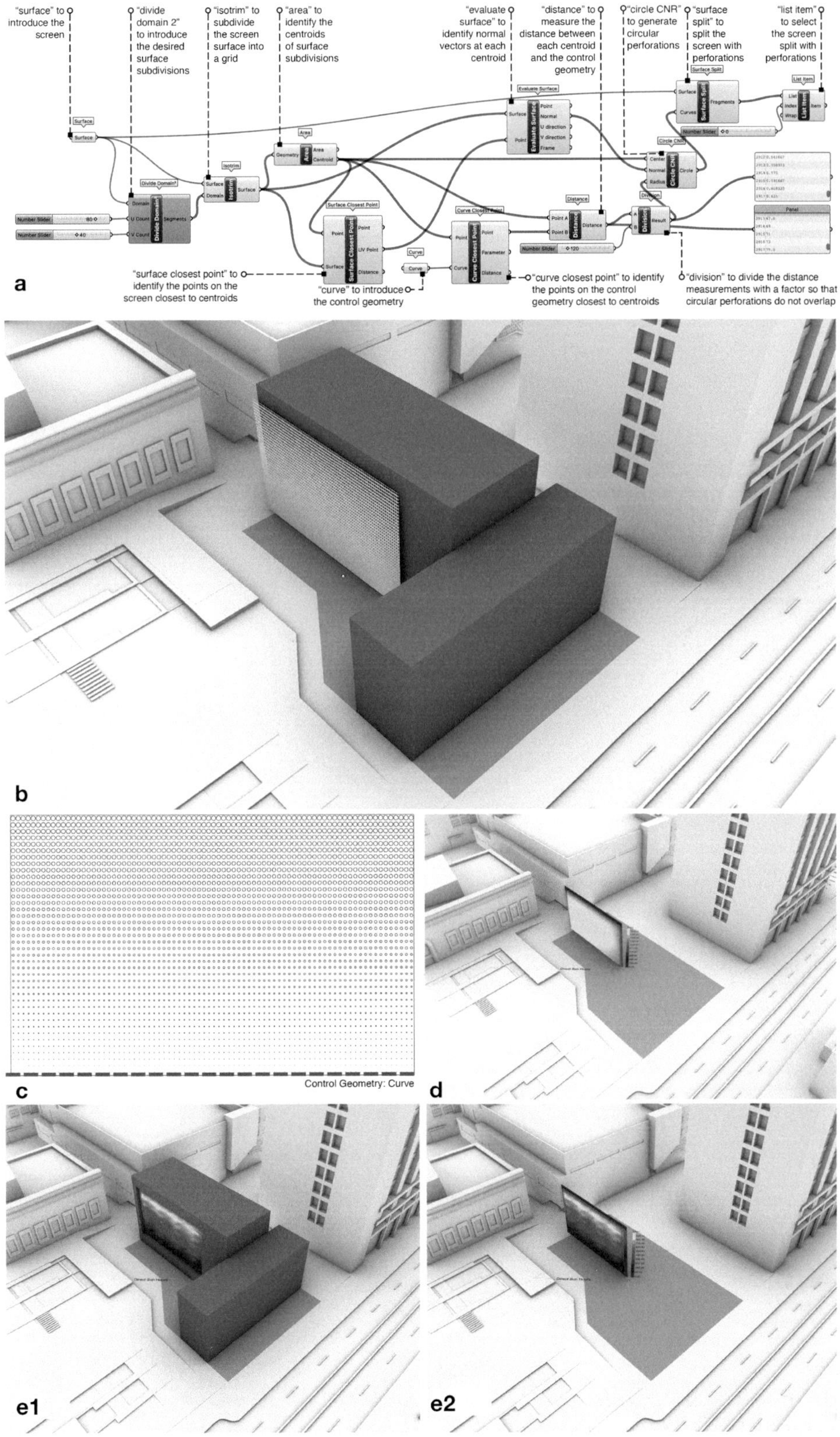

Figure 6.7 *(a) The Grasshopper script for developing a perforated screen in response to the direct sun hours analysis introduced in Section 6.2.1; (b and c) The resulting perforated screen with the desired circular perforations on a grid pattern; (d) annual direct sun hours of the aperture without the screen introduced by Approach 1; (e1 and e2) annual direct sun hours of the aperture with the screen introduced by Approach 1.*

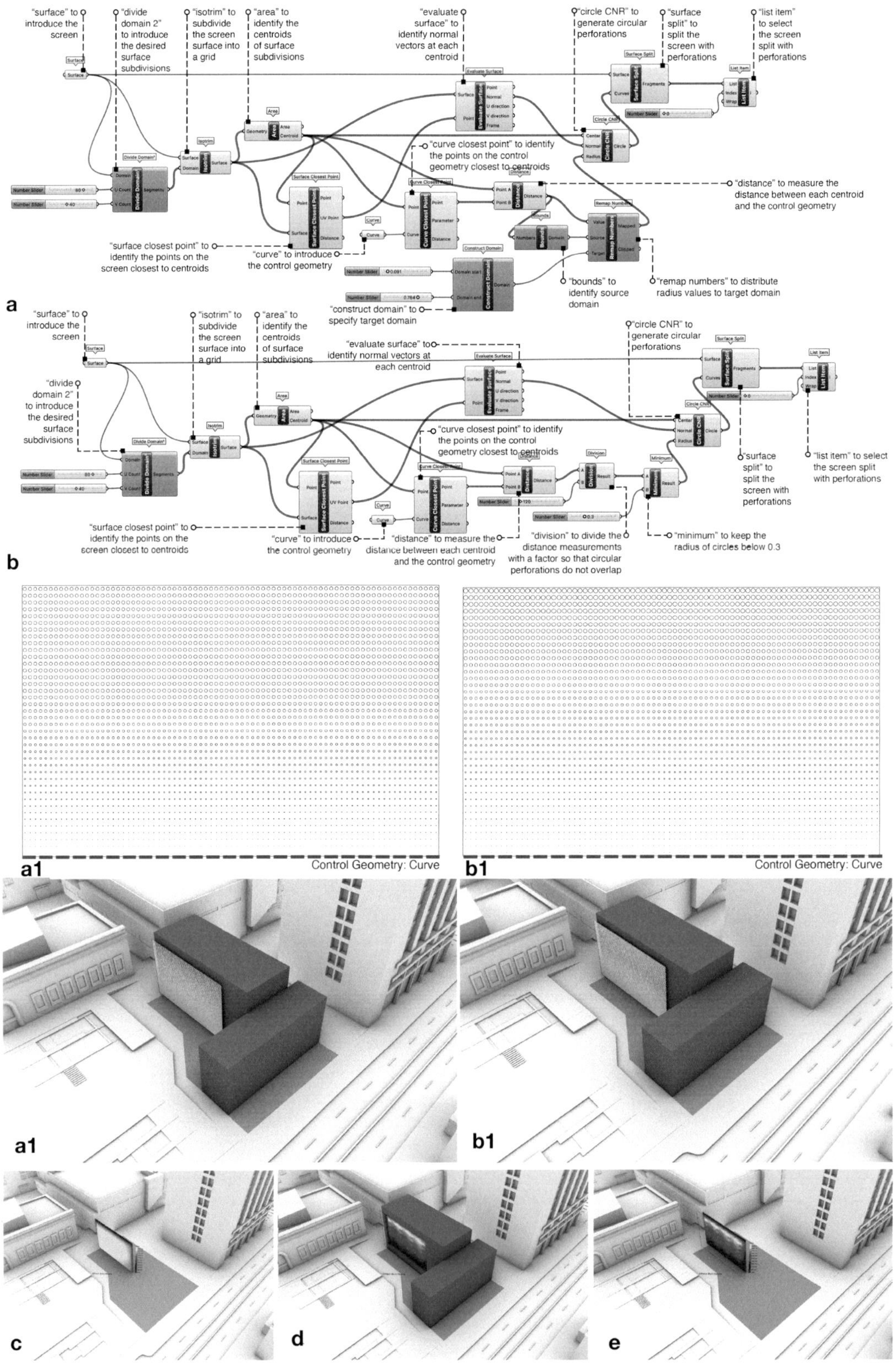

Figure 6.8 *(a) The parametric screen development operation using Number remapping; (b) the parametric perforated screen system using the "Min" (minimum) component; (a1) the resulting parametric screen pattern using Number remapping; (b1) the resulting parametric screen pattern using the script limits the radii so that all values larger than 0.3 is replaced with a radius of 0.3; (c) annual direct sun hours of the aperture without the screens introduced in Approach 2; and (d and e) annual direct sun hours of the aperture with the screens introduced in Approach 2.*

be converted into a bitmap image, and the resulting image can be fed into the "Image Sampler" component of Grasshopper. The Image Sampler component can then be used to inform the size of the perforations on a perforated screen based on the number of direct sun hours across an aperture.

Using the same sample building and the same sample screen, the screen is first subdivided into a grid of subsurfaces using the Isotrim and "DivideDomain²" components. The centroids of the subsurfaces are then identified using the "area" component, after which their corresponding uv points are identified on each subsurface using the "SrfCP" component. As in previous approaches, the circles for perforations are created using the Circle CNR component, whose centers are identified using the centroids of the subsurfaces. Using the "EvalSrf" component, the normal vector for each circle is identified for each centroid uv point on the subsurfaces. A standard radius of 0.375 foot (4.5 inches) is specified for each circle.

Following these steps, the circles need to be scaled in proportional to the number of annual direct sun hours they receive. The scaling operation introduced in previous sections is initiated, with the "Scale" component, where the circles constitute the geometry to be scaled, and the uv centroid points on subsurfaces constitute the center points of scaling. In the next step, the "Image Sampler" component is used to influence the scaling factor for each of the circles.

The gradient-coded analysis mesh from Ladybug's sun hour analysis is exported to an image-editing software as a raster image (i.e., JPG, PNG, etc.) (Figure 6.9a). Since the scaling operation in

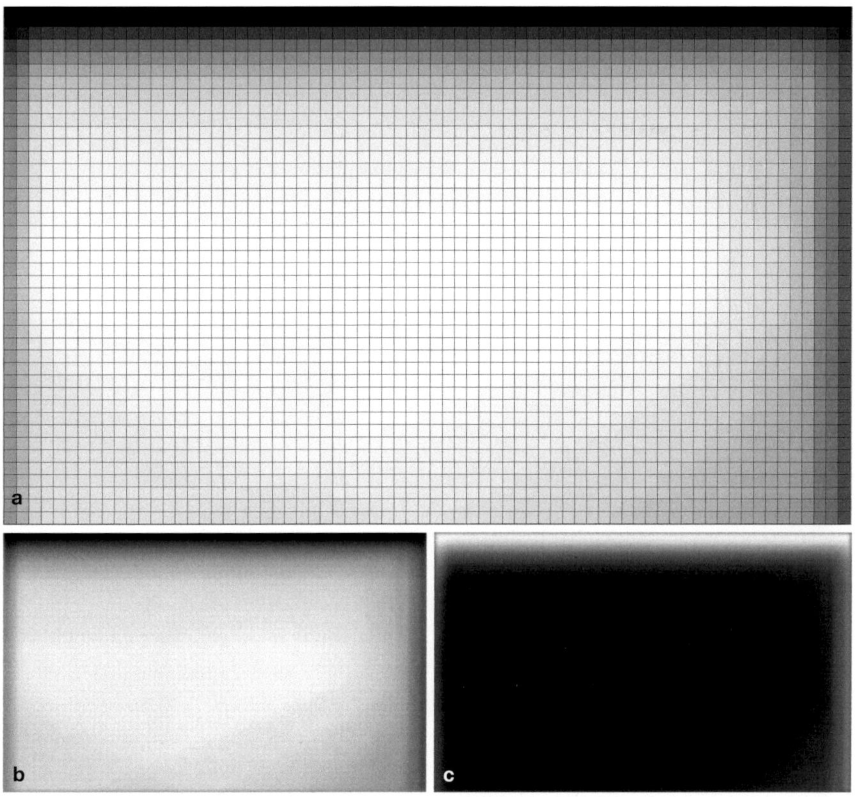

Figure 6.9 (a) The grayscale version of the analysis mesh from Ladybug's gradient-coded sun hour analysis; (b) blurred analysis results to achieve a continuous gradation; and (c) the inverted version of the blurred analysis.

progress is two-dimensional (i.e., on u and v axes), it is converted into grayscale (as opposed to and RGB or CMYK format), and inverted, since the Image Sampler component converts darker tones to smaller values, and lighter tones to larger values. The intent here is to make smaller perforations for high direct sun hour areas and larger perforations for low direct sun hour areas of the aperture (Figure 6.9b). Finally, the image is blurred to achieve a continuous gradation (Figure 6.9c). The resulting raster image is then inverted and fed into the Image Sampler component by double-clicking on the component and specifying the path to the grayscale direct sun hours image created. At this point, since the default domain input of the Image Sampler component is from 0 to 1, the original surface component is "reparameterized," so its u and v dimensions are equivalent to one unit.

The uv points from the "SrfCP" component are then connected to the "Image Sampler" component, which generates numerical values for each pixel on the image based on its relative uv location. These values can now be used as the scaling factor input on the "Scale" component to influence the radii of perforations based on their direct sun hours. However, using these raw values will often cause the apertures to be out of scale, or too small to realistically affect the aperture. Therefore, the values are remapped to a target domain between 0.1ft (1.2 inches) and 0.3 ft (3.6 inches) using the "Bnd" (bounds), "Dom" (Construct Domain) and "ReMap" (Remap Numbers) components as introduced in Approach 2. The resulting values are now used as the scaling factor for the "Scale" component, yielding circular perforations whose radii have been precisely customized according to the number of hours they receive sunlight on an annual basis. As a last step, the perforated screen surface is created by using the "SrfSplit" (Surface Split) component and selecting the perforated using the List Item component. A close look illustrates how the radii of the perforations vary based on the annual direct sun hours.

Annual direct sun hours analysis of the sample building with the new screen, which was developed using the "Image Sampler" component, shows that the screen provides a highly customized response to direct sun hours. In doing so, the screen limits exposure to normally overexposed areas of the aperture and allows exposure to underexposed areas (Figure 6.10). An advantage of using the "ReMap" component in Approach 3 is the designer's control over the minimum and maximum perforation radii. For example, in this analysis the top part of the aperture has a highly exposed area. Based on performance analysis, if one was to target further controlling this exposure, it is possible to decrease the maximum value of the domain from 0.3 ft (3.6 inches) to a smaller value.

Approach 4: Using Surface Population

Another common approach to designing parametric skin systems is surface population. The processing power and efficiency of parametric software have made surface population operations possible and more accessible to designers. Surface population operations involve three main steps:

1. Subdivision and simplification of a surface
2. Creating derivative(s) of original subdivided geometries
3. Relating the original subdivisions and their derivatives to one another, yielding a complex surface populated with additional elements

Based on environmental factors such as the ones discussed in the first three approaches, one may also want to introduce an intermediary step between steps 2 and 3, altering the scale and depth of the populated surface modules as desired. In Approach 4, main surface population steps will first be introduced using the sample surface from Sections 6.1.2 and 6.1.3. The surface of the skin system surface from our sample building will then be populated using a variety of techniques, altering scale and depth of the modules.

In Section 6.1.1, subdivision and simplification of a curved surface was introduced (Figure 6.4). Using the simplified subsurfaces from that section, the original surface can be populated. In

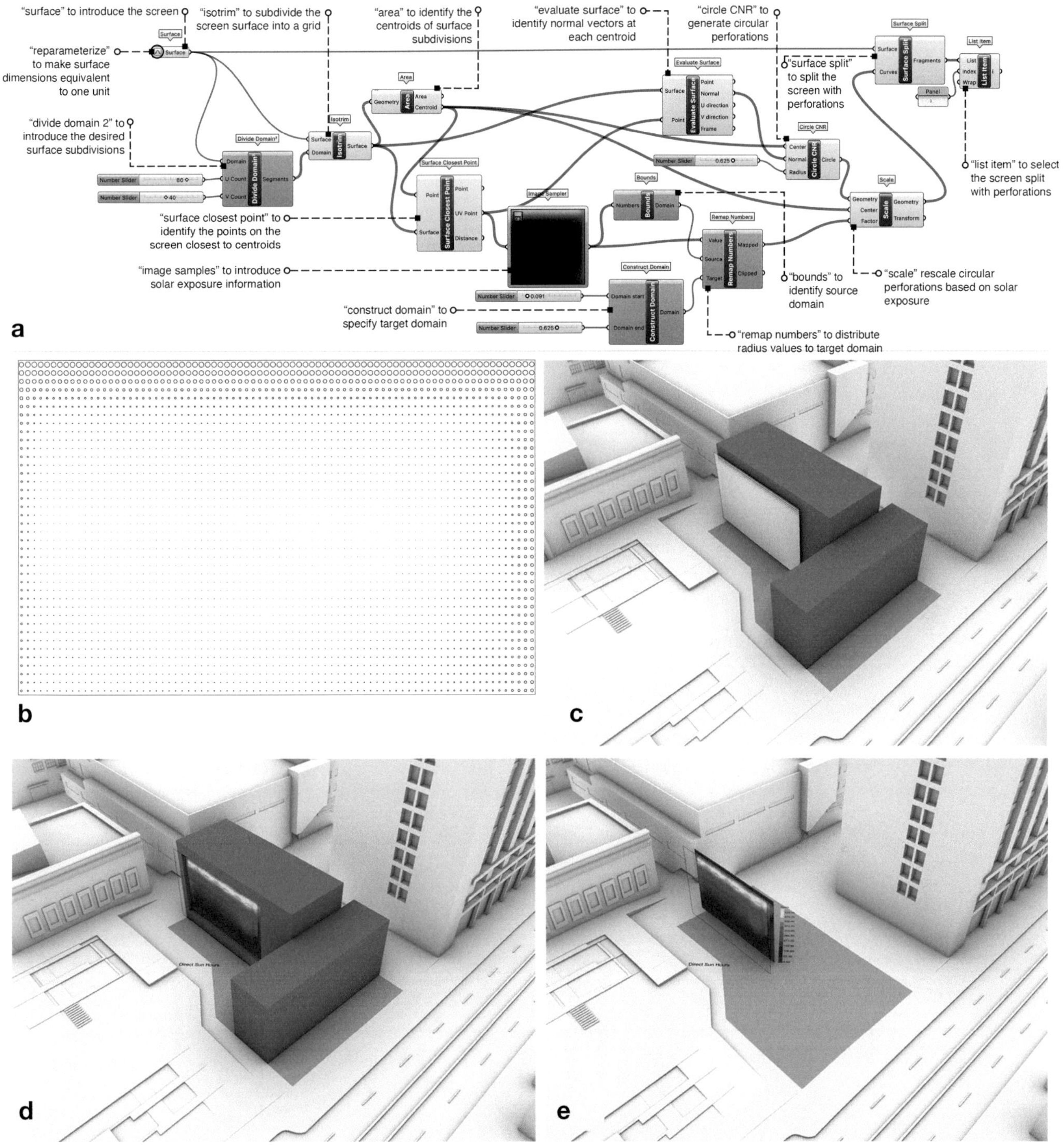

Figure 6.10 (a) The Grasshopper definition for scaling perforations using the "image mapper" component; (b) the resulting perforated screen, with perforations whose radii have been precisely customized according to the number of hours they receive sunlight on an annual basis; (c) the resulting perforated screen on the fictitious building; (d) annual direct sun hours of the aperture with the screen introduced in Approach 3, with the building elements surrounding the aperture; and (e) direct sun hours of the aperture with the screen introduced in Approach 3, without the building elements surrounding the aperture.

this case, the edges of the subsurfaces are joined using the "Join Curves" component. The joined curves are then scaled down with a scale factor using the centroids of the subsurfaces identified using the "Area" component. The scaled, joined curves are then moved using the "Move" component on the normal vector direction of the subsurfaces, which are identified using the "SrfCP" and "SrfCP" components with a certain amplitude (in this example, 7).

Joined curves are finally lofted with the scaled and moved curves using the "Loft" component (Figure 6.11). In this example, scaling and moving factors were given fixed values. However, one could also determine these values using control geometries, Graph Mapper, or Image Sampler, as discussed in the earlier sections.

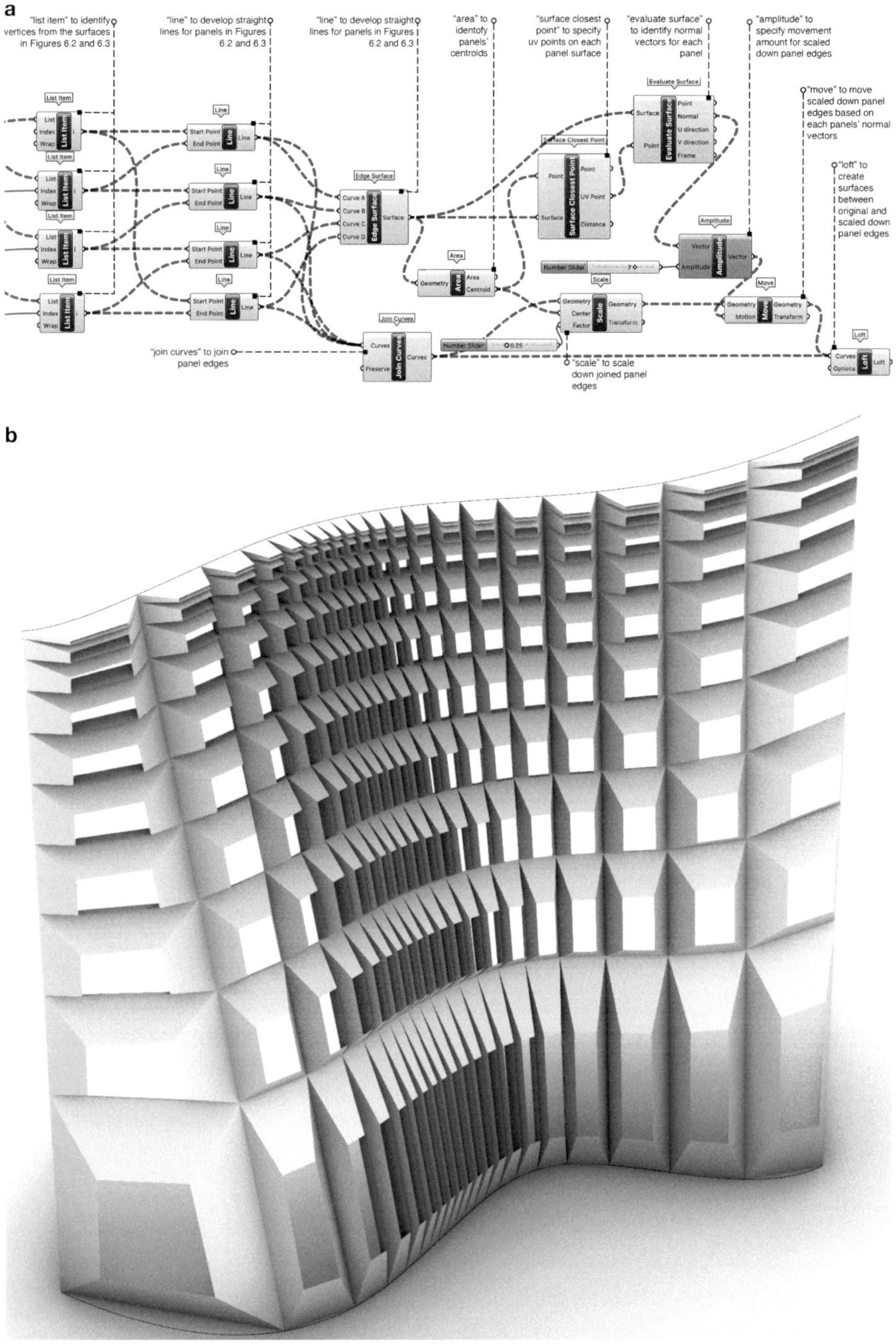

Figure 6.11 (a) the surface population operation and (b) its outcome using the curved surface that was subdivided and simplified in Section 6.1.3.

The same approach can be utilized in designing a parametric screen system for the sample building discussed in previous sections. In the following paragraphs, surface population will be used to exemplify screen system alternatives for the same sample building.

In the first example (Screen System Example A), surface population is used to create a screen system with non-varying aperture sizes (a constant value, which, in this case, is 0.5 ft or 6 inches). In Figure 6.12, one can observe the surface population operation and the resulting screen system, the original annual direct sun hours analysis of the sample building's aperture, and outcomes of the same analysis when Screen System Example A is included in the context geometry. Figure 6.12 indicates that a further customized solution to the direct sun hours analysis is desirable when using the surface population technique.

In the second example (Screen System Example B), surface population is used to create a screen system with varying aperture sizes using a control geometry, which, in this case, is the bottom edge of the original screen surface. In Figure 6.13, one can observe the surface population operation, the original annual direct sun hours analysis of the sample building's

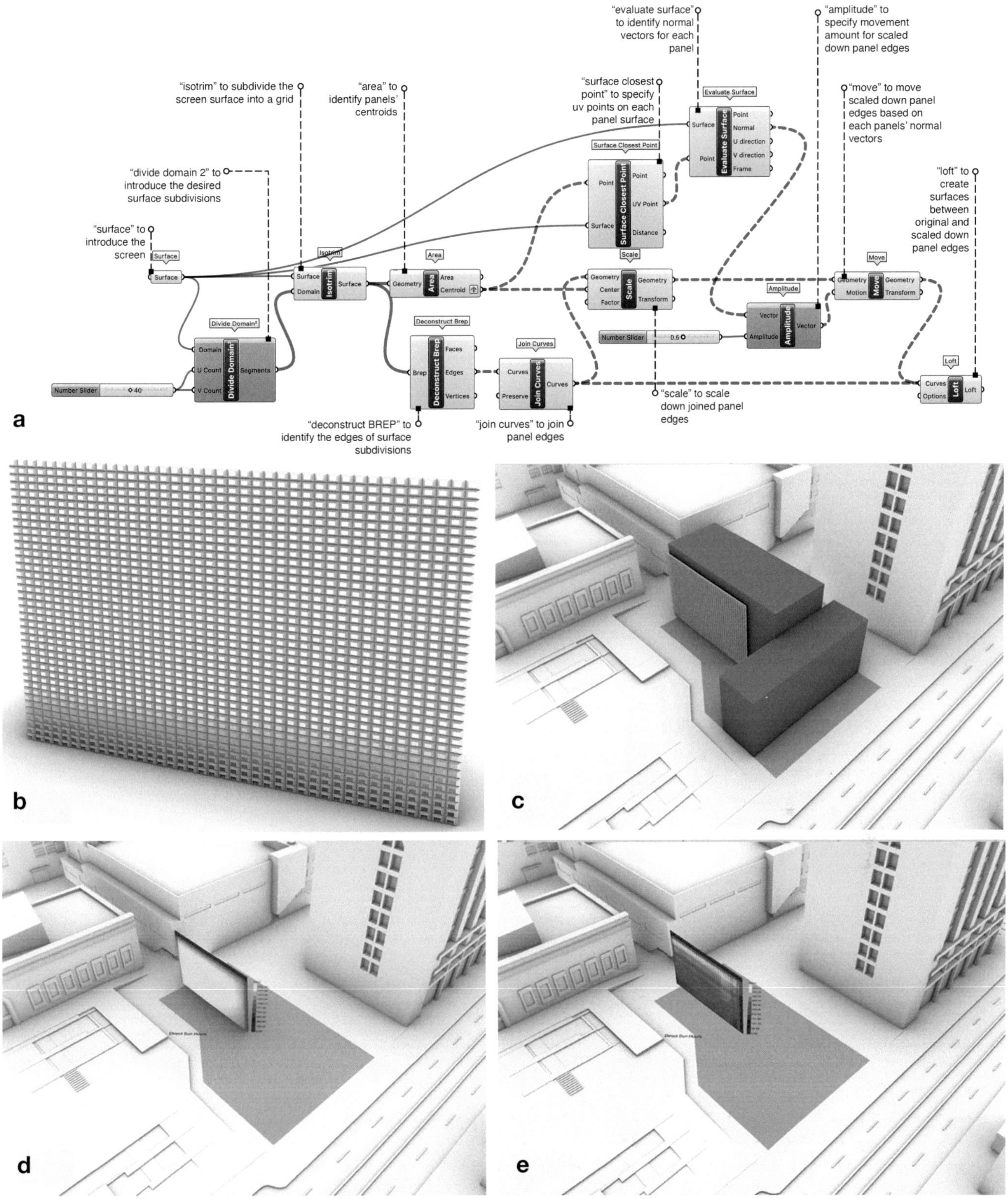

Figure 6.12 *Screen System Example A: (a) The Grasshopper definition developed for the surface population operation; and (b and c) the resulting screen system; (d) original annual direct sun hours analysis of the sample building's aperture; and (e) the outcomes of the same analysis when Screen System Example A is included in the context geometry.*

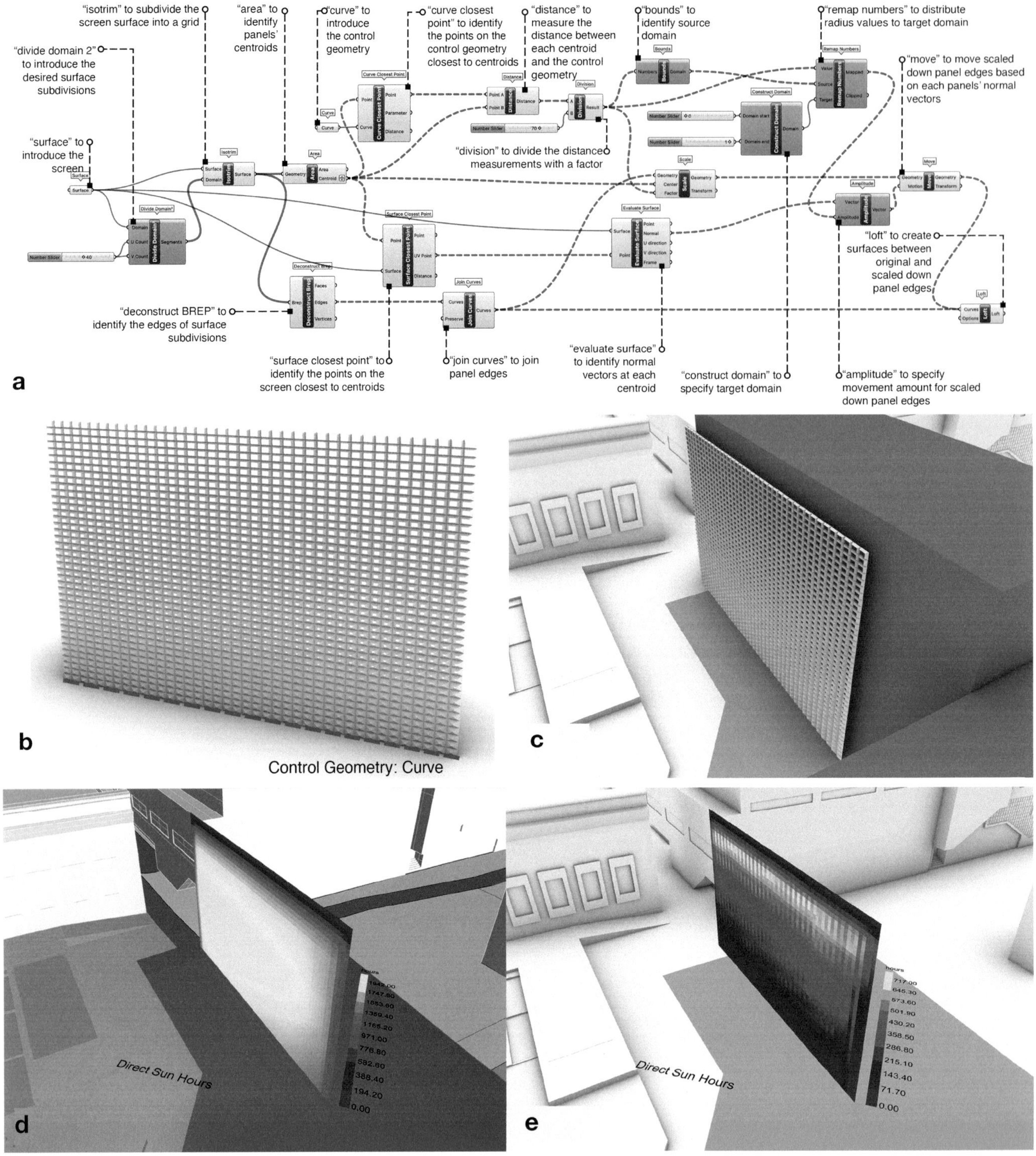

Figure 6.13 *Screen System Example B: (a) surface population operation and the resulting screen system; (b) original annual direct sun hours analysis of the sample building's aperture; and (c) outcomes of the same analysis when Screen System Example B is included in the context geometry.*

aperture, and outcomes of the same analysis when Screen System Example B is included in the context geometry.

In the third example (Screen System Example C), surface population is used to create a screen system with varying aperture sizes using an image sampler, which, in this case, is the

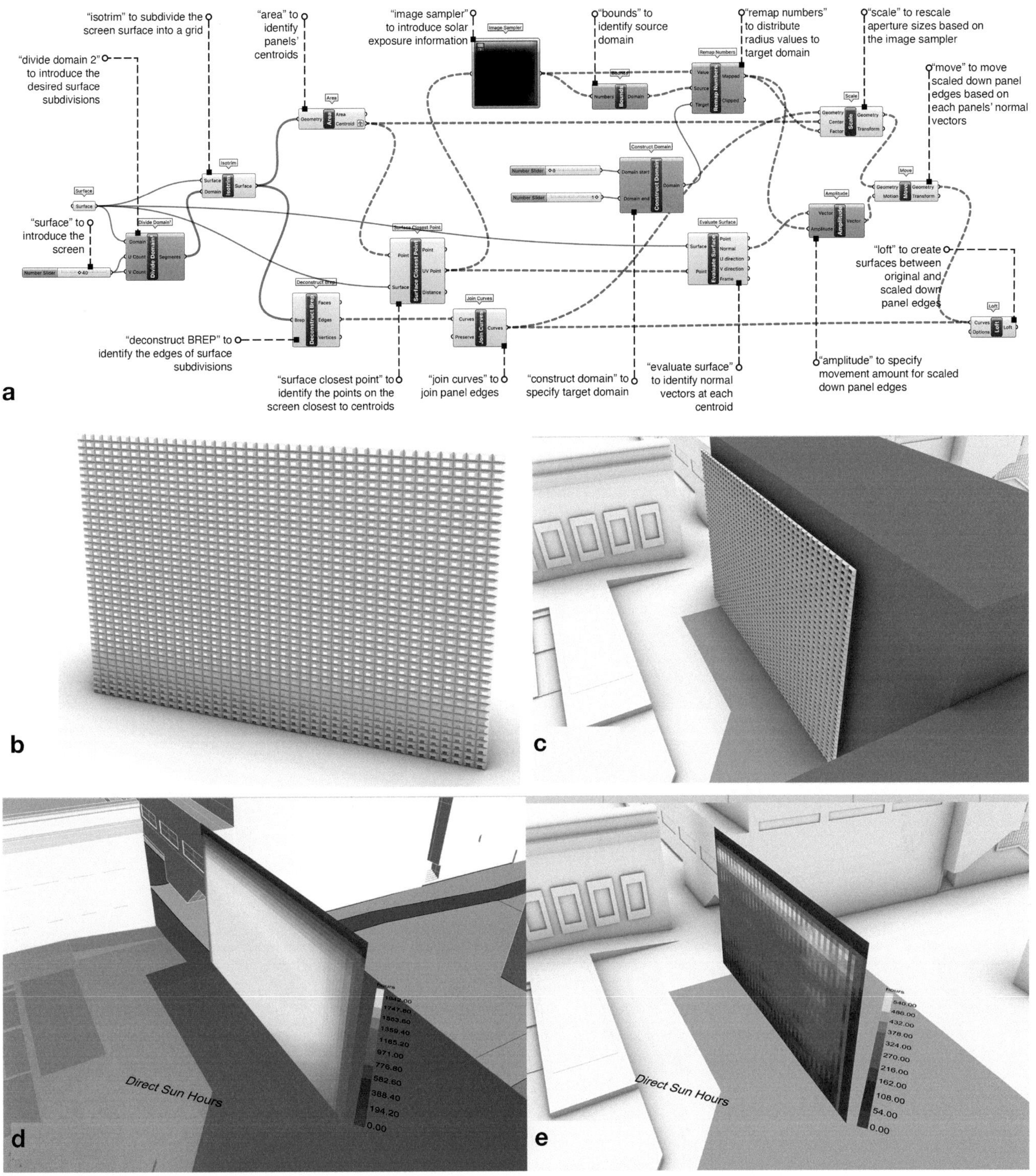

Figure 6.14 Screen System Example C: (a) The Grasshopper definition used for surface population; and (b and c) the resulting screen system; (d) original annual direct sun hours analysis of the sample building's aperture; and (e) the outcomes of the same analysis when the sample Screen System Example C is included in the context geometry.

outcome image from the original gradient-coded sun exposure analysis. In Figure 6.14, one can observe the surface population operation and the resulting screen system, the original annual direct sun hours analysis of the sample building's aperture, and outcomes of the same analysis when Screen System Example C is included in the context geometry.

Based on the orientation and location of the building, one can also choose to use surface population by omitting portion(s) of the modules created by the technique. In the fourth

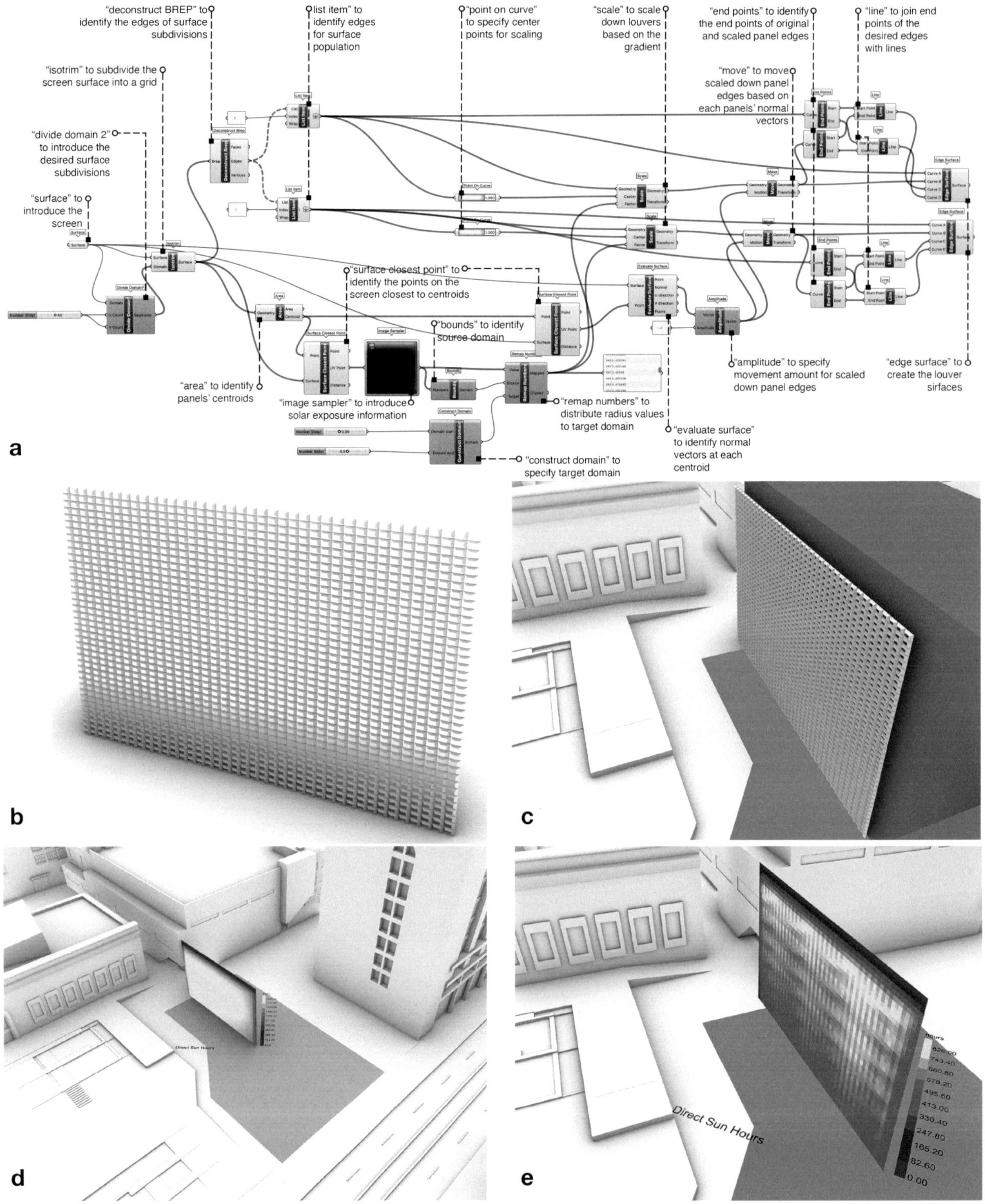

Figure 6.15 *Screen System Example D: (a) The Grasshopper definition used for surface population operation; (b) original annual direct sun hours analysis of the sample building's aperture; and (c) outcomes of the same analysis when Screen System Example D is included in the context geometry.*

example (Screen System Example D), surface population is used to create a screen system with varying aperture sizes using an image sampler, which, in this case, is the outcome image from the original color-coded sun exposure analysis. However, in this case, the bottom and north-facing elements of the apertures are not included in the screen system due to the building's orientation. In Figure 6.15, one can observe the surface population operation, the original annual direct sun hours analysis of the sample building's aperture, and outcomes of the same analysis when Screen System Example D is included in the context geometry.

6.3 OTHER REPETITION AND PANELING APPROACHES TO SUBDIVIDING SURFACES

Environmental factors are very important for designing parametric screens; however, they do not constitute the only informers. Depending on design objectives other patterning strategies may come into consideration. In this section, four additional parametric screen design strategies will be introduced, all of which use various control geometries. As discussed in earlier sections, Grasshopper's LunchBox plug-in can be used to create a variety of surface subdivisions. The strategies introduced in this section start each script using the "Diamond" component of LunchBox plug-in to generate parallelogram-based subsurfaces.

In the first example, a single point is placed on the screen of our sample building's skin. The objective is to minimize exposure around this point and create apertures gradually growing in size, based on their distance from this point. In an actual project, this may be a space that needs more privacy, more solar protection, or less visibility, based on design objectives. In the script for the first example, the centroids of diamonds are identified by using the "Area" component. Each diamond is assigned a circle using Grasshopper's "circle" component, and the normal vectors for each circle are identified using the SrfCP and EvalSrf components.

In order to specify the circular radii based on their distance from our attractor point, the distance between each centroid and the control point is measured using the "Distance" component. The output of this "Distance" component is then "Remapped," limiting the radius values to a domain with a minimum of 0.05 and a maximum of 0.6 feet. The resulting circles are then used to split the original base screen to create the desired circular apertures (Figure 6.16).

Depending on design and program objectives, one might want to provide more privacy for various parts of an aperture using control geometries. It is possible to introduce multiple control geometries to influence parametric screen aperture sizes, such as multiple points, multiple curves, etc. In the second example, two points are introduced as control geometries on different portions of our sample building's screen. The script developed is remarkably similar to our first example, except that the aperture sizes now need to be affected by the location of two different points. Using a very similar script to the first example, two points are introduced to Grasshopper using the "Point" component. The distance between each circular aperture's centroid and the two points are then measured individually using two different "Distance" components. Since the objective is to have both points affect aperture radii, one needs to relate the distance data. In this script, the data are related to one another using the "Addition" component, however one could also use other basic mathematical operations. The resulting distance data is then limited to a domain with a minimum of 0.05 and a maximum of 0.6 feet and connected to the circular apertures' radius input, yielding a screen where aperture radii get larger based on the increasing distance of their centroids from the two control points (Figure 6.17).

Design objectives may also require various other control geometries to influence outcomes. In the third example, a curve is used as a control geometry to influence the size of circular apertures on the sample building's parametric screen. In this script, a curve control geometry is introduced, and the distance between the apertures' centroids and the control geometry curve is measured using the "Curve Closest Point" and "Distance" components. Limiting the distance data to a domain between 0.05 and 0.5 feet, the radii of target circular apertures are identified to inform screen design (Figure 6.18).

In the fourth example, the same strategy is followed. A large circle is being used as the control geometry, and the desired parametric screen's circular aperture radii are controlled based on

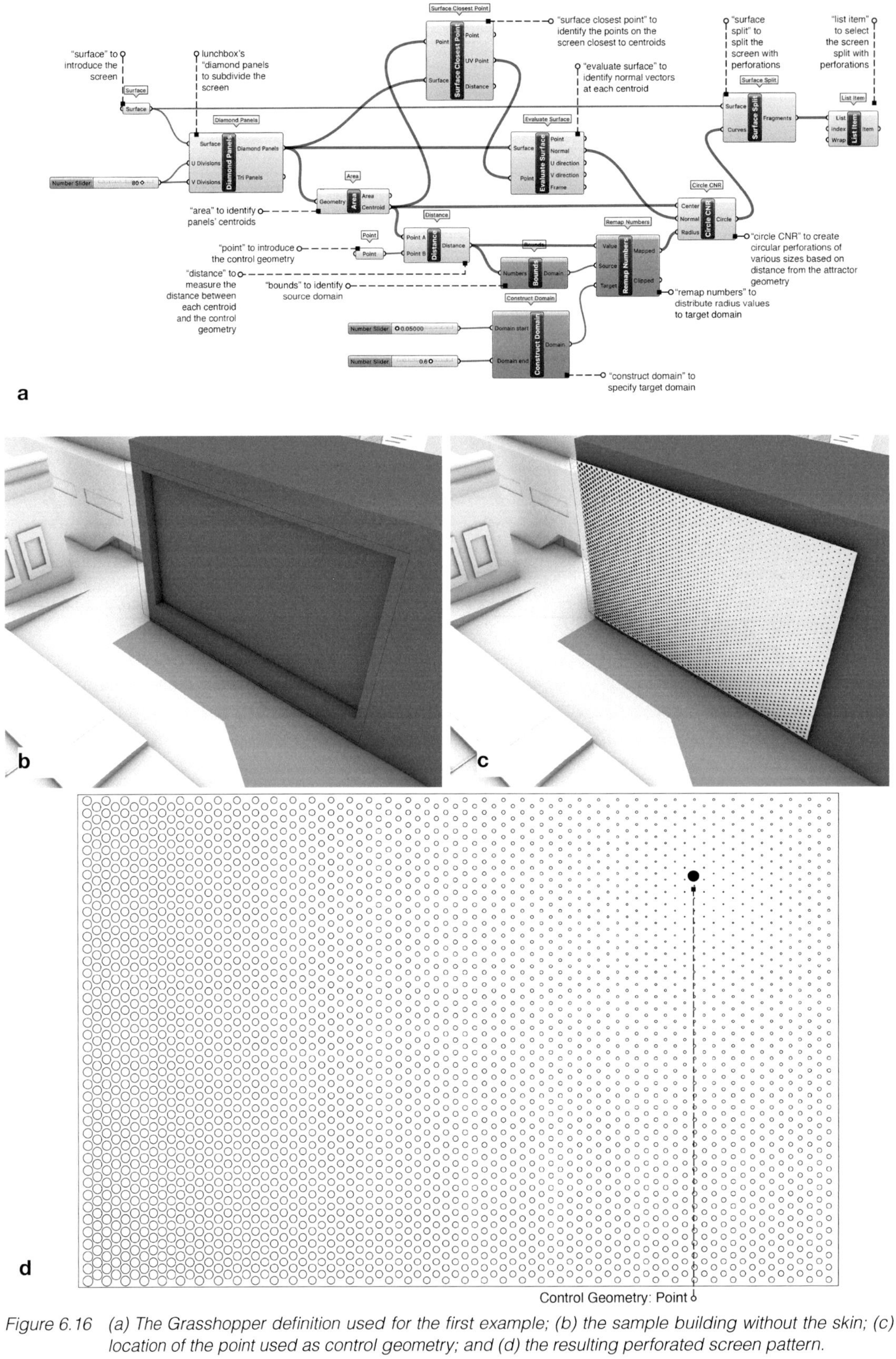

Figure 6.16 *(a) The Grasshopper definition used for the first example; (b) the sample building without the skin; (c) location of the point used as control geometry; and (d) the resulting perforated screen pattern.*

their centroids' distance from the circle control geometry (Figure 6.19). It is important to note that, based on the same principles and techniques, all of these examples can be replicated by using different paneling strategies (either using Grasshopper or the LunchBox component),

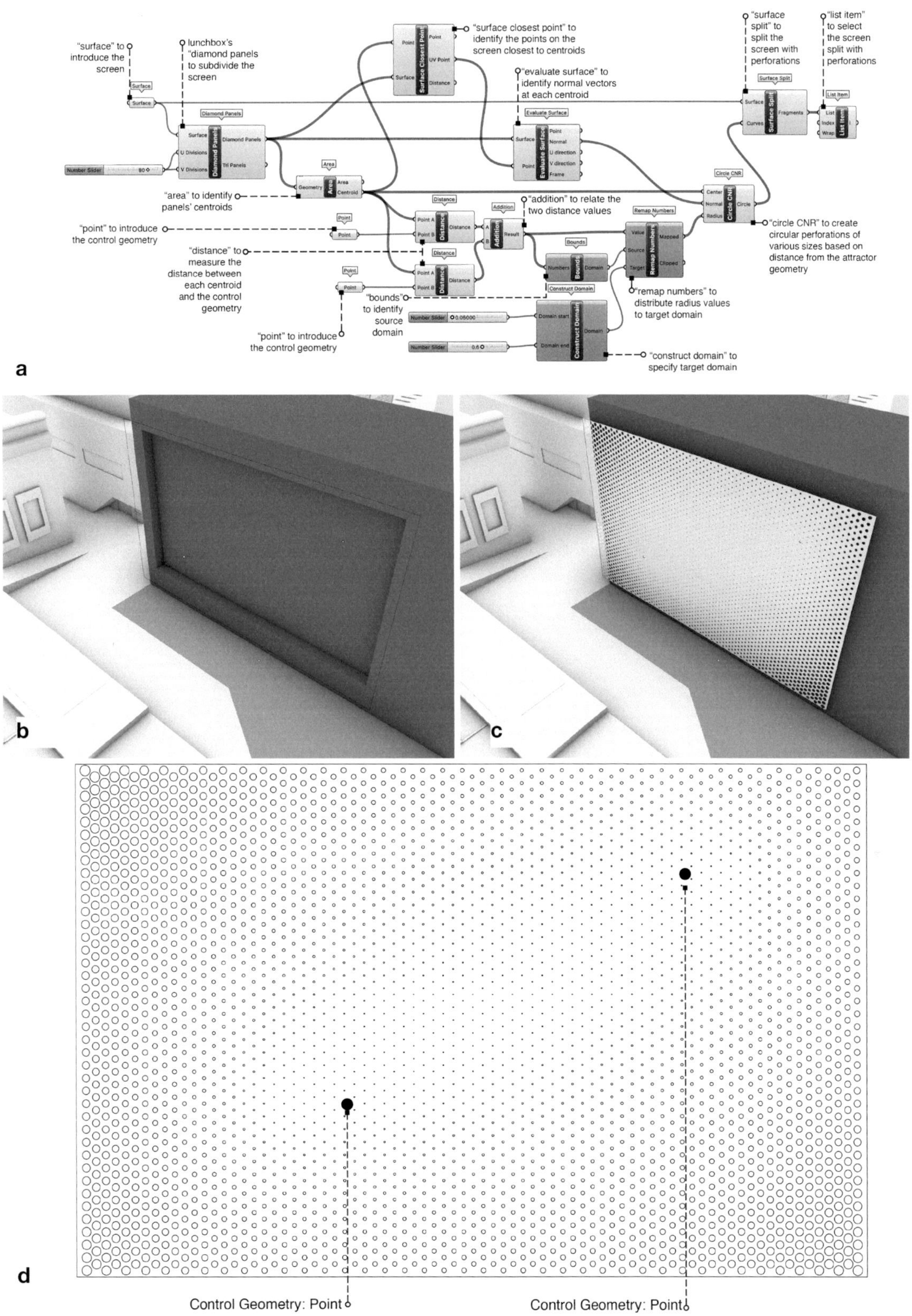

Figure 6.17 *(a) The Grasshopper definition used for the second example; (b) the sample building without the skin; (c) location of the points used as control geometries; and (d) the resulting perforated screen pattern.*

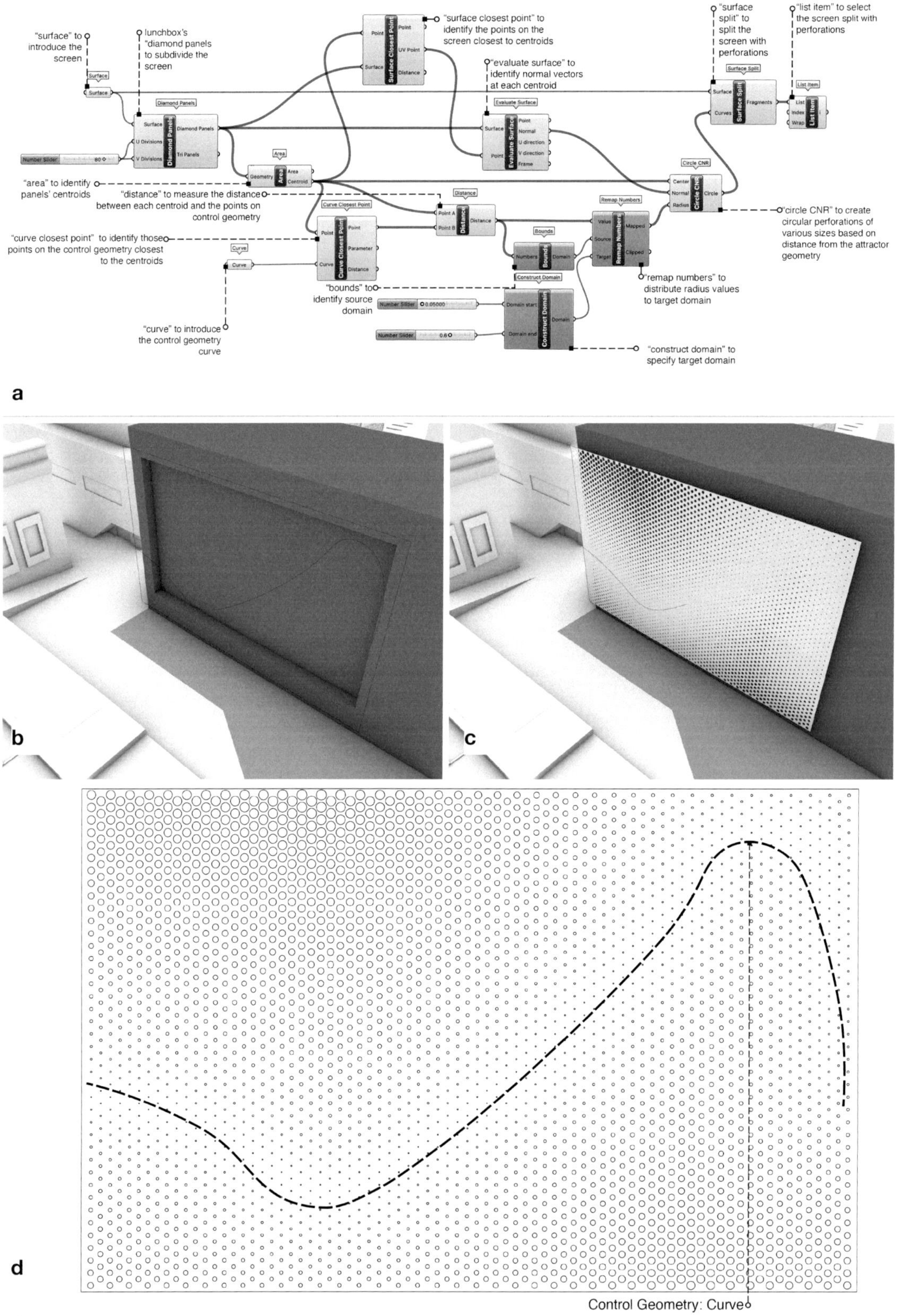

Figure 6.18 (a) The Grasshopper definition used for the third example; (b and c) location and shape of the curve used as control geometry; and (d) the resulting perforated screen pattern.

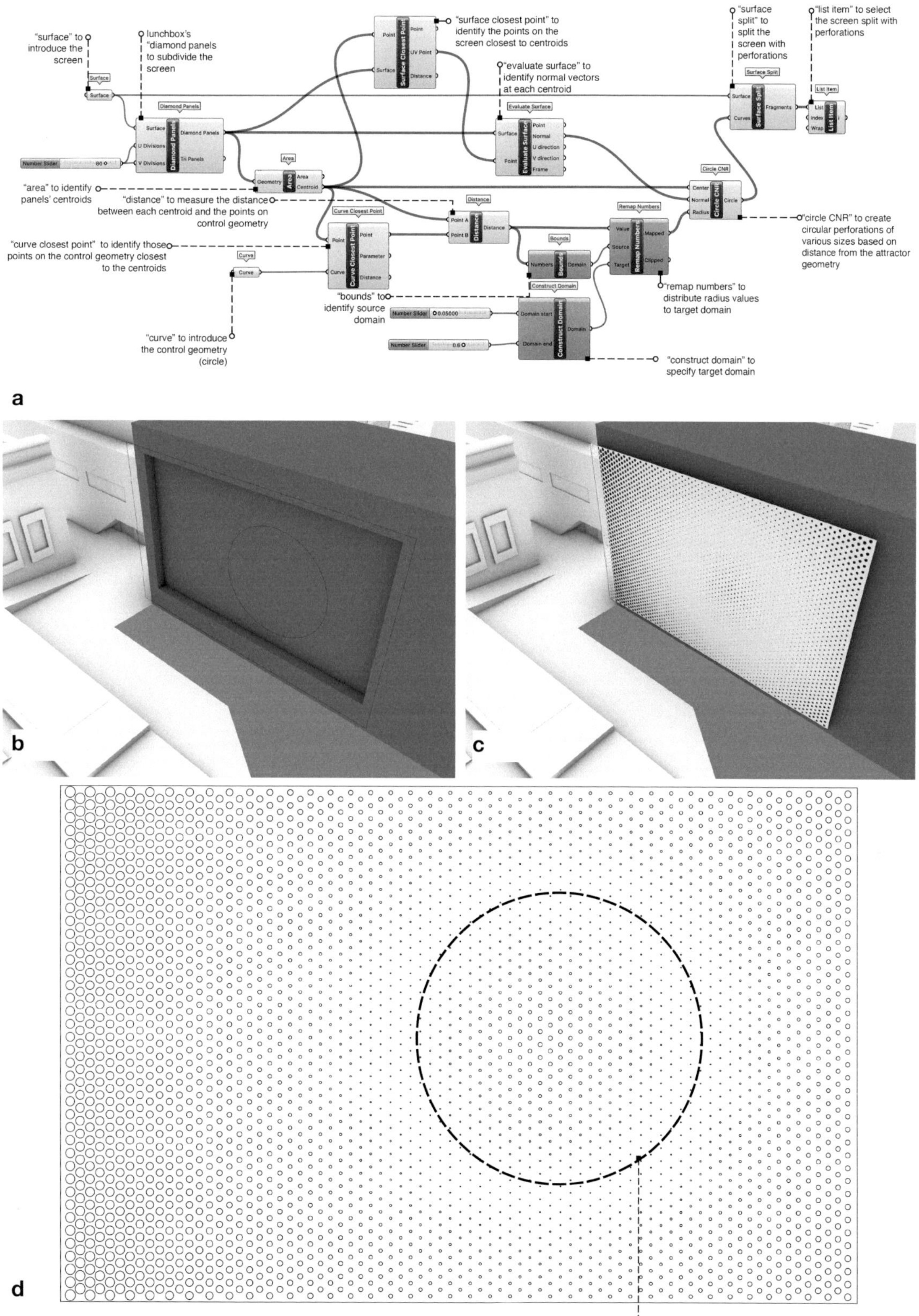

Figure 6.19 *(a) The Grasshopper definition used for the fourth example; (b and c) location and shape of the circle used as control geometry; and (d) the resulting perforated screen pattern.*

using various aperture geometries (i.e., rectilinear, hexagonal, etc.), or using a variety of two- or three-dimensional control geometries (i.e., points, curves, surfaces, or polysurfaces).

6.4 REPETITION AND PANELING APPROACHES SUBDIVIDING COMPLEX GEOMETRIES

Having covered paneling and repetition for simple rectilinear surfaces, in this section we will discuss using similar approaches on more complex geometries. Depending on the design objectives, one may need to generate skin systems using complex geometries. In this section, a complex curved surface is subdivided and perforated (Figure 6.20). In this example, the curved surface is first subdivided using LunchBox's "Diamond" subdivision tool. The centroids of the diamonds are identified using the Area component, and using the "Polygon" component, in which polygons are created, each taking a centroid as its center. Using a slider, the number of polygon sides is set to four to create square apertures. The corners of the squares are then rounded, setting the "Fillet Radius" to 2.

At this point, the squares are parallel to the xy plane, since the Polygon component's "P" input defaults to the ground plane (XY). In order to make the squares parallel to the original surface,

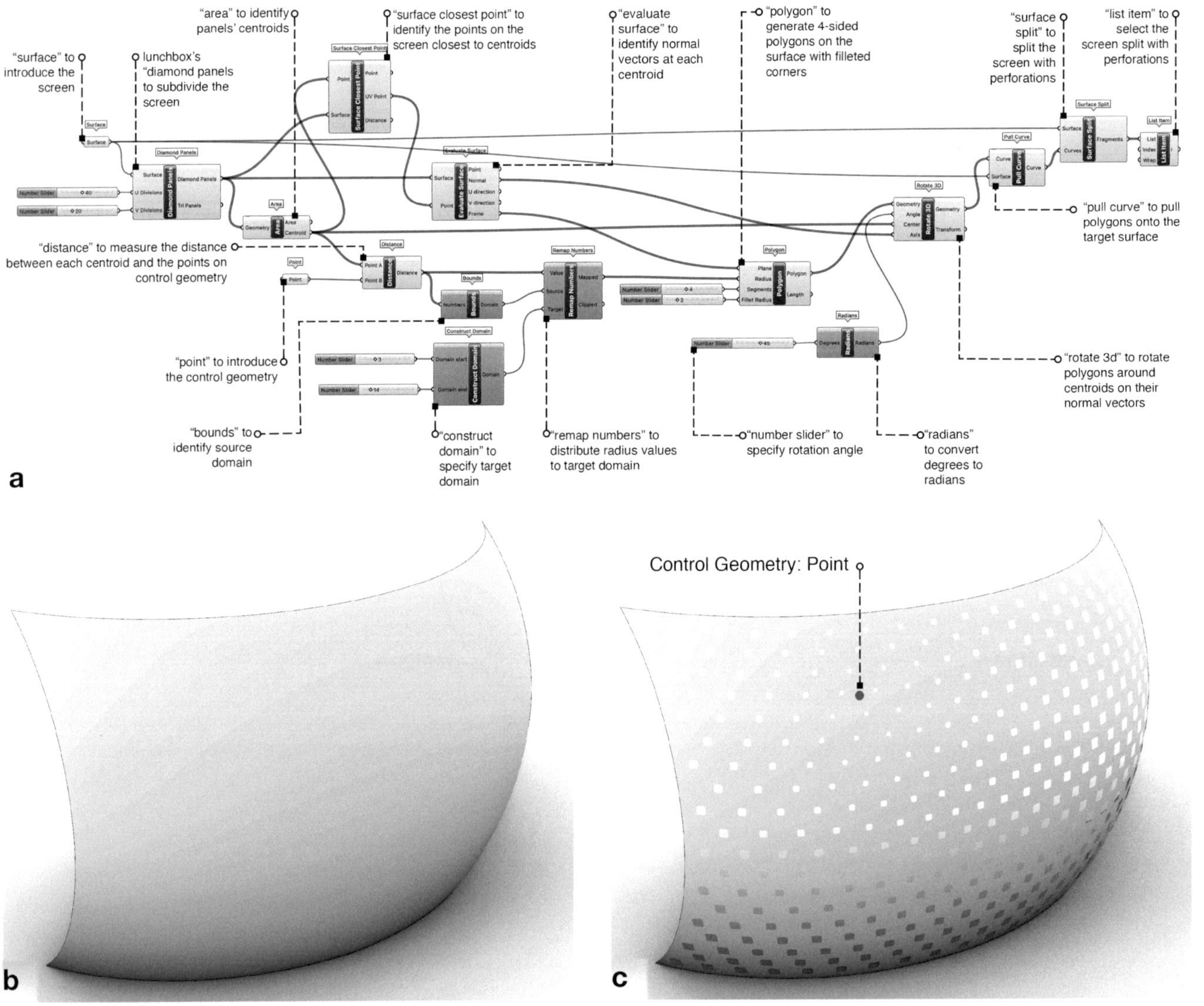

Figure 6.20 (a) The Grasshopper definition used for creating perforations on a complex curved surface; (b) the original surface and the location of the control point; and (c) the resulting perforated surface with the control geometry point depicted.

the surface is evaluated at each centroid using the EvalSrf component. Connecting the "F" (frame) output of the "EvalSrf" component to the "P" (plane) input of the Polygon component, each square is rotated on the surface, making their normal vectors parallel to the surface's normal vectors at each centroid. Using a point on the surface as a control geometry, the radii of the polygons are set so that their size increases as their distance from the control geometry point increases. To do this, the distance between each centroid and the control geometry point is measured, and the output is then remapped to a domain between 3 and 16.

Finally, the rotation angle of the squares is edited, rotating each square on its normal axis for 45 degrees, making them parallel to the ground line. To split the original surface using the squares, the square curves are first pulled onto the curved surface using the "Pull Curve" component and then the surface is split using the "SrfSplit" component. Figure 6.20c illustrates the resulting perforated screen. This approach can be used to create skins systems on a variety of curved surfaces.

6.5 POPULATING COMPLEX SURFACES WITH PREDESIGNED UNITS: REPEATING MODULAR UNITS ON COMPLEX SURFACES

A common approach to façade design, including controlling daylight and visibility among other factors, is the use of modular units. Modular units, such as concrete masonry units (CMUs) and similar elements, have also been historically used as design elements to create rhythm on the façade, and light effects in interiors. Parametric techniques help save time and effort in populating complex surfaces with predesigned, modular units. In this section, a sample predesigned façade module is introduced, much like a CMU or other similar unit (Figure 6.21b).

In order to populate and panelize the complex curved surface introduced in Section 6.4, the sample predesigned façade module is first introduced to Grasshopper using the "Geometry" component, while the curved surface is introduced into Grasshopper using the "Surface" component. In order to populate the curved surface, the "Surface Box" component is used to subdivide the surface using a 14 × 14 divided domain. Finally, the thickness of the populated curved surface is specified using the "H" (height) input of the "Surface Box" component, which, in this case, is set to 20 units using a slider.

Now that rectangular prisms have been created on the original surface using the "Surface Box" component, the individual predesigned modular units can be used to populate the curved surface. To do this, Grasshopper's "Box Morph" component is used to morph the original geometry, the individual predesigned module, into the surface boxes created. In doing so, the geometry to be "morphed" is the original geometry, the reference input for needed for the BoxMorph component is the bounding box of the original module (created using the "Bbox" component), and the output of the "Surface Box" component constitutes the "Target" input of the Surface Box component (Figure 6.21a). Figure 6.21 illustrates the script used for this operation (Figure 6.21a), the sample predesigned modular unit (Figure 6.21b), as well as the original curved surface (Figure 6.21c) and the resulting populated surface (Figure 6.21d).

6.6 POPULATING COMPLEX SURFACES WITH PREDESIGNED UNITS: REPEATING MODULAR UNITS ON COMPLEX SURFACES TO AVOID DISTORTION

The complex surface population method discussed in Section 6.5 is efficient; however, it distorts predesigned units, which may not be desirable in many instances. Instead of using the "Box Morph" component of Grasshopper, we can also use additional native Grasshopper components to populate a surface with predesigned units avoiding distortion. Figure 6.22 demonstrates an example of this process.

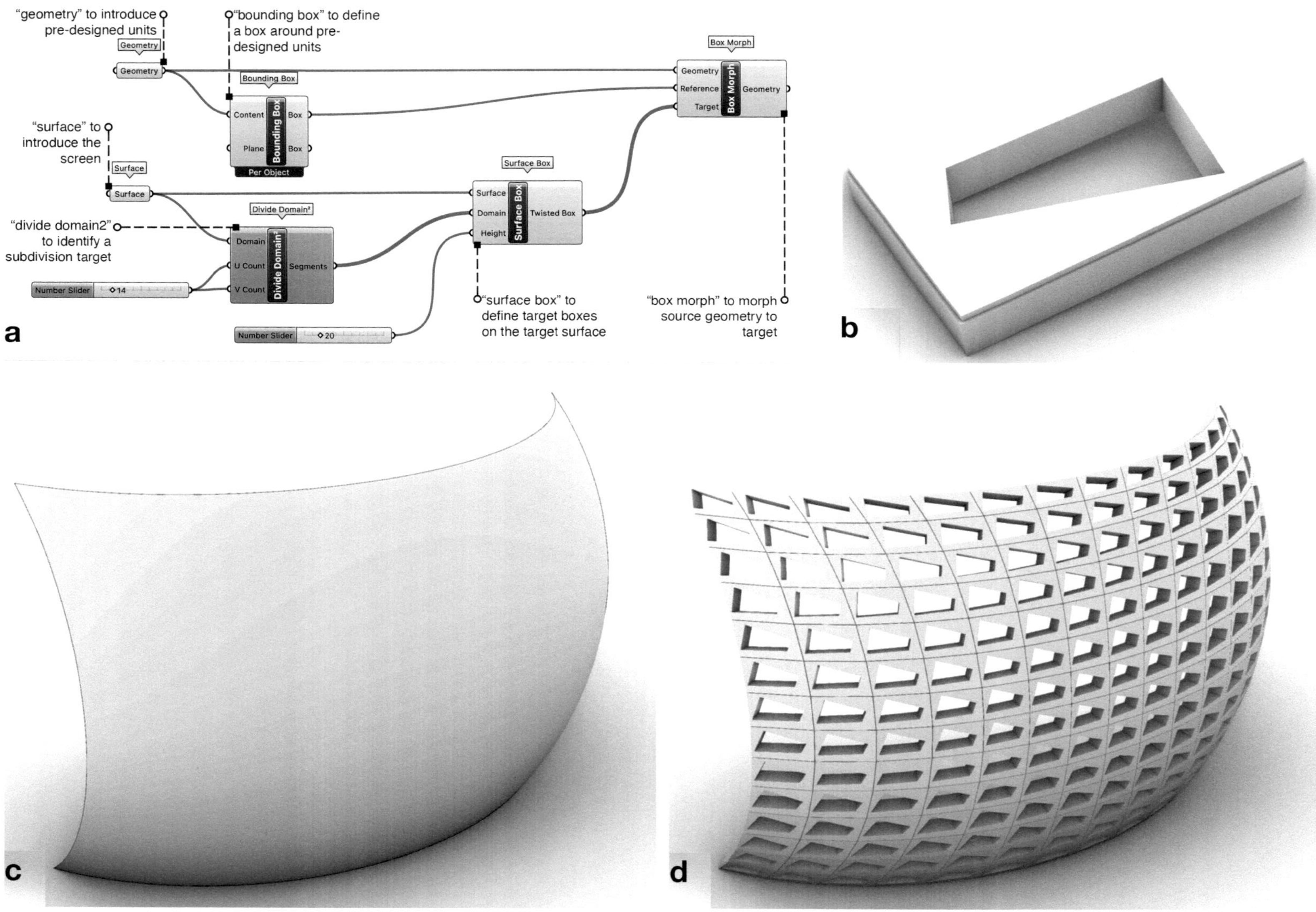

Figure 6.21 *(a) The Grasshopper definition used for panelizing and populating a curved surface with predesigned units; (b) a single unit; (c) the original complex curved surface; and (d) the resulting panelized surface populated with predesigned units.*

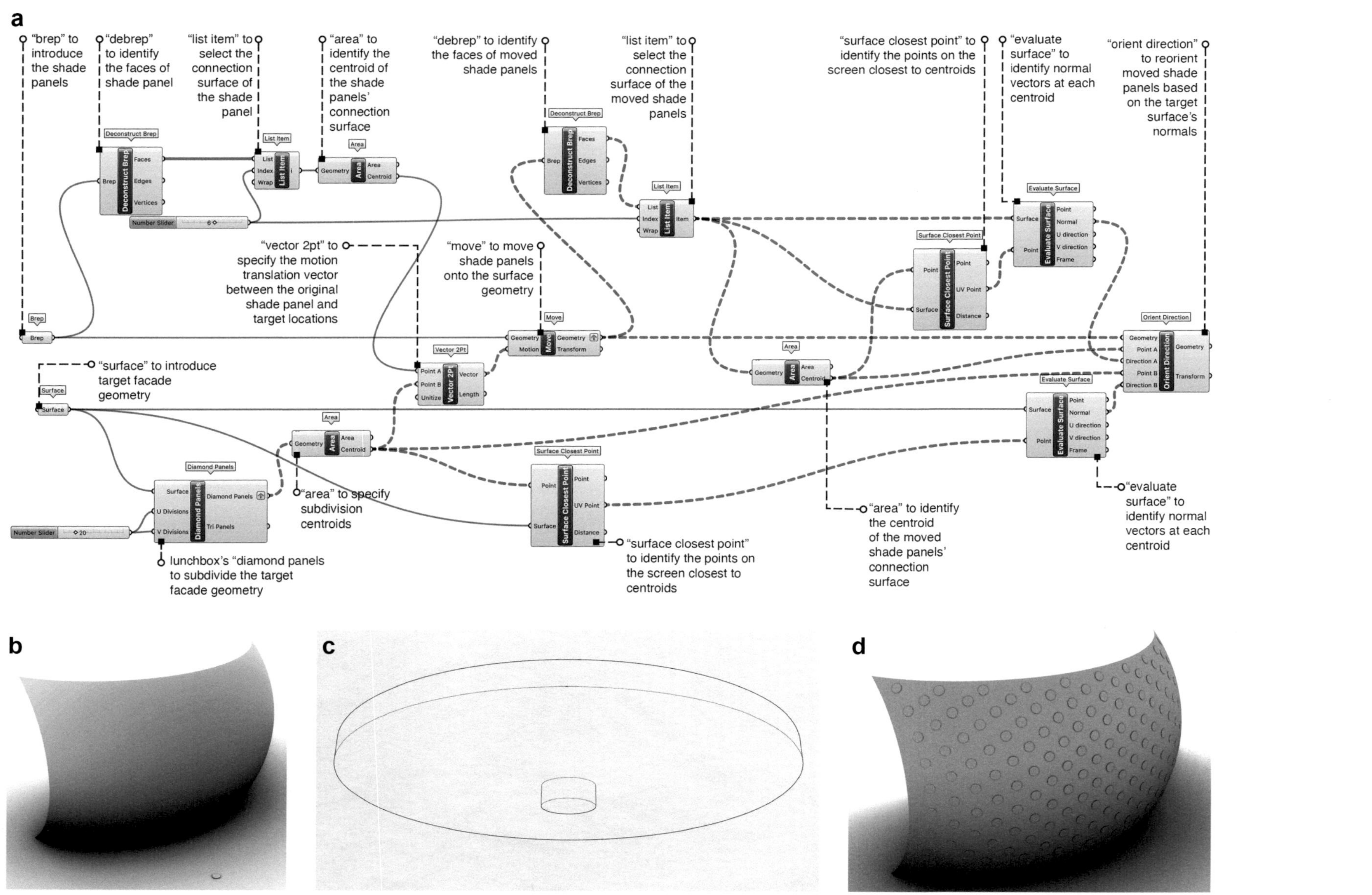

Figure 6.22 *(a) The Grasshopper definition developed for populating a curved surface with predesigned shading panel units avoiding distortion; (b) the identical curved surface introduced in Section 6.5; (c) the fictitious circular shading unit; and (d) the resulting composition of the target curved surface and the reoriented source predesigned shading panel units.*

Figure 6.22b illustrates the same curved surface introduced in Section 6.5, and Figure 6.22c illustrates a fictitious circular shading unit. Figure 6.22a demonstrates the Grasshopper definition developed for this operation. First, the sample shade panels are introduced into Grasshopper using the Brep component. Likewise, the target curved surface is introduced using the Surface component. Using Lunchbox's Diamond Panels component, the target surface is panelized, and the centroids of panels are identified using the Area component. These centroids constitute the target locations for the shading panels.

To identify the connection points between the curved surface and shading panels, the predesigned units are deconstructed using the "Deconstruct Brep" (DeBrep) component, and using the List Item component, the connection surface of the shading panels' bases are selected. The centroids of these connection surfaces constitute the source points for the movement of the predesigned shading panels.

Now the Move component needs to be used to move the source shading predesigned unit to the centroids of the target surface's panels. To specify the translation vector for the movement, the "Vector 2Pt" component is used. The starting point of the translation vector is the source point selected for the predesigned shading panel, and the target movement points are the centroids of the target surface's panels. Following the moving operation, the panels are replicated on the centroids on the target surface's diamond panels, however the shading panels do need to be reoriented based on the normal vectors at the centroid of each target panel.

For reorientation, first, the target panels' normal vectors are identified using the SrfCP to evaluate surface components. Then, the copied shading panels' connection surfaces and their centroids are selected using the DeBrep, List Item, and Area components. Now, for the reorientation, the "Orient Direction" component needs to be used. The replicated shading panels are introduced to the "Geometry" input. The copied shading panels' connection surfaces' centroids are introduced as the source "Point A," and the normal vector for the shading panels' connection surfaces' centroids are introduced as the source "Direction A." The target panels identified using the SrfCP component are introduced as the target "Point B," and the target panels' normal vectors are introduced as the target "Direction B" (Figure 4.22a). The resulting composition of the target curved surface and reoriented source shading panels are illustrated in Figure 6.22d.

6.7 CONCLUSION

In this chapter, the basics of generating façade and skin systems using various repetition, geometry subdivision, and paneling approaches – as well as external factors, such as solar exposure and visibility analysis options – were introduced. Chapter 8 will introduce how such approaches can be utilized in coordination with parametric building performance analyses with metrics, such as energy use intensity, annual solar exposure, and solar daylight autonomy using Grasshopper and contemporary plug-ins.

NOTE

1 Individual curves, surfaces, and various other complex geometries can also be introduced to Grasshopper as a Brep or sets of Breps.

CHAPTER 07

EVOLUTIONARY APPLICATIONS Using Parametric Applications to Generate, Analyze, and Select Design Iterations

Evolutionary solvers in parametric design are relatively new applications. They can help the designer in multiple phases of the architectural design process. The main principle of these applications is that they enable the identification of "best" possible solution(s) for one or more dependent variables, based on the modification of an independent variable. An important advantage of evolutionary solvers is their capability of evaluating the results of thousands of independent variable iterations automatically, thus finding the "best" possible dependent variable outcomes.

It is important to note at this point, that the use of evolutionary solvers should be for better informed design decision-making and should not be the sole driver. The complexity of architectural design thinking requires that multiple factors be considered simultaneously. Optimization may end up hampering the uniqueness of a design proposition. Therefore, it is important to remember that evolutionary solvers are meant to provide information for decision-making, and they cannot be decision-makers by themselves.

Different evolutionary solvers can optimize for single or multiple variables. When a solver is used to optimize one dependent variable, the process is termed single-objective optimization. When multiple variables are optimized simultaneously, the process is referred to as multi-objective optimization.

Although evolutionary solvers can be used in multiple phases of the architectural design process, they require at least intermediate level knowledge of parametric methods. Therefore, we will look into evolutionary solvers in this chapter. We will address single-objective optimization by discussing the Galapagos solver, and multi-objective optimization by discussing the Octopus solver – both of which operate within the Grasshopper interface. First, let us visit the background and development of evolutionary solvers in architecture.

7.1 EVOLUTIONARY APPLICATIONS: BACKGROUND

The conceptual framework of evolutionary solvers in parametric design is based on the idea of natural selection. First, the solver calculates the "suitability" of several randomly developed propositions for a criterion or multiple criteria defined by the user. The "unsuitable" propositions are then eliminated or altered, leading the way to another round of calculations with the remaining propositions. During the new round of calculations, the remaining propositions are altered by emulating mutation or eliminated by emulating natural selection based on their

DOI: 10.4324/9781003230052-7

"suitability". During this round of calculations, new propositions can also be created by emulating the breeding of "parent" propositions. This entire process is repeated as many times as it is necessary to identify the most suitable propositions based on the original criterion or criteria. At the end of the process, propositions are organized from the most suitable proposition to the least suitable.

We introduced "the original proposition" earlier in this chapter as the independent variable, since it is not affected by any other factor than the evolutionary solver's process. In evolutionary solver terminology, the modified proposition is referred to as the "genome." We introduced the "suitability of the modified proposition" earlier in this chapter as the dependent variable since it is affected by the modification of the proposition. In evolutionary solver terminology, the "suitability of the genome" is referred to as "fitness." Therefore, in this artificial process, genomes constantly get evaluated based on their fitness. In essence, an artificial selection process takes place, akin to the natural selection process.

David Rutten, the developer of the commonly used Galapagos (Vukorep and Kotov, 2021) evolutionary solver, provides a history of evolutionary solvers in his 2010 paper. Early computational work in this area dates to the 1960s and 1970s. During this period, interest in and the use of evolutionary solvers were mostly limited to the world of computer programmers. With the advances achieved in personal computing and its increasing accessibility to the masses, evolutionary solvers became accessible to all computer users in general (Rutten, 2010). Since their development for accessible computer-aided design platforms, such as Rhinoceros and Revit, evolutionary solvers have become more commonly visible in architectural design processes. Solvers such as Galapagos and Octopus provide interfaces accessible to architects and designers; thus, one no longer needs to be a computer programmer to use evolutionary solvers. In this book, the term evolutionary solver is used to identify such solvers (Vukorep and Kotov, 2021).

7.2 THE SOLUTION PROCESS

In this section we will introduce the evolutionary solver process by explaining a simple single-objective visibility analysis example. Figure 7.1a illustrates an imaginary downtown plan with an empty lot A surrounded by imaginary buildings in neighboring lots and blocks. Two of the neighboring lots are also empty. The objective is to find the vantage point "V" on "lot A" that has the highest possible visibility from its surroundings within a 200-foot radius. If we dedicate the horizontal bottom edge of the lot as "u axis," and the vertical left edge of the lot as "v axis," then any given point on the lot will have a coordinate that we can specify using a (u,v) coordinate (Figure 7.1b). By moving a vantage point "V" to all possible (u,v) coordinates and measuring the visibility of its isovist at all (u,v) points, we can find the location that has the highest visibility on lot A within a given radius.

In this scenario, the "u" and "v" coordinates of the moving vantage point V constitute ***genes***, and the moving vantage point V constitutes a ***genome*** (an individual). The area of the vantage point V's isovist constitutes the ***fitness*** criterion: the larger the visibility area, the more fit the genome. In this scenario, we can ask an evolutionary solver to keep changing the "u" and "v" values of the genes and measuring each genome's visibility until it finds the genome that has the highest visibility. This constitutes a "single-objective optimization" task. If multiple variables are analyzed with an evolutionary solver, this would constitute a "multi-objective optimization" task.

Once the solver is assigned with the task, it creates a random set of genomes, each with their (u,v) coordinates, yielding the initial generation, ***generation 1***. Once all genomes are evaluated, the solver eliminates the worst performing genomes, and "mutates" or "breeds" the remaining genomes (generating new genomes) to yield the next generation of genomes,

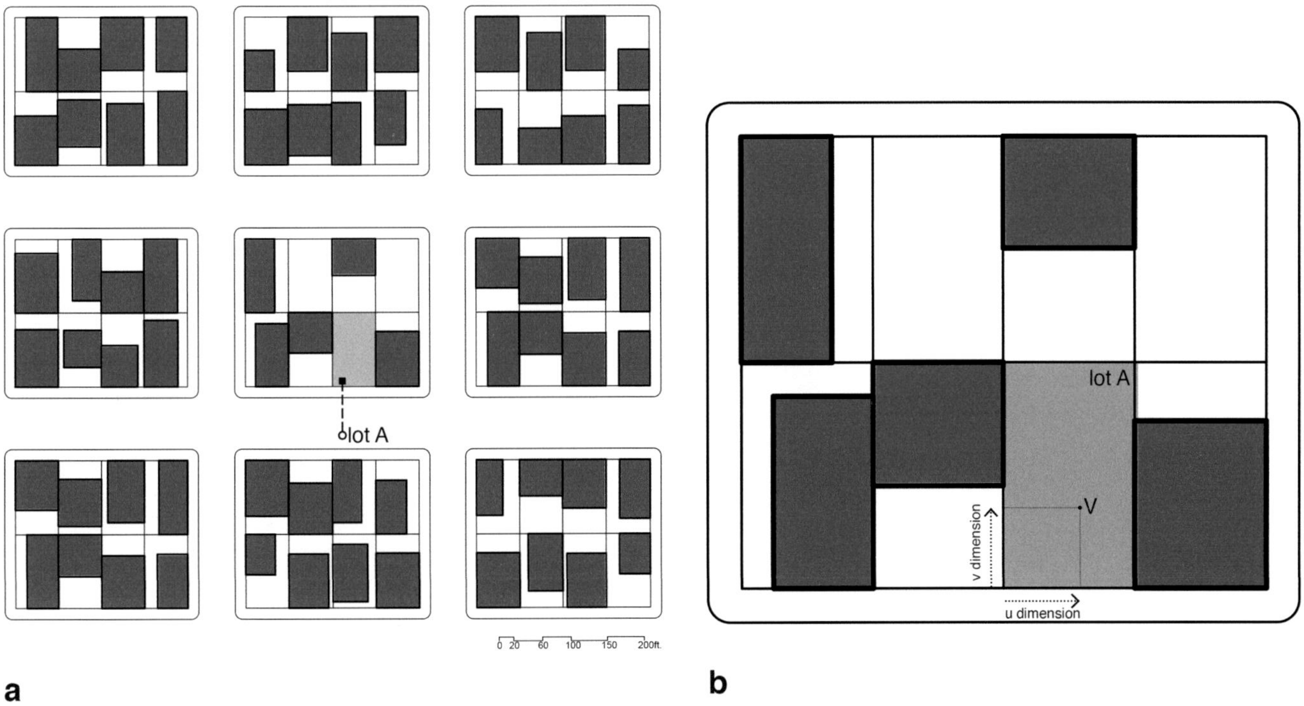

Figure 7.1 *(a) Lot A in an imaginary downtown environment; (b) vantage point "V" on lot A, u and v dimensions of lot A.*

generation 2. The solver then repeats this task until the "best-performing genome," the vantage point that has the highest visibility, is identified (Figure 7.2). The remaining genomes are organized and listed based on their fitness. Since geometrically there are an infinite number of points in a given plane, the accuracy of the solution depends on the number of digits of the u,v coordinates – the number of divisions defined on the u and v axes.

At this point, it is important to note that the example discussed in Figure 7.1 represents a well-scoped, straightforward problem, and it has an optimum solution. Therefore, the calculation process for this problem is not too time-consuming. As we will see in subsequent sections of this chapter, more complex and especially multiple-variable problems can be a lot more time-consuming to resolve. In cases of multiple-variable problems, the outcome also is not the "best" solution, but of maximum fitness. In such situations, based on time availability, it may be helpful to run the solver multiple times to find options with higher levels of fitness.

7.2.1 Advantages and Disadvantages of Evolutionary Solvers

Rutten (2010) discusses the advantages and disadvantages of evolutionary solvers. One disadvantage that becomes clear immediately when one uses an evolutionary solver is that the process tends to be slow. Depending on the selection criteria and the kind of analysis underway, each iteration can take a long time. Considering the number of iterations created and analyzed in the process, a full optimization process can take hours or days. The visibility analysis example discussed in Figure 7.1 represents a relatively simple and well-scoped example; therefore, the optimization process does not take an incredibly long period of time.

As we will discuss in the upcoming sections of this chapter, more complex analyses, such as direct sun hours of a space based on its orientation, may take significantly more time; and rather than yielding a "best" solution, an option with maximum fitness may be the result. Therefore, based on time availability, running the simulation multiple times may be helpful in identifying more than one feasible option. This implies that there is no "guaranteed" solution. The problem needs to be clearly defined, and often a "good enough" solution needs to be identified. Otherwise, the process may continue indefinitely (Rutten, 2010).

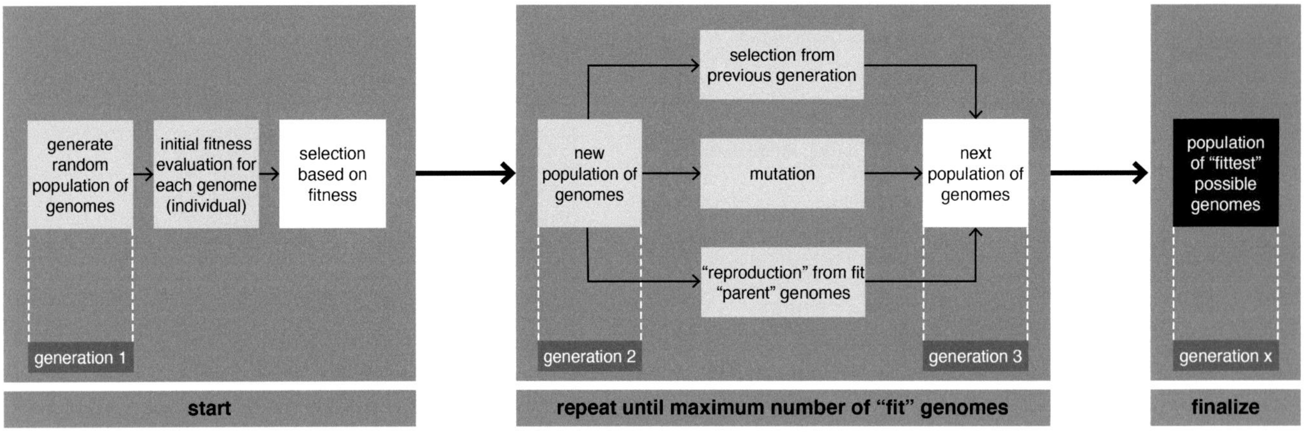

Figure 7.2 The solution process undertaken by evolutionary solvers.

On the other hand, Rutten considers their flexibility and transparency among the advantages of evolutionary solvers. One can work on very diverse problems, and the process tends to be fairly transparent through the solvers' interface. Evolutionary solvers also tend to be fairly forgiving: for instance, if the user realizes that an ill-defined problem has been identified, the problem definition can be easily altered. The process also allows the user to stop and collect intermediate results when needed (Rutten, 2010).

7.3 SINGLE-OBJECTIVE OPTIMIZATION

Let us observe the optimization process introduced in Section 7.2 in more detail using the Galapagos solver. In Figure 7.3a, the surface of the parcel is first introduced to Grasshopper using the "Surface" component. To specify the location of vantage points on the lot, the "Evaluate Surface" component is used, and the surface is "reparameterized," a process which equalizes the surface's edge lengths to 1 unit. To specify the (u,v) coordinates of the vantage points, the "construct point" component is used, and two sliders with a minimum of 0, and maximum of 1 are connected to x and y coordinate inputs of this component. Now, the two sliders can control the location of the vantage point on the lot's surface, essentially creating a new ***genome*** for each (u,v) coordinate.

The "Isovist" component introduced in Chapter 3 can now be deployed to analyze the isovist of each genome. The buildings around lot A are introduced to the "isovist" component using a "geometry" component and setting it to multiple geometries. The analysis radius is set to 200 feet, and the number of isovist points is set to 300, using panels. The resulting isovist points are then used to build a closed isovist polyline, whose area is calculated by the "Area" component. To see the isovists more clearly, an optional "Boundary Surfaces" component is used, highlighting the isovist outputs. Now, isovist areas can be calculated for each genome. Since we want to find the highest visibility vantage point, the ***fitness*** of ***genomes*** will be analyzed based on their isovist areas: the larger the isovist area, the more fit a genome is.

The Galapagos solver has two connection points: the "genome" input, and the "fitness" input. Since our objective is to find the vantage point with the highest visibility, each vantage point's isovist area will be calculated, therefore the isovist area will constitute the fitness input. In the meantime, the sliders that dictate each vantage point's (u,v) coordinates (genes), thus creating genomes, will constitute the genome input.

Now that the genomes and our fitness criteria of maximum visibility have been provided for Galapagos, we can run the analysis. Double-clicking the component brings up the Galapagos Editor with the options panel (Figure 7.3b). The editor also has tabs for solver options and records of the optimization process. The left side of the options panel presents

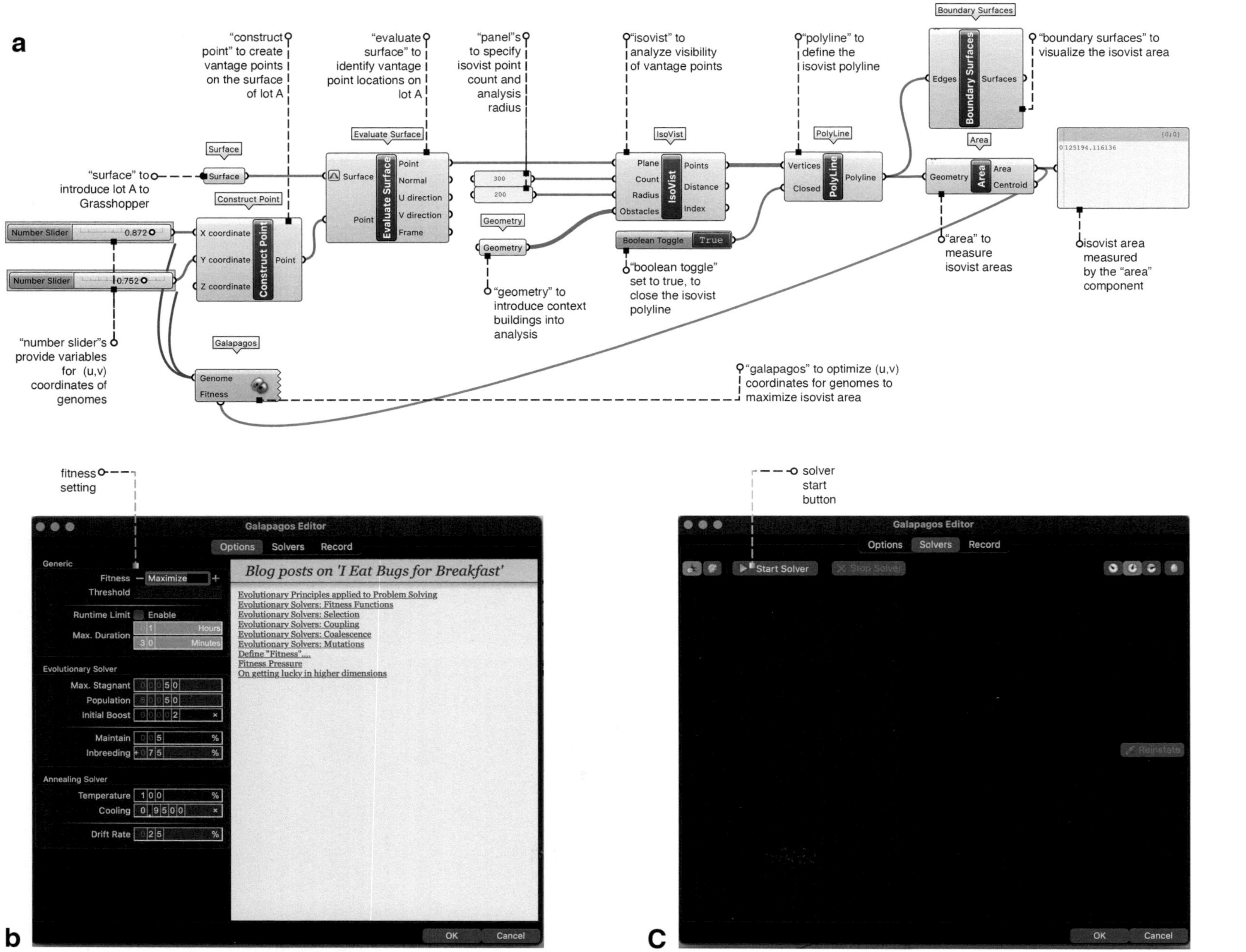

Figure 7.3 (a) The Grasshopper definition used to set up the Galapagos optimization process; (b) Galapagos options in default state; (c) Galapagos solver in its default state.

the component's settings, while the right shows links to Galapagos developer David Rutten's blog on evolutionary solvers. The top setting in this panel is the fitness criterion, which can be set to "minimize," "maximize," or a specific numeric value. For this illustration, we will set the fitness function to "maximize" to find the point with the highest visibility. When one activates the "solvers" tab, the "Start Solver" button appears (Figure 7.3c).

Once the solver is activated using the "Start Solver" button, Galapagos generates a random set of genomes (generation 1) and analyzes each genome based on the fitness criteria (Figure 7.4a). Through multiple iterations, successive generations are created in which genomes get evaluated – they go through elimination due to lack of fitness, they mutate, or they coalesce. The fitness of the genomes improves with each generation. When the "fittest"

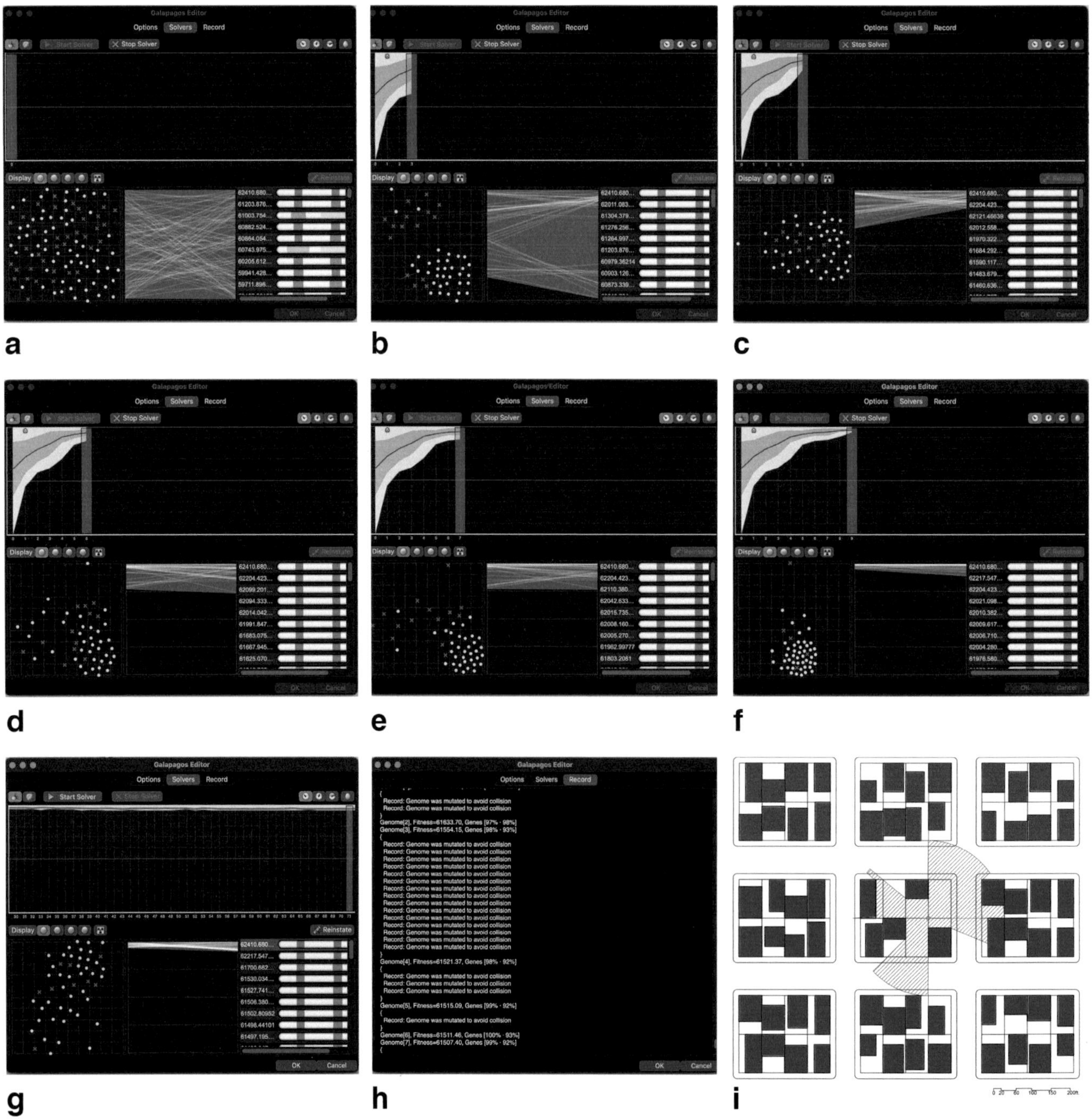

Figure 7.4 (a) Generation 1 of genomes in Galapagos; (b to g) successive generations of more fit genomes; (h) records of the optimization process; (i) the "fittest" genome – the vantage point with the largest isovist area, thus highest visibility within a 200-foot radius.

genome is found, the process stops (Figures 7.4b–g). Once the optimization process is complete, one can click on iterations and click the "Reinstate" button to visualize them on the Rhinoceros screen. Each iteration's isovist area can be viewed by connecting a panel to the Area component, and any desired iteration can be baked into the Rhinoceros environment.

Now that we introduced the basic functions of the Galapagos solver, let us look into its options in more depth. The Galapagos solver offers a variety of options to customize the optimization process. The example we have been discussing so far has only used the default settings in Galapagos solver. In this section we will have a closer look into the options provided by Galapagos. Figure 7.5 illustrates the options provided.

As illustrated in the previous section, the main option is the fitness option, which allows the user to set the optimization to minimize or maximize the best fit value. One can also set this to a specific numeric value. The threshold option allows the user to set a specific maximum or minimum value instead of the absolute maximum or minimum. For example, the maximum value in a genome set may be 70, but the user may be looking for a maximum value of 60. In this scenario, it is possible to set the fitness value to "maximize" and set the threshold to 60. The runtime limit option sets a time limit to the optimization process when enabled. As discussed earlier, sometimes optimization processes can take long periods of time. Using the runtime limit option, one can set Galapagos to stop the process after a selected amount of time.

What Is the "Annealing Solver"? On the Galapagos options screen, one will notice that there is an "annealing solver" option as well. Since in this book the objective is to introduce evolutionary solvers, we will not go into the details of the annealing solver option. However, it is worth providing a brief note about its rationale and difference from the evolutionary solver.

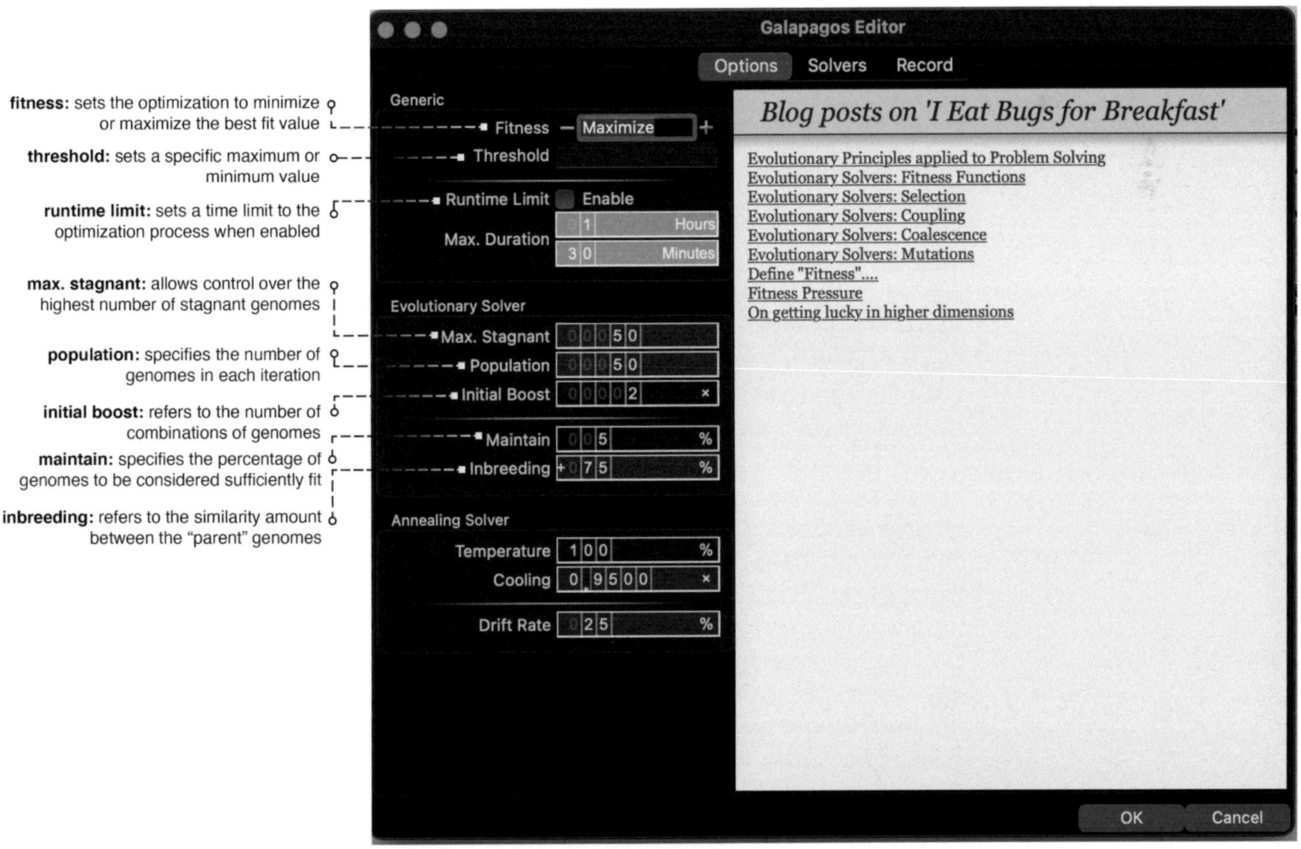

Figure 7.5 Galapagos solver's generic options and options for the evolutionary solver.

We discussed that the evolutionary solver emulates the natural selection process that happens in nature to generate and analyze genomes. The annealing solver, on the other hand, emulates a process termed "annealing" in materials science. The term annealing refers to the process of heating a material such as metal to a high temperature, keeping it at the designated temperature for a given period of time, and slowly cooling it back to room temperature. During this process, the atoms of the material gain mobility, and reorganize into new patterns (Callister and Rethwisch, 2019). The annealing solver emulates this process of atom mobility and reorganization in the generation of solutions. This is the rationale behind the "temperature" and "cooling" options of the annealing solver. The annealing solver therefore essentially provides an alternative method for the genome creation method of the evolutionary solver.

7.4 EVOLUTIONARY SOLVERS IN ARCHITECTURE: SINGLE OBJECTIVE OPTIMIZATION EXAMPLES

Thanks to the flexibility of evolutionary solvers, they can be used in various phases of the architectural design process, and in many specific decision-making tasks: site analysis phase, conceptual development phase, spatial organization tasks, skin system design tasks, and so on. This section will introduce examples on how evolutionary solvers can help in architectural decision-making.

7.4.1 Identifying the Orientation of Workspaces to Minimize Direct Sun Access and Glare

An important objective in workspace design is to minimize glare. Glare on work surfaces and computer screens hinders comfort during the work process, negatively affecting productivity. Direct sun exposure of a space is one of the major contributors of glare problems. Let us imagine we need to identify possible orientations of a proposed workspace during the ongoing design process of a multi-functional building. Clearly, many factors will need to be taken into consideration, one of which will be minimizing glare. Using a given design proposal, evolutionary solvers can be used to identify spatial orientation possibilities that can help minimize glare. In this section, we will use the Galapagos solver to address this sample scenario.

Figure 7.6 illustrates a fictitious workspace design proposal with a strip window around its corner in progress for a site in San Luis Obispo, CA. An orientation vs. direct sun hours analysis using the Galapagos solver can be conducted to help better inform the decision-making process so that glare problems can be minimized. The "Direct Sun Hours" component of the Ladybug plug-in for Grasshopper was introduced in Chapter 3. Results of a given direct sun hours analysis can be visualized to identify potential areas that may cause glare using the "LB Legend Parameters" component of Ladybug. Since higher numbers of direct sun hours will cause more glare problems, the objective in this example will be minimizing the direct sun hours through the window of the workspace design proposal. Minimizing the highest number of direct sun hours will provide the conditions for minimum possible glare.

In the scenario introduced in Figure 7.6, first, the sun path for San Luis Obispo was plotted to get solar vectors, which is necessary to calculate direct sun hours. The procedure for plotting direct sun hours was introduced in Chapter 3, Section 3.3.4, therefore we will not describe that procedure at length in this chapter.

Our workspace design proposal's ground surface is raised to 3 feet and identified as the test geometry, while our workspace design proposal's outer surfaces are identified as the opaque geometry around the test geometry. Both the test geometry surface and the space's outer shell are set to rotate 360 degrees using a slider set to yield integers (rotation axis is not specified, since the component's default rotation axis is the Z-axis). The outcomes of the rotation are connected to the LadyBbug's "LB Direct Sun Hours" component for the test geometry, so that the impacts of each rotation can be observed on the test surface in terms of direct sun

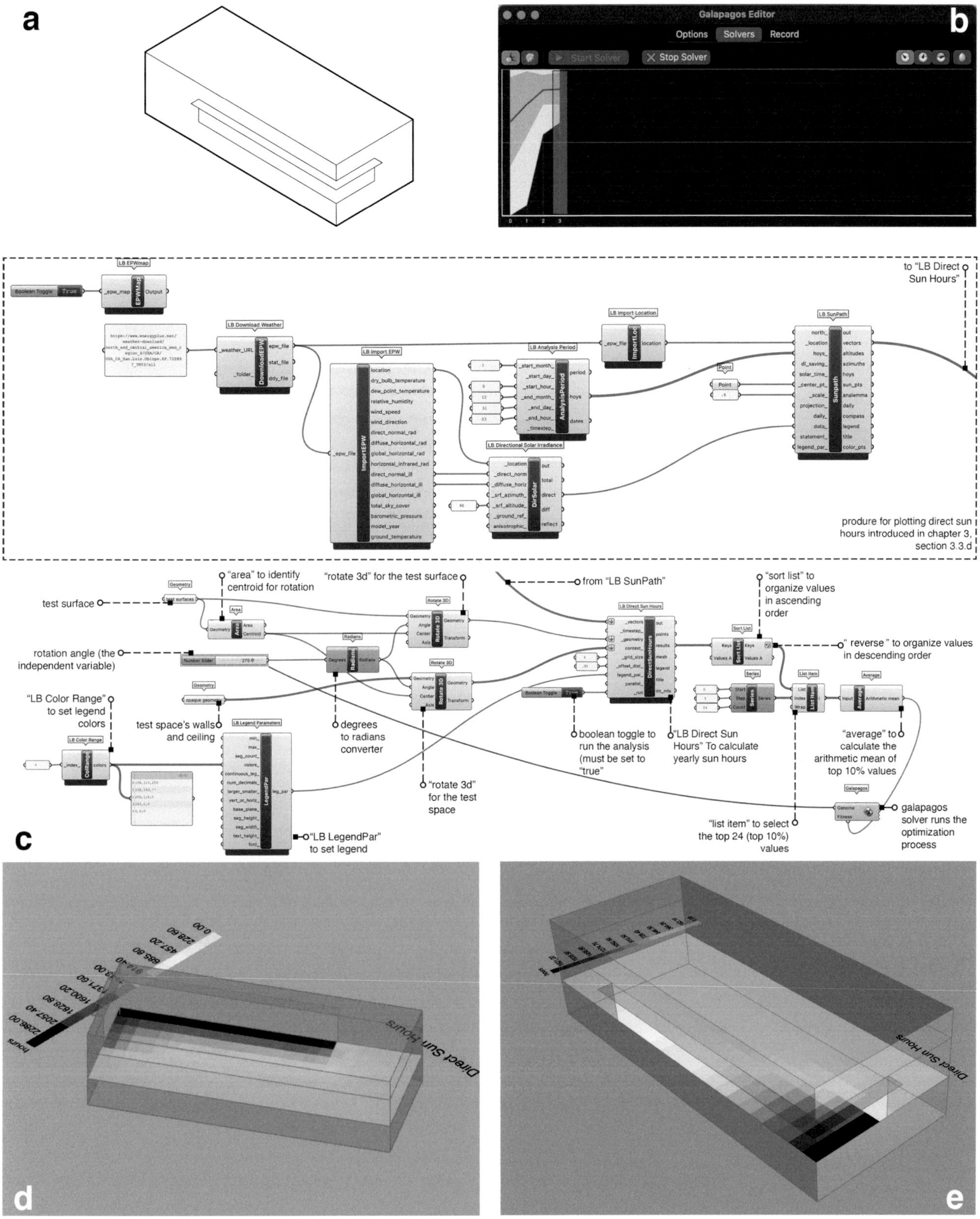

Figure 7.6 *(a) The workspace design proposal; (b) Galapagos solver during the analysis process; (c) the Grasshopper definition used for analysis; (d) Rhinoceros screen during analysis showing one of the iterations (darker tones indicate higher glare potential); (e) the orientation with minimal glare potential.*

hours. For purposes of visualization related to glare issues, Ladybug's LB Legend Parameters is used, and its "colors" setting is set to number 6 (the setting for glare) using Ladybug's "LB Color Range" component to illustrate potential high glare areas.

The question here is how to pick the potential high glare area. In this example, the "grid size" for the LB Direct Sun Hours is set to 4, which means that the component will subdivide the test surface (which is equal to the square footage of the workspace) into a grid of 4 feet × 4 feet. This yields direct sun-hours results for a total of 240 squares for each orientation iteration. Since we are interested in minimizing the number of squares with the highest direct sun hours access, selecting the squares with the highest values, and minimizing those values becomes important. Using the Sort List component, the results of each iteration is ordered in ascending order, and the list is reversed to list the highest values first. Then, using the "List Item" component along with the "series" component, the top 24 values are selected. This yields the top 10% of direct sun hours from each iteration since each iteration yields 240 values. Finally, using the "average" component, the arithmetic mean of the top 10% direct sun hours values is taken, which is our dependent variable that needs to be minimized.

At this point, our independent variable, the space's orientation value as well as the dependent variable, the test surface's mean highest direct sun hour values are set and ready to be connected to the Galapagos solver. While the mean highest sun hours value is set as the "Fitness" value, the slider for the rotation angle is set as the "Genome" value. Once the Galapagos solver is double-clicked, the fitness criteria is set to "minimum" to find the orientation that will yield minimum annual sun hours for the test surface, thus intending to minimize potential glare problems.

Clicking the "Start Solver" button initiates the optimization process. Galapagos solver measures the direct sun hours calculation for each rotation iteration by creating new genomes through elimination, mutation, and breeding. The optimization process continues until the minimum value for the mean maximum direct sun hour measurement for all orientation possibilities. The measurements are organized from minimum to maximum, and each iteration can be visualized on the Rhinoceros interface by clicking on the measurement value and selecting the "Reinstate" option on the Galapagos interface. The reinstated solution(s) based on the desired direct sun hour measurements are now ready to be baked into the Rhinoceros environment, to be evaluated with other design objectives in mind.

7.4.2 Identifying the Building Orientation That Allows Maximum Access to Desired Views

Another example for using single-objective optimization is the identification of a building orientation that allows maximum access to desired views. Often, during the site analysis process we identify and note desirable and undesirable views around the project site. Using an evolutionary solver in early stages of the design process can help increase informed decision-making about the orientation of the project, or its various spaces and massing, to maximize access to desired views (or minimize access to undesired views). In this example, we will look into optimizing the orientation of a sample building massing to maximize its access to ocean views.

Figure 7.7 illustrates a fictitious site close to an ocean front. In this scenario, some buildings are between our sample site and the ocean, partially blocking access to desirable ocean views. We will illustrate the use of the Galapagos solver to find a building massing orientation that allows maximum access to ocean views.

A rectangular prism represents the proposed building. Since we are interested in the ocean view from the building's façades, for the purposes of analysis the rectangular prism is only composed of four vertical surfaces representing the building's façades. The building is set

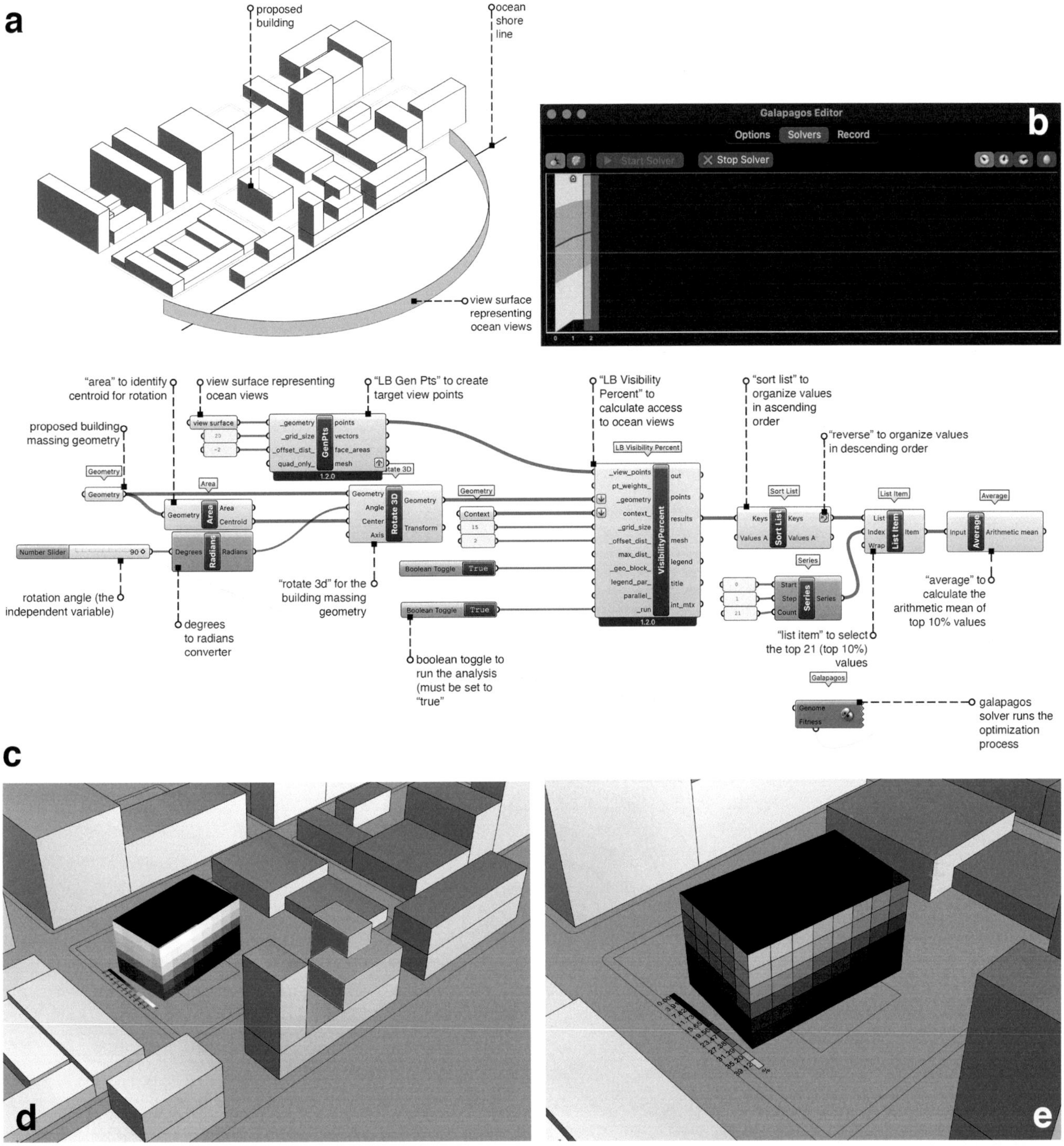

Figure 7.7 *(a) The building design proposal; (b) Galapagos solver during the analysis process; (c) the Grasshopper definition used for analysis; (d) Rhinoceros screen during analysis showing one of the iterations (lighter tones indicate better access to ocean views); (e) the orientation with the highest average maximum visibility values.*

to rotate around its centroid between –90 and 90 degrees using an integer-based slider. To calculate views to the ocean, Ladybug's "LB Visibility Percent" component is used. This component requires a set of target points representing the view. To achieve the target view, a semi-circular surface is created, centered around the site's centroid (Figure 7.7). A simple subdivision of the target surface can provide the target points. For this, Grasshopper's native "Isotrim" component, the LunchBox plug-in, or Rhinoceros's "Paneling Tools" (among others) can be used. For purposes of demonstration, in this example, Ladybug's "LB Generate

Points" component is used, and it is subdivided into a grid of 20 feet × 20 feet. A "geometry" component is set to represent the multiple buildings that are partially blocking the proposed building's ocean views.

At this point there are a few remaining settings needed to run the LB Visibility Percent component. First, the proposed building's surface is subdivided into a 20 foot by 20 foot grid by setting the "_grid_size" input to 20. An offset distance of 2 is set to be able to see analysis results slightly off the proposed building's surface. The "_geo_block" input is set to "true" to make the proposed building's façade surfaces opaque to one another, so that in any orientation, a surface facing the land cannot "see through" the surface(s) facing the ocean. Finally, the component is started by setting the "run" input to "true" using a Boolean toggle, yielding 156 visibility percent values per iteration at the end of the optimization process.

Similar to the process demonstrated in Section 7.4.1, the results are organized in ascending order using the Sort List component and reversed into descending order. The highest 10% of visibility values are selected using the List Item component, and the arithmetic mean of these values is calculated for each iteration. The resulting value is used as the "Fitness" criterion (the dependent variable) for the Galapagos solver. The genome, on the other hand, is provided by the changing angle values of the slider controlling the "Rotate 3D" component.

When the Galapagos solver is set to maximize the view percentage values and run, it yields the orientation that has the highest top 10% visibility values. It is important to note, at this point, that in both examples from Section 7.4.1 and this section the fitness criterion can be identified in various ways, since the outcomes are provided as a grid of values. In the last two examples, the top 10% of the values were selected, and their average was used as the fitness criterion to minimize or maximize. One can also use the arithmetic median and its accompanying standard deviation as the fitness criteria.

7.4.3 Identifying the Highest Visibility Point for Multiple Storefronts for a Commercial Space

The last single-objective optimization example we will introduce is about isovist area optimization. In this scenario, we will create an imaginary commercial space with two storefronts, and our objective will be to find the point in this space that has the highest visibility from the two available storefronts. The idea is to find the most visible point, so that the store owner can display the most prominent item sold in the store.

Figure 7.8a depicts the imaginary commercial space with two storefronts. First, a test surface 3 feet above the floor is introduced. In order to define the location of the target point (independent variable), the "evaluate surface" component is used. The surface is reparameterized to make the length of the two sides of the surface equivalent to 1, and two sliders set from 0 to 1 are introduced to specify the location of the target point. The "point" output of the "Evaluate Surface" component is introduced to the "isovist" component, the number of isovist points is set to 1000 for a fine level analysis, and the isovist radius is set to 300 feet. The obstacle geometry (walls of the commercial space) is introduced using a "geometry" component. Finally, using a "polyline" component, closed polylines are identified for each isovist, and, using the Area command, the area of each isovist is calculated (Figure 7.8c).

At this point, the dependent variable (isovist area) and independent variable (location of the target point identified by the two sliders) are ready for optimization using the Galapagos component. The Area component is connected to the Fitness input, and the two sliders are connected to the Genome input. Once the Galapagos solver is started by double-clicking it and selecting Start Solver, generations of target points are created and evaluated based on their isovist area (Figure 7.8b). To visualize the isovists more clearly during the optimization process, a "boundary surfaces" component may be added to the "polyline" component

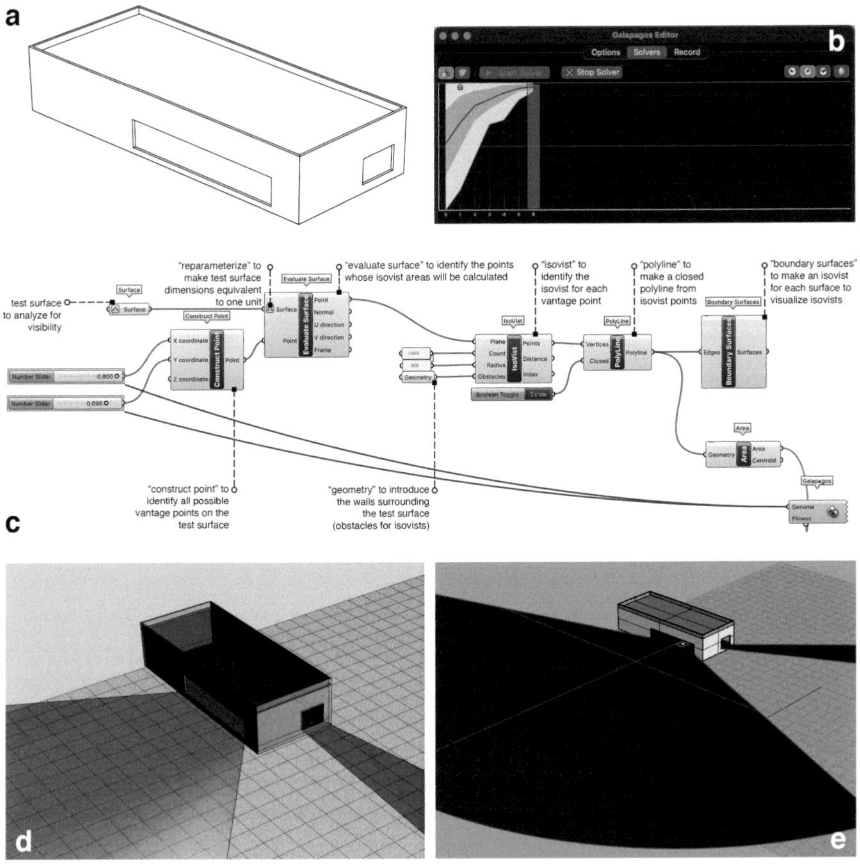

Figure 7.8 *(a) The imaginary commercial space with two storefronts; (b) Galapagos solver during the analysis process; (c) the Grasshopper definition used for analysis; (d) Rhinoceros screen during analysis showing one of the iterations; (e) the point with the highest visibility when both storefronts are considered.*

(Figure 7.8d). The process ends once the point with the highest isovist area with a radius of 300 feet is identified (Figure 7.8e).

7.5 MULTI-OBJECTIVE OPTIMIZATION

In optimization with evolutionary solvers, the decision-making process becomes more complicated since there is more than one dependent variable involved. In multi-objective optimization, the objective is to find genomes that meet more than one criterion at the same time. Nineteenth-century economist Vilfredo Pareto introduced the conceptual framework of multi-objective optimization in welfare economics. The "best decision" the idea relies on making a decision that works best for multiple factors. Making the best decision for one factor may affect another factor adversely, so trade-offs are involved. It may be necessary to compromise the best solution for one factor for the benefit of another, yielding a result that is good for both factors, but not necessarily the best (Radford and Gero, 1988).

The concept of multi-objective optimization is commonly explained using the "Pareto optimum." In the late-nineteenth century, Vilfredo Pareto introduced the Pareto optimum. The idea is that optimum allocation of resources in an economy is not achieved as long as at least one person can still be better off while other individuals are kept as well off (Radford and Gero, 1988).

For design processes, Radford and Gero (1988) suggested that Pareto optimization is realistic and useful since it allows subjective decision-making through consideration of trade-offs.

Such solutions are referred to as "Pareto front solutions," where the solution is based on the "best" compromise ultimately identified by the decision-maker in charge – the designer. Unlike single-objective optimization where the "best" fit is identified by a solver, in multi-objective optimization the results are interpreted by the designer, and the final decision is made through the designer's rationale and preferences. The Pareto optimum is commonly illustrated using a two-dimensional curve graph (Figure 7.9). In this graph, the round points have various values for both criteria 1 and 2. The objective is to select a round point that provides good results for both criterion (Radford and Gero, 1988).

The Octopus solver, a multi-objective solver developed by Robert Vierlinger based on the SPEA-2 and HypE algorithm, was developed at ETH Zurich. Based on the Pareto optimum idea, Octopus works on the premise of minimizing the values for multiple objectives (Vukorep and Kotov, 2021). Since minimizing the values for one objective will tend to maximize the other, findings require the user to consider trade-offs and pick the most reasonable option. Let us demonstrate a multi-objective optimization process using the Octopus solver.

7.5.1 Defining a Multi-objective Optimization Problem

In order to define a multi-objective optimization problem, we need to identify at least two dependent variables with criteria. In Section 7.4.1, we used the Galapagos solver to identify a building orientation that allows maximum access to desired views in an imaginary context. That was an example of a single-objective optimization process with one dependent variable. There may be additional orientation criteria in addition to maximizing access to desired views. For this example, we will introduce maximizing winter direct sun hours as the second dependent variable, since it would help decrease winter time heating energy use. We can therefore define a sample problem as "maximizing total winter direct sun hours and access to desired views based on orientation" for a sample building mass. To make the optimization results more recognizable, the proposed building mass is modified to slightly different proportions.

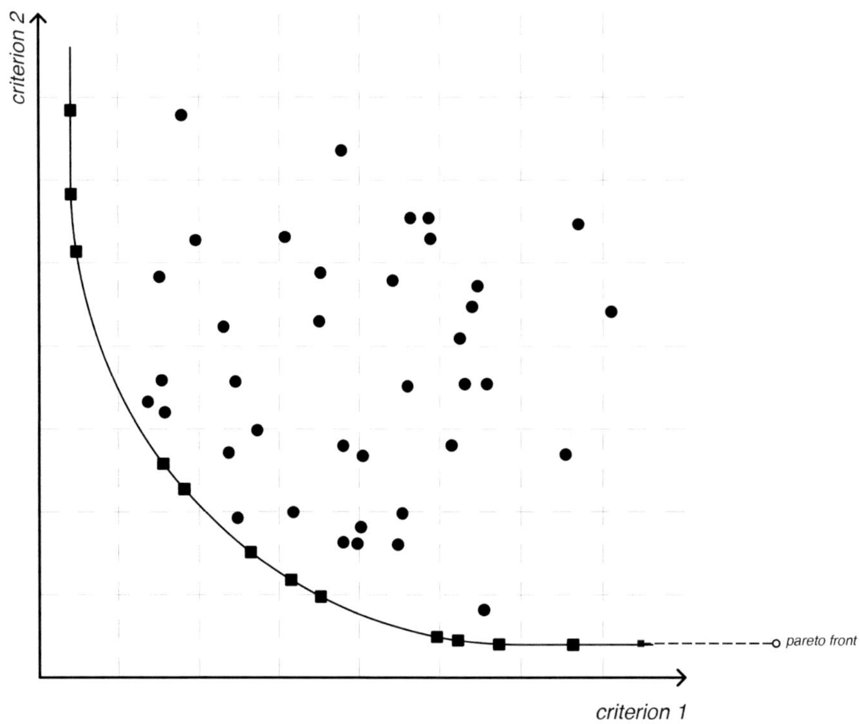

Figure 7.9 Pareto front for a sample optimization problem with two criteria.

7.5.2 The Optimization Procedure

The Grasshopper definition introduced in Figure 7.7c provides values for the first dependent variable, views to scenery. Using the same definition, Figure 7.10 illustrates the addition of the second dependent variable, winter direct sun hours, and the optimization process. Since we will need climate data to calculate winter direct sun hours, climate data is first imported into Grasshopper using Ladybug's "LB EPWMap" and "LB Download Weather" components. Location information (using the "LB Import Location" component), and the proposed building's footprint centroid are provided to the "LB Sun Path" component. Then, using the "LB Analysis Period" component, the analysis period is created: from November 1, 12:00 am to February 28, 11:00pm for winter. By connecting the "vectors" output to the LB Direct Sun Hours component's "vectors" input, sunlight vectors are provided.

The rotating modified building proposal from the definition in Figure 7.7c is used as the analysis geometry, and the context from the same figure is used to input the geometry of the buildings surrounding the proposed building. Grid size for analysis is set to 15 feet, and the numeric results of the LB Direct Sun Hours component are mass added using the "mass addition" component, yielding the total number of direct winter sun hours.

We now have the values for the two dependent variables to be optimized by the Octopus solver. The dependent variables, winter direct sun hours and views to scenery, are connected as the objectives, identified with an "O" on the Octopus solver component. Once the objectives are provided, it is time to specify the genomes, identified with a "G" on the Octopus solver component. The rotation angle provided by the rotation slider constitutes the genomes; therefore, it is connected to the "genomes" input of the Octopus solver. The optimization definition is now ready to run.

To start the Octopus solver, one needs to double-click on the Octopus solver. This opens the Octopus interface, showing the axes for dependent variables, and a series of settings component (Figure 7.10c). Under the navigation tab, settings such as population size, mutation rate and crossover rate are provided on the right column. These settings are similar to the settings discussed under the Galapagos solver interface introduced under single-objective optimization. On the left column, current conditions of an ongoing optimization process are provided. The middle panel is reserved for the Pareto front graph to display findings. The "export" tab allows exporting image and text information from the interface at various points during optimization – i.e., every generation.

The optimization process is started using the "start" button on the "navigation" tab. During optimization, the Rhinoceros and Grasshopper interfaces disappear, and findings slowly start appearing on the graph. The process is time consuming; however, it can be temporarily stopped using the "stop" button and restarted if necessary – the solver continues the process from where it left off.

7.5.3 Interpreting Findings

As discussed earlier, multi-objective optimization yields a number of solutions from which the user needs to make an informed selection. Figure 7.11 illustrates the optimization process findings at the end of 8 hours running the Octopus solver using a mid-range laptop with 16gB of RAM. The Pareto front for this process is displayed in a central location on the Octopus interface (Figure 7.11a). Taking a closer look into the graph, once can see that the most feasible options maximizing access to views as well as total winter direct sun hours exist around the central portion. The options on the top left of the graph maximize access to views, but fail to maximize the total winter direct sun hours. Likewise, the options on the bottom right maximize the total winter direct sun hours, but fail to maximize access to views (Figure 7.11b).

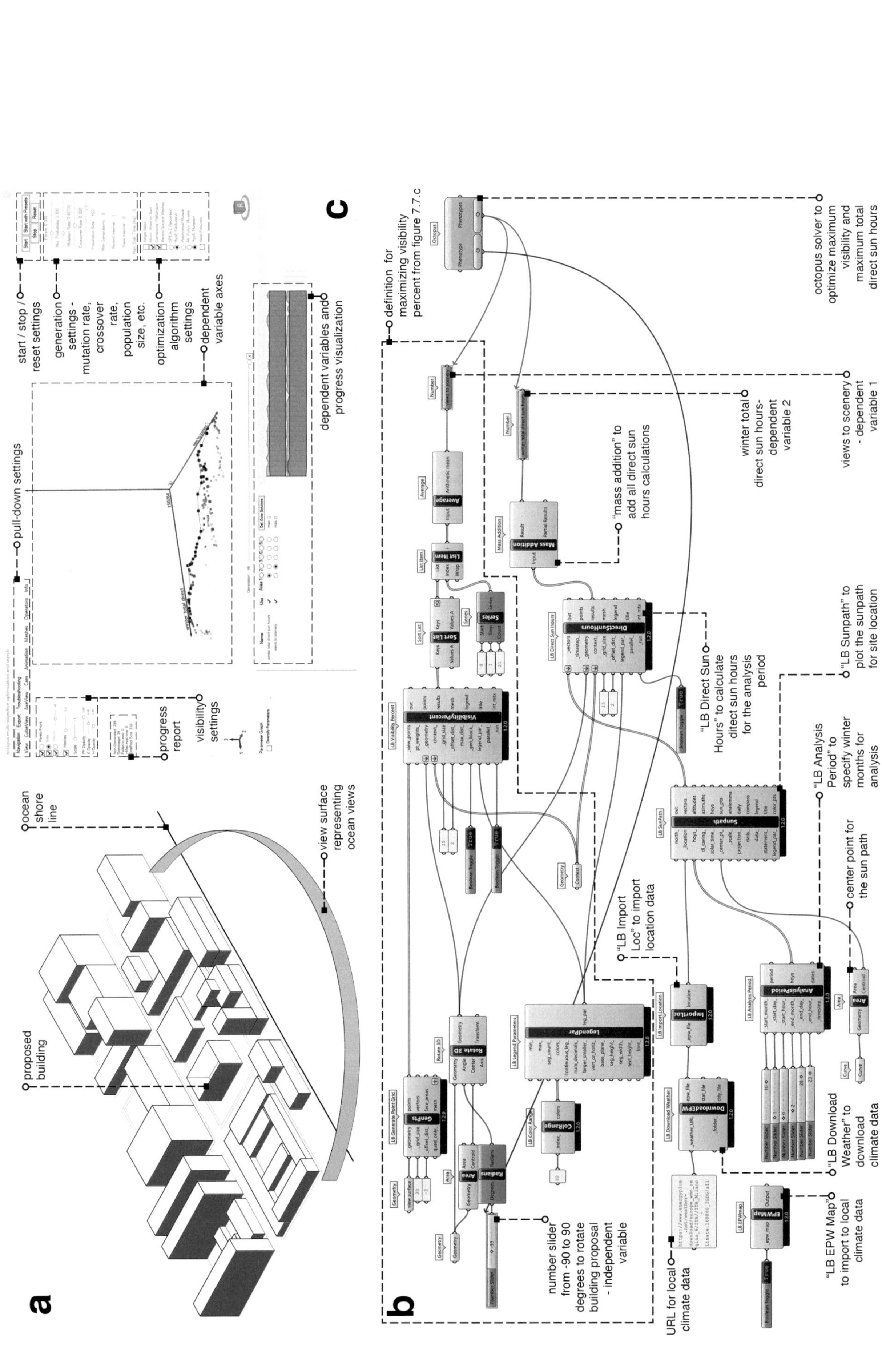

Figure 7.10 (a) The modified building design proposal from Section 7.4.2; (b) The Grasshopper definition used to set up the multi-objective optimization process; (c) Octopus solver interface.

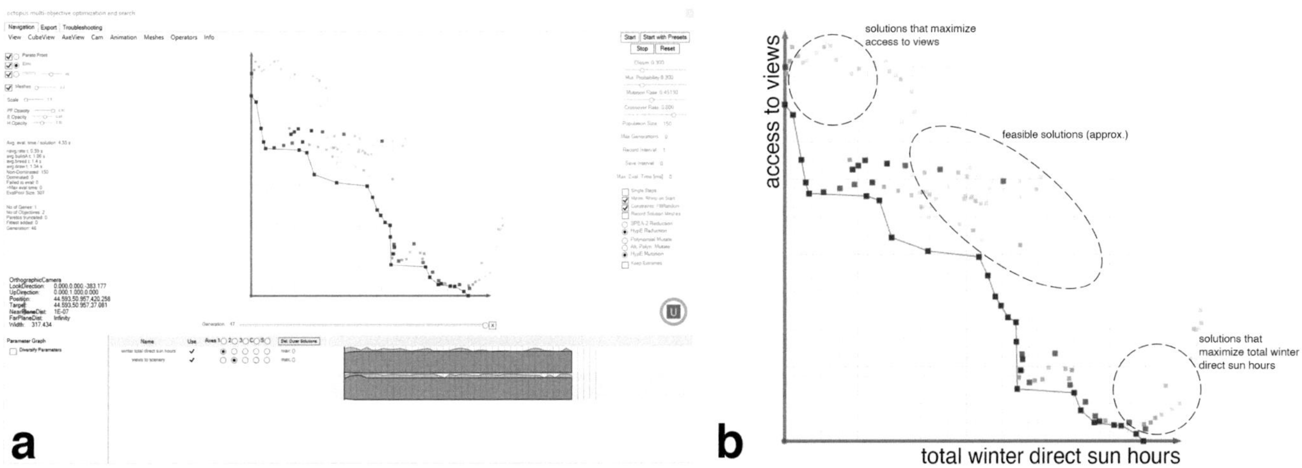

Figure 7.11 (a) Octopus solver interface at the end of eight hours of optimization; (b) optimization findings at the end of eight hours of optimization.

At this point we need to look at the options in the central portion of the graph and make an informed decision. Figure 7.12 illustrates three selected feasible options that maximize both access to views and total winter direct sun hours based on a 15' by 15' grid. While options a and b have a similar orientation, option c has a very different orientation. This shows the advantage of multi-objective optimization: by considering additional factors, one can make decisions about different orientations that satisfy both criteria. In this example, the designer needs to make an informed decision about orientation by taking additional factors into consideration.

It is important to note that none of the three options in Figure 7.12 are "best" options, but options that that approach the best-case scenario. Furthermore, there is no clear "end" to the optimization process. At the end of eight hours, the options displayed in Figure 7.12 were available. Had the optimization process be run longer, other, better performing options could be identified. Nevertheless, this is not guaranteed either. This exemplifies the user reliant nature of the multiple objective optimization process.

7.6 EVOLUTIONARY SOLVERS IN ARCHITECTURE: MULTI-OBJECTIVE OPTIMIZATION EXAMPLES

7.6.1 Optimizing Building Orientation to Minimize Energy Consumption

Let us consider a slightly more complicated scenario. In the example in Section 7.5, the objective was to maximize both criteria. Nevertheless, when energy consumption is considered, maximizing direct winter sun hours may not be sufficient. To minimize energy use, we usually wish to minimize direct sun hours in summer, and maximize direct sun hours in winter. This adds complexity to the equation: one of the dependent variables needs to be minimized, and the other needs to be maximized. We will discuss how to approach this problem in the following paragraphs. Let us first define the setting.

In Section 7.1, an imaginary urban lot was introduced. We can build a three-dimensional imaginary urban environment by using the same lot, and by assigning random heights to its surrounding buildings (Figure 7.13). To demonstrate the optimization problem defined, a simple sample building mass is introduced. The Grasshopper definition needs to be written such that Octopus calculates the minimum total summer direct sun hours and maximum total winter direct sun hours for every degree of rotation from 0 to 359 degrees.

Since we will need climate data to calculate direct sun hours, climate data are first imported into Grasshopper using Ladybug's "LB EPWMap" and "LB Download Weather" components (Figure 7.14). Location information (using the "LB Import Location" component) and

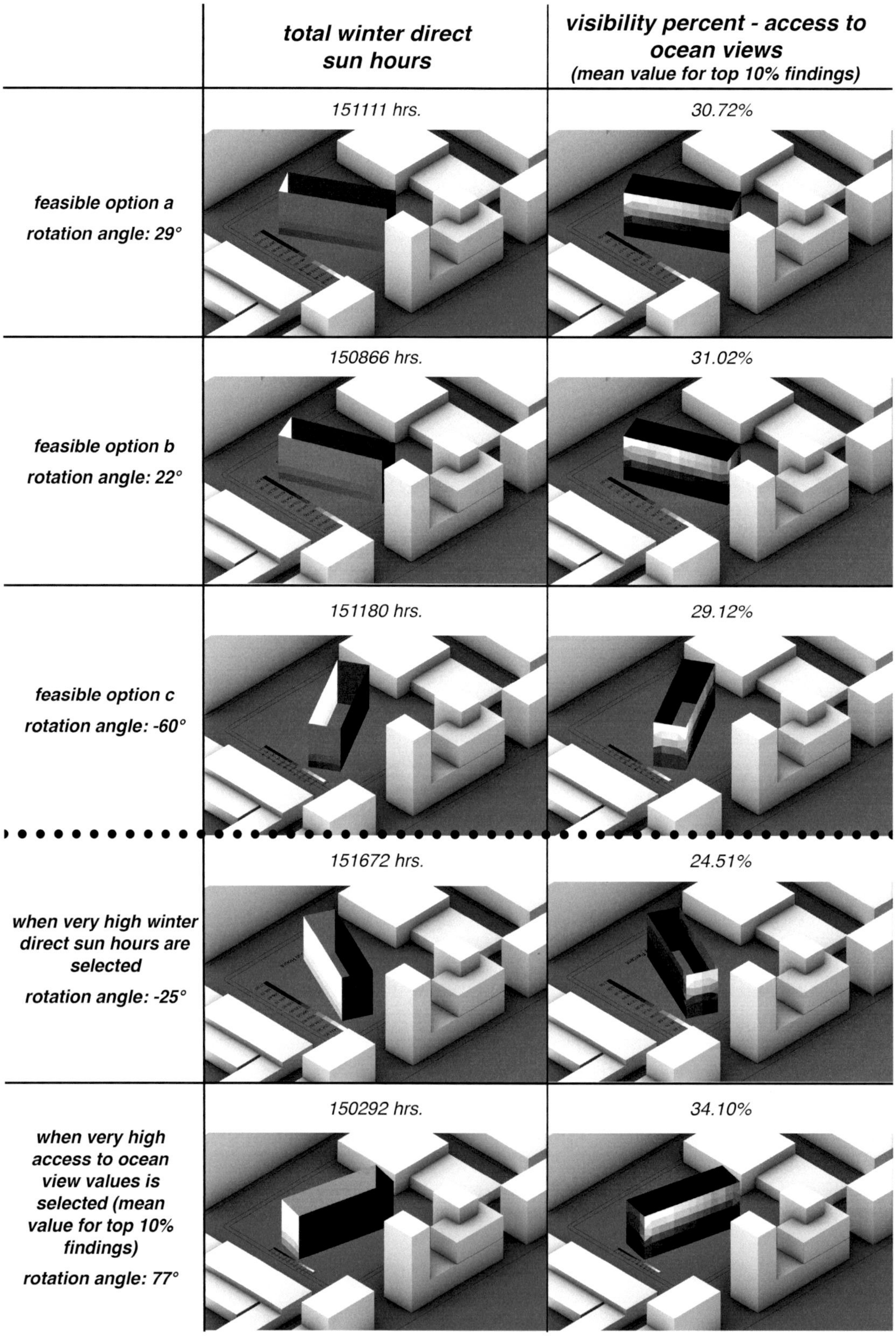

Figure 7.12 Matrix illustrating three selections from feasible options, one selection with very high winter direct sun hours, and one selection with very high access to ocean view values.

the building's footprint centroid (using "Point") are provided to the "LB Sun Path" component. Since we will analyze two time periods, two separate "LB Sun Path" components are created. Then, using two "LB Analysis Period" components, two analysis periods are created: from November 1, 12:00 am to February 28, 11:00pm for winter, and from June 1, 12:00 am

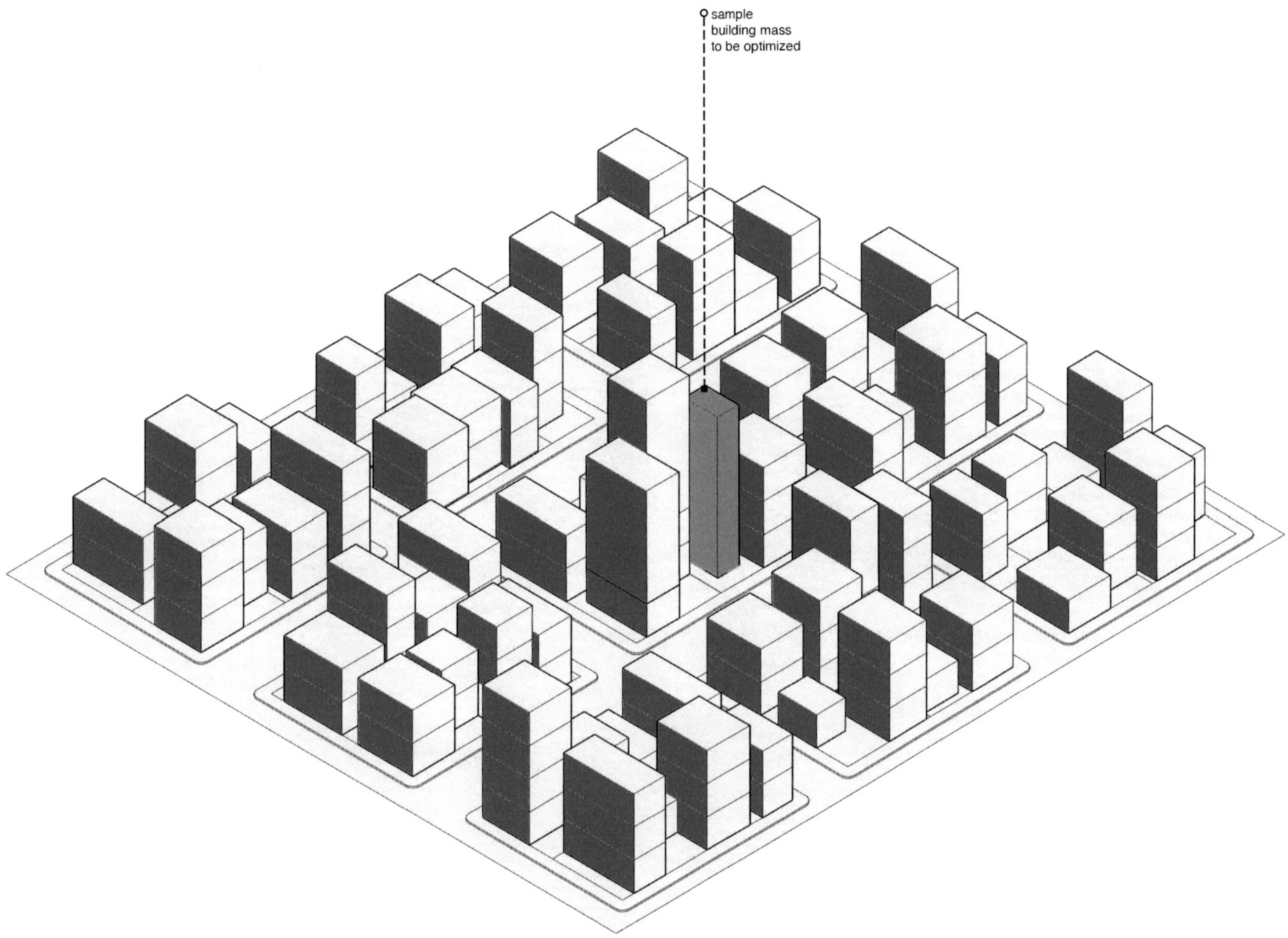

Figure 7.13 The sample urban context with the sample building mass. The orientation of the building will be optimized based on direct sun hours in winter and summer.

to September 30, 11:00pm. By connecting the "vectors" output to the LB Direct Sun Hours component's "vectors" input, sunlight vectors are provided. The context geometry is input by using a "geometry" component, setting it to "select multiple geometries," and connecting to the buildings surrounding the proposed building.

The proposed building mass' height is set up such that it is taller than two of its neighbors, and it is shorter than its third neighbor. Its geometry is input using a "geometry" component, and its rotation around its footprint's centroid is set up from 0 to 359 degrees using the Rotate 3D component. The output is then provided to LB Direct Sun Hours as the geometry to be analyzed, using the "_geometry" input. Finally, the "_grid_size" input is set to 3 feet to specify the size of the cells for which direct sun hours will be calculated. It is important to note here that the smaller the grid size, the higher resolution and detailed the analysis will be. However using smaller grid sizes, the analysis will take longer. One can decide the size of the grid based on time availability and desired analysis resolution. We now have access to direct sun hours for the proposed building through summer and winter, for each degree of rotation. Since the objective is to minimize the results for summer and maximize them for winter, both results from the LB Direct Sun Hours are mass added using the "mass addition" component.

The independent and dependent variables are now ready to be provided as input to the Octopus solver. The dependent variables, summer and winter direct sun hours, need to be connected as the objectives, identified with an "O" on the Octopus solver component. In doing so, since winter direct sun hours need to be maximized, and Octopus solver works by minimizing variables, we will set the total winter direct sun hours to negative, using the "negative"

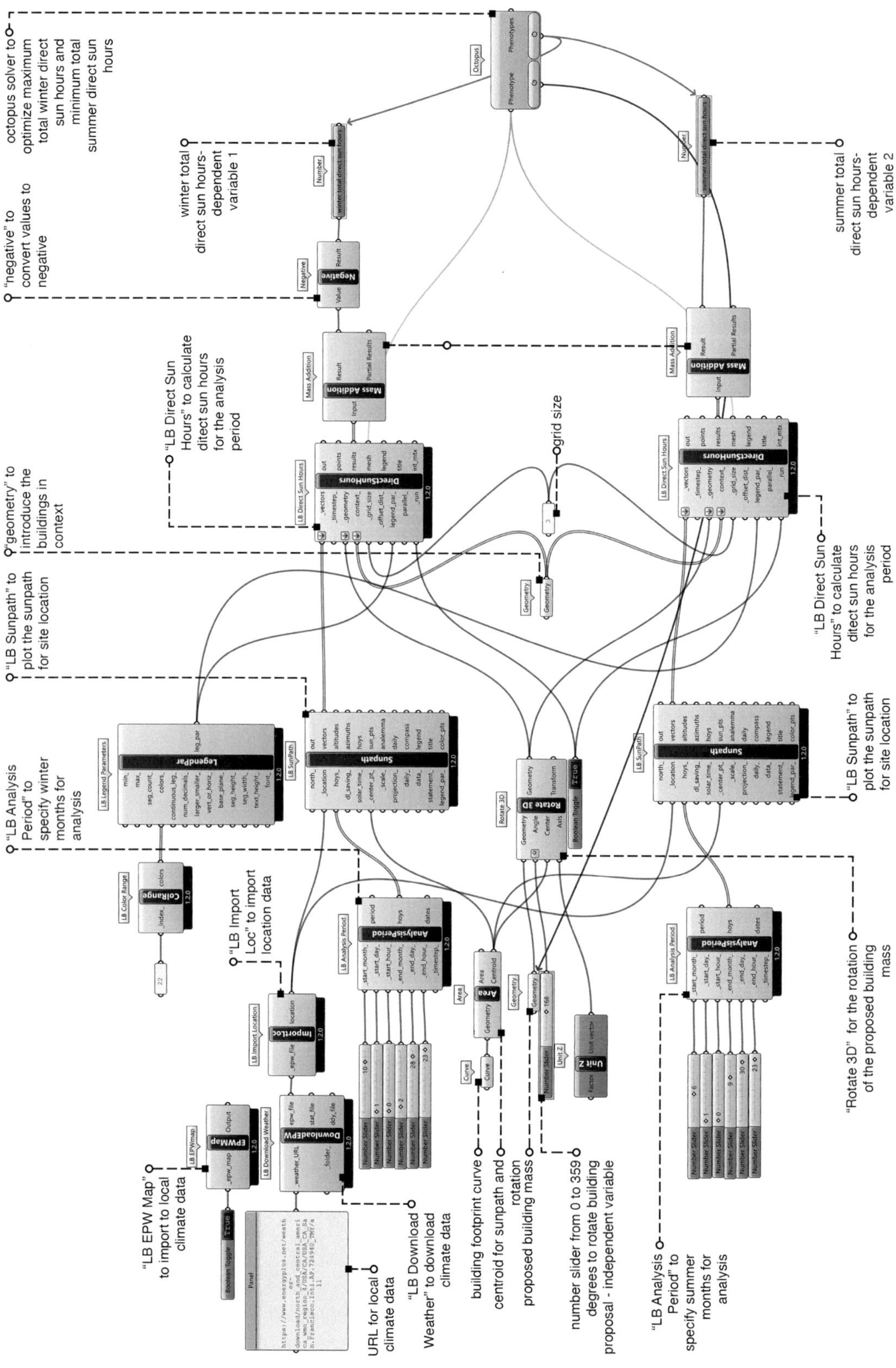

Figure 7.14 The Grasshopper definition used to set up the multi-objective optimization process.

component. This way, the smallest negative winter direct sun hour value will constitute a maximum. Once the objectives are provided, it is time to specify the genomes, identified with a "G" on the Octopus solver component. The rotation angle provided by the rotation slider constitute the genomes, therefore it is connected to the "genomes" input of the Octopus solver. The optimization definition is now ready to run (Figure 7.14).

Once the Octopus solver is started, it calculates maximum winter and summer direct sun hours for the proposed building mass for numerous generations of genomes. In this example, the optimization process was run for ten hours. Figure 7.15 illustrates the findings from the optimization process based on a 3' by 3' grid.

Three of the orientation options from the feasible solutions area of the Pareto front (Figure 7.15b) were selected and compared. As in the previous example, diverse orientation options were feasible according to the two optimization criteria (Figure 7.16).

Figure 7.16 shows that diverse orientation options can maximize winter direct summer hours and

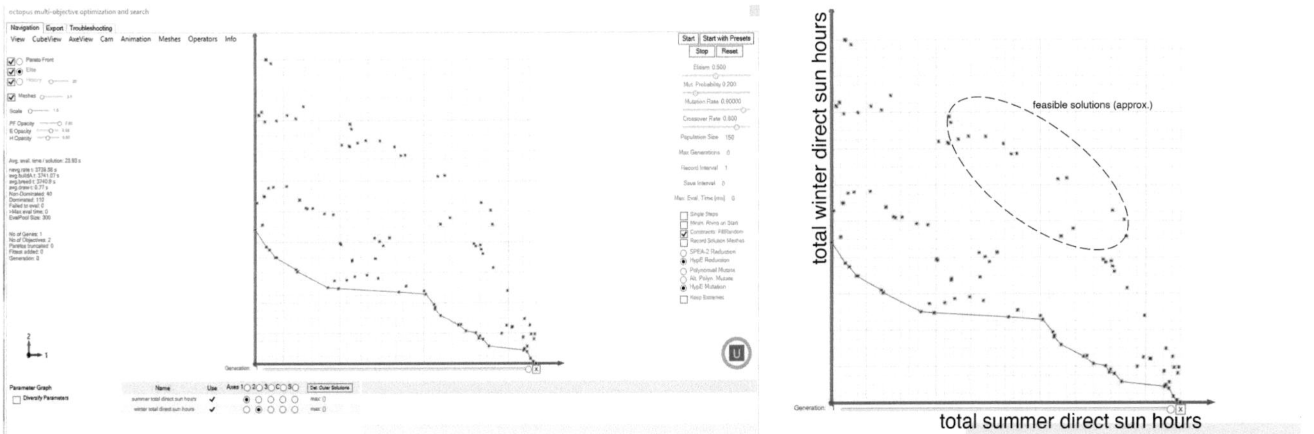

Figure 7.15 (a) Octopus solver interface at the end of 10 hours of optimization; (b) optimization findings at the end of 10 hours of optimization.

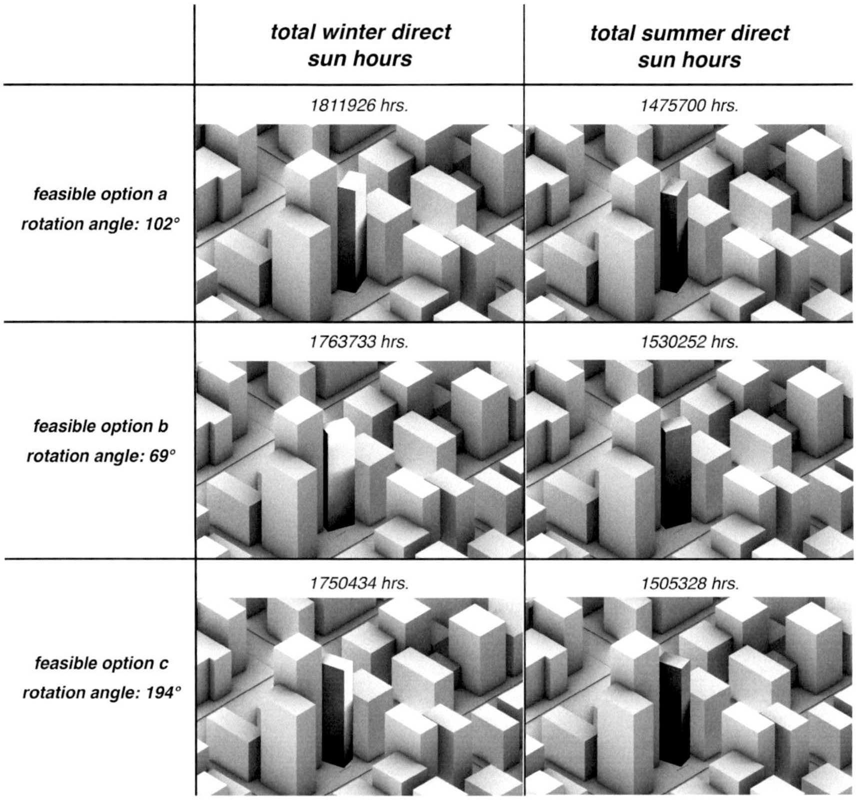

Figure 7.16 Matrix illustrating three selections from feasible options, one selection with very high winter direct sun hours, and one selection with very high access to ocean view values.

minimize summer direct sun hours. As in the previous example, the three options selected do not constitute the "best" options. Once again, by considering other design objectives and the outcomes of this optimization process, the designer can make a better-informed decision about orientation.

7.6.2 Optimizing Views and Square Footage to Increase Real Estate Value

The final multi-objective optimization example we will introduce entails optimization in regard to views and square footage. In many cases, it will be in the interest of the project to maximize not only access to desirable views, but also square footage for financial reasons. In Section 7.4.2, we demonstrated a single-objective optimization process to maximize access of a proposed building massing to desirable views by varying its orientation. In this example, we will revisit the imaginary environment created for the example from Section 7.4.2. In this scenario, instead of changing the building's orientation, we will introduce randomized pop-outs to the sides of the building. The randomized pop-outs will not only alter the building proposal's access to desirable views, but also its total square footage. Therefore, the introduction of randomized pop-outs will constitute the independent variable. The building proposal's access to desirable views and square footage will constitute the dependent variables. The optimization process will target maximizing the dependent variables.

Figure 7.17 illustrates the imaginary waterfront environment from Section 7.4.2 with a different proposed building mass. The proposed building is 96 feet tall with eight 12-foot floors, and its footprint dimensions are 180 feet × 100 feet. Assuming that we are not allowed to change the orientation of the building to maximize access to ocean views, random 14 foot × 45 foot pop-outs are proposed for the sides of the building. Accordingly, there is space for a total of 32 pop-outs on each side of the building. To allow pop-outs (that are further away from

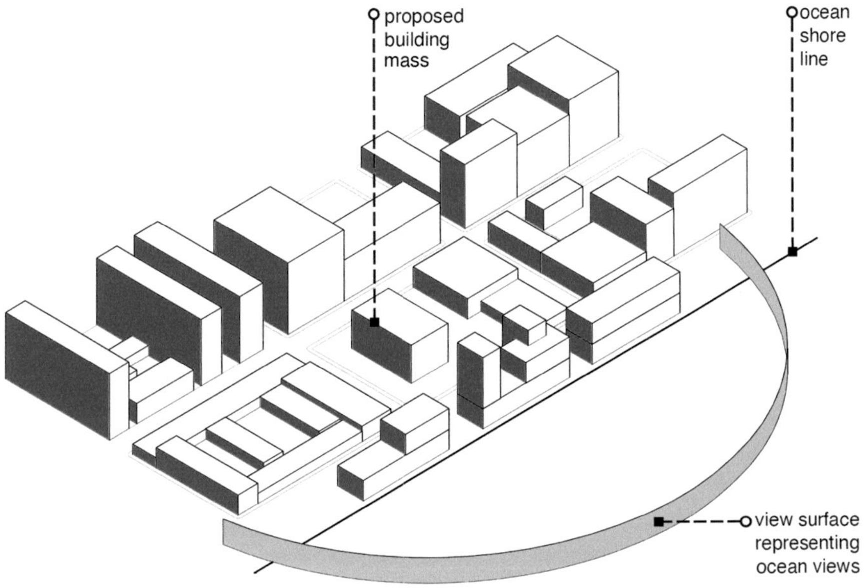

Figure 7.17 The imaginary waterfront environment from Section 7.4.2 with a different proposed building mass.

the waterfront) some access to ocean views, a maximum of eight pop-outs per side will be allowed.

The definition developed for maximizing square footage and access to ocean views generates five main tasks for Grasshopper: (i) create the maximum number of 32 pop-outs on both sides of the building and randomly select a maximum of 8 of them (maximum of 16 total pop-outs), (ii) join the selected pop-outs with the main building mass, (iii) measure the total square footage of each iteration including the selected pop-outs, (iv) measure the total ocean view iteration including the selected pop-outs, and (v) optimize iterations to maximize square footage and access to ocean views.

Creation and Random Selection of Pop-outs. First, the main building mass, a rectangular prism, is introduced to Grasshopper as a "Brep," and it is deconstructed using the "Deconstruct Brep" component. The two longitudinal sides of the building are selected using the List Item component, yielding two faces. Each of the faces are then subdivided into 32 rectangles, which constitute the base for the pop-outs that will be created. Since the two parts of the definition so far yield two lists with 32 pop-outs each, random selection will be executed using the List Item component (Figure 7.18a).

For random selection of a maximum of eight pop-outs per side, two "Random" components are used. Using the "construct domain" component, an integer domain from 0 to 31 is developed, and the output is provided as the "range" input for the "Random" component, so that the randomly created numbers are between 0 and 31 (since Grasshopper creates lists starting with 0, a total of 32 values are created using a slider from 0 to 31). The number of random numbers to be created is set to 8, and the "seed" value is connected to two integer sliders that operate between 0 and 20. Random selection is executed by setting the Octopus solver to continuously alter the "seed" value. To generate one set of random numbers, the output is flattened. The random values created may not be integers, therefore the values are rounded to the nearest possible integer using the "Round" component. To avoid any duplicate values, the output is fed into the "Sort Duplicate Values" component, and the output list is grafted to ensure individual item selections. Now, the randomly selected eight rectangles for each side of the building are ready to be extruded.

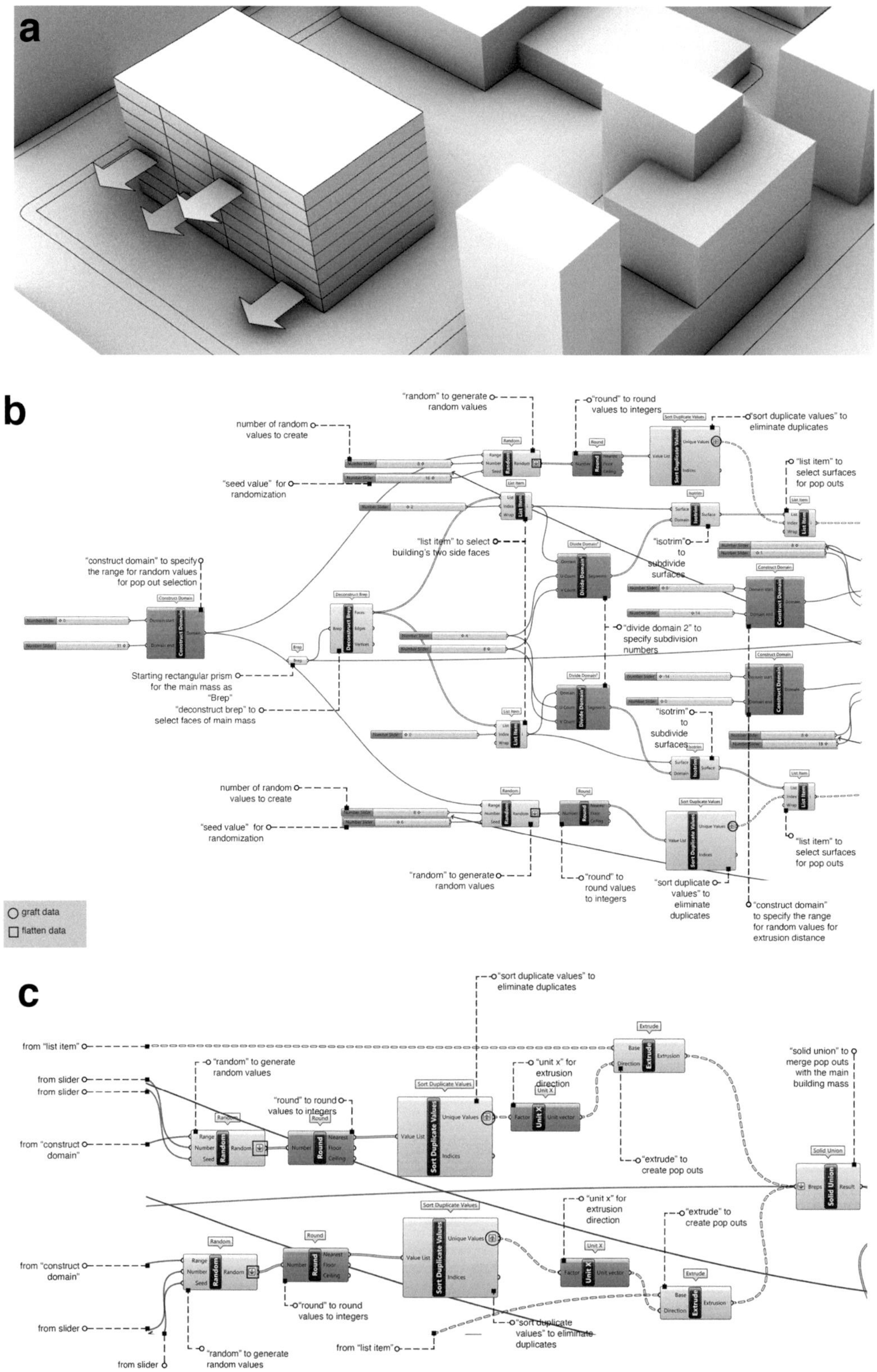

Figure 7.18 *(a) Surface subdivision for extrusion of pop-outs; (b) portion of the Grasshopper definition for random selection of surfaces to extrude; (c) portion of the Grasshopper definition for generating random extrusion values, extrusion, and union with the main building mass.*

Instead of assigning a constant depth value to the pop-outs, the extrusion value is also randomized. Using a randomization procedure similar to the random selection of rectangles, two domains are defined using the "Construct Domain" component: one from 0 to 14 (for the positive X direction), and one from –14 to 0 (for the negative X direction). The domains are connected to the "range" input of the "Random" component, the number of values to be created is set to 8, and sliders from 0 to 20 are used to provide the seed value. Since altering the "seed" values will randomly alter the extrusion depth, the seed sliders will also act as independent variables. Finally, the "extrude" component is used on the X direction and –X direction to assign random extrusion values to randomly selected rectangles (Figure 7.18b).

Joining the Selected Pop-Outs with the Main Building Mass. Once the extrusion is set up, the resulting selection of pop-outs are joined with the main building mass using a "Solid Union" component. The portion of the Grasshopper definition that generates mass composition iterations is now complete, and the outcomes are ready to be connected to area and visibility percent measurement tasks (Figure 7.18c).

Measuring the Total Square Footage of Each Iteration Including the Selected Pop-Outs. Now that the building mass iterations are ready to run, the procedure that will measure the total square footage of each iteration needs to be developed. For this procedure, a cutting plane above each "floor" of the building needs to be set, so that the square footage of each floor of the building can be measured. To generate the cut planes, the centroid of the main building mass is generated using the Area component. Using the "rectangle" component, a rectangle is created around the centroid point. Using the Construct Domain component, a domain from –200 feet to 200 feet is defined (so that the rectangle is large enough to slice the main building mass and its pop-outs), and the outcome is connected to the X and Y dimension inputs of the "Rectangle" component. Finally, using the "Boundary Surfaces" component, a rectangular surface is created. The cutting plane is now ready.

In the following step, the rectangles are copied vertically. To make sure each cut accurately represents a floor, using the "Series" component, a series that starts at 3 feet is created, and a total of eight height values are created with 12 foot intervals representing floor height. The resulting series is connected to the "Z Unit" component, and the cutting planes are created vertically at 12 foot intervals using the "Move" component. The building mass from the "Solid Union" component is then sliced with the cutting plane using the "Brep | Brep" component, yielding the outline of each floor's footprint. The area of each floor is measured using the Area component, and the results are mass-added using the "Mass Addition" component. The output of the "Mass Addition" component yields the first dependent variable in our scenario: the building's total square footage for each iteration.

Measuring the Total Ocean View Percentage of Each Iteration. To measure the ocean view percentage of the iterations, Ladybug's LB Visibility Percent component is used. The iteration outputs from the "Solid Union" component are provided as the geometry to be analyzed. The surrounding context is set to multiple geometries, and buildings surrounding the proposed building mass are introduced as the context.

As in Section 7.4.2, a semicircular surface is introduced as the target geometry representing ocean views, and it is subdivided to create target points using a "LB Generate Point Grid" component. The offset distance from analyzed surfaces is 5.5 feet, and the maximum analysis distance is set to 10,000 feet. The "_geo_block" input is set to "true" to take pop-outs blocking each other's views into consideration. For visualization purposes, Ladybug's "LB Legend Par" and LB Color Range components are used, and the color index is set to 5 to get a black and white visualization of results. Finally, the visibility percent analysis results are connected to the Mass Addition component to calculate the total ocean view percent. The output of Mass Addition component yields the second dependent variable in our scenario: the building's total ocean view percentage (Figure 7.19).

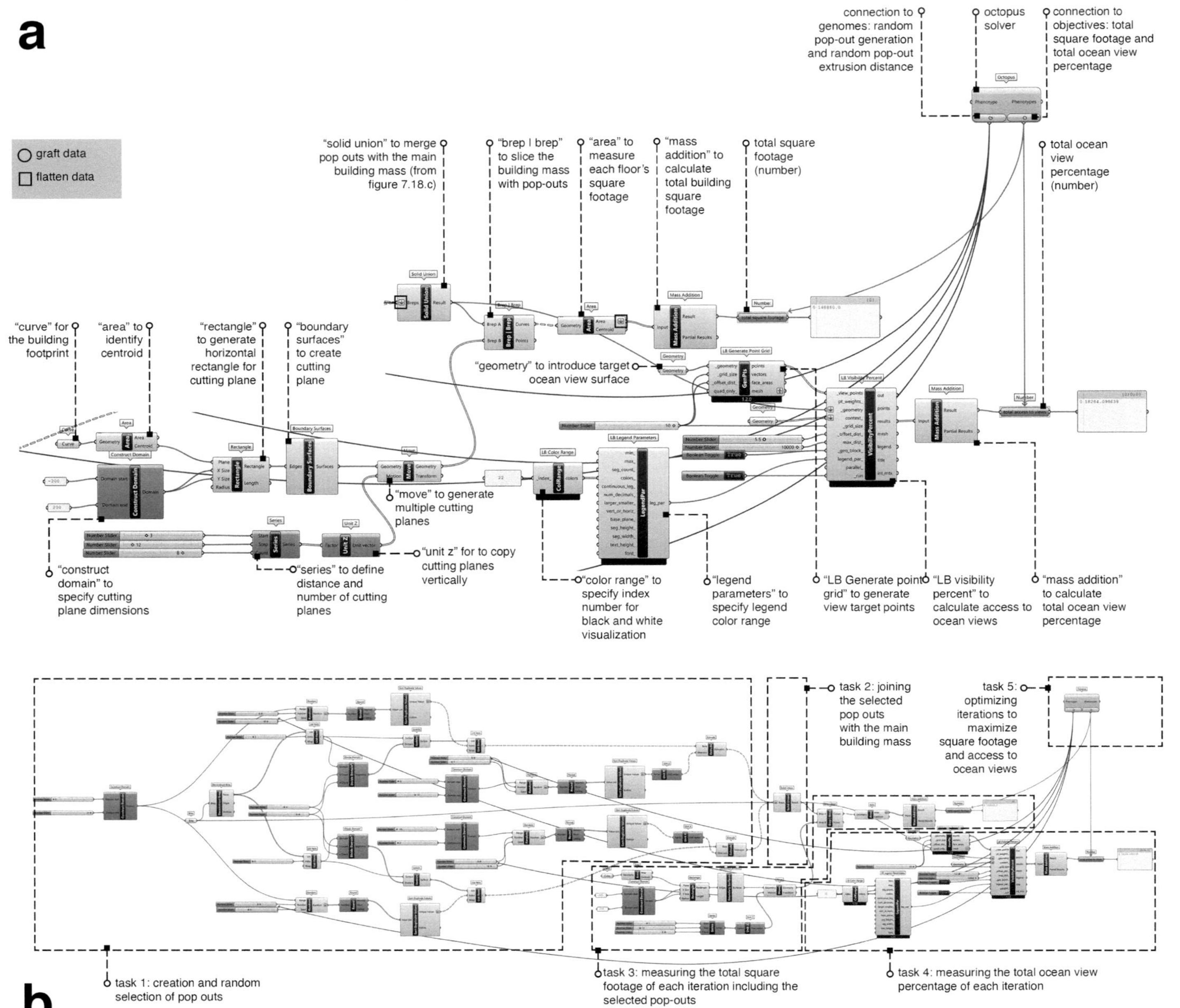

Figure 7.19 *(a) Measuring the total square footage of each iteration including the selected pop-outs, measuring the total ocean view percentage of each iteration, and optimizing iterations to maximize square footage and access to ocean views; (b) summary visualization of the complete Grasshopper definition used for all five tasks introduced.*

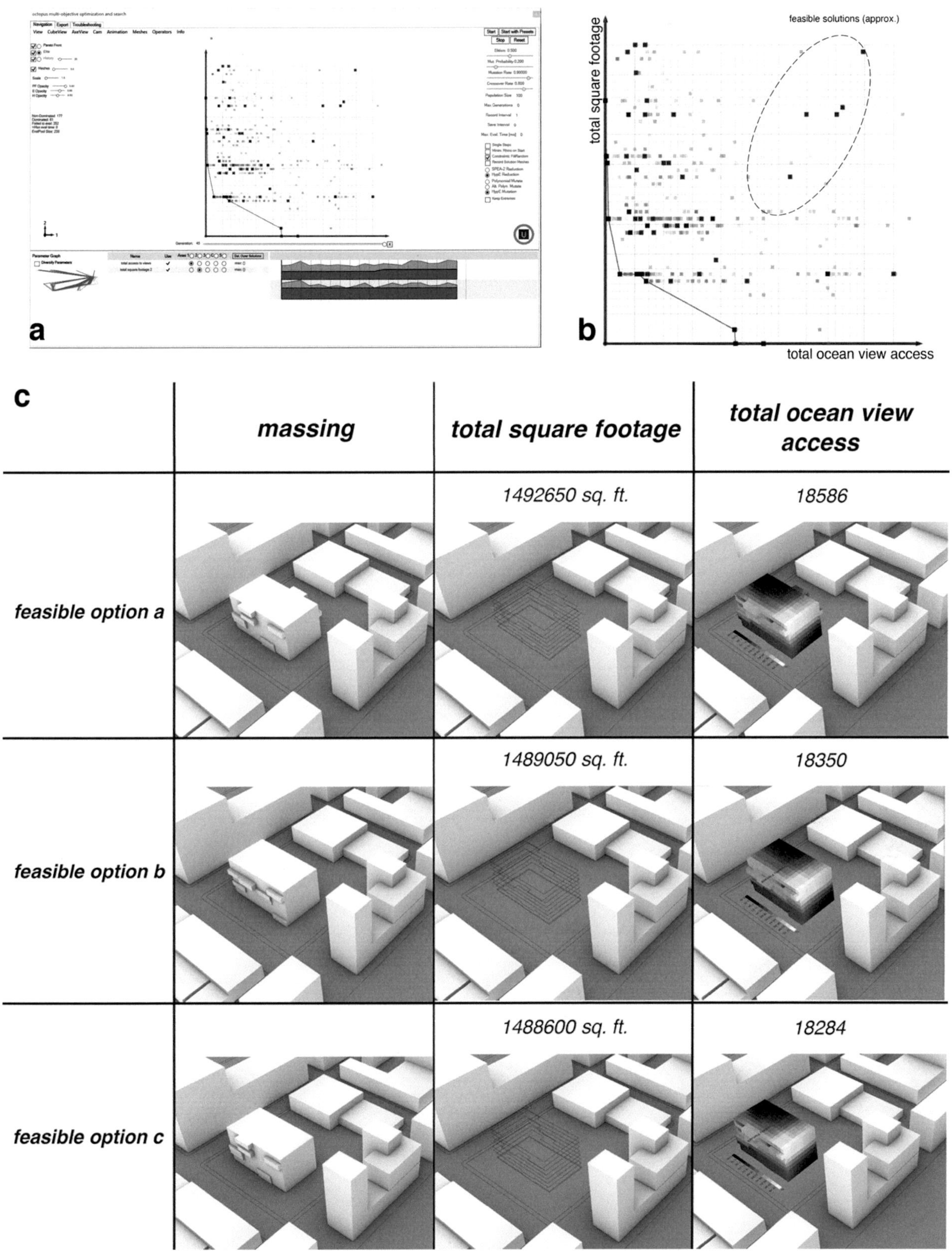

Figure 7.20 (a) Octopus solver interface during optimization; (b) optimization findings; (c) three feasible options.

Optimizing Iterations to Maximize Square Footage and Access to Ocean Views. The Grasshopper definition is now ready to run the optimization task. The Octopus solver is introduced, and first, the two dependent variables are connected as the objectives (the "O" input of the Octopus solver): the building's total square footage and total ocean view percentage. Then, the independent variables are introduced to provide the genomes: the randomly generated pop-outs and their randomly generated depth. The sliders that randomize the location of the pop-outs and the sliders that randomize the extrusion value are connected to the phenotypes ("P" input) of the Octopus solver (Figure 7.19a). We are now ready to run the optimization process. Figure 7.19a illustrates the Grasshopper definition developed for the last two tasks, and Figure 7.19b illustrates a summary visualization of the complete Grasshopper definition used for all five tasks introduced.

With two dependent variables and four randomization sliders, the optimization process is time intensive. For this example, the optimization process was run for 45 generations of genomes for approximately 12 hours. At the end of the 45-generation optimization process, the findings were clear. The Octopus solver was able to identify a good number of feasible options, with five iterations especially successful in meeting the criteria. Figure 7.20 illustrates the three feasible mass composition iterations that yield the highest square footage and ocean view access. As in the previously discussed multi-objective optimization tasks, the high-performing iterations introduced in this section are not the "best" options, but are iterations that perform better than many others. Had the optimization process been run for a longer time, the Octopus solver might be able to find better-performing iterations.

CHAPTER 08

PARAMETRIC METHODS FOR INTRODUCTORY ENVIRONMENTAL PERFORMANCE ANALYSES

Parametric methods prove helpful for evaluating the environmental performance of building proposals in early and more advanced design development stages. In this chapter, we will introduce environmental performance indicators for buildings and discuss how parametric methods can support design decisions in various design phases. Our focus will be on the environmental performance indicators of building proposals, with emphases on energy and human comfort issues. More specifically, we will discuss energy use and daylight-related indicators.

8.1 ARCHITECTURAL DESIGN AND ENERGY

Anytime humans build an object, the process and the product have energy impacts. All production processes require energy. Energy consumption for the built environment starts as early as the beginning of the design process. We use energy not only for producing the tools we use daily, but also for making our physical environments comfortable during the design process. Production of a simple pencil, running a computer for drawings and simulations, and heating and air conditioning an office all require energy consumption.

The construction and occupancy of the buildings we design consume extremely high amounts of energy. During construction, it is not just the production of building materials that consumes energy: transportation of materials, their assembly, and finishing all require energy. Following occupancy, energy consumption continues. Heating, ventilation, air conditioning, mechanical systems, maintenance, cleaning, elevators, etc. all use energy.

The materials we use to build elements of the built environment also require energy consumption for material extraction, preparation, and manufacturing. This is commonly referred to as embodied energy. This implies that all design processes for the built environment have energy consumption implications from the manufacturing of materials to the occupancy of the built environment.

This requires architects to be informed about the energy use implications of the project site (as discussed in Chapter 3) as well as the energy use implications of every design decision made, since energy is expensive. Energy is not only expensive from an economical point of view, but also from an environmental point of view: harnessing and generating energy have *both* economic and environmental costs. For example, extracting and using fossil fuels, such as oil, not only costs money but also negatively impacts the natural environment by increasing emissions of greenhouse gases (GHG), which contribute to global warming.

Over the past decades, architectural researchers and designers have developed measurement and simulation methods to quantify energy use prediction. Using these methods,

DOI: 10.4324/9781003230052-8

we have been able to calculate estimated energy implications for design proposals. More recently, architectural researchers and designers have also developed guides to help architects design toward minimizing energy consumption and dependency while contributing to human comfort.

Parametric methods in architecture can contribute to early and later design process phases by enabling rapid and efficient analyses of building proposals' energy consumption and comfort. Energy use in an occupied building is also related to the connections between the sun as a source of light, and the proposed building's spaces based on their lighting needs. Based on a building's location, different light levels and, therefore, different energy consumption levels may be required. Architectural design can address these issues during design stage to optimize the use of daylight and reduce energy consumption. In the following sections, we will look into an influential set of architectural guides that target minimizing energy consumption. This will be followed by a discussion of specific energy use-related measures and related parametric methods.

8.1.1 Architecture 2030

Over the recent decades, it has become evident that the worldwide building sector is one of the greatest contributors to global warming due to the carbon emissions associated with energy consumption. Carbon emissions are not only a result of building operations, but also the embodied energy of building materials through material extraction and production processes. Global climatic changes recorded by the scientific community in recent decades have triggered responses in many disciplines including architecture and related disciplines with a focus on built environment. Academia, nonprofit organizations, as well as think tanks worldwide have contributed to idea generation on potential actions to eliminate global warming and minimize its adverse effects.

One of these organizations is Architecture 2030, a US-based independent, nonprofit organization intending to respond to the climate changes we are currently experiencing. Led by Edward Mazria, FAIA, Architecture 2030 highlights that about 40% of annual carbon dioxide emissions worldwide are generated by buildings, and an estimated 11% of carbon contributions to the system (referred to as embodied carbon) is due to building materials and construction. Consequently, Architecture 2030 sets as its main objectives to significantly reduce fossil fuel-based carbon emissions, and to build foundations for an equitable, resilient, and zero-carbon emissions built environment. A key step for achieving these objectives is to reduce energy use, and then power new and existing buildings using renewable energy – thus cutting or minimizing carbon emissions. The common metric used for energy consumption is the site energy use intensity (EUI), measured in kBtu/sq. ft./yr (thousands of British thermal units used per square foot, per year), based on the building type (i.e., the programmatical use intent of the building). The "Zero Tool", developed by Architecture 2030, has identified the average energy consumption of building design proposals based on building use and its climatic context. It also helps identify an energy consumption target for the building design proposal that can meet the Architecture 2030 challenge (Architecture 2030, n.d.).

8.1.2 Energy Use Intensity

Energy use intensity indicates the total energy consumption of a building per unit area (i.e., square feet or square meters). The EUI acts as a method to evaluate a building's energy consumption. Using the Imperial system, the EUI is commonly calculated as kBTU/sq. ft./year; while using the International System of Units (SI), it is calculated as kilowatt hours per square meter per year (kWh/m^2/year). The EUI calculations for a building prove helpful in comparing its performance against energy use standards or against other buildings of the same type. Since different building types have different energy needs and consumption requirements, cross-comparisons are made within the same typology. Calculating estimated EUI of design proposals in the early phases of the design process can help the designer in decision-making about mass composition as well as aperture strategies.

8.1.3 Surface Area to Volume Ratio

The "Surface Area to Volume Ratio" (SA/V) is another important metric relating to the energy consumption of a building. A significant value also in science and engineering, SA/V is calculated as an object's surface area per unit volume of that object. The SA/V value of a building can impact its energy consumption since a high SA/V value means more interface with the external environment. Depending on the building's context, SA/V values may mean high heating or cooling needs, thus affecting the energy consumption of that building. High SA/V values mean more exposure to the external environment.

A simple cube example can help illustrate the relationships between surface area and volume. Let us consider a 10' × 10' × 10' cube. The surface area of the cube is 6 × 10 × 10, therefore a total of 600 square feet. Its volume, on the other hand, is 10 × 10 × 10, therefore a total of 100 cubic feet. This cube's SA/V equals 6. If we simply increase the size of the cube to 20' × 20' × 20', its SA/V value will significantly decrease. While the cube's surface area would rise to 2,400 square feet (6x20x20), its volume would increase to 8,000 (20 × 20 × 20), causing the cube's SA/V value to drop to 0.3. Calculating SA/V values of building mass composition proposals in the early design phases can prove helpful in making decisions in relation to local climatic factors.

8.2 PARAMETRIC METHODS FOR ANALYZING ENERGY USE IMPLICATIONS

Now that we looked into the basic definition of EUI and SA/V values, let us discuss the use of parametric methods in the evaluation of design proposals. Parametric methods offer time and effort saving strategies in early and more advanced design phases in the architectural design process.

8.2.1 EUI: Basic Simulation Using Ladybug, Honeybee, and Honeybee Energy

As we discussed in Chapter 3, Ladybug Tools provide time efficient methods for calculations and analyses of environmental data. It is possible to calculate EUI values for design proposals using a combination of the Grasshopper Plug-ins, Ladybug (LB), Honeybee (HB), and Honeybee Energy (HB-E). These plug-ins allow the user to analyze a design proposal as a single use zone or a building composed of multiple use zones. In this section, we will start the discussion on using Ladybug Tools on a simple house design proposal, which will be defined as a single use zone building. In the following sections we will go into more complex options of analysis with multiple use zones.

As an introduction to basic energy simulation, we will develop an energy use simulation definition for a simple fictitious single-family house design proposal in San Francisco, CA. The house is composed of an L-shaped mass with a flat roof, with 11 transparent apertures – windows as well as glass sliding doors for access to an outdoor patio. Honeybee and Honeybee Energy plug-ins require that for energy simulations, building masses are modeled as closed polysurfaces, and apertures are modeled as simple open surfaces coplanar with the walls of the main closed polysurface. Therefore, in this example, the house was modeled as a single closed polysurface with apertures coplanar with its surfaces (the flat roof parapet was added for visualization purposes only) (Figure 8.1a and 8.1b).

In Honeybee, a "use zone" can be defined as a simple geometry, using a "HB Room from Solid" component. Since our intent is to conduct an energy use simulation on a single-use zone residential unit, a closed polysurface is introduced into Grasshopper using a basic "geometry" component to represent the L-shaped, single-floor, and flat-roof house. On the HB Room from Solid component, the "_conditioned" input is set to "true" using a Boolean toggle.

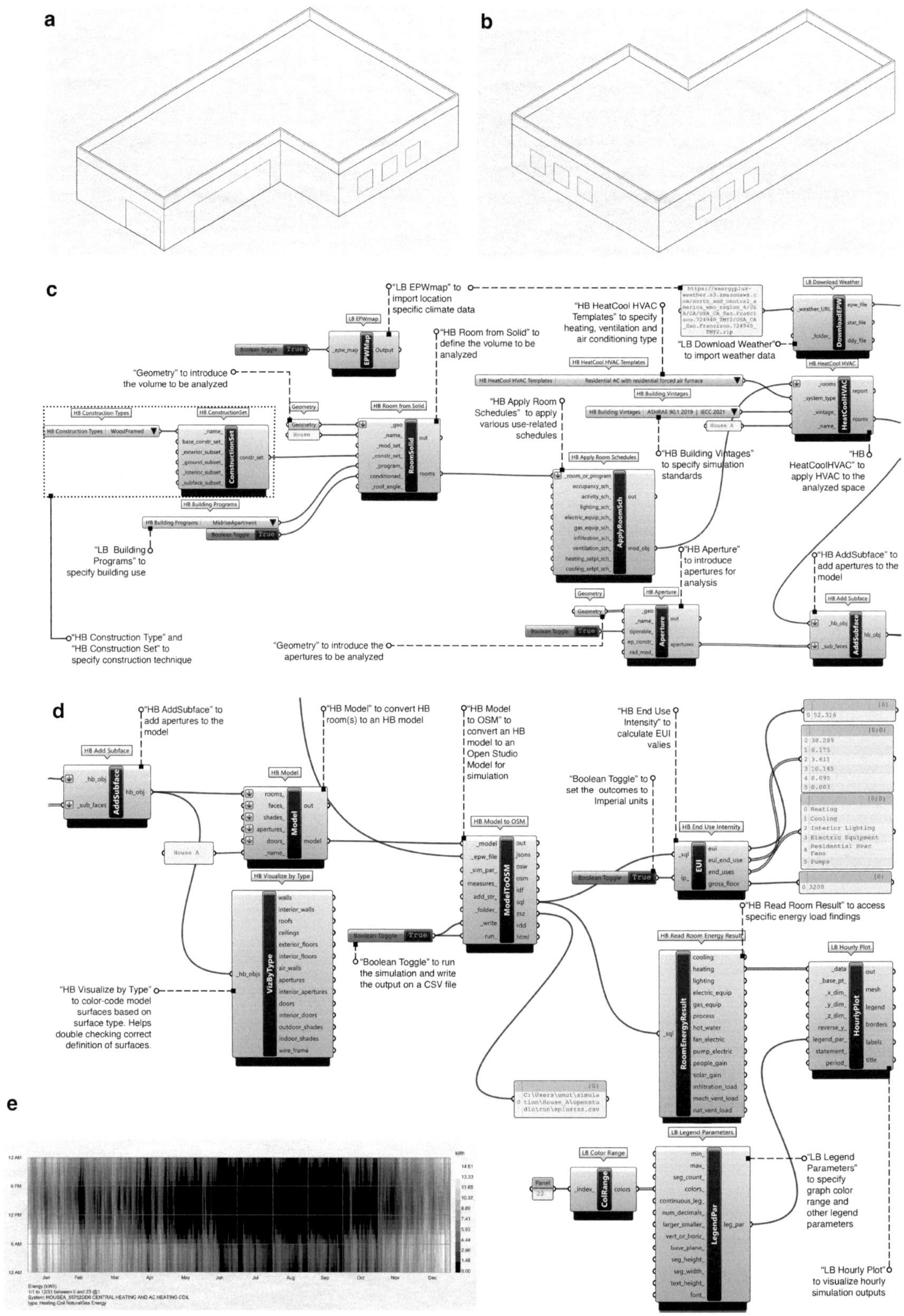

Figure 8.1 *(a) The fictitious L-shaped San Francisco house with a flat roof, 11 transparent apertures, and a southeast view; (b) the same fictitious L-shaped San Francisco house with a flat roof, 11 transparent apertures, and a northwest view; (c) preparation of Rhinoceros geometry and data inputs for energy use simulation; (d) running the analysis with the HB Model to OSM component, reading EUI results using the "HB End Use Intensity" component; and (e) an example of reading the yearlong hourly heating energy loads using the HB Read Room Energy Result and "LB Hourly Plot" components. The legend output was set to black and white using the LB Legend Parameters and "LB Color Range" components.*

To emulate a small residential environment, the building type was set to the closest option, "midrise apartment" using the "HB Building Programs" component. The "_conditioned" input was set to "true" using a Boolean toggle to indicate that the house's interiors will be mechanically conditioned. Finally, to specify the construction technique for the house, Honeybee's "HB ConstructionSet" component was used and "woodframed" was selected as the construction type, since the proposed house design is in San Francisco, CA, USA – a common construction technique for this location (Figure 8.1c).

The resulting HB Room was further edited using the "HBHeatCool HVAC", specifying the heating and cooling system type as "residential air conditioning with residential forced air furnace" (a common HVAC system for residential units in the United States), and setting the standard for calculations to "ASHRAE 90.1 2019" using the "HB Building Vintages" component (Figure 8.1c).

To add apertures to an existing analysis use zone (in this case, the house), Honeybee's "HB Add Subface" component needs to be used. Using the "HB Aperture" component and a standard "Geometry" component, apertures modeled as open planar surfaces coplanar with the building's geometry are introduced to the analysis. On the HB Aperture component, the "operable" input is set to "true" with a "Boolean toggle" component to indicate that the house's windows and doors will be operable. The house then is redefined as an "HB Room" with its massing and apertures using the HB Add Subface component. Using the "HB Model" component, the combination of HB Room and its apertures are defined as a Honeybee model and is now ready for running an energy simulation (Figure 8.1d).

For energy simulation calculations, Honeybee-Energy uses Open Studio Model (OSM) and Energy Plus standards introduced in Chapter 3. Now that our single zone house is ready for simulation, we can use Honeybee's "HB Model to OSM" component to run an energy simulation. To run the energy simulation, first, the "model" output of the HB Model component is connected to the "model" input of the HB Model to OSM component. Using the steps introduced in Chapter 3, weather data about San Francisco is downloaded and introduced to the HB Model to OSM component as an EPW file. Finally, the "_write" input and "run_" inputs of the HB Model to OSM component are set to "true" using a "Boolean toggle," which runs the simulation and requires the HB Model to OSM component to record the quantitative outcomes in multiple formats (Figure 8.1d).

The HB Model to OSM component of Honeybee-Energy provides data outputs in multiple formats, including "SQL" and "HTML" formats among others. HTML format is particularly useful since it can be accessed through a regular web browser. SQL and other data formats, on the other hand, prove helpful in converting data into readable formats for Honeybee-Energy components. For energy use intensity readings, Honeybee's "HB End Use Intensity" component uses SQL format data. When SQL data from the HB Model to OSM component are fed into the HB End Use Intensity component, we can observe that the sample house's EUI is 165.037 kWh/m^2 for the default analysis period that covers from January 1, 00:00 (midnight) to December 31 23:00 (11:00 pm). Imperial system measurements can be used instead by setting the component's "ip_" input to "true" with a Boolean toggle: EUI for the proposed house in IP reads as 52.316 kBtu/ft2 for the same analysis period. We can also observe the EUI values for specific uses such as cooling, interior lighting, electric equipment, residential HVAC fans, and pumps by connecting panels to the "eui_end_use" and "end_uses" outputs of the HB end use intensity component.

By connecting the SQL output of the "Model to OSM" component to the "HB Read Room Energy Result" component, we can also observe the yearlong hourly heating energy loads on a graph (Figure 8.1d and 8.1e). Using the HB Read Room Energy Result component, one

Table 8.1 The yearly energy use intensity (EUI) calculated for the sample house's heating, cooling, interior lighting, electrical equipment, and pumps per year. The last column on the right shows the total yearly EUI. All findings have the same unit: kBtu/ft2.

Sample house in San Francisco, CA	*Heating*	*Cooling*	*Interior lighting*	*Electrical equipment*	*Residential HVAC fans*	*Pumps*	*Total EUI*
EUI values by type (kBtu/ft2)	38.289	0.175	3.611	10.145	0.095	0.003	52.316

can also observe other yearlong hourly loads such as cooling, lighting, electrical equipment, and so on (Figure 8.1d). Table 8.1 summarizes the total and equipment specific EUI values for this sample house based on the illustrated single zone analysis. As one would expect, a residential unit such as this house in San Francisco area has higher EUI values for heating and electrical equipment as opposed to cooling and residential HVAC fans.

During this process, the HB Visualize by Type component proves helpful. Various Honeybee components representing Honeybee surfaces, objects or models can be connected to the HB Visualize by Type component. The component color-codes surfaces and objects based on their object type – be it an aperture, roof, or wall. This feature enables the designer to check and make sure whether objects in the model have been to their appropriate types (Figure 8.1d). Having looked into a smaller scale building for EUI calculation and related representations, let us discuss more complex buildings with multiple programmatic elements.

8.2.2 EUI: Multiple Building Use Zone Simulation Using Ladybug, Honeybee, and Honeybee Energy

In Chapter 6, Section 6.5, we looked into the direct sun hours of a large aperture on a large public building in San Francisco, CA surrounded by buildings of various heights, where the large aperture faced southwest. In order to demonstrate EUI calculation for a multiple building zone building using Ladybug, Honeybee, and Honeybee Energy, we will use a sample fictitious building similar to the building from Section 6.5 as a multi-zone office building in Albuquerque, NM, with an atrium facing southwest, with a number of individual offices with their apertures facing northeast, and their entrances facing the atrium (southwest direction). Figure 8.2a illustrates the building under discussion, Figure 8.2b illustrates the southwest facing atrium space, and Figure 8.2c illustrates the individual offices with their apertures facing northeast while their entrances are facing the atrium, therefore southwest direction. This fictitious building constitutes a multi-zone building with a larger open, shared space and 24 individual office spaces (Figure 8.2).

Now, let us look into the process for EUI calculation as well as more specific energy use calculations for this building using the Ladybug, Honeybee, and Honeybee Legacy plug-ins for Grasshopper. To prepare for the analysis, each space that needs to be analyzed is modeled as closed polysurfaces in Rhinoceros (in this case, the atrium and the individual offices were introduced to Grasshopper using a "Geometry" component as multiple geometries). To define these volumes in Grasshopper as interrelated volumes in a single building, Honeybee's "HB Intersect Solids" component is used. The solids are defined as Honeybee "rooms" using the "HB Rooms from Solid" component. In Section 8.3.1, using the "HB Construction Types" and "HB Construction Set" components, construction criteria are specified. Program type and space conditioning are specified using the HB Building Programs component – in this case, the building program is set to "Large Office" using the HB Building Programs component (Figure 8.3a).

The "rooms" (defined by the HB Room from Solid component) are then fed into the "HB Solve Adjacency" component. This component analyzes the rooms, and identifies which surfaces

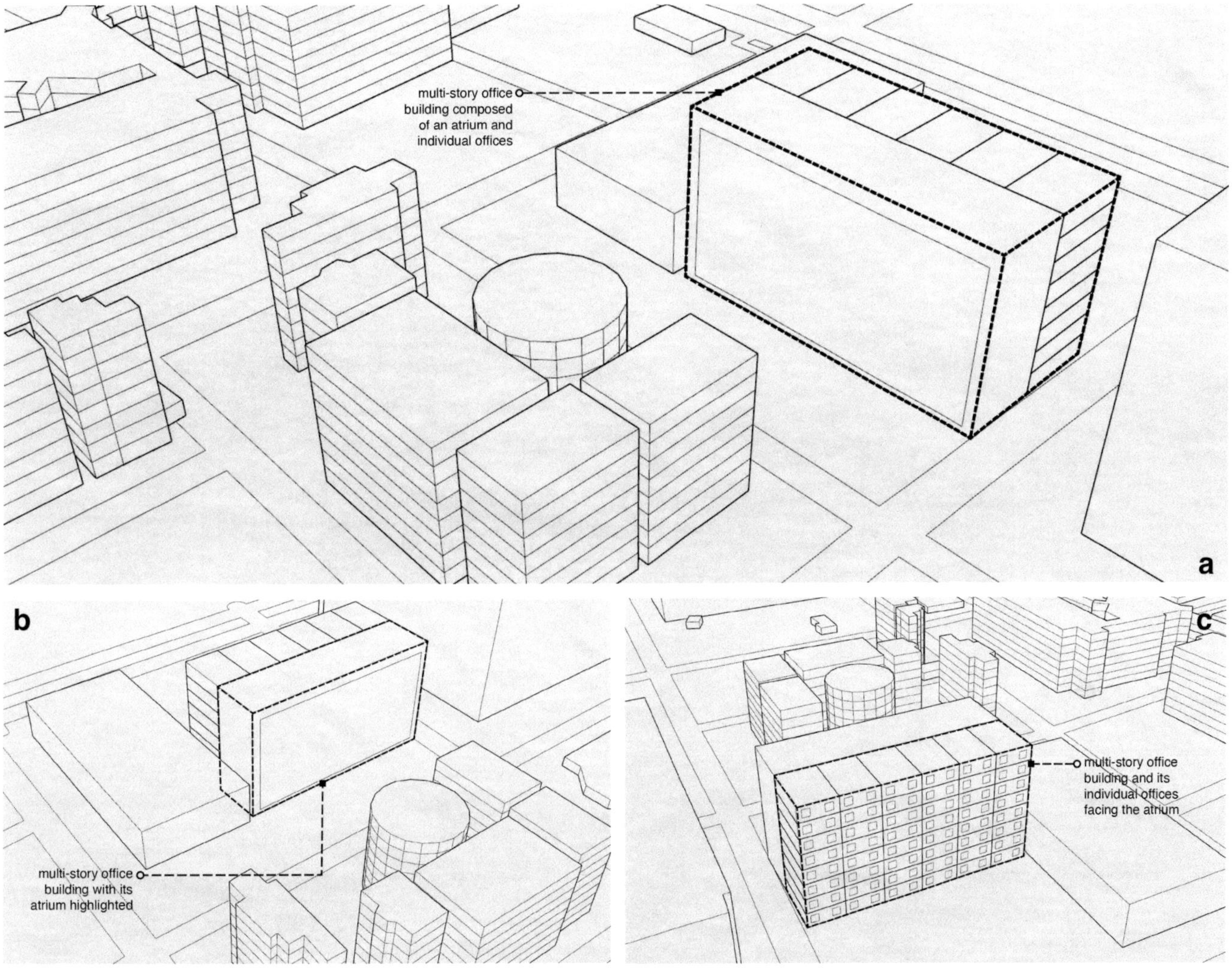

Figure 8.2 (a) A large public office building surrounded by buildings of various heights in an urban setting (Albuquerque, NM) with a south-facing large aperture; (b) the mass of the atrium space with the south-facing aperture; and (c) individual offices in the building facing the atrium, and their apertures facing east.

are adjacent to other "rooms", and which surfaces are exposed to the outside – either the ground surface, or outside space. At this point, the "rooms" can be used to build a Honeybee model simply by adding apertures. Nevertheless, to emulate a more realistic analysis, an HVAC system WAS ADDED to the building prior to adding apertures and running the EUI calculations (Figure 8.3c).

In Figure 8.3c, a heating, ventilation, and air conditioning system is introduced to the building using the "HB All-Air HVAC" component. The "HB All-Air HVAC Templates" component provides an extensive list of heating, ventilation, and air conditioning system options to select from. In this example, a variable air volume chiller with a gas boiler was selected. The next step involves the introduction of apertures into the analysis model. First, apertures are modeled three-dimensionally in Rhinoceros as surfaces that are coplanar with surfaces of the building's volumes. At this point it is advisable to place the aperture surfaces on their own layer in the Rhinoceros model. The aperture surfaces are then introduced to Grasshopper as multiple surfaces using a "geometry" component (Figure 8.3c).

This geometry is then defined as a set of apertures using the HB Aperture component, and they are defined as operable apertures using a Boolean toggle to set the "operable_" input to

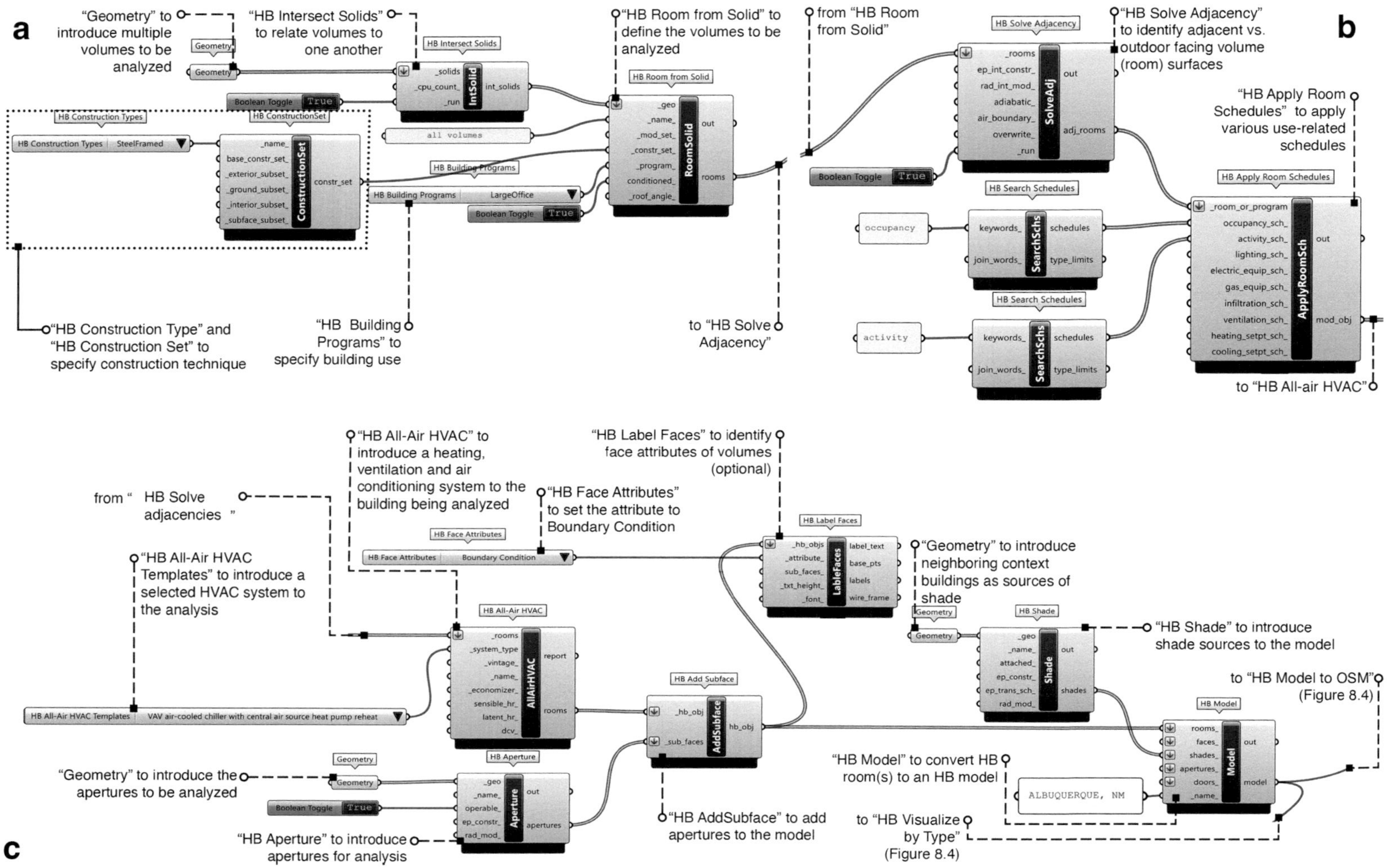

Figure 8.3 *(a) Preparing the basic building volumes for analysis; (b) identifying shared surfaces as well as outside facing surfaces; and (c) introducing apertures, HVAC settings, and neighboring buildings as obstacles to solar access to prepare the model for simulation (continued in Figure 8.4).*

"true". Like the example we discussed in Section 8.2.1, the aperture geometry is introduced to the main building model as subsurfaces using the HB Add Subface component. At this stage, to double-check whether the orientation of surfaces is true, "HB Label Surfaces" component is used, and the "attribute" is set to "boundary condition" using the "HB Face Attributes" component. Following this double-check, the Honeybee Energy model needs to be defined and contextual surfaces need to be introduced to count for obstacles to solar access. The Honeybee objects output of the HB Add Subface component is connected to the "rooms_" input of the HB Model component. The buildings surrounding the building under analysis are ten introduced to Grasshopper as multiple geometries using the "geometry" component, and the "geometry" component is connected to the "shades_" input of the HB Model component (Figure 8.3c).

Our model containing the building with the additional settings, as well as the context is now ready for analysis. The accuracy of the Honeybee model can be double-checked by visualization through the HB Visualize by Type component, which color codes all the model components, such as HB rooms, subfaces (i.e., apertures), shade (i.e., neighboring buildings, louvers, etc.). Following the color-coding check, the key component is Honeybee-Energy's HB Model to OSM component, which uses the Open Studio Model (OSM). First, the HB Model component's "model" output is connected to the "model" input of the HB Model to OSM component. Prior to running the OSM, we need the weather data, which, as discussed in Chapter 3 and earlier in this chapter, are downloaded and imported into the definition using Ladybug's "LB EPWMap" and "LB DownloadEPW" components. The output EPW URL address is connected to the "_epw_file" input of the HB Model to OSM component (Figure 8.4).

Previously, we did not introduce any simulation parameters, which yielded a yearlong analysis. In this example, we will look into another yearlong analysis, but this time specifying the analysis period to demonstrate how we can specify the analysis period down to the hour throughout the year. To introduce simulation parameters to the analysis, "HB Simulation Parameter" is used. This component can help control many parameters (i.e., run period, holidays, etc.) to customize the process. In Figure 8.4, the "LB Analysis Period" we are familiar with from Chapter 3 is used to specify the run period parameter. Although the HB Simulation Parameter component's default analysis period is the whole year, for demonstration purposes in Figure 8.4, the analysis period is set from January 1, 00:00 to December 31, 23:00. Once all inputs are ready, the HB Model to OSM component simulation is run by using a Boolean toggle to set the "_write" and "run_" inputs to "true". While the "_write" input enables the saving of the simulation results in multiple formats, the "run_" input initiates the simulation running process. As we discussed in Section 8.2.1, the HB Model to OSM component yields OSM outputs in many formats. Like in Section 8.2.1, the HB End Use Intensity component yields EUI calculations and details for the analysis periods, which can be accessed using Grasshopper's native panels (Figure 8.4).

For more specific analysis results, it is possible to use the HB Read Room Energy Result component. In this example, the "sql" output of the HB Model to OSM component was fed into the HB Read Room Energy Result component, and the energy use calculations for the analysis period were plotted on a graph using the "HB Hourly Plot" component for an entire year. Figure 8.5 illustrates the cooling energy loads of our fictitious building in kWh (Kilowatts per hour), after the color scheme is edited by using the "LB Legend Parameters" and "LB Color Range" components. Analyzing the results through Figure 8.5, one can observe, as expected, that cooling loads maximize for our sample building from the beginning of May to the end of October.

Looking into the yearly EUI calculations and their details for our sample building, one can observe that the energy use intensity for the sample multistory office building is much higher than the sample house we analyzed in Section 8.2.1. Table 8.2 illustrates a higher number of

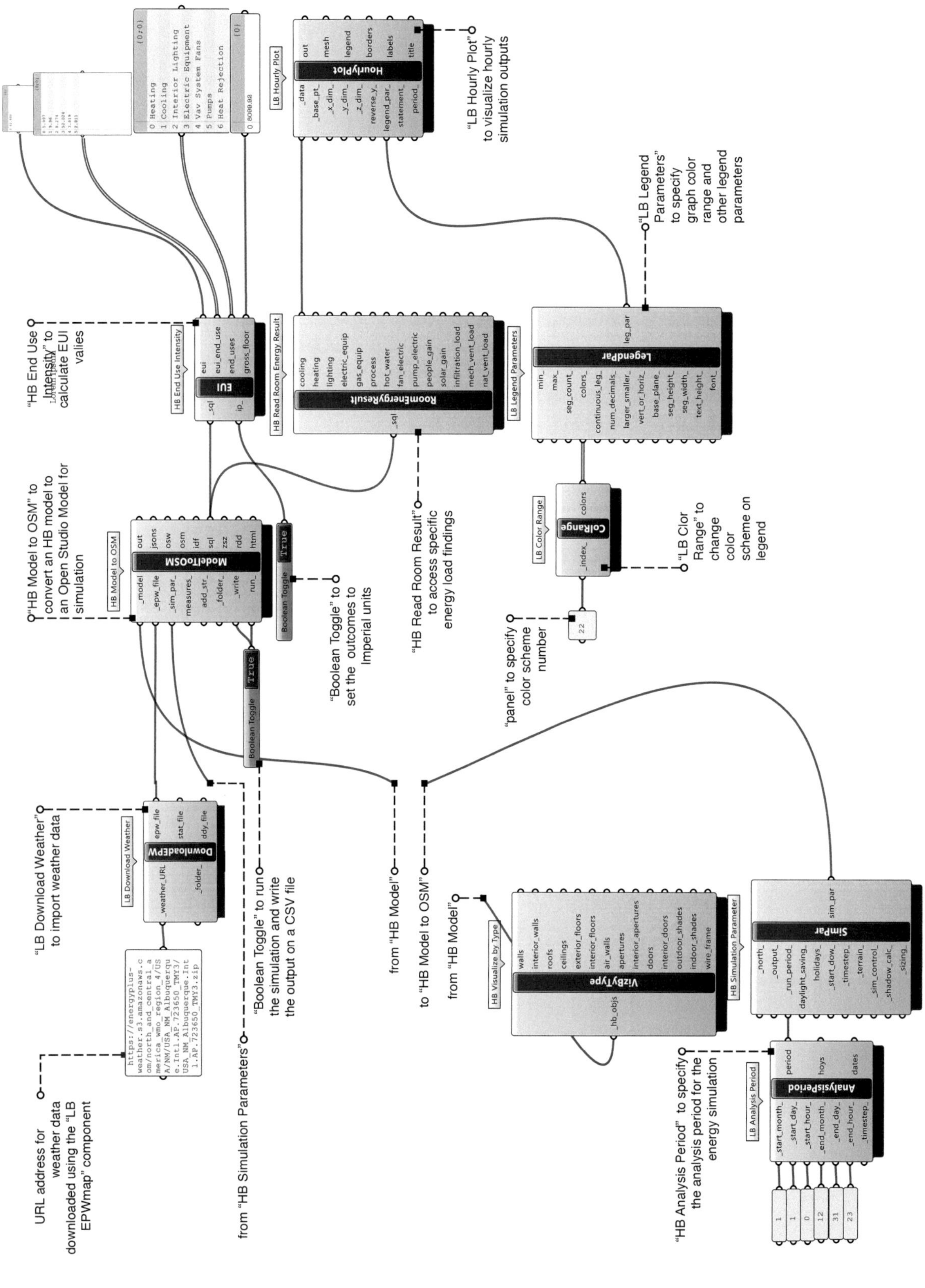

Figure 8.4 Preparing and running the Honeybee model using OSM and extracting EUI calculations and individual room energy results (continued from Figure 8.3).

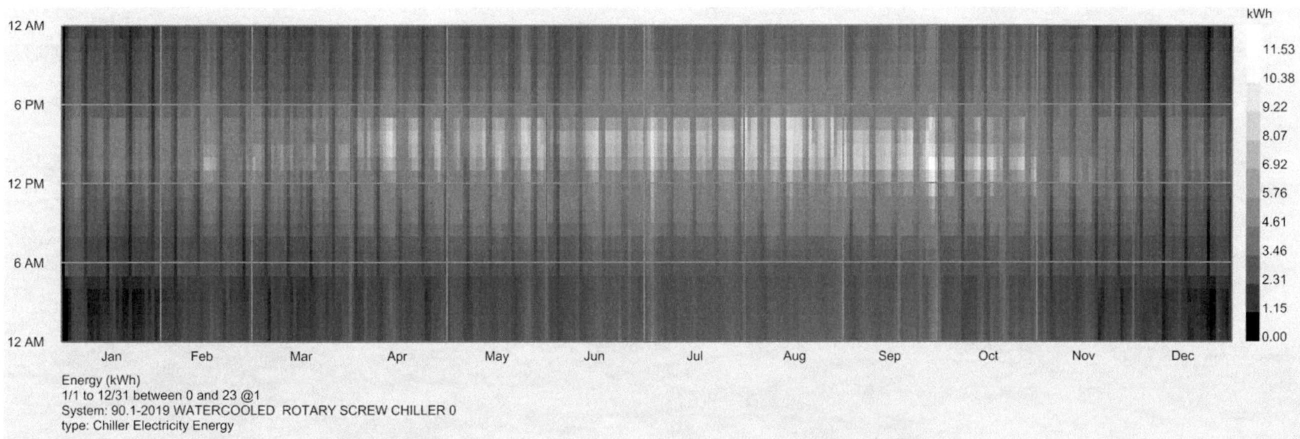

Figure 8.5 *Visualizing the total cooling energy use needs for the sample office building in kWh (kilowatt/hour) using the "HB Read Room Energy Result," "LB Hourly Plot," "LB Legend Parameters," and "LB Color Range" components.*

Table 8.2 The yearly energy use intensity (EUI) calculated for the sample office building's heating, cooling, interior lighting, electrical equipment, VAV system fans, pumps, and yearly EUI. The last column on the right shows the yearly EUI. All findings have the same unit: kBtu/ft2.

Sample office building in Albuquerque, NM	*Heating*	*Cooling*	*Interior lighting*	*Electrical equipment*	*VAV system fans*	*Pumps*	*Yearly EUI*
EUI values by type (kBtu/ft2)	5.993	10.013	8.274	52.024	3.839	2.822	82.965

variables than the sample house from Section 8.2.1, since in this example we introduced an HVAC system (in this case, a variable air volume chiller with a gas boiler) as well as multiple spaces with adjacency to the simulation. As one would expect, in the context of Albuquerque, NM, heating energy use intensity seems to be much higher due to the climatic and programmatic requirements.

8.2.3 Looking into EUI With a Louver System

Having looked into the yearly EUI calculations for our fictitious building in Albuquerque, NM, let us look into the potential effects of protection from solar heat gain to decrease the building's energy use intensity. In Section 8.2.2, we calculated the EUI values for our fictitious office building with a large south-facing aperture which, one could argue, may have a fairly strong effect on the EUI findings.

Now that we started analyzing EUI values using Ladybug Tools and Honeybee Energy, we can explore to what extent these decreased direct sun hours affect energy use intensities. To illustrate how louvers, secondary skin systems, and similar measures may affect energy use intensity of a building, we will introduce a horizontal louver system and recalculate the EUI values on our sample fictitious building on the exact same site in Albuquerque, NM.

To conduct this analysis, a horizontal louver system is introduced into the same Rhinoceros model (Figure 8.6). Then, using the exact same Grasshopper definition introduced in Figures 8.3 and 8.4, the EUI values are calculated. The only difference in the workflow is that the louvers introduced into the Rhinoceros model as surfaces are introduced into the Grasshopper definition as shade geometries in addition to the surrounding context buildings.

Running the same Grasshopper definition, one can easily observe the impacts of the horizontal louver system on the sample building's energy use intensity values. The results of this

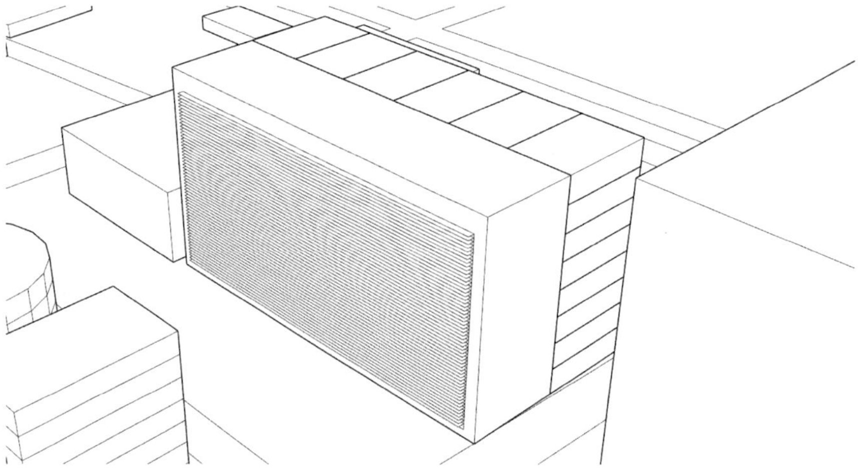

Figure 8.6 *The horizontal louver system from Section 6.2.2 introduced into the same Rhinoceros model used for direct sun hours analysis conducted in Section 8.2.2.*

Table 8.3 The yearly energy use intensity (EUI) calculated for the sample office building's heating, cooling, interior lighting, electrical equipment, VAV system fans, and pumps with the additional louver system. The last column on the right shows the yearly EUI. All findings have the same unit: kBtu/ft2.

Sample office building in Albuquerque, CA	*Heating*	*Cooling*	*Interior lighting*	*Electrical equipment*	*VAV system fans*	*Pumps*	*Yearly EUI*
EUI values by type (kBtu/ft2)	6.696	7,024	8.274	52.024	2.51	2.293	78.822

analysis indicate that the simple non-parametric louver system increased EUI for heating from 5.997 to 6.696, while lowering it for cooling from 9.96 to 7.34 (Table 8.3).

Clearly, the simple horizontal louver system introduced earlier and this section do not provide an ideal solution. Nevertheless, by observing the EUI calculations provided by Ladybug Tools and Honeybee Energy, one can get a quick overview of how EUI outcomes are affected by design decisions. Based on these simple observations larger scale aperture and skin-related decisions can be subjected to early performance analysis processes to inform more detailed design decisions to maximize building energy use efficiency.

8.2.4 Surface Area to Volume Ratio (SA/V) as It Relates to EUI

Having discussed the EUI calculations for single zone and multi-zone buildings in an urban context, let us now look into the implications of surface area to volume ratio for buildings. As introduced in Section 8.1.3, high SA/V values mean more exposure to the external environment, thus triggering a need for higher energy usage for heating and/or cooling, depending on the context and climate.

In this section, we will look into the SA/V values of two sample massing ideas for a fictitious structure in San Francisco, CA. The two masses under consideration have the same indoor volume (96,000 cu. ft.); nevertheless, the masses have different building footprint areas and different total surface areas in sq. ft. Table 8.4 displays the total floor area per story, number of floors, total floor area, total building floor area, total surface area, and SA/V ratios for the two masses.

While both massing options have the same volume and total building area, mass 1 has twice the footprint area of mass 2, thus only six floors for a total building area of 9,600 sq. ft. Mass

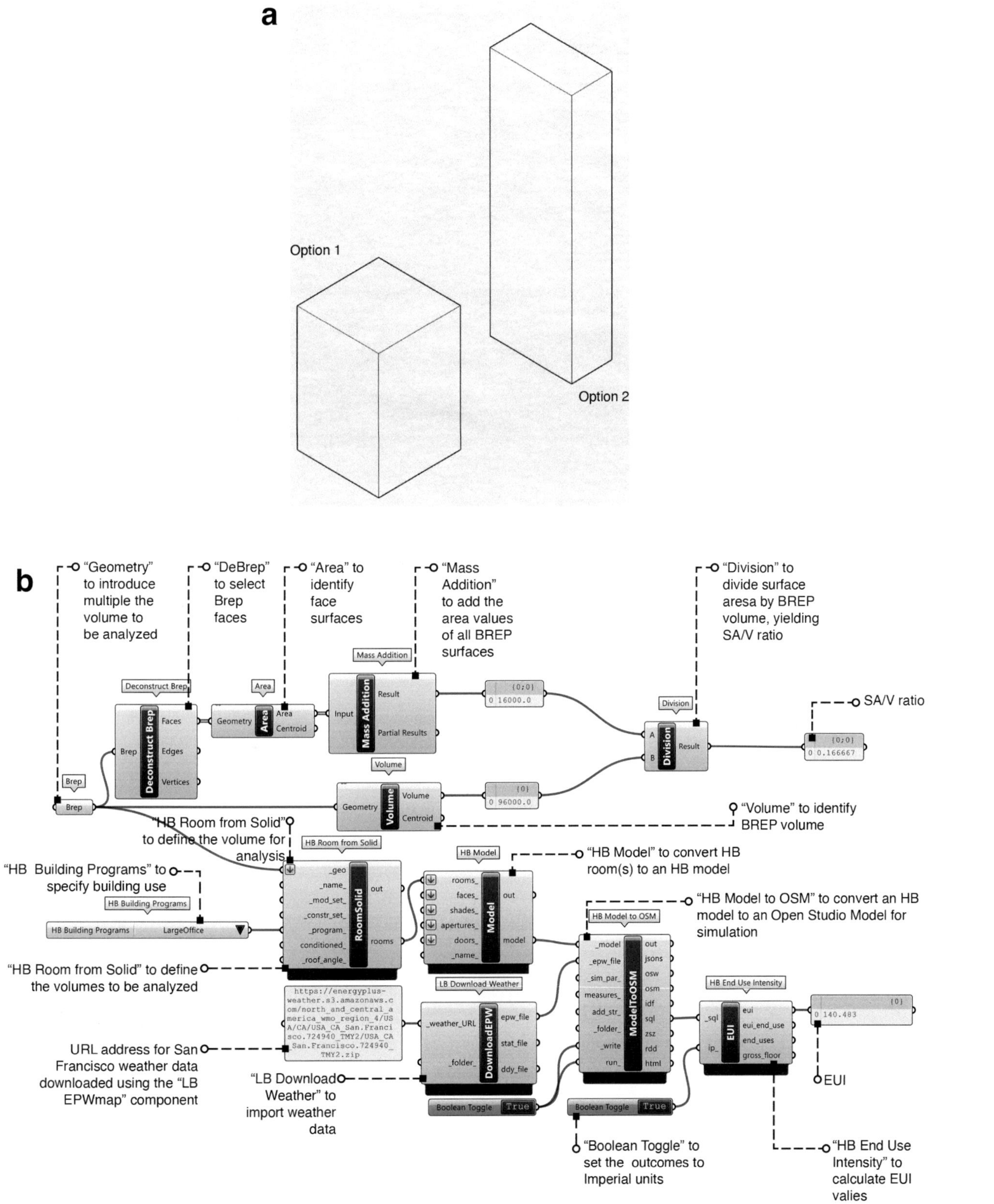

Figure 8.7 *(a) Two building massing proposals for San Francisco, CA; (b) the Grasshopper definition was used to calculate the SA/V ratio and yearly EUI for building massing proposal 2.*

2, on the other hand, has a footprint area of 800 sq. ft., thus allowing the same total 9,600 sq. ft. in 12 floors. As a result, while mass 1 has a total surface area of 12,800 sq. ft. and a SA/V ratio of 0.13333, mass 2 has a total surface area of 16,000 sq. ft. and a SA/V ratio of 0.16667. Figure 8.7a illustrates the difference between the two massing options while mass 1 has a larger footprint and a shorter building height, mass 2 has a smaller footprint and a taller building height.

Figure 8.7b illustrates the Grasshopper definition developed using native Grasshopper components as well as Ladybug and Honeybee components to calculate the SA/V ratios and EUI values for the two masing options. Initially, each options is introduced into Grasshopper as Breps, whose volumes are calculated by the native Grasshopper and "Volume" component. To calculate the surface area for the two options each Brep is deconstructed using the "DeBrep" component, the surface area of each of the Brep surfaces are calculated using the "area" component, and the total surface areas of the Breps are calculated using the "mass addition" component. The "division" component yields the SA/V ratio for each option by dividing the total surface area of each proposal by their volume.

Once the SA/V ratios are calculated, the two Breps for the two options are introduced to Ladybug and Honeybee plug-ins. Each Brep is defined as a Honeybee "room" using the HB Room from Solid component. Each resulting HB Model is then analyzed using the HB Model to OSM component, with weather data being imported from Ladybug's "Download EPW" component. Finally, the EUI for each option is calculated using Honeybee's HB End Use Intensity component (Figure 8.7).

The findings indicate that the total surface area and SA/V ratios of the two massing options differ despite having the same volume (96,000 cu. ft.) and total building area. Since option 2 has a smaller footprint and a higher total surface area, its SA/V ratio is 0.16667. Option 1, with its footprint area twice that of option 2, has a smaller total surface area, thus yielding a SA/V ratio of 0.13333 (Table 8.4).

Table 8.4 illustrates a comparative analysis of the two massing options. Both options have the same total building area and volume. Nevertheless, due to the difference in the two proposals' massing differences, option 1 has a total surface area of 12,800 sq. ft, and a SA/V ration of 0.13333; while proposal 2 has a total surface area of 16,000 sq. ft, and a SA/V ration of 0.16667. Consequently, the yearly EUI value for option 1 is 79.045 kBtu/ft2, while the yearly EUI value for option 2 is 140.483 kBtu/ft2 (Table 8.2). Based on these findings, we can observe that despite equal total building area and volume values, yearly EUI values for the two massing option significantly differ due to the SA/V ratios. Since option 2 has a higher SA/V ratio, its exposure to external factors is higher. As a result, heating and cooling option 2 proves more energy-intensive than option 1. Thus, the SA/V ratio proves to be a helpful indicator of potential energy consumption needs for a building during the design proposal and development stage.

8.3 ARCHITECTURAL DESIGN AND DAYLIGHT

Heating, ventilation, and air conditioning constitute only a portion of a building's energy consumption. Lighting and relationships with daylight contribute to the energy consumption needs

Table 8.4 The yearly energy use intensity (EUI) calculated for the sample office building's heating, cooling, interior lighting, electrical equipment, VAV system fans, pumps, and heat rejection. The last column on the right shows the yearly EUI. All findings have the same unit: kBtu/ft2.

Building massing option for San Francisco, CA	*Volume (cu. ft)*	*Number of floors*	*Footprint area (sq. ft)*	*Total floor building floor area (sq. ft)*	*Total surface area (sq. ft)*	*SA/V ratio*	*Yearly EUI values by option (kBtu/ft2)*
Option 1	96,000	6	1,600	9,600	12,800	0.13333	79.045
Option 2	96,000	12	800	9,600	16,000	0.16667	140.483

of a building as well. Therefore, when energy consumption-related performance measures are considered, a building's relationships with daylight access are critical. A building's location, orientation, mass composition, and location as well as size and materiality of its apertures can significantly affect a building's energy consumption. In this section, we will look into how access to daylight may affect a building's dependency on daylight and energy.

8.3.1 Spatial Daylight Autonomy (SDA)

Daylight autonomy of a building refers to the percentage of number of hours during which the daylight levels exceed a particular percentage. Spatial Daylight Autonomy (SDA), on the other hand, is the percentage of floor area that receives 30 foot-candles (fc) for a minimum of 50% of a workday. As a measurement of light intensity, "foot-candle" (also referred to as lumen/square foot) refers to the amount of light sufficient to saturate a one square-foot surface with one lumen of light. In metric terms, the same measurement is identified as a "lux," and it refers to the amount of light sufficient to saturate a ***one square-meter*** surface with one lumen of light. Spatial Daylight Autonomy (SDA) has recently become a commonly used metric due to its being a part of LEED building standards.

Daylight autonomy is important for a building from an energy consumption point of view, primarily because less daylight autonomy for a space means more dependency on artificial lighting. Besides energy use-related concerns, daylight without glare also means higher levels of comfort for people occupying the building, since it implies less dependency on artificial lighting options. Let us now look into the use of parametric methods for analyzing daylighting and energy use implications using Grasshopper and Ladybug Tools, including Honeybee and Honeybee Radiance.

8.4 PARAMETRIC METHODS FOR ANALYZING LIGHTING AND ENERGY USE IMPLICATIONS

Once again, let us look into the fictitious San Francisco example we analyzed in Chapter 6, and calculate the spatial daylight autonomy values for the fictitious building's atrium and offices. The Honeybee Radiance plug-in and Honeybee and Ladybug Tools prove helpful in SDA calculations. For this analysis, the same Rhinoceros file used in Chapter 6 and earlier in this chapter was used by removing the office spaces and apertures on the ground floor. The atrium space was modeled as a single closed polysurface (Figure 8.8a), along with the 18 office spaces modeled as individual closed polysurfaces (Figure 8.8b).

Initially, all building volumes are introduced to Grasshopper as multiple volumes using the "geometry" component. The volumes are then related to one another using the HB Intersect Solids component, which identifies the surfaces adjacent to other spaces, surfaces adjacent to outside, and surfaces adjacent to the ground plane. The volumes are also defined as HB "rooms" using the HB Room from Solid component, and the building program is identified as a "large office" building using the HB Building Programs component. For SDA calculations, apertures need to be introduced into the Grasshopper environment. To do this, all apertures (surfaces coplanar to building volumes) are introduced to Grasshopper as multiple geometries using the "geometry" component. Using the HB Aperture component, aperture surfaces are defined as apertures, and they are deemed "operable" by setting a "Boolean toggle" to "true". The apertures are then associated with the building volumes (i.e., Honeybee "rooms" using the HB Add Subface component). The last step in this setup process is to set up the geometry around the building to be analyzed as obstacles to sunlight. To achieve this, the surfaces of the surrounding buildings are introduced into Grasshopper as multiple geometries and defined as sources of shade using the "HB Shade" component (Figure 8.8c). An important point to remember during this process is that, in the model, surface normal vectors need to be oriented so that they are facing outwards. When the surface normal vectors are not oriented outwards, they may fail to accurately interact with light, receiving light or casting

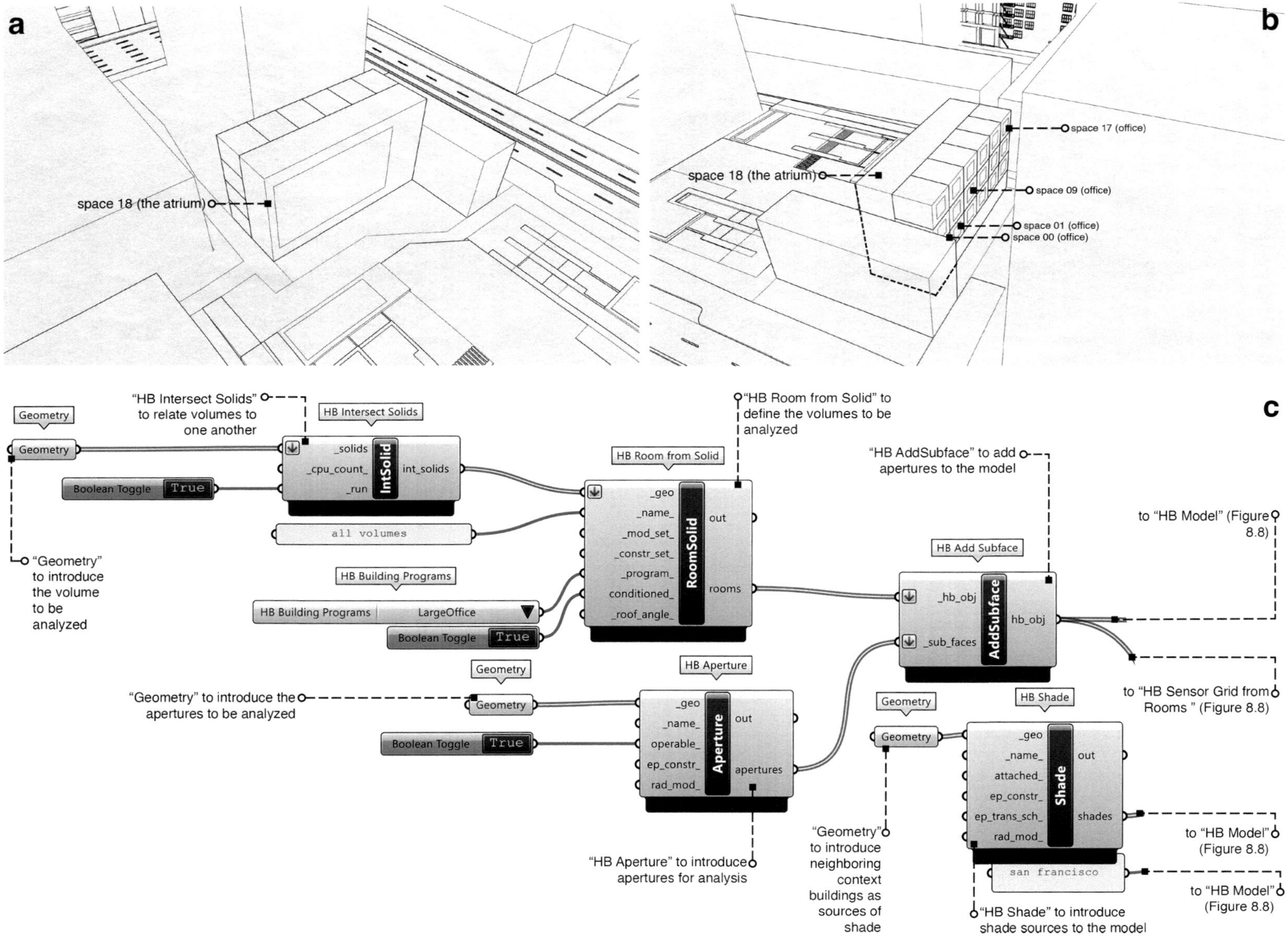

Figure 8.8 *(a) The sample San Francisco building with its atrium facing the public plaza; (b) its individual office spaces facing the neighboring urban alley; and (c) the portion of the Grasshopper definition used to set up Honeybee volumes and their apertures.*

shadows. In case of unexpected or counterintuitive results, one can double-check the normal vectors of surfaces using the "Dir" command of Rhinoceros and, if necessary, correct their orientation using the "Flip" command in Rhinoceros.

In the next step, all Honeybee geometries defined as rooms and apertures are defined as a Honeybee model using a HB Model component. Now that the Honeybee model is ready for analysis, the "HB Annual Daylight" component is used to start the analysis. The HB Annual Daylight component requires weather data as well as a model with sensor grids defined to calculate annual daylight access. To download and import the weather data, Ladybug's "LB Download Weather" and "LB Weather from EPW" components are used as introduced in Chapter 3 of this book. These data are fed into the HB Annual Daylight component using an "HB Weather from EPW" component. To create a sensor grid, on the other hand, Honeybee's "HB Sensor Grid from Rooms" is used to define the points of the 5' × 5' grid. (As explained in Chapter 7, selecting smaller grid sizes, while increasing precision, may also increase the time required to run the analysis.) Following this, the HB Sensor Grid from Rooms component is used to define the points of the grid as sensors. Finally, Using the "HB Assign Grids and Views" component, the sensors are assigned to the Honeybee model, which is fed into the "_model" input of the HB Annual Daylight component. To calculate SDA for each building volume, Daylight Analysis (DA) values need to be calculated by converting the "results" output of the HB Annual Daylight component using the "HB Annual Daylight Metrics" component. Finally, the "DA" output of the "HB Annual Daylight Metrics" component is fed into the "HB Spatial Daylight Autonomy" component, which yields yearly SDA values for each space in the model (Figure 8.9).

Table 8.5 summarizes the SDA calculation findings for the atrium and individual offices. The results indicate that, as expected, due to its large aperture, the atrium has plenty of access to daylight, and has a high SDA value. Some of the individual offices facing the alleyway, however, will need more daylight – or a better spatial configuration – to reach the 50% value in terms of their yearly spatial daylight autonomy. Although most spaces with an SDA below 50% are still close to the target with an SDA over 40%, spaces with Grasshopper numbers 0, 1, 6, 7, 12, and 13 need more daylight if the objective is to meet the 50% minimum SDA. Based on these findings, the designer(s) may decide to revise the design proposal by revisiting spatial organization decisions as well as orientation and aperture-related decisions.

8.4.1 Looking into SDA With a Louver System

In Section 8.2, we discussed using Ladybug and Honeybee Energy to calculate yearly energy use intensity values for a fictitious San Francisco building and followed up in Section 8.2.3 to recalculate the values after the introduction of a louver system on the building's southwest façade. To investigate how this louver system affects the spatial daylight autonomy values of the spaces in this building, we can replicate this process for SDA values using Ladybug and Honeybee Radiance.

Using the exact same Rhinoceros model from Section 8.2.3 (Figure 8.6), the same Grasshopper definition introduced in Figures 8.8 and 8.9 was run for SDA values of the building's spaces. Since all variables for the individual office spaces remained the same, no changes were identified in their yearly SDA values. For the southwest-facing atrium, however, the yearly SDA dropped from an above-target 94.7% to a below-target 32%.

As in the EUI comparison we discussed in Section 8.2.3, this comparative analysis shows that the louver system introduced does not provide a perfect solution. Nevertheless, we can see that by conducting comparative analyses like these in early design phases, design proposal iterations can be incrementally fine-tuned based on the findings. Furthermore, since the Grasshopper definitions remain the same, it is quick and easy to test multiple massing and aperture alternatives by simply changing Rhinoceros geometry and running the analysis.

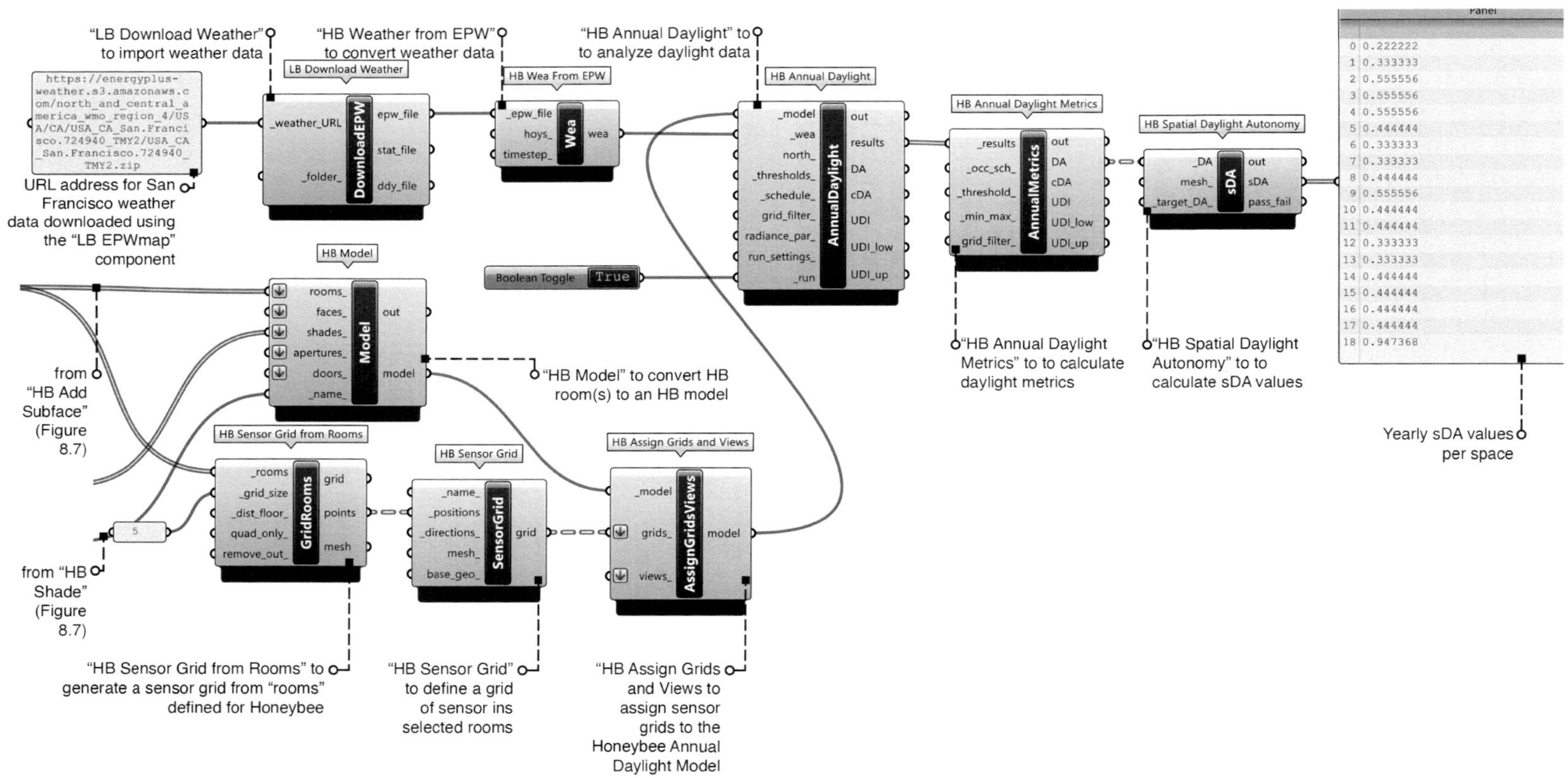

Figure 8.9 Calculating the SDA values for each space in the sample fictitious San Francisco office building by taking the local weather and surrounding context into consideration.

Table 8.5 SDA calculation findings for the sample fictitious office building's atrium and individual offices. Some of the individual offices facing the alleyway will need more daylight – or a better spatial configuration – to reach the 50% value in terms of their yearly spatial daylight autonomy.

Space	*Grasshopper no.*	*Yearly spatial daylight autonomy (%)*	*Comments*
Individual office	0	22.2	Below 40%, below target
Individual office	1	33.3	Below 40%, below target
Individual office	2	55.5	Above 50%, above target
Individual office	3	55.5	Above 50%, above target
Individual office	4	55.5	Above 50%, above target
Individual office	5	44.4	Below 50%, below target
Individual office	6	33.3	Below 40%, below target
Individual office	7	33.3	Below 40%, below target
Individual office	8	44.4	Below 50%, below target
Individual office	9	55.5	Above 50%, above target
Individual office	10	44.4	Below 50%, below target
Individual office	11	44.4	Below 50%, below target
Individual office	12	33.3	Below 40%, below target
Individual office	13	33.3	Below 40%, below target
Individual office	14	44.4	Below 50%, below target
Individual office	15	44.4	Below 50%, below target
Individual office	16	44.4	Below 50%, below target
Individual office	17	44.4	Below 50%, below target
Atrium	18	94.7	Above 50%, above target

8.5 MEASURING BUILDING ENVIRONMENTAL PERFORMANCE USING "LADYBUG TOOLS": OBSERVATIONS

As we move deeper into the twenty-first century, we have been observing an accelerating expansion of digital tools for environmental performance analyses. Some of these tools can operate on personal computers, while others can help with environmental performance analyses online through servers. In this chapter, we discussed Ladybug Tools, only one of the many available tools that can conduct such analyses. The advantage of a Grasshopper-based environmental analysis software is that the tools can easily be integrated with ongoing parametric explorations using Grasshopper. Furthermore, preliminary design decisions can easily be evaluated based on environmental performance by staying in the Rhinoceros/Grasshopper environment. Nevertheless, it is the designer's responsibility to identify the most efficient and productive tool option(s) for the project at hand.

Specifically, with Ladybug Tools, one can observe that the tool set is ever changing with newer, better versions through time. We must recognize at the outset, that plug-in tools such as Ladybug Tools are ever changing, and the crucial task for designers is to understand the logic and rationale behind such tools. It is only through such a recognition that designers can continue adapting to and adopting ever-developing tools such as Ladybug Tools.

Finally, it is important to underline that Ladybug Tools can conduct many additional layers of environmental performance analysis in much finer scales. In this chapter, we limited the discussion to large-scale analyses since such software will keep developing with newer and newer versions. Readers can explore finer scales of analysis with this basic understanding of the main principles. Nevertheless, in order to avoid software and version-specific discussions that may not be relevant with newer versions or other software, the main principles and large-scale analyses methods were introduced in this chapter.

CHAPTER 09

PRACTICAL MATTERS Parametric Methods and Digital Fabrication for Architectural Model Making

Architectural model making is a key part of design and representation processes. Models help designers visualize design proposals, generate reiterations, and fine-tune the physical expression of the building being designed. As representations of design proposals, architectural models also help designers communicate their ideas to clients, community members, and colleagues. Driscoll (2013) classifies architectural models into two categories, as (i) study/sketch models and (ii) presentation models. While study/sketch models constitute experimentation tools during design development, presentation models can target a variety of audiences and scales: planning models for urban scale decision-making (1/128" = 1' or 1/64" = 1' scale), marketing models for communication with community members or commercial interests (1/16" = 1' or 1/8" = 1' scale), museum models for providing information about a specific phenomenon, teaching models for illustrating architectural details (1/4" = 1' or 1/2" = 1' scale), and landscape design models for communicating open space design features. One-to-one scale models are also often built by architecture offices to test specific design features and performance. Parametric methods and digital fabrication can contribute to the building of these various types of architectural models in various ways.

Parametric methods and digital fabrication techniques help architectural model making immensely. They not only help save valuable time and energy through efficiency but also contribute to the precision and quality of models. Since parametric methods can be very efficient in repetitive tasks, they tend to be time-savers in the generation of repetitive iterations. Since digital fabrication techniques are machine-based, they tend to strongly contribute to the precision of model parts. Furthermore, digital fabrication techniques enable rapid prototyping, making it possible to generate physical representations of many design iterations in a short amount of time, supporting the idea generation and evaluation process. This can be especially helpful for communicating design ideas to clients and community members during the design process.

Digital fabrication techniques can be used to precisely cut existing manufactured materials such as paper products, acrylic, wood products, and even metal. We will refer to such processes as cutting operations. A second set of digital fabrication operations are additive: they reshape and add layers of manufactured materials to build forms created using computer-aided design (CAD) and parametric methods. Commonly used materials include PLA (Poly Lactic Acid), ABS (Acrylonitrile Butadiene Styrene) as well as metals. Finally, subtractive

 DOI: 10.4324/9781003230052-9

operations sculpt manufactured materials by carving them, generating three-dimensional forms created using CAD design and parametric methods.

Scaling Operations for Architectural Models. Regardless of the digital fabrication technique that will be used, correctly scaling the architectural model parts prior to fabrication is crucial. The architectural scaling method used in the United States is based on the Imperial numeric system, using feet and inches. In most other regions of the world, the International System of Units (SI system) is used, with metric units such as millimeters, centimeters, and meters.

Scaling model parts for the target model scale works somewhat differently in Imperial and IS systems. Using the SI system, the scaling factor for model building is the same as the target model. If a commonly used SI-based 1/200 scale model is targeted, the real dimensions of the designed building is divided into 200. This means that a one-meter (100 centimeters) distance in real life need to be represented using 100/200 centimeters, or 0.5 centimeters (5 millimeters) in the architectural model.

Using the Imperial numeric architectural scaling system, there is an additional step involved identifying the scaling factor for the architectural model. Using the Imperial system, the commonly used 1/16" = 1' scale requires a scale factor of 1/192 (or, 1/[12 × 16]), since one-foot equals 12 inches, and one needs to multiply 12 by 16 to identify the scaling factor. Table 9.1 illustrates commonly used Imperial architectural scales, their related scaling factors, the common architectural modeling use for these scales, and the closest SI system scales for architectural modeling. While this table covers commonly used scales, it is not exhaustive – intermediate architectural modeling scales are also used.

Digital 3D Model to Digital Fabrication Tools. Whether cutting, additive or subtractive operations are used, digital fabrication tools utilize digital files that provide X, Y, and Z coordinates for tools' moving parts to complete the operation. The term for this file is "g-code", and its common file extension is ".gcode." Typically, an intermediary piece of software is used to convert data from the CAD software into a "g-code" file. In this chapter, we will look into combinations of parametric methods and digital fabrication techniques that help with precise

Table 9.1 Commonly used Imperial architectural scales, their related scaling factors, the common architectural modeling use for these scales, and the closest SI system scales for architectural modeling. While this table covers commonly used scales, it is not exhaustive – intermediate architectural modeling scales are also used.

Architectural modeling scale using Imperial System	*Scaling factor for digital fabrication*	*Common architectural modeling use: to communicate*	*Closest architectural modeling scale using SI system*
1/128" = 1'	1/1536	Environmental context and mass composition relationships	1/2000
1/64" = 1'	1/768	Close context and mass composition relationships in more detail	1/1000
1/32" = 1'	1/416	Building mass composition and basic floor plate information	1/500
1/16" = 1'	1/192	Basic spatial organization, building skin, and massing information	1/200
3/32" = 1'	1/128	Spatial organization, building skin, and massing information	1/100
1/8" = 1'	1/96	Detailed spatial organization and building skin information	1/100
1/4" = 1'	1/48	Basic building detail information	1/50
1/2" = 1'	1/24	Design details	1/20
1" = 1"	1 to 1	Prototyping	1 to 1

time- and effort-efficient architectural models. We will first look into cutting operations, which will be followed by additive operations and subtractive operations.

9.1 CUTTING OPERATIONS AND PARAMETRIC METHODS IN ARCHITECTURAL MODELING

Cutting operations in digital fabrication became increasingly prominent during the last decade. The decreasing costs of equipment made cutting operations more and more affordable to architecture practices and schools. Today most architecture firms and schools have access to one or more types of cutting methods. Commonly used digitally guided cutting methods are laser cutting, plasma cutting, and waterjet cutting.

9.1.1 Laser Cutting

Laser cutters are equipped with a laser gun that can cut through the material, a mechanism that can move the laser gun on X and Y axes based on the g-code, and a computer processing unit that can read the g-code and direct the movement of the mechanism. Since the laser beam essentially cuts through the material by burning it, laser cutters need a ventilation mechanism to discharge resulting toxic fumes safely (Figure 9.1a).

With most laser cutters, the user can alter the intensity of the laser beam depending on the material to be cut and its thickness: the thicker the material, the higher the laser intensity. Lower laser intensities can also be used to etch or score the material, which can be helpful in creating abstract textures to represent differences in surface materials (i.e., an etched grid on a surface to represent a tiled surface) or introducing text (Figure 9.1b). Another approach to control the effects of the laser beam is to control the laser gun's movement speed. While the laser beam can burn through thicker materials in slower speed, thinner materials can easily be cut at higher movement speeds.

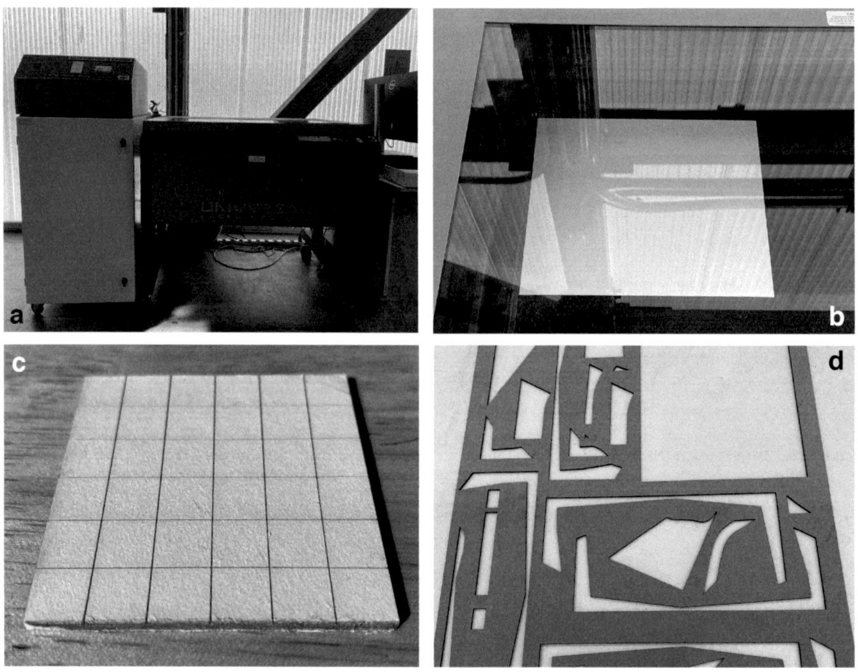

Figure 9.1 *(a) A laser cutter and its ventilation mechanism at California Polytechnic State University's (San Luis Obispo) digital fabrication laboratory; (b) the laser cutter's cutting bed; (c) a process board surface etched to represent floor tiles; and (d) the leftover unused material waste following a laser cut job with unorganized parts. Photographs a and b courtesy of Andrea Garavaryan, author's former student. Process board etching in (c) courtesy of Katherine Neuner, author's former student – the post-laser cutting board was photographed by the author.*

Etching or scoring thinner materials, such as thin process board, also enable easy folding of materials. Quick laser cutting and etching/scoring of material can be used to create fast and accurate prototypes and architectural models. The cutting, etching, and scoring operations of laser cutters are typically color-coded on the CAD software. Based on the model, laser cutters cut the material for a set color (i.e., red), etch the material for a second set color (i.e., blue), and score the material for a third set color (i.e., green).

Common materials that can be laser cut for architectural models include various types of paper, paper-based boards (i.e., corrugated cardboard, process board, museum board), extruded acrylic, and various wood products, such as medium density fiber (MDF) boards. However, infilled materials should not be cut using laser cutters, since the infill material may flammable, and can create a fire hazard during the cutting process. Overall, any flammable materials should not be cut using a laser cutter.

The precision and time efficiency of laser cutting makes it a desirable method in architectural model making. However, since during the cutting process the material is burned, the resulting parts often need to be cleaned before being used. Laser cutting can also cause material waste. Depending on the geometry of the parts that are being cut, and how the parts have been organized in the CAD software, the remaining parts of the material can end up unused and/or unusable. Therefore, it is good practice to pay attention to how much material will remain uncut/unused and how material waste can be minimized through the organization of the parts that will be cut (Figure 9.1d).

Laser Cutting Operations for Study Models. Laser cutting can be especially helpful in the conceptual development phase of projects. Due to their fast and time-efficient nature, laser cutting operations empower designers in rapid production of numerous early design alternatives in a short amount of time. Coupled with a to-scale site context model, laser cutting also enables precision in the development and rapid evaluation of design alternatives.

One such example is the development of study models using Rhinoceros' "UnrollSrf" (unroll surface) and "DupBorder" (duplicate border) commands. Following the development of a massing concept model in Rhinoceros, the designer can use the "UnrollSrf" command to create surfaces of the model that are placed flat on a surface. In doing so, deselecting the "explode" option ensures that the surfaces are attached to one another at their adjacent edges. The "UnrollSrf" operation positions the unrolled surfaces at the origin (0,0,0) of the model space (Figure 9.2a).

Once the unrolling operation is complete, it is possible to either draw lines around the unfolded surfaces as well as their adjacent edges or use the DupBorder command to get the geometry's outer boundaries and add the adjacent edges. After assigning the appropriate color for the appropriate operation (i.e., cutting, etching, or scoring) based on the laser cutter, the CAD file is ready for the laser cutter. Following the cutting process, the model can be created in a short time, folding the material at its etched or scored locations (Figure 9.2b). For such operations, thicker paper types such as Bristol (100 lb or 270 gr/m^2) can be preferred so that the resulting study model is reasonably sturdy.

Laser Cutting Operations for Presentation Models. The speed and precision of laser cutting operations make them ideal for presentation models. As in analog model building, one needs to account for the thickness of model materials. Another aspect to be mindful of is that the laser beam cutting the material is perpendicular to the material's surface, yielding a 90-degree cut. Therefore, laser cutting does not produce clean corner joints that are conventionally possible using an analog 45-degree bevel board cutter. Building a presentation model, one needs to consider the potential color or texture differences between the material's surface and its cross section. One such material is process board, whose cross-section

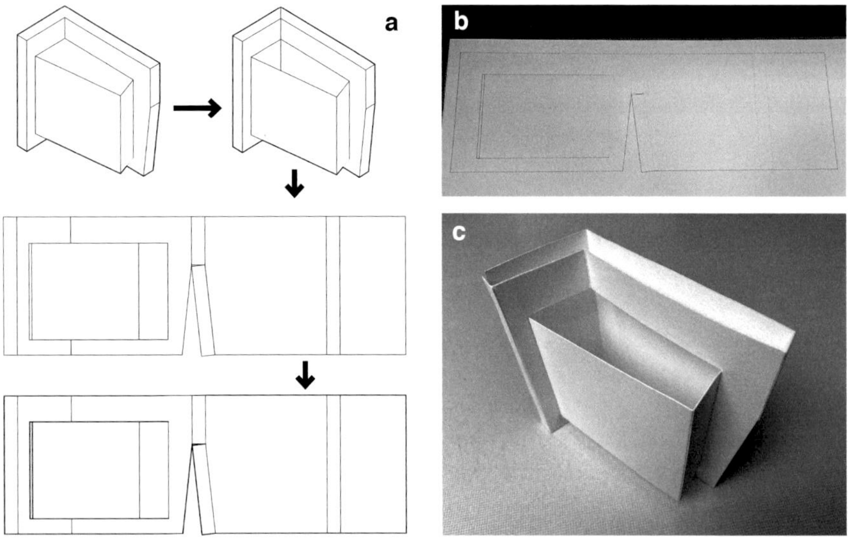

Figure 9.2 *(a) The proposed mass concept model in its original, simplified, unrolled, and laser cutting-ready states (thick lines: cut, thin lines: score); (b) the material after cutting; and (c) the final folded model. Photograph b and laser cutting operations courtesy of Andrea Garavaryan, author's former student. Photograph c by the author.*

Figure 9.3 *1/16" = 1' scale final presentation model prepared for a third-year final studio review at California Polytechnic State University, San Luis Obispo (Spring 2018). Materials: MDF (slabs), acrylic (façade), process board (walls and façade structural trusses), 3D printed PLA (stairs), basswood (columns). Courtesy Logan Kozlik, author's former student. (The site model was collaboratively built using cardboard and Bristol paper using laser cutting techniques by all the members of author's studio in Winter/Spring 2018).*

material and color is different from its surface. If such a material is used, paint can be integrated to the process. Alternatively, materials with an identical cross section and surface color can be preferred when laser cutting. In either case, the cut material will need to be cleaned of burn marks caused by the laser beam.

Laser cutters' cutting capability of thicker materials also have positively impacted architectural model building for presentations. Materials that could not be easily cut manually prior to digital fabrication's prominence, such as MDF and acrylic, can now be integrated into presentation models. A good example is the use of MDF for representing the thickness of floor slabs from the bottom of a suspended ceiling to the floor surface in a typical cross section. On a 1/16" = 1' scale model, 1/4" thick MDF can represent a 4 foot distance from the bottom of the suspended ceiling to the upper floor surface. In this scenario, a simple laser cutting operation followed by coloring can save precious time, replacing the analog cutting and layering of a thinner material. Similarly, the extruded acrylic sheet, a material that could not be easily cut manually, has made its way into the architectural modeling palette. Extruded acrylic's various colors and transparency options can easily be coupled with laser cutting techniques to represent a variety of materials and textures in architectural models. Such materials help expand the visual palette, contributing to designers' options for abstracting real building materials (Figure 9.3). Overall, it is also recommended that the material that needs to be laser cut is first tested using a small size sample prior to purchasing large sheets of material.

9.1.2 Plasma Cutting

While it is not used as commonly as laser cutting, plasma cutting constitutes another digital fabrication method used in architecture schools and firms. Since plasma cutters can cut through electrically conductive materials such as steel sheets, plasma cutting is conducive for large-scale fabrication such as furniture prototypes. As a fundamental state of matter, plasma contains a gas consisting of ions and free electrons. Consequently, the plasma cutting process requires creating an electric circuit through the plasma torch and the cutting material by means of grounding. An extremely hot electrically charged gas, such as oxygen, executes the cutting process.

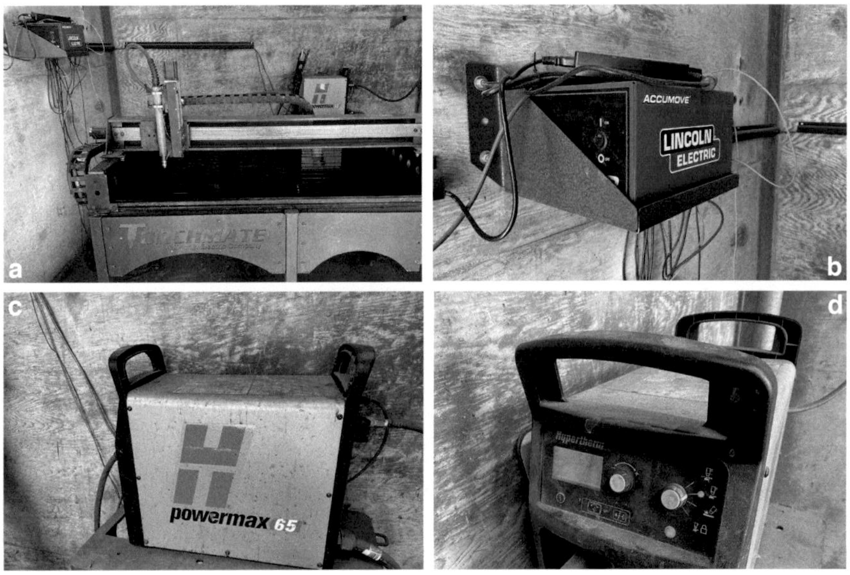

Figure 9.4 *(a) The plasma cutting equipment at California Polytechnic State University San Luis Obispo, College of Architecture facilities with the robot and cutting bed in the front, the power unit to the left, and the electrically charging air compressor and clamps in the back; (b) the power unit; (c) the electrically charging air compressor; and (d) the electric circuit power setting interface. Photographs by the author.*

Basic plasma cutters are typically equipped with a plasma torch which is connected to a moving mechanism that carries the torch on the X and Y axes toolpath generated using a CAD file (i.e., the robot). In addition to the robot, the cutter employs a power unit, electrically charging air compressor, and clamps and wiring for grounding the conductive cutting piece (Figure 9.4).

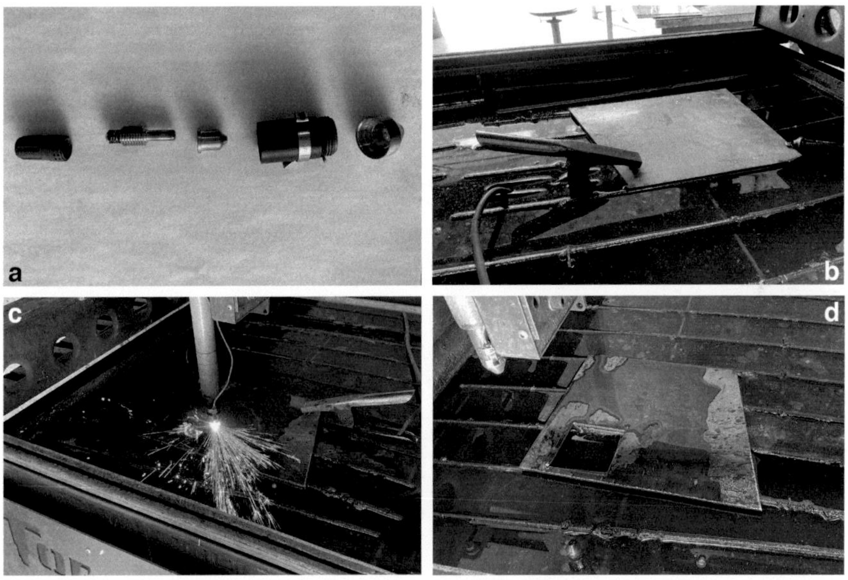

Figure 9.5 *Details from the plasma cutting equipment at California Polytechnic State University San Luis Obispo, College of Architecture facilities. (a) The torch in its disassembled state; (b) a sample cut piece in its grounded state on the cutting bed; (c) the sample cut piece during the cutting operation; and (d) the remaining cut piece after the cutting operation on the cut bed. Photographs by the author.*

The cutting bed contains water, which is for cooling down the cut piece after the operation. Based on the thickness of the material to be cut, the power of the electric current is adjusted. Thicker materials require higher electric current power, which is measured in amperes (Figure 9.5). Similar to some laser cutters, plasma cutters use their proprietary software for toolpath generation. After drawing the desired cut shape, a vector file such as a dxf file is exported and loaded onto the proprietary software. Depending on the plasma cutter's manufacturer and the size and shape of the material to be cut, the robot may need calibration, or the origin point may have to be redefined on the cutting bed. Following the settings, the cut piece is cut using a run command. During the cutting process, a safety mask needs to be worn to protect the eyes.

9.1.3 Waterjet Cutting

Although rarer in architecture firms and schools, waterjet cutting is another digital fabrication method that is capable of cutting through hard-to-cut materials, such as aluminum and steel, with precision. Due to their precision, waterjet cutters are more commonly preferred for industrial production, although they can also be used for architectural and industrial design production and presentations. Similar to laser and plasma cutters, waterjet cutters are equipped with a "gun" that can move on the XY plane based on g-code coordinates, where the "gun" can shoot a very high-pressure stream of water mixed with an abrasive material. Unlike plasma cutting, this technique is more preferable if the material to be cut is sensitive to higher temperatures. Due to the technique's industrial orientation, and the relatively limited use of waterjet cutting in architectural model building, we will not go into further details of the technique in this section.

9.1.4 Time-Saving Model Building Strategies Using Parametric Methods with Cutting Operations in Mind

A combination of parametric methods and cutting operations can help accelerate architectural model building while decreasing the amount of manual labor required. In this section, we will look into three examples of mixing and matching parametric methods and cutting operations. First, we will look into serial sectioning techniques to prepare contours of a selected sloped topography and a sample building mass for laser cutting. The second example will focus on creating a "waffle" structure similar to the Metropol Parasol in Seville, Spain, designed by Jurgen Mayer H. Architects using parametric methods. The third and final example builds on the procedure for surface population of building façades to intervene in solar exposure of large building apertures.

Rapid Contouring for Site Topography and Massing Models. Topography and massing concept models are among the most commonly built model types in architecture schools and firms; not only for design development, but also for presentation. Prior to the availability of digital and parametric methods, designers would need to find topography information for a given terrain and manually cut contours to build site topography models. Similarly, floor plan outline-based massing models were prominent in design development and presentation. Nevertheless, CAD models of terrains and building massing are now commonly accessible, enabling rapid contouring and laser cutting for quick site and massing models.

In this example, we will look into rapid contouring and laser cutting a sloped terrain modeled as a closed polysurface (Figure 9.6a). The site terrain is first introduced into Grasshopper as a "boundary representation" (Brep). In order to create a surface that can precisely contour the terrain, the "Bounding Box" component is used to create a bounding box for the Brep. Since the terrain needs to be contoured horizontally, the bottom face of the bounding box is selected using the "Deconstruct Brep" (DeBrep) and "List Item" components. Using the "move" and "series" component, the bottom face of the bounding box is copied vertically on the Z-axis at one-foot increments (Figure 9.6b). Contouring is completed using the "Brep|Brep" component, which yields closed polylines that can be laser cut (Figure 9.6c). Using the "move" and "series" components, each contour polyline is moved on the Y-axis to avoid overlaps. The contour polylines are then projected onto the c-plane of Rhinoceros using the "project" component. Once baked into a separate Rhinoceros layer, contours can be reorganized to fit into the laser cutter's template (Figure 9.6d and e). In this example, since the three straight sides of the contour pieces enable proper alignment, numbering the pieces is not crucial. Depending on the scale of the target model, appropriate material thickness can be selected to ensure model accuracy.

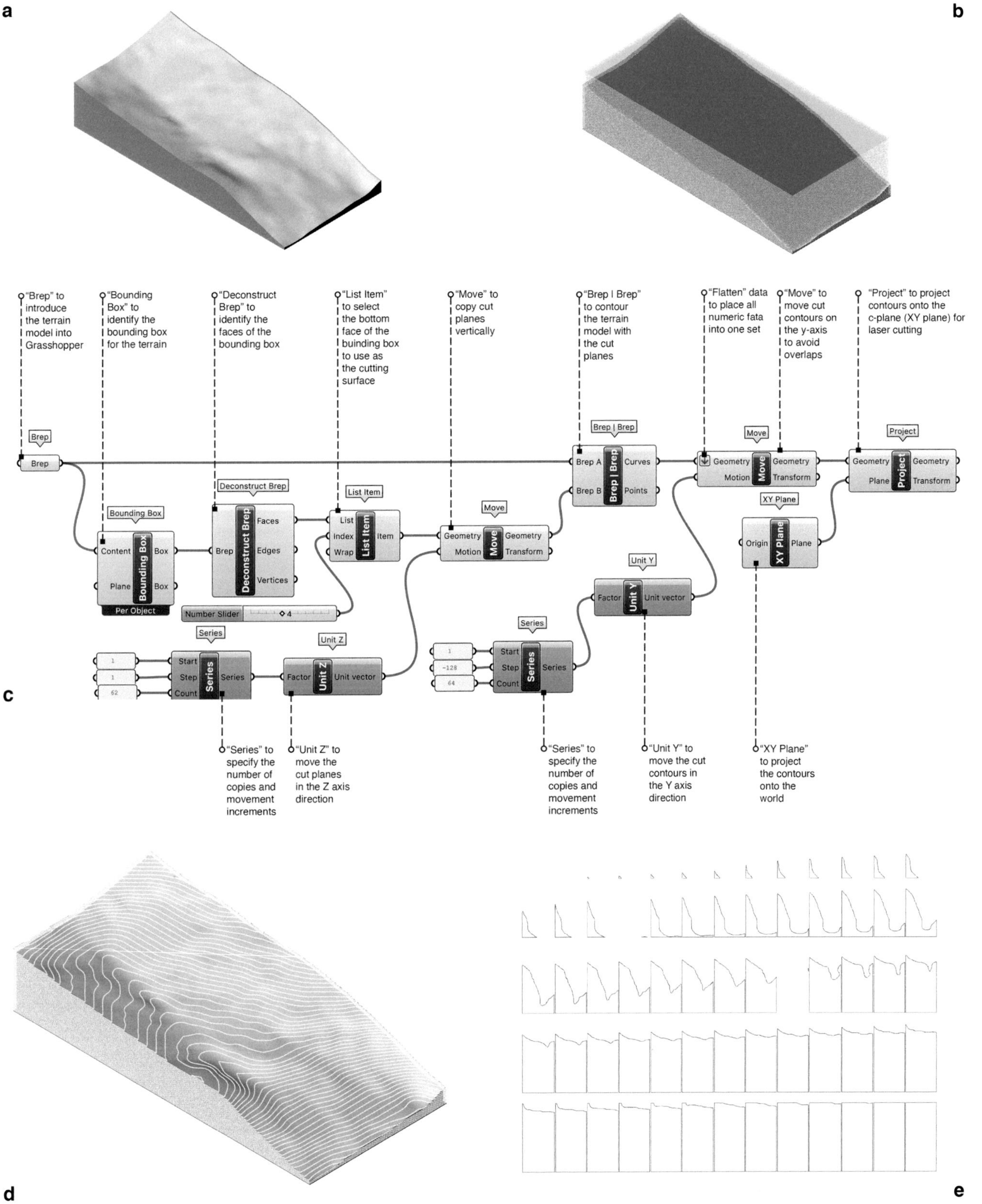

Figure 9.6 *(a) The sloped terrain modeled as a closed polysurface; (b) cut plane copied vertically on Z-axis at one-foot increments; (c) the Grasshopper definition to create closed polylines that can be laser cut; (d) contour polylines to be projected onto the c-plane of Rhinoceros using the "project" component; and (e) contours projected on the c-plane reorganized to fit into the laser cutter's template.*

Interlocking Slices: the "Waffle." Another common approach to representing three-dimensional masses is to create interlocking slices of the mass to be represented, creating an object that resembles a "waffle". The Metropol Parasol in Seville, Spain, designed by Jurgen Mayer H. Architects, represents a well-known example of this approach. This approach is an efficient way to represent both regular and amorphous three-dimensional objects.

In this example we will look into modeling a site terrain using the interlocking slices "waffle" technique. Figure 9.6a illustrates the sample site terrain that we will model using the interlocking slices technique. The sample site terrain model in Figure 9.6 is a closed polysurface which can be easily sliced horizontally and vertically on the XY plane. The Grasshopper definition in Figure 9.7a introduces the terrain's closed polysurface object into Grasshopper using a boundary representation ("Brep") component. To identify horizontal and vertical cutting surfaces on the x and y axes, the "bounding box" component is used, and using the DeBrep and List Item components, the initial horizontal and vertical cutting surfaces are selected. The initial horizontal and vertical cutting surfaces are then copied on the X and Y axis using 12.5-unit increments, and the site terrain Brep is sliced using the "Brep|Brep" (BBX) component (Figure 9.7a).

The resulting Brep slice outlines are then converted into surfaces using the "boundary surfaces" component, and another instance of BBX component is used to find the intersection lines between "waffle" surfaces. Now, for the perpendicular laser cut surfaces to have interlocking notches, U-shaped cuts in opposite directions are necessary to the horizontal and vertical cuts. To ensure that the interlocking notches start at midpoints of intersection lines between "waffle" surfaces, the "point on curve" component is used to identify the midpoints of intersection lines. Then, cylinders in positive and negative directions are introduced with a 1/16" radius, which will enable 1/8" thick materials (i.e., process or chip board) to be used to put together interlocking surfaces (Figure 9.8).

Finally, for digital fabrication purposes, the parts that are ready to be laser cut need to be organized and oriented onto the XY plane. Once the waffle surfaces are trimmed using the notch cylinders, they are projected onto XZ and YZ planes so that the pieces are co-planar. As a last step, the pieces are rotated onto the XY plane using the "Rotate 3D" component. Once baked, the parts that need to be laser cut can be organized to minimize material waste, and the cut pieces can be assembled to represent the target terrain. Figure 9.9 illustrates versions of the final "waffle" terrain model in (a) Grasshopper/Rhinoceros interface with selection; and (b) rendered in Rhinoceros interface. Once laid flat on the XY plane, the "waffle" parts can be "baked" into Rhinoceros. Rhinoceros creates parts as surfaces when baked from Grasshopper. Using Rhinoceros' DupBorder, the parts can be prepared for cutting.

Numbering parts. Whether rapid contouring or making an interlocking slices model, numbering model parts helps organization and assembly. Using Grasshopper for numbering is fast and efficient. A small addition to the Grasshopper definition we used for the interlocking slices section can add numbers to the parts that will be cut. Figure 9.10a illustrates that small addition. First, the rotated, laid flat "waffle" parts from Figure 9.9 are connected to the "Area" component to identify their centroids. The centroids are then connected to Grasshopper's "Text Tag 3D" component through the "location" input, specifying the location of the numbers and ensuring that numbering will appear inside the parts' boundaries. In the next step, the numbers of parts are specified using a "series" component, where the numbers start at 1, the increase steps are set to 1, and the count of elements are set to 21, the total number of parts produced by the "Rotate 3D" component in Figure 9.9. The output of the "Series" component is grafted to generate one-to-one connections between the parts and numbers. Finally, the numbers' text size is specified, which, in this case, is set to 5 units for readability. Once the numbers are "baked" into Rhinoceros, they need to be exploded to get the number text outlines for etching or scoring using the laser cutter.

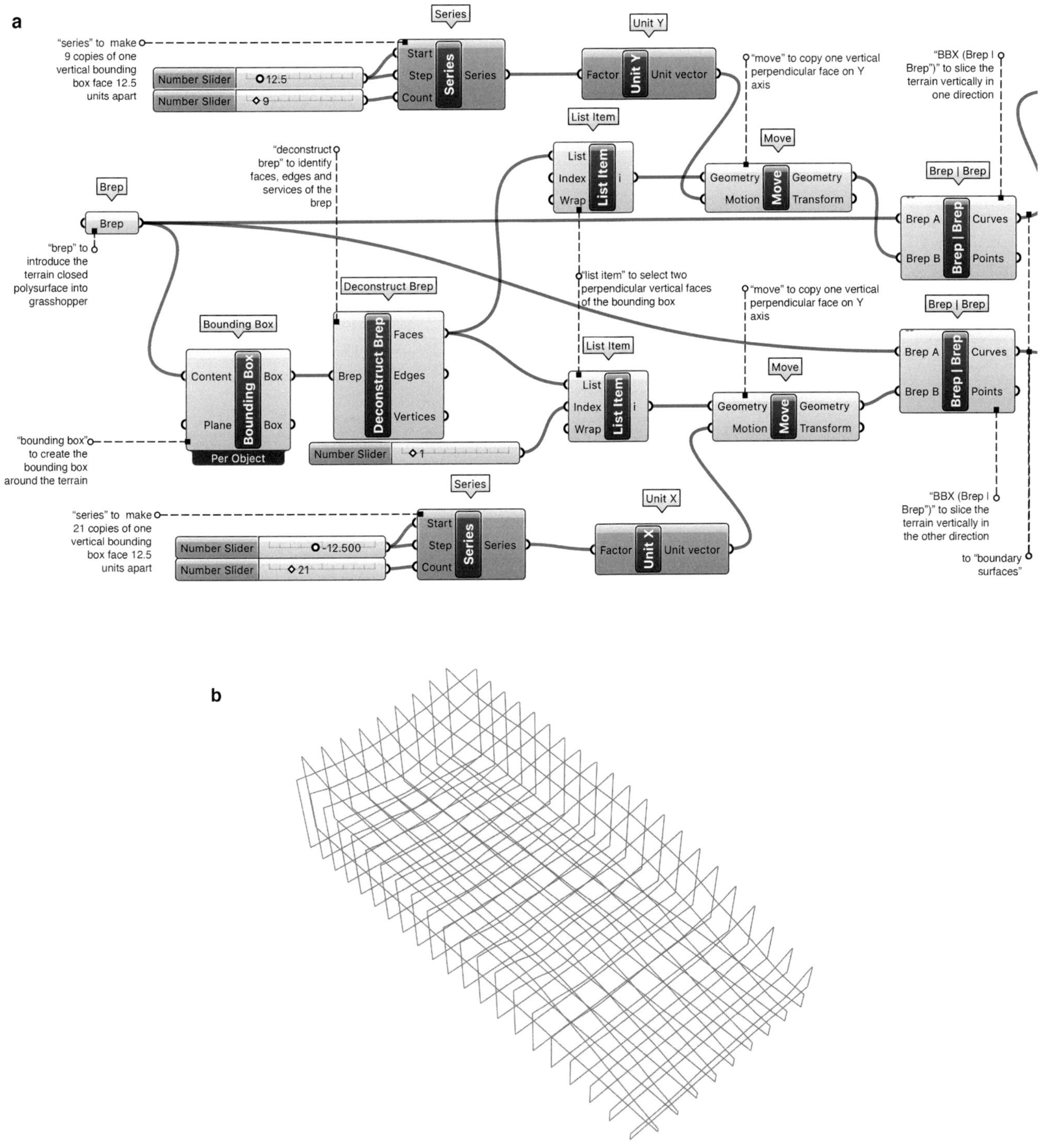

Figure 9.7 (a) the portion of the Grasshopper component used to create vertical cuts of the terrain in X and Y axes; (b) the resulting terrain slices ready for developing an interlocking slices model.

9.2 ADDITIVE TECHNIQUES: THREE-DIMENSIONAL PRINTING

Three-dimensional printing technology has been available since the 1980s. However, within the second half of the last decade, three-dimensional printing has become a lot more prominent in architecture firms and schools. The primary reasons behind this development are the decreasing cost of three-dimensional (3D) printers, and the increasing user friendliness of available equipment. Thanks to the affordability and user friendliness of 3D printing tools today, it is not uncommon to see a number of 3D printers when one walks into a studio in an architectural school or firm.

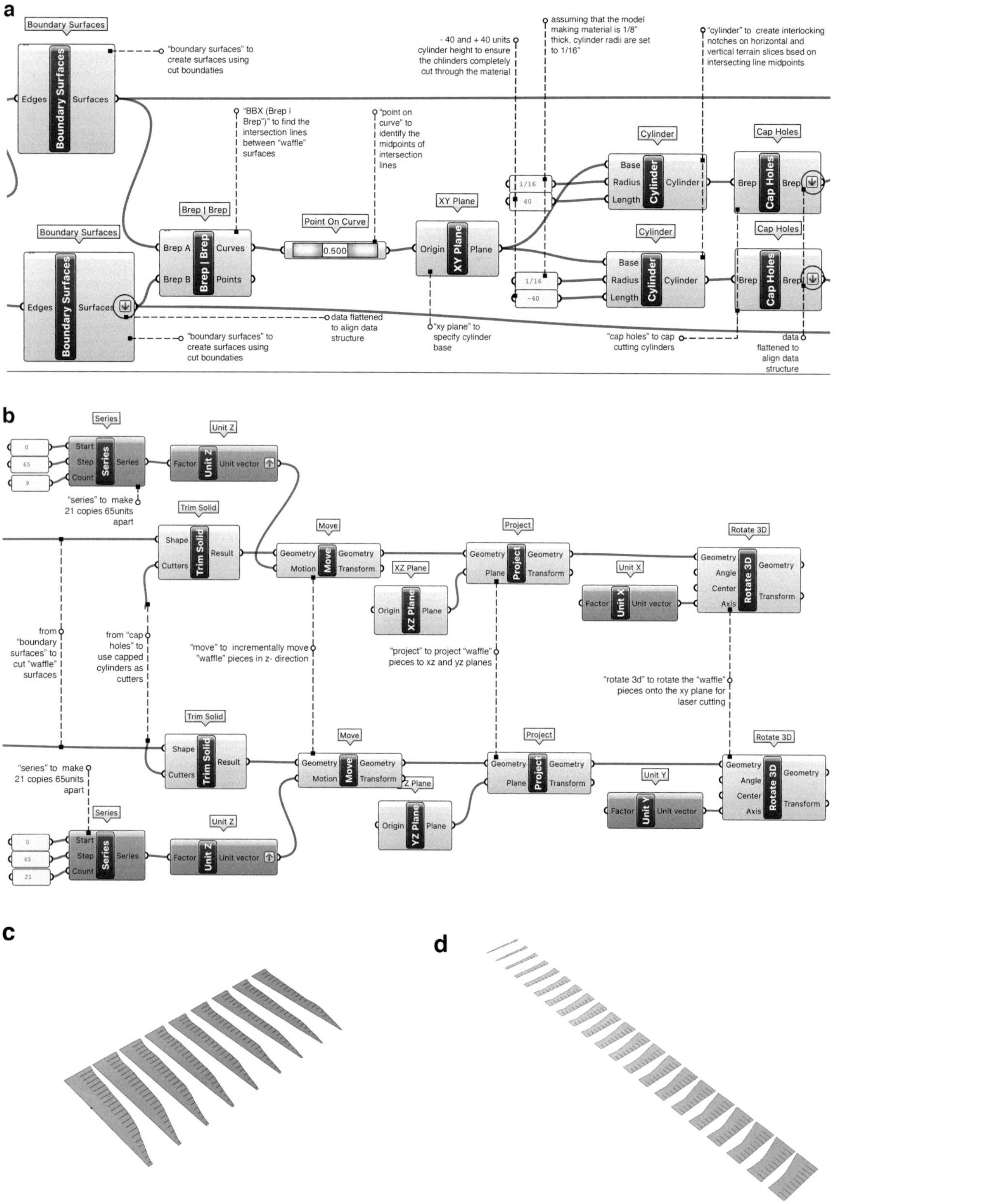

Figure 9.8 The portion of the Grasshopper script used (a) to generate cylinders for trimming notches; (b) to project and lay parts flat for laser cutting; (c and d) model parts laid flat on X and Y axes.

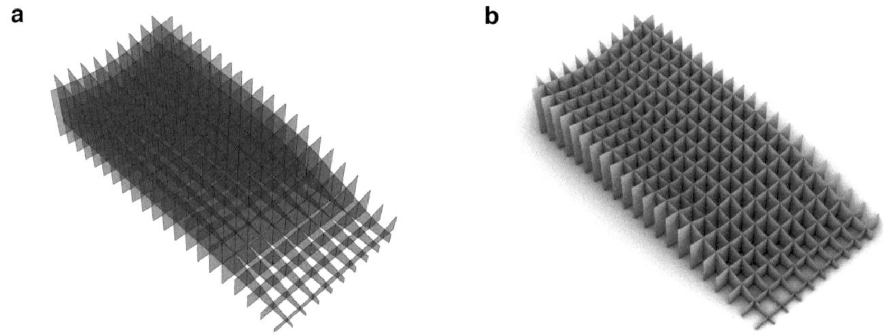

Figure 9.9 *The interlocking terrain model parts (a) in Grasshopper/Rhinoceros interfaces with selection; and (b) rendered in Rhinoceros interface.*

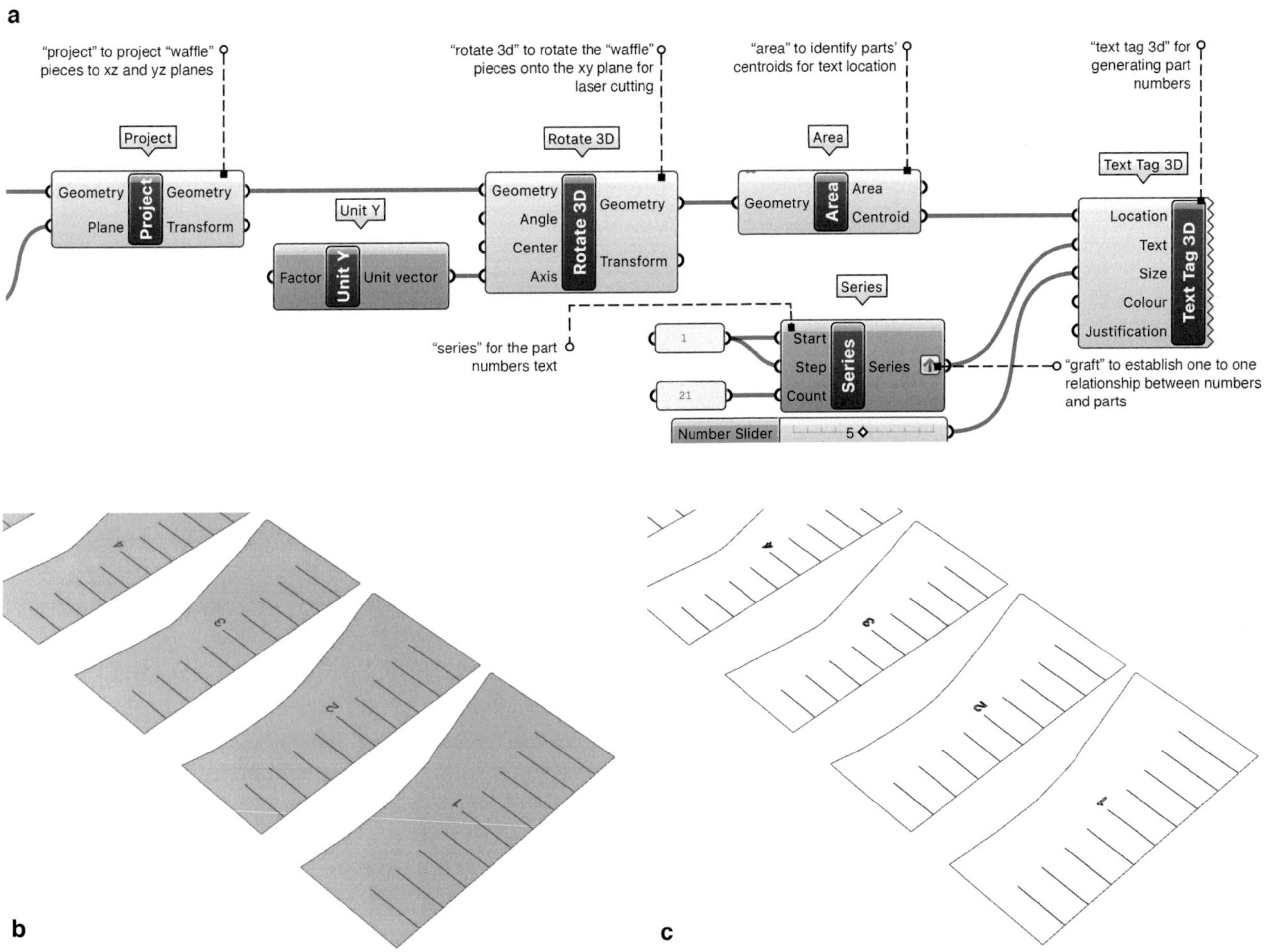

Figure 9.10 *(a) The portion of the Grasshopper script used to number interlocking slices; (b) numbered terrain model parts on X-axis as Grasshopper selection; and (c) numbered terrain model parts baked and ready for laser cutting in Rhinoceros.*

There are three main types of 3D printing technologies: stereolithography (SLA), selective laser sintering (SLS), and fused deposition modeling (FDM). Currently, FDM is the most commonly used 3D printing technique, and we will primarily look into this most accessible 3D printing technique. Prior to that, however, it is important to briefly introduce stereolithography and selective laser sintering as additional techniques which were developed earlier and are still in use in various design and manufacturing disciplines.

Stereolithography (SLA) 3D printers convert liquid resin into hard formed plastic using a laser beam. Their accuracy and capability of providing high levels of detail make SLA 3D printers desirable for industrial applications and precise rapid prototyping. Selective laser sintering (SLS) 3D printers, on the other hand, convert a polymer powder such as nylon into solid form using high-power lasers. The laser beam selectively targets the volume(s) that need to be solidified within the polymer powder. Since the 3D printed object remains within the material powder, no support material is required for complex geometries. SLS printers and their materials tend to be cost effective.

Finally, fused deposition modeling (FDM), the most accessible technique today, uses a system where a heated filament is extruded through a nozzle and onto a printing bed. Polylactic acid (PLA), Polyethylene Terephthalate Glycol (PETG), and Acrylonitrile Butadiene Styrene (ABS) are among the commonly used materials for FDM.

FDM-oriented materials are cost effective, but the technique and the materials do not provide the durability and precision afforded by SLA and SLS 3D printing. Nevertheless, the affordability and user-friendliness of equipment along with the affordability of materials make FDM 3D printing the most accessible 3D printing technique for architecture students, firms, and beginning enthusiasts. Let us look into more details and uses of FDM 3D printing.

9.2.1 Fused Deposition Modeling 3D Printing Basics

FDM 3D printers build by moving a heated nozzle extruding the filament over a heated printing bed. Common FDM 3D printers employ a variety of methods to move the nozzle extruding the filament. Some 3D printers move just the nozzle, and others can move both the nozzle and the 3D printing bed in various ways. Commonly referred to as "delta" printers, some 3D printers only move the nozzle in X, Y, and Z directions over a fixed printing bed, slowly moving the nozzle on the Z axis after each layer of printing is completed using the X and Y axes. Another type of printer moves the nozzle on X and Y directions only, but move the bed in the Z direction downwards, slowly lowering the print bed after each layer is completed by the nozzle using X and Y axis movements. A more commonly used 3D printer type since the early 2020s, on the other hand, moves the nozzle in X, Y, and Z axes and the bed in X and Y axes simultaneously, increasing the height of the nozzle gradually. All types of FDM 3D printing have to print the object from bottom to top. Due to this, cantilevering parts of the object being printed may need a support structure, which will be discussed in the following paragraphs.

Preparing CAD Geometry for FDM 3D Printing. For an object to be 3D printed using the FDM technique, the geometry needs to be "watertight"; in other words, a closed polysurface or mesh surface without any holes. Consequently, it is important to generate 3D models in CAD software that are clean and devoid of overlapping surfaces and openings.

Many CAD programs offer commands that enable differentiating between closed or open polysurfaces or problematic geometries. For example, using Rhinoceros, one can use the "SelClosedPolysrf" (select closed polysurfaces) component, which identifies closed polysurfaces, or "SelOpenPolysrf" (select open polysurfaces) component, which identifies open polysurfaces that can be problematic for FDM 3D printing. Versions of the same commands can be used to identify closed or open meshes as well. Once the closed geometry is ready for 3D printing, it needs to be scaled and exported to an intermediary "slicing" software that will generate the 3D print layers for the printers to follow.

Preparing the Geometry for 3D Printing Using Intermediary Software. The scaled and ready to print geometry needs to be exported into an intermediary "slicer" software to generate the "g-code" file for the 3D printer to properly extrude the filament. "Slicer" software essentially generates contours of the object to be 3D printed in the intervals of the target resolution, which refers to the height of each 3D print layer. For a 3D print to be "sliced," the

3D model needs to be exported from the CAD file in STL (stereolitography) format with the ".stl" file extension. During the exporting process, the CAD program being used will provide options to double-check whether or not the geometry being exported is "watertight."

Today, a variety of "slicer" software is available, most of which can be downloaded and used free of charge. Some 3D printers may also require their own proprietary software for slicing. When the STL file is imported into the slicer software, the software interface shows the object to be printed on a virtual copy of the print bed. At this point, 3D printing settings need to be specified. 3D printing settings, such as nozzle and print bed temperature and printing speed, are usually provided by the slicing software as the default based on commonly used settings: for example, for PLA, nozzle temperature is set to 200–210°C, print bed temperature is set to 50–60°C, and printing speed is set to 50–60 mm/s.

Other key settings for the designer include the infill type and amount, support type and amount, and finally, the print bed adhesion type. Based on the geometry of the object to be printed, the infill type and amount need to be selected carefully. While high-density infill types and amounts can make the print sturdier, they also increase the time and material amount required for the print. Similarly, the type and amount of support need to be carefully considered. Higher support densities may afford higher precision; however, they also increase printing time, and it may be more challenging to separate the support geometry from the printed object. Finally, a variety of print bed adhesion types are provided by various slicing software. In general, for geometries with small footprints, "brim," a thin first layer of the expanded footprint, and for geometries with very small footprints and high vertical distances, "raft," a thicker initial mass of print bed base need to be chosen (Figure 9.11).

Generating Supports. Since FDM 3D printers build objects from the bottom up, if the printed object has cantilevering parts, building a removable support structure below the cantilevering parts may be required. Commonly used slicer software provides options for selecting a variety of support densities and geometries. Since FDM printers build each layer on the layer below, many cantilevering parts that make a large angle with the XY plane can be printed without a support structure. A common indicator of the need for a support structure is the angle between an object's cantilevering part and the XY plane – also the printing bed. Usually, if this angle is below 45 degrees, a support structure below the cantilevering part is needed.

Many affordable FDM 3D printers have a single nozzle, which means that the support structure and the 3D printed object are built by the same nozzle using the same material. This also means that once the printing is complete, the designer needs to clean up the support structure using a tool such as a plier. For the 3D printed object to be smoother and more presentable, the support structure needs to be separated from the main object. In addition,

Figure 9.11 Previewed in slicer software: (a) an object to be 3D printed with a medium amount of infill; (b) the object to be 3D printed with a "brim"; and (c) the object to be 3D printed with a "raft."

if the support structure is too dense, separating the support structure from the main object tends to be fairly time consuming. Therefore, it is important to carefully consider the density of the support structure. Using the slicer software, the designer can adjust the support structure density based on previous personal experience (Figure 9.12).

9.2.2 FDM 3D Printing in the Architectural Design Process

Since it is not a labor-intensive technique (except for 3D modeling using CAD software), FDM 3D printing can greatly contribute to the architectural design process. One of the advantageous uses involves printing the site context of the project and evaluating alternative massing responses to the context and the program. In the early stages of the process, this technique enables rapid testing of multiple mass composition ideas with relative ease. The technique also enables rapid testing of mass composition in relation to sun path on the site (Figure 9.13).

FDM 3D printing can also help the architectural design process by decreasing the amount of labor needed for study models. Parts of study models that may be time consuming to build using conventional methods can be 3D printed, and the time and effort required to build those parts can be invested in other tasks. A good example is the rapid modeling and 3D printing of staircases. Since building models of staircases tends to be time consuming, the designer can easily build simple 3D models of the staircases considered for a building in the design process and then 3D print it. The time and effort needed for conventionally modeling staircases can be invested in other portions of the study model (Figure 9.14).

9.3 SUBTRACTIVE TECHNIQUES

Subtractive digital fabrication techniques involve the removal of material from a given mass of material using a rotating tool. The origins of subtractive machines date back to the nineteenth century. With the advances in CAD and digital fabrication techniques, computer numeric controlled (CNC) machining (or milling) started to become more accessible to architecture schools and firms. Today many architecture schools and firms own various types of CNC milling machines.

Common CNC milling machines are equipped with a rotating drill bit that moves in X, Y, and Z directions based on three-dimensional data from a CAD file. The drill bits' rotation frequency can be adjusted based on the type of material that needs to be milled. Likewise, bits of various sizes can be replaced based on the task and material. The material to be milled is secured on a static bed after which the rotating mill starts removing material based on the CAD data provided. Common materials that can be milled for architectural models include, but are not limited to wood, wood products such as MDF, and "foam" products, such as extruded polystyrene boards.

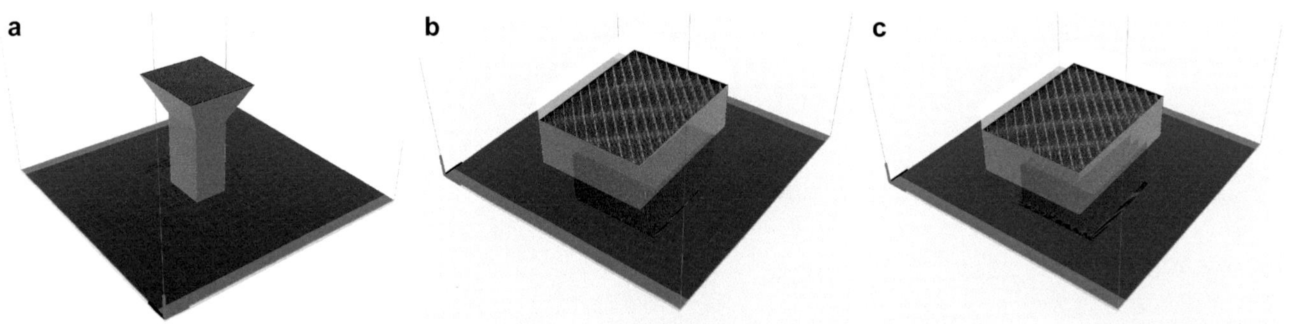

Figure 9.12 Previewed in slicer software: (a) an object to be 3D printed that does not need support due to the slope angle of its cantilever; (b) an object with a cantilever to be 3D printed with high-density support; (b) an object with a cantilever to be 3D printed with low-density support.

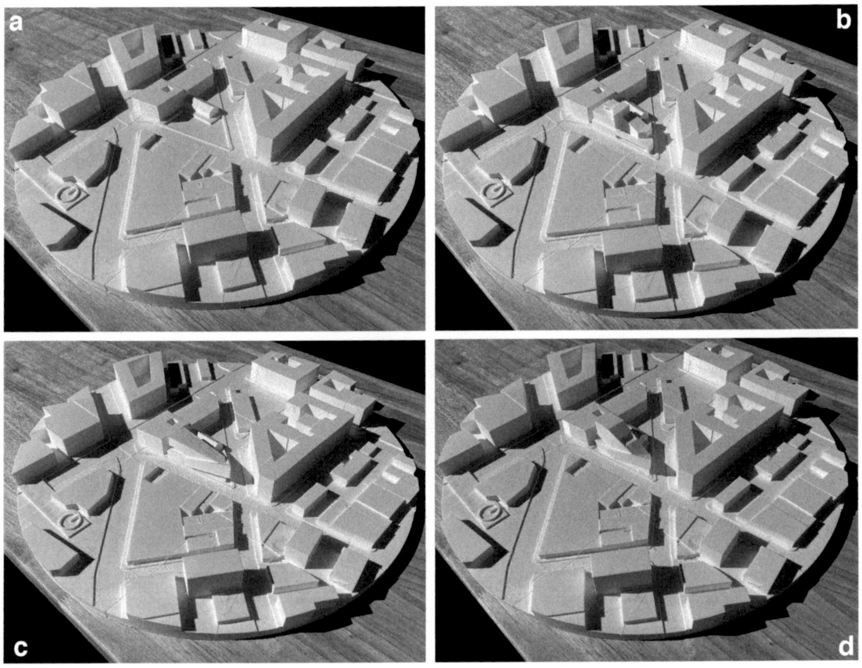

Figure 9.13 *(a) A 1/64" = 1' scale context massing model 3D printed by the author for a project in Los Angeles; (b), (c), and (d) three iterations of a contemporary arts center proposition being tested on the site in early stages of the design process. Massing models on b, c, and d courtesy of Katherine Neuner, author's former student. The site was 3D modeled, printed, and photographed by the author.*

Figure 9.14 *3D printed staircases and laser cut scaled human figures for a study model. Study model Courtesy Graci Lusk, author's former student. Photograph by the author.*

CNC milling can be employed for various tasks in architectural modeling, but it is more commonly used for modeling site(s) with diverse topographical features. Therefore, CNC milling can constitute an alternative to rapid contouring of sheet materials discussed in Section 9.1.4. CNC milling can also be employed for building furniture depending on the design and target materials. In this section we will look into basic steps and examples of CNC milling for architectural model building.

9.3.1 Basic CNC Milling Steps

Basic CNC milling steps involve preparing the 3D model, developing the toolpath, securing the material on the cutting bed, and running the milling job. Similar to 3D printing slicer software, there are a number of software packages that can analyze 3D geometry and generate a milling toolpath for a variety of machines. Many of these require an STL file based on a closed polysurface for toolpath generation. Different CNC routers may also offer their own proprietary software for toolpath generation. In this section, we will look into the milling of the sample topography introduced in Section 9.1.4 using extruded polystyrene board.

After scaling the 3D file that will be milled, it is exported in the STL format. The file is then imported into the software. At this point, it is important to select a milling material that has sufficient depth, so that the drilling bit does not hit and damage the CNC router's bed due to the use of a thin material. Once the material with sufficient thickness is selected, the X, Y, and Z axes dimensions of the material are introduced to the software package. Following this step, in this example, the material to be milled is secured on the CNC router's bed using double-sided tape. Using other CNC routers, the material may also have to be secured on the milling bed using other means, such as using screws and a customized jig.

After securing the material to be milled on the CNC router bed, rough and fine milling toolpaths are generated. Depending on the target milling resolution, only the rough milling toolpath, or fine milling toolpath can be used. While rough toolpath milling consumes shorter amounts of time, the resulting resolution is low. Likewise, fine toolpath milling yields a higher resolution and finer surfaces but consumes more time.

The following step involves informing the CNC router about the location of the material on the bed and the starting point (the origin). This step can vary according to the CNC router being used. While some CNC routers accept origin information through mechanical means, others may accept digital information. Similar to 3D printing slicer software, CNC milling software often offers static and animated previews of the toolpath and the upcoming milling process (Figure 9.15).

Figure 9.15 *(a) The topography STL file imported into the CNC router's software; (b) setting up the milling resolution; (c) generating the toolpath for the milling process; and (d) preview of the upcoming milling outcome. Screenshots courtesy of Andrea Garavaryan, author's former student.*

The final step involves the actual milling task. Depending on the CNC router being used, the router may be able to select and install the required drill bits based on the resolution. Alternatively, the user may have to manually change drill bits during the milling process. It is advisable to be present to observe the CNC router during the milling process. Most CNC routers are equipped with an emergency stop button to stop the process in case of an unexpected or damaging move. All such observations need to be conducted using safety gear, such as goggles for the eyes and masks to avoid inhaling fine particles of the material being milled.

In this example, a fine-scale CNC router was used for demonstrating the milling of the sample 3D topography. The CNC router used offered protection from the milling process using an oven-like glass lid that separates the user from the milling process. In many cases, CNC routers also provide a vacuuming mechanism to safely absorb and store the particles of the milled material. Despite such mechanisms, in many cases, the user still needs to vacuum and clean up the equipment and milling space following the milling process. Following the milling process, many materials such as medium density fiber (MDF) and extruded polystyrene board may need manual sanding and finishing (Figure 9.16).

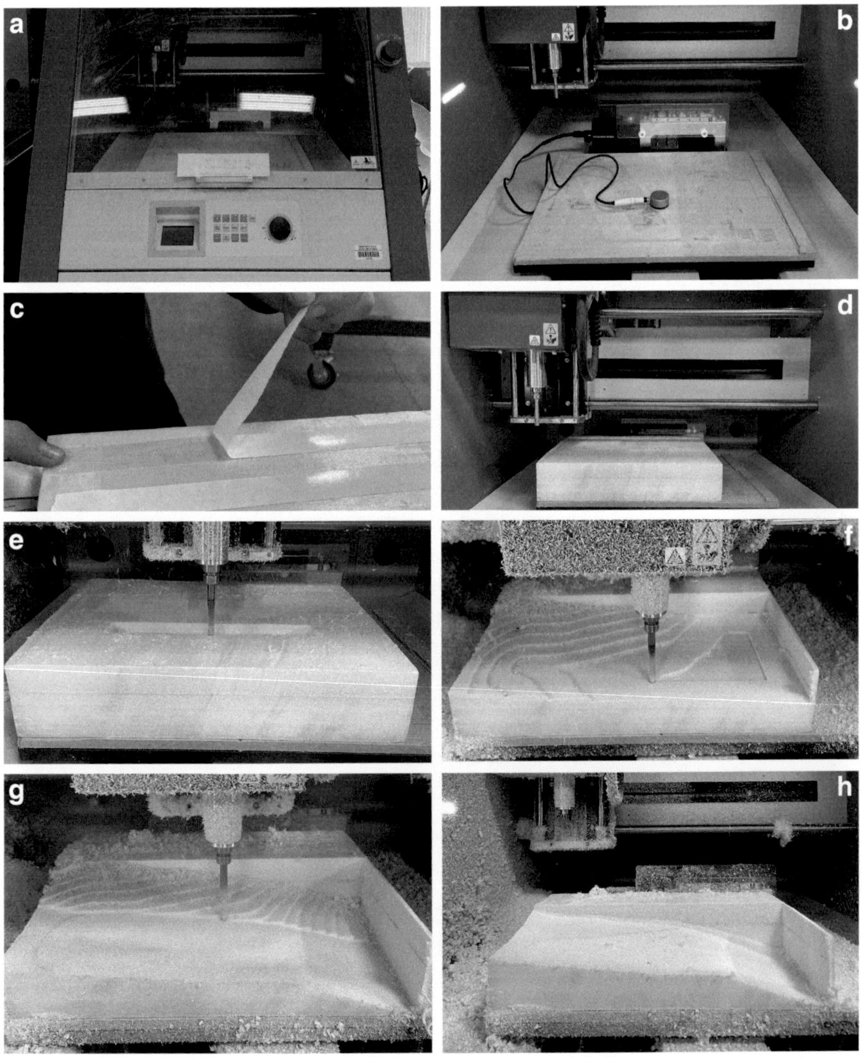

Figure 9.16 *(a) High resolution CNC router with protective screen; (b) CNC router being calibrated with its calibration device; (c) extruded polystyrene being prepared for securing on CNC bed using double-sided tape; (d) extruded polystyrene secured on the CNC router bed prior to milling; (e) beginning stages of the milling process; (f) rough milling; (g) detailing in progress; and (h) final topography model at the end of the milling process. The CNC milling process and photographs courtesy of Andrea Garavaryan, author's former student.*

9.4 MIXING AND MATCHING METHODS AND MATERIALS: DIGITAL FABRICATION TECHNIQUES AND ARCHITECTURAL MODEL BUILDING MATERIALS

Similar to building a real structure, architectural models need to be designed for stability for presentation and transportation, so that they can perform structurally, and parts of the model do not fall off. Mixing and matching materials not only makes architectural models more presentable, but also helps with time saving and stability. Whether students or professionals, designers need to design the architectural model: how structural elements and the model sit on the site, how structural elements connect to representations of building slabs, how façade materials connect to the slabs and structural elements, how vertical circulation elements are represented, and how entourage is prepared and represented. In this section, we will look into a variety of digital fabrication methods and material selection strategies for building architectural models.

9.4.1 Representing the Site

Depending on the site location and type, various site representation materials and digital fabrication methods are available. For flat and urban sites, a combination of laser cutting and 3D printing methods can help advance precision and presentation quality. A good example is the use of laser cutting and etching sheet materials for the site and 3D printing for context buildings' models. For sites with a slope, whether they be urban or rural, laser cutting with rapid contouring or CNC routing tend to offer precision and time efficiency. Using either combination usually requires additional steps for achieving presentation quality. While laser cut model parts may need to be cleaned (and in some cases painted), CNC milled topography models may need to be finished by sanding. After sanding, if the material is absorptive, or sensitive to paint materials, it may need to be covered with gesso before any potential painting decisions (Figure 9.17). For painting, it is good practice to use paint products that do not have negative impact(s) on the environment, such as spray paint.

9.4.2 Representing the Structural System and Slabs

When building an architectural model, representing the structural system and slabs often creates challenges in aligning and continuity of materials. To overcome such challenges, it is advisable to ensure the continuity of vertical elements through horizontal elements. Specifically, it is good practice to precut voids on horizontal elements, such as slabs, for the vertical elements such as columns and egress staircases to go through. In doing so, material selection is important for accurate scale representation. Precut materials such as basswood can be helpful in representing columns and beams. Based on the target model scale, sheet materials that offer a variety of thicknesses may be considered. For example, on a 1/16" = 1' scale architectural model, to represent a floor plate thickness of 4' (including the slab and

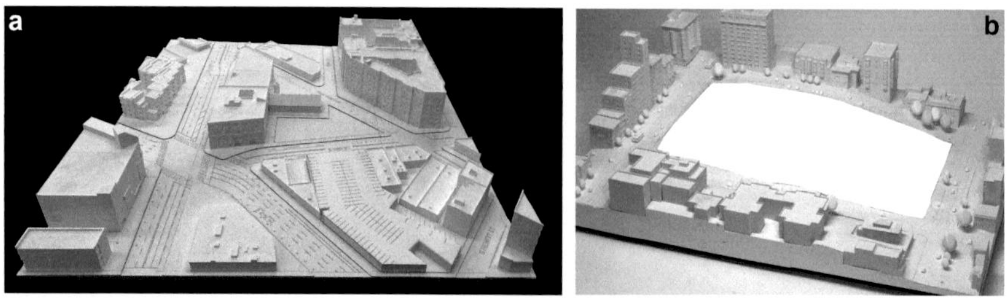

Figure 9.17 (a) A site model for a flat urban site using MDF, process board, 3D printing, and laser cutting (this model was collaboratively built using process board and PLA filament using laser cutting and 3D printing techniques by all the members of author's studio in Fall 2021); (b) a site model for a sloped site built using extruded polystyrene boards, gesso, white acrylic paint and CNC milling (this model was collaboratively built using extruded polystyrene, PLA filament, and Bristol paper using CNC milling, laser cutting, and 3D printing techniques by all the members of author's studio in Winter/Spring 2019). Photographs by the author.

the distance between the floor surface and the suspended ceiling below, to accommodate mechanical systems), a 1/4" MDF sheet can be laser cut. Similarly, 1/8" thick sheet materials can be laser cut to represent 2' × 2' columns on a 1/16" = 1' scale architectural model (Figure 9.18).

9.4.3 Representing Vertical Circulation Elements

Traditionally, representing staircases has been among the most time-consuming tasks in architectural model building. The advent of digital fabrication methods has decreased the amount of time required for such tasks. For study models, rapid laser cutting and etching can help create quick 3D representations of staircases. For presentation models, the popularity of 3D printing techniques continue to increase due to the level of detail that can easily be integrated (i.e., steps and railings) and the ease they provide in creating staircases with complex geometries. For more conventional vertical circulation elements, such as elevator cores and rectangular egress stairs, rectangular prisms cut out of sheet materials are advisable with the current technologies available (Figure 9.18).

9.4.4 Representing Façade Materials

Representing façade materials and textures requires abstraction due to scale differences and the differences between building materials and available modeling materials. While it is common to use sheet materials for façade representations, 3D printing can also be occasionally used for complex geometries. Common sheet materials for representing façade elements include process board, chipboard, acrylic, and various commercially available perforated paper types. Perforated façade elements will often need to be represented (a) with exaggerated scale if using digital fabrication techniques, or (b) abstracting the perforation scale using commercially available perforated paper. Despite being more time consuming, 3D printing façade elements remains to be an additional option for representing façade elements (Figure 9.19).

9.4.5 Entourage

Entourage is a critical element of any architectural model, which helps provide a sense of scale, thereby increasing the understanding of the objects represented in relation to human scale. Entourage in architectural modeling includes, but is not limited to human figures, vehicles, street lighting, trees, as well as interiors and street furniture. The precision and time efficiency afforded by digital fabrication methods also make building entourage into study

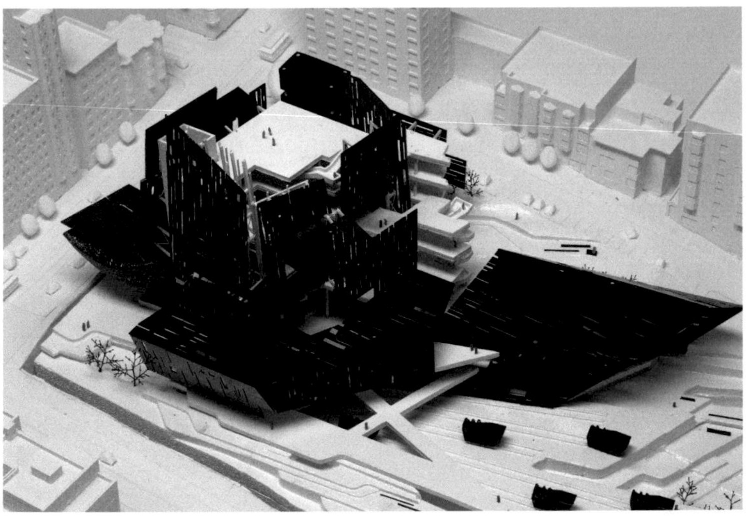

Figure 9.18 A 1/16" = 1' architectural model representing slabs using (a) laser cut 1/4" thick MDF sheet material; (b) columns using basswood; (c) staircases using 3D printed scaled elements; and (d) egress stairs using laser cut and sheet materials to build rectangular prisms. Architectural Model courtesy of Violeta Smart, author's former student. Photograph by the author.

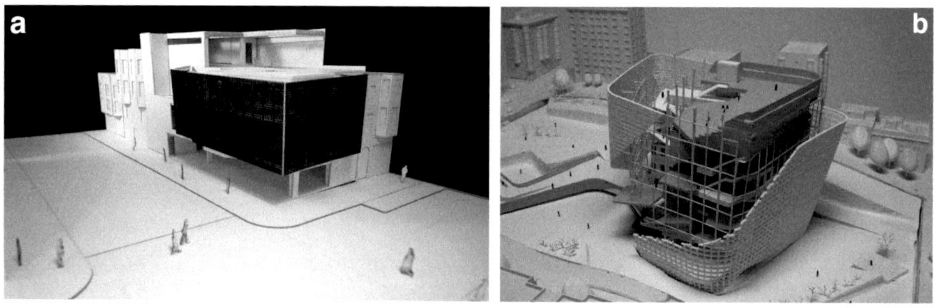

Figure 9.19 *Secondary façade skin system representation (a) using exaggerated scale and commercially available perforated paper (architectural model courtesy Michele Triantafillidis, author's former student); (b) using exaggerated scale and 3D printing (architectural model courtesy Tammy Nguyen, author's former student). Photographs by the author.*

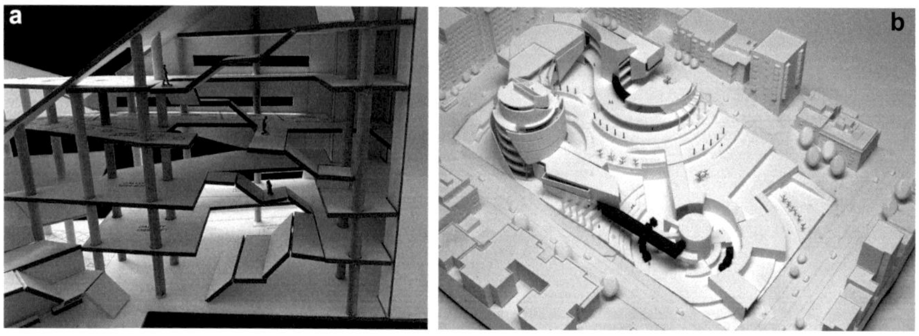

Figure 9.20 *(a) Study model with human figure entourage built using the laser cutting technique (study model courtesy Katherine Neuner; author's former student); and (b) final presentation model with vehicle and tree entourage built using 3D printing (final presentation model courtesy Kiah Hixon, author's former student). Photographs by the author.*

and presentation models a relatively easy task. Laser cutting and 3D printing are currently common methods for generating entourage for architectural models. For smaller scale models, laser cutting human figures and furniture items tend to be fast and efficient. For larger entourage elements such as vehicles, street lighting, and trees, one needs to make a decision between laser cutting and 3D printing based on the scale, abstraction level, and precision that is needed (Figure 9.20).

9.5 POSSIBLE DEVELOPMENTS: PARAMETRIC METHODS, DIGITAL FABRICATION, AND THE FUTURE OF ARCHITECTURAL MODEL MAKING

In this chapter, we looked into parametric and digital fabrication methods that are instrumental for architectural model building as of the year 2022. Approximately since year 2010, parametric and digital fabrication methods have developed immensely, which has also made them accessible to a much larger audience of architecture schools and firms worldwide. It would not be surprising to see the expanding use and availability of these methods to a much larger portion of the architecture community within the immediate years to come. Having taken a snapshot of the current uses and availability of parametric and digital fabrication methods in architectural model making, let us move into our last chapter, where we will delve into a deeper discussion about possible routes for future development.

CHAPTER 10

RECONTEXTUALIZING PARAMETRIC METHODS IN ARCHITECTURE
Routes for Further Development

In the previous nine chapters of this book, we discussed multiple facets of parametric design in architecture. In Chapter 1, we discussed the basics that differentiate parametric design from other design methods available to us. Chapter 2 introduced the history and contemporary debates about parametric design in architecture. Starting with the third chapter, we looked into specific parametric methods that may contribute to various phases of the architectural design process. Chapter 3 focused on parametric methods that may help with precision and time efficiency during site analysis. In Chapter 4, we discussed parametric methods that can contribute to conceptual development and early mass composition. Chapter 5 introduced various spatial analysis methods to evaluate spatial organization decisions. While Chapter 6 introduced parametric methods to custom design skin systems, Chapter 8 introduced parametrically evaluating their environmental performance outcomes. In Chapter 7, we looked into evolutionary solvers, which can help immensely with decision-making based on a number of variables: while the Galapagos plug-in for Grasshopper is helpful with single criterion decision-making processes, the Octopus plug-in can help us evaluate options based on multiple design criteria. Finally, in Chapter 9, we looked into digital fabrication methods and how they can help support the architectural design process in a variety of phases. In the current chapter, we will step back and look into the world of parametric design in architecture in light of all issues, methods, and concerns discussed so far. Our objective is to recontextualize parametric methods in architecture and discuss routes for future development.

10.1 CONTRIBUTIONS OF PARAMETRIC METHODS IN THE ARCHITECTURAL DESIGN PROCESS

In Chapters 1 and 2, we discussed that pre-digital parametric design methods already contributed to architectural explorations via descriptions that defined interrelationships between design elements, and their proportions instead of imposing an architectural style. This fundamental contribution of parametric design continues to be a major advantage in architectural design today.

How about digital parametric methods and their contributions in the architectural design process? They certainly yield efficiency in time consumption and effort. Beyond efficiency, however, parametric methods do contribute to the fluency of architectural design processes in various ways. Let us look into these advantages as we prepare to discuss potential futures for parametric design methods in architecture.

DOI: 10.4324/9781003230052-10

10.1.1 Contributions to Development, Analysis, and Manipulation of Complex Geometries

Among the key contributions of digital parametric design methods in architectural design have been in development, analysis, and manipulation of complex geometries. Simplifying and manipulating complex geometries using CAD software has been traditionally challenging due to the dependence of many CAD software on Euclidian geometry. As of 2022, it seems like advanced CAD software coupled with parametric tools provide many time and effort-efficient advantages about this challenge.

Development, Analysis, and Manipulation of NURBS Geometries. As discussed earlier, NURBS stands for non-uniform rational B-splines, which is essentially a mathematical description of two or three-dimensional geometries. Novel tools introduced to Rhinoceros within the recent years have made development and manipulation of complex NURBS geometries for many Rhinoceros commands such as "CageEdit," and tools such as "SubD" save time and effort during the development and manipulation of complex geometries.

Parametric methods have added a new dimension for quick and time/energy saving NURBS analysis tools. A good example is the "Paneling Tools" suite developed by Rajaa Issa and McNeel Associates. The suite is not limited to Rhinoceros but has a set of tools offered in the Grasshopper environment. This set of tools can easily analyze and subdivide complex geometries using both the Rhinoceros and Grasshopper interfaces. It is especially useful when complex and curved geometries are considered. Available for download free of charge, this suite is representative of contemporary parametric tools that can help make designers' lives easier given the contemporary level of digital developments.

As we discussed in earlier chapters, Grasshopper's "isotrim" and "divide domain 2" components provide efficiency and precision during the subdivision of complex curved geometries. Grasshopper plug-ins such as "Lunchbox" can further streamline complex subdivision and paneling processes. Overall, parametric tools and methods have greatly contributed to experimentation with complex NURBS geometries.

Development, Analysis, and Manipulation of Mesh Geometries. While many complex geometries may be easier to analyze and manipulate in mesh format, they also tend to be more challenging to control when it comes to form manipulation. We now know based on our discussion in Chapter 4 that mesh geometries use a lot more vertices, edges, and surfaces to define surfaces compared to NURBS geometries. This becomes advantageous particularly with complex and curved geometries.

One can easily manipulate and make complex mesh geometries presentable by using commonly available, free of charge Grasshopper plug-ins. We discussed such plug-ins in Chapter 4 in this book. Although it is harder to manipulate the end product, manipulations through plug-ins such as Weaverbird can help make complex geometries more accessible for many designers, especially making physical modeling more accessible through desktop 3D printers. The key point in this process is to learn about the fundamentals about the differences between NURBS and Mesh geometries, which we discussed in earlier chapters in this book. Overall, parametric methods and tools have made experimentation with complex mesh geometries possible, which would have been almost impossible for beginners about 20 years ago. The recommendation here is to delve further into the geometric properties of NURBS and Mesh geometries after getting a good basic understanding of basic geometry definition in CAD software and parametric methods that involve digital geometric manipulation.

10.1.2 Contributions by Bringing in Empirical Approaches and Methods into the Architectural Design Process

Another contribution of parametric methods is making empirical approaches and methods a better integrated part of the architectural design process. Configurational analysis and visibility analysis have been a part of architectural research for a long time. However due to their data-intensive nature, their use in design and research processes tended to be time consuming. The data-driven approach of parametric methods has made it possible to integrate such analyses into the architectural design process. Using native Grasshopper components or freely available plug-ins, students and professionals can now analyze their design proposals empirically for visibility and configurational implications. This brings an additional analytical capability to the large arsenal of tools we already have, such as building physical models and line-drawing iterations.

Another set of analytical tools that have long been an integral part of architectural design and research processes involves environmental performance analysis. Energy use and daylighting are key factors not only in architecture's responsibility in response to the climate crisis but also in our responsibility about the well-being and productivity of people occupying buildings. As we discussed in Chapters 6 and 8, parametric methods streamline such analyses and can make them integral to the design process. The energy use and daylighting implications of a proposed skin system can now be quickly analyzed. If the skin system has been designed parametrically, it can be altered in a short amount of time by altering parameters and reanalyzing. Overall, parametric methods have proven efficient in environmental performance analysis during the architectural design process.

10.1.3 Decreasing the Number of Third-Party Software and Streamlining the Design Process

Parametric methods in architecture can also decrease dependency on third-party software used for streamlining the design process. Due to their data-intensive nature, processes such as environmental performance analysis and configurational analysis tend to have separate software for such analyses. A number of online environmental performance analysis tools, as well as offline configurational analysis software, exist. While such tools can be very efficient and precise, they usually require their users to complete some form of export/import procedure from the user's preferred CAD software into the tool itself. Parametric tools can eliminate this need.

A good example is Ladybug Tools for environmental data and performance analysis. Both at the environmental data analysis and environmental performance analysis levels, architects have conventionally had to rely on third-party software and tools. The toolkit provided by Ladybug eliminates this need for users of Rhinoceros and Grasshopper. Similar advantages exist for users of other CAD/parametric counterpart software packages. Eliminating the need for exporting/converting/importing drawings or data, such tool sets save time and effort. The advantage lies not only in the time efficiency of the tool, but also in the elimination of the need for switching back and forth between additional software or tools. An additional positive is the avoidance of concentration loss during the workflow.

10.1.4 Time- and Effort-Saving Optimization Techniques in Design Decision-making: Evolutionary Solvers

A big leap in the development of digital parametric methods in architecture comes in the form of evolutionary solvers. By generating and evaluating multiple genomes against single or multiple criteria, evolutionary solvers can help decision-making processes through optimization. Conventionally, architects and designers do not take optimization as the ultimate objective in the design process – the idea is to develop a solution that not only responds to problems but also is a solution that displays a unique character. Nevertheless, evolutionary solvers do prove useful for decision-making on one criterion, or a small number of criteria, in the process. Essentially, evolutionary tools prove helpful for repetitive testing of alternatives.

As we discussed in Chapter 7, one can test design alternatives based on a single criterion or multiple criteria. While the Galapagos plug-in for Grasshopper can optimize alternatives based on a single criterion, the Octopus plug-in for Grasshopper can optimize alternatives based on multiple criteria. We have discussed examples of single criterion and multiple criteria optimization processes in Chapter 7. As of the time of this writing, it is possible to state that optimization processes using evolutionary solvers tend to be time consuming. As of now, once multiple criteria optimizations get in the picture, the process can be even more time consuming. Clearly, the complexity and size of the NURBS geometry being analyzed also affects the data processing time required.

Nevertheless, hardware and software developments in computing seem to continue at an ever-increasing pace. There is a gigantic gap between computer hardware capabilities and parametric computing capabilities between 2017 and 2022. Therefore, it would not be unreasonable to anticipate that in the upcoming years evolutionary solvers can become more efficient and offer better streamlined processes. Overall, one can anticipate that parametric optimization methods and tools will continue to advance in the upcoming years.

10.1.5 Advances in Digital Fabrication Methods and Tools

Advances in digital fabrication methods and tools have had a profound impact on architectural design processes – both for students and professionals – over the last decades. These advances can be primarily categorized under the titles "economic accessibility," "interface accessibility," "time and effort efficiency," and "precision."

Economic Accessibility. Especially since year 2015, prices for digital fabrication tools have been dropping, making them more and more accessible to architecture students and professionals. Among these, low-cost 3D printers that can use PLA, ABS, and PETG as well as smaller scale CNC routers come to the forefront. Similarly, 3D printing materials such as PLA, ABS, and PETG seem to be getting cheaper as the demand and production increases. As of today, it is not uncommon to see many self-owned 3D printers on student desks as a part of studio culture in architecture schools. Over the past few years, this has enabled architecture students to develop, 3D print, and evaluate more and more prototypes and mass compositions in relation to the project context. Similarly, architecture offices rely more and more on 3D printing technologies for rapid prototyping and evaluating design iterations.

As the costs of digital fabrication tools and materials decrease, the architectural design process is positively affected in terms of precision and efficiency. More and more architecture students and offices can now test ideas using time-efficient digital fabrication tools for physical modeling. It would not be unreasonable to expect this trend to continue, and digital fabrication tools to become more economically accessible worldwide.

Interface Accessibility. As parametric methods and digital fabrication methods advance, the interface between parametric tools and digital fabrication tools become more user-friendly and accessible. While many digital fabrication tools have their proprietary software, within the last few years we have been witnessing the release of more and more software packages that can process three-dimensional data in multiple formats. These include, but are not limited to 3D printing, laser cutting, and CNC routing methods. More and more architecture students and beginning professionals can now use accessible interfaces between their software and digital fabrication tools, expanding student and professional architectural designers' reach.

Time and Effort Accessibility. The advances achieved in the mechanisms of digital fabrication tools have made them less time and effort consuming. Pre-prototype development now takes less time and effort since digital fabrication tools can achieve increasing amounts of detail. A good example is the rapid development of economically accessible desktop 3D printers. Not only do the printers now print faster and with more precision but also pre-prototype development software for 3D printers has decreased the amount of preparation time needed. Over time, software developers have added new infill patterns and support structures that leave fewer tasks to the designer.

Precision. Especially within the past five to seven years, many digital fabrication tools have become increasingly precise. One good example is CNC routers that employ smaller-sized drill bits. Although they may be more time intensive, these routers can achieve increasing amounts of precision using smaller drill bits. Some newer CNC router models also do not require manual drill bit change, automatically changing drill bits based on the level of precision required. Another similar example is the newer economically accessible desktop 3D printers. Advances in the design of their software and mechanisms have increased their 3D printing precision, allowing the designers to print smaller and more precise model parts.

10.2 COMPUTER-AIDED DESIGN, PARAMETRIC DESIGN, DIGITAL FABRICATION, AND EMERGING CONCERNS IN ARCHITECTURAL DESIGN

As architects and designers, we have many "conventional" design methods and tools in our arsenal that have been tested and perfected over time. Pencil and ink sketching helps us in idea generation and communicating the observed or desired atmosphere and scale in a space. Whether two- or three-dimensional, hand-drafted line-drawings (i.e., plans, sections, axonometric illustrations) help ***and*** require us to always keep the scale of spaces we are creating in mind. Manually building physical study models immensely helps with visualizing spaces, studying their potential atmospheres, as well as idea generation and developing iterations. Manually building physical presentation models can help us add a humane feel to the presentation through analog interventions.

CAD, parametric design, and digital fabrication have altered the dynamics of two- and three-dimensional architectural representation. It is not uncommon to observe in architecture schools that students do not sketch their design ideas and observations as often as they used to. Study and presentation models are now heavily dependent on digital fabrication methods. The almost limitless capability of CAD methods in zooming in and out of line-drawings as well as 3D models weaken the link between the designer and a sense of scale in the spaces being designed. Three-dimensional rendering and physical modeling are now heavily dependent on digital models.

These developments have triggered an expected and natural series of concerns about the quality of architectural design production among experienced professionals as well as academics. First off, it is fairly easy to observe that many architecture students and beginning designers are more distant to well-established, tested, perfected, and advantageous design methods, tools, and techniques. This distancing seems to be especially observable on the disconnection of student and beginning architectural designers from a sense of scale as well as the sense of atmosphere of the spaces being designed.

Such concerns especially seem to be elevated due to the use of "fashionable" parametric physical expressions by beginning designers around the world. Many professionals and academics are concerned that the similarities among "fashionable" parametric physical expression proposals from many architecture schools are causing an "impersonalization" of architectural design proposals.

A similar set of concerns comes to the forefront when it comes to architectural representation using CAD, parametric design, and digital fabrication. With respect to line-drawings, architecture students seem to be more distant from an understanding of line weights and line types due to their dependence on computers. With respect to renderings, a higher and higher number of architecture students seem to solely rely on rendering engines rather than using composite methods.

Although it is wonderful for architecture students and beginning professionals to embrace computer-based technology, it is important not to dismiss the "conventional" set of analog methods and tools we have in our arsenal. In this respect, it might be beneficial to take a look at the points of discussion that are common among practitioners, academics, as well as practitioners who also teach in adjunct positions in architecture schools. Therefore, what would be commonly proposed practices for architecture students and beginning professionals who are interested in digital and parametric methods and tools? Below are commonly discussed proposals by many practicing architects and academics.

The Common Practice of Keeping a Sketchbook. It is good practice to always keep a sketchbook for design ideas, observations, and notes. Although parametric and digital methods and tools provide many advantages, they do not provide the humane, tactile experience of recording thinking and elaborating on a mental process. Keeping an analog sketchbook not only allows one to keep a track record of experiences, but it also encourages and allows recording design ideas through sketches of observations and design ideas. Practicing sketchbook-based analog representation skills also contributes to manual precision and eye-hand coordination, which can help with other analog skills, such as physical model building for study and presentation models.

Printing CAD-based Line-drawings to Sketch Over and Get a Sense of Scale. Many academics and practitioners observe that when one stays in the CAD environment for a prolonged period of time, the sense of scale tends to disappear. Crucial building elements, such as walls, façade elements, and interior atria, seem to lose their three-dimensional meaning to be perceived merely as lines on computer software. Therefore, it is good practice to frequently print scaled drawings from CAD software using the appropriate line weights and line types. This will not only help with regaining a sense of scale of the spaces being designed, but also contribute time-saving steps to the design process, such as laying trace paper over line-drawings to reflect and develop more advanced iterations. At the same time, it will help the designer keep an eye on and fine tune the settings for line weights and line types.

Analog Preparation of Physical Study Model Parts to Save Time. In many architecture schools, it is not uncommon to witness architecture students trying to laser cut or 3D print simple, rectilinear model pieces. Although digital fabrication tools have great advantages, they may not be offering the best solution when time is limited and pieces that need to be fabricated can easily be prepared manually. This is especially the case when study models are considered. Study models, as the name implies, are meant to be draft models that will help design development through exploration and experimentation. In such cases, quickly prepared analog pieces can offer great time-saving solutions. Instead of waiting in line to use a laser cutter or waiting for a 3D printer to print simple parts, using analog techniques to build study models saves time. This is another reason for architecture students and beginning professionals not to lose connection with time-tested design tools and methods.

Use of Composite Methods for Line-drawings and Renderings. For most architecture students, relying on a single software package is convenient and time-efficient. Most CAD and rendering software, however, do not offer the diverse effects that can be achieved with analog methods, such as using multiple drawing tools to enhance the representation. For example, a combination of trace paper, pencils of various hardness and a few ink pigment liners can easily be combined to create a drawing that has depth and character. Relying on a single software package, on the other hand, can be limited when it comes to depth and character. Therefore, it is advisable to enhance drawing and renderings through superimposition and layering of outputs from multiple software packages. Just like a combination of linework and toning using pens, pencils, and markers, a superimposition of multiple outputs from different software packages can easily add depth and character to two- or three-dimensional drawings and renderings.

Design Development Using a Combination of Digital and Analog Methods to Maintain a Sense of Scale and Atmosphere. As we discussed in the previous sections, each analog, digital method, and tool offers distinct advantages. It is advisable to go back and forth between digital and analog tools so that one can maintain a sense of scale and atmosphere for the project. Printing to scale line-drawings and sketching over them before developing digital reiterations is distinctly advantageous for the design process and can contribute to the creation of a humane environment with the desired atmosphere.

10.3 PARAMETRIC FUTURES

Following decades of developments in computational design, parametric design, and digital fabrication, what are our routes for future development? Observing the developments within the last 20 years, it is not hard to anticipate that computational design, digital design tools, parametric design, and digital fabrication will continue to advance at an unprecedented pace. It would not be unreasonable to expect that architects and designers will increasingly use digital design tools, parametric design tools, and digital fabrication methods in their design processes. So, making the best of what parametric design can offer in architecture, what would our parametric futures look like?

10.3.1 Stronger Connections Between Design Disciplines and Basic Science

Given the data-intensive nature and close connections of parametric design methods with basic sciences, one can anticipate that architects and designers will need to strengthen the connections between their work and basic science. This indicates that beginning architects and professionals may need to have deeper understanding of sciences such as physics, mathematics, biology, and chemistry. In order to make good sense of analyses outcomes, beginning architects and professionals may also need to have a solid understanding of statistics. Conventionally, architects and design professionals have been less proficient when it comes to connections with basic science. The introduction of data-intense parametric methods in architecture may require architecture students, beginning architects and professionals to have stronger connections with basic science, so that they can make reasonable sense of data from scientific building analyses – either through post-occupancy evaluations of existing buildings or parametric interventions in building design as they utilize advanced data analysis.

Especially following World War II, many architects and designers have increasingly distanced themselves from empirical scientific data. The "Parametric Future" may require architects and designers to be more fluent with principles of basic science, so that they can take advantage of data-intensive parametric methods to advance their design proposals – not only for increasing quantitative environmental performance, but also to increase the desired experiential quality of design proposals.

10.3.2 Key Skills Remain Crucial

Although we have been experiencing a proliferation of computational design, parametric design, and digital fabrication methods in architecture, the key skills in architectural design processes remain crucial. Observation and imagination-based sketching, hand-drawing, tactile material-based explorations, and real life, in-person experimentation still remain crucial foundations of idea generation in architectural design. Many skills and methods we have been exposed to, such as analog physical model building, sketching, and line-drawing remain essential in the architectural design process and will help architects and designers keep in close contact with issues of scale and spatial atmosphere. In this sense, it follows that analog design and representation skills will continue to contribute to the foundation of design processes, but computational design, parametric design, and digital fabrication methods will accompany analog design and representation skills with varying degrees of production.

10.3.3 Architects and Designers Mastering Data Management

Although architectural design processes tend to be heavily influenced by human intuition, we always remain connected to empirical data, whether it be environmental factors or spatial interrelationships or behavioral information or environmental performance. With digital fabrication methods expanding beyond model making and increasing labor costs, it is also likely that more and more building components will rely on being digitally fabricated. In this sense, it probably would not be out of line to anticipate that building design and construction will be more dependent on digital tools and methods.

Based on the latest developments as of year 2022, one can see that more and more architects and designers will need to master their data management skills in addition to more conventional architectural design and production skills. As we enter a world of advanced computerization of architectural design and production, one could argue that it would be a solid investment to expand digital and data management skills for beginning architecture students and professionals. At the end of the day, so far, the early years of the twenty-first century have been characterized by humanity's reliance on all sorts of data. At least within the foreseeable future, architects and designers will need to expand, develop, and master their data management skills.

10.3.4 Looking into the Future

We are still artists and craftspeople, and the pencil remains one of the most amazing technological developments that afford the use of so many ideation techniques and design avenues. So, let us move forward and make progress – not just relying on computers, but with our pencils, pens, markers, and tracing paper. We need to embrace the potential of our centuries-old methods and techniques while recognizing that progress also depends on new tools and novel ideas based on science and technology.

REFERENCES

Agresti, A., and Finlay, B. (2000). *Statistical Methods for the Social Sciences*. Upper Saddle River, NJ: Prentice Hall.

Amin, A. (1994). Post-Fordism: Models, Fantasies and Phantoms of Transition. In A. Amin (Ed.), *Post-Fordism: A Reader* (pp. 1–39). Hoboken, NJ: Blackwell Publishers.

Architecture. 2030 (n.d.). Action for Zero Carbon Buildings. Retrieved January 2022 from https://architecture2030.org.

Becker, J., and Weissenbacher, R. (2020). Fordism. In O. Kaltmeier, A. Tittor, D. Hawkins, and E. Rohland (Eds.), *The Routledge Handbook to the Political Economy and Governance of the Americas* (1st ed., pp. 113–118). London: Routledge.

Benedikt, M. L. (1979). To Take Hold of Space: Isovists and Isovist Fields. *Environment and Planning B: Planning and Design*, *6*, 47–65.

Block, P. (2016). Parametricism's Structural Congeniality. *Architectural Design*, *240*, 68–75.

Bolstad, P. (2019). *GIS Fundamentals: A First Text on Geographic Information Systems*. Hoboken, NJ: John Wiley & Sons.

Burry, M. (2016). Essential Precursors to the Parametricism Manifesto: Antoni Gaudi and Frei Otto. *Architectural Design*, *240*, 30–35.

Callister, W. D., and Rethwisch, D. G. (2019). *Materials Science and Engineering: An Introduction*. New York: Wiley.

Carpo, M. (2016). Parametric Notations: The Birth of the Non-Standard. *Architectural Design*, *240*, 24–29.

Catmull, E., and Clark, J. (1978). Recursively Generated B-Spline Surfaces on Arbitrary Topological Meshes. *Computer Aided Design*, *10*, (6), 350–355.

Cross, N. (1982). *Designerly Ways of Knowing*. London: Springer.

Cruz, T. (2015). The Architecture of Neoliberalism. In M. Poole and M. Shvartzberg (Eds.), *The Politics of Parametricism: Digital Technologies in Architecture* (1st ed., pp. 189–199). London, New York: Bloomsbury.

Deamer, P. (2015). Parametric Schrizophrenia. In M. Poole and M. Shvartzberg (Eds.), *The Politics of Parametricism: Digital Technologies in Architecture* (1st ed., pp. 178–188). London, New York: Bloomsbury.

Driscoll, M. (2013). *Model Making for Architects*. Marlborough: The Crowood Press Ltd.

EnergyPlus. (n.d.). Retrieved March 2021, from *Energy Plus Web Site*: https://www.energyplus.net.

European Climate and Health Observatory. (n.d.). Retrieved 2021 from https://climate-adapt.eea.europa.eu/observatory

Frazer, J. (2016). Parametric Computation: History and Future. *Architectural Design*, *240*, 18–23.

Guzowski, M. (2018). *The Art of Architectural Daylighting*. London: Laurence King.

Hillier, B. (1996). *Space is the Machine: a Configurational Theory of Architecture*. Cambridge, New York: Cambridge University Press.

Hillier, B., and Hanson, J. (1984). *The Social Logic of Space*. Cambridge: Cambridge University Press.

Hillier, B., and Penn, A. (1991). Visible Colleges: Structure and Randomness in the Place of Discovery. *Science in Context*, *4*(1), 23–49.

Jabi, W. (2013). *Parametric Design for Architecture*. London: Laurence King Publishing.

Korn, G. A., and Korn, T. M. (2000). *Mathematical Handbook for Scientists and Engineers: Definitions, Theorems, and Formulas for Reference and Review*. New York: Dover Publications.

Kwok, A. G., and Grondzik, W. T. (2011). *The Green Studio Handbook: Environmental Strategies for Schematic Design*. New York: Architectural Press.

Ladybug Tools LLC. (n.d.). *Ladybug Tools*. https://www.ladybug.tools. Retrieved May 2021, from https://www.ladybug.tools.

Ladybug Tools LLC., Publications. (n.d.). *Ladybug Tools Publications*. Retrieved May 2021, from https://www.ladybug.tools/publication.html.

Lechner, N. (2015). *Heating, Cooling, Lighting: Sustainable Design Methods for Architects*. Hoboken, NJ: John Wiley & Sons.

Loutzenhiser, P.G., Manz, H., Felsmann, C., Strachan, P. A., Frank, T., and Maxwell,G. M. (2007). Empirical validation of models to compute solar irradiance on inclined surfaces for building energy simulation. *Solar Energy, 81*, 254–267.

Makstutis, G. (2018). *Design Processes in Architecture: From Concept to Completion.* London: Laurence King.

Murray, S. (2009). *Contemporary Curtain Wall Architecture.* New York: Princeton Architectural Press.

National Oceanic and Atmospheric Administration's National Weather Service (n.d.). Retrieved 2021 from https://w1.weather.gov

Olgyay, V. (1963). *Design with Climate: Bioclimatic Approach to Architectural Regionalism.* Princeton, NJ: Princeton University Press.

Otto, F., and Rasch, B. (1995). Finding Form: On the Way to an Architecture of the Minimal. In Schanz, S. (Ed.), Frei Otto, Bodo Rasch : finding form : towards an architecture of the minimal: the Werkbund shows Frei Otto, Frei Otto shows Bodo Rasch : exhibition in the Villa Stuck, Munich, on the occasion of the award of the 1992 Deutscher Werkbund Bayern prize to Frei Otto and Bodo Rasch (Edition Axel Menges, pp. 13–14). Stuttgart: Deutscher Werkbund Bayern, Frei Otto and Bodo Rasch.

Oxman, R. (2007). Digital Architecture as a Challenge for Design Pedagogy: Theory, Knowledge, Models and Medium. *Design Studies, 29*, 99–120.

Oxman, R. (2017). Thinking Difference: Theories and Models of Parametric Design Thinking. *Design Studies, 52*, 4–39.

Oxman, R., and Oxman, R. (2014). Introduction: Vitruvius Digitalis. In R. Oxman and R. Oxman (Eds.), *Theories of the Digital in Architecture* (1st ed., pp. 1–9). London: Routledge.

Palmer, J. M., and Chapman, K. S. (2000). Direct Calculation of Mean Radiant Temperature Using Radiant Intensities. *ASHRAE Transactions, 106* (Part 1), DA-00-03-2.

Penn A., Desyllas, J., and Vaughan, L. (1999). The Space of Innovation: Interaction and Communication in the Work Environment. *Environment and Planning B: Planning and Design, 26*, 193–218.

Poole, M., and Shvartzberg, M. (2015). Introduction. In M. Poole and M. Shvartzberg (Eds.), *The Politics of Parametricism: Digital Technologies in Architecture* (1st ed., pp. 1–18). London, New York: Bloomsbury.

Pressman, A. (2012). *Designing Architecture: The Elements of the Process.* New York: Routledge.

Radford, A., and Gero, J. (1988). *Design Optimization in Architecture, Building and Construction.* New York: Van Nostrand Reinhold.

Rutten, D. (2010). Evolutionary Principles applied to Problem Solving. Retrieved 2022 from https://www.grasshopper3d.com/profiles/blogs/evolutionary-principles

Sadeghipour R. M., and Pak, M. (2013). Ladybug: A Parametric Environmental Plugin for Grasshopper to Help Designers Create an Environmentally-conscious Design. In Proceedings of the 13th International IBPSA Conference Held in Lyon, France, Aug 25–30th.

Schon, D. A. (1983). *The Reflective Practitioner: How Professionals Think in Action.* New York: Basic Books.

Schumacher, P. (2008). Parametricism as Style - Parametricist Manifesto. Presented and discussed at the Dark Side Club, 11th Architecture Biennale, Venice, 2008. Retrieved January 2021 on http://www.patrikschumacher.com.

Schumacher, P. (2016). Parametricism 2.0: Gearing Up to Impact the Global Built Environment. *Architectural Design, 240*, 9–17.

Steinberg, S. L., and Steinberg, S. J. (2015). *GIS Research Methods: Incorporating Spatial Perspectives.* Redlands: ESRI Press.

Tait, J. (2020). *The Architecture Concept Book.* London: Thames & Hudson.

Tedeschi, A. (2014). Algorithms-aided Design: Parametric Strategies using Grasshopper. Brienza (Potenza): Le Penseur Publisher.

Thomas, G. B., Hass, J., Heil, C., and Weir, M. D. (2018). *Thomas' Calculus* (14th ed.). New York: Pearson.

Toker, U. (2006). Workspaces for Knowledge Generation: Facilitating Innovation in University Research Centers. *Journal of Architectural and Planning Research, 23*(3), 181–199.

Toker, U., and Gray, D. O. (2008). Innovation Spaces: Workspace Planning and Innovation in U.S. University Research Centers. *Research Policy, 37*, 309–329.

Turner, A., Doxa, O'Sullivan, and Penn, A. (2001). From Isovists to Visibility Graphs: A Methodology for the Analysis of Architectural Space. *Environment and Planning B: Planning and Design*, *28*, 103–121.
Van Doesburg, T. (1970). Towards a Plastic Architecture. In U. Conrads (Ed.), *Programs and Manifestoes on 20th-Century Architecture* (1st ed., pp. 78–80). Cambridge, MA: The MIT Press.
Vukorep, I., and Kotov, A. (2021). Machine Learning in Architecture: An Overview of Existing Tools. In As, I. and Basu, P. (Eds.), *The Routledge Companion to Artificial Intelligence in Architecture*. New York: Routledge.
White, E. T. (1983). *Site Analysis: Diagramming Information for Architectural Design*. Tucson, AZ: Architectural Media.
Woodbury, R. (2010). *Elements of Parametric Design*. London, New York: Routledge.
Yuan, P. (2016). Parametric Regionalism. *Architectural Design*, *240*, 92–99.

INDEX

3D analog modeling 48–49
3D printing 19, 175, 177; fused deposition modeling (FDM) 178; generating supports 179, 180; materials 178; preparing CAD geometry 178; slicer software 178–179; *see also* fused deposition modeling (FDM)

additive operations 166; 3D printing 175, 177–180
Alberti, L. B. 11
algorithms 10–12, 15, 84; Catmull-Clark Subdivision 58–60, 62–63; HypE 132; Loop 63; SPEA-2 132
anisotropic sky model 29
annealing solver 125, 126
apertures 87, 161
architectural concept 48
architectural design 2; algorithms 11, 15; daylight 160, 161; and energy consumption 147–148; "-isms" 13; key skills 193; mesh geometries 63; phases of 9; spatial daylight autonomy (SDA) 161; *see also* conceptual and preliminary development; site analysis
architectural research: operationalization 17–18; parametric methods 17–18
Architecture 2030 148
archival research 20, 21
area component 41
avant-garde movements 13–15

Babbage, C. 11
Bartlett School of Architecture 83
basic even subdivision of surfaces 44, 45
Benedikt, M. L. 37
Bezier function 90, 91
Block, P. 16
Boolean Toggle component 58–59
Boundary Representations (Breps) 92, 172, 174
boundary surfaces command 65
bounds component 47
BoxMorph component 115
Brep join component 53
Burry, M. 11, 14, 16

Carpo, M. 12, 13
carrier 83, 84
Cartesian coordinate system 44
Catmull-Clark Subdivision component 58–60, 62–63
chain-linking, components 8–9
Circle CNR component 96
climate change: Architecture 2030 148; greenhouse gases (GHG) 147
cognitive models of design thinking 4
commands 2; boundary surfaces 65; DupBorder 169; sweep 51; UnrollSrf 169
complex geometries, subdividing, repetition and paneling approaches 114, 115
complex surfaces: repeating modular units on 115, 118; subdividing 91–92
components: area 41; Boolean Toggle 58–59; bounds 47; BoxMorph 115; Brep join 53; Catmull-Clark Subdivision 58–59; chain-linking 8–9; Circle CNR 96; Construct Domain 143; CrvCP 97; custom preview 47; DeBrep 53, 92, 118; Deconstruct Brep 172; deconstruct domain 47; Delauney Mesh 63; Dist 97; Divide Domain 2 44, 45, 90, 91; Download EPW 160; EPWMap 23; EvalSrf 97; evaluate surface 45, 130; Graph Mapper 53, 87, 89–91; Grasshopper 7, 8; Grasshopper, coordinated interrelationships 8–9; HB All-Air HVAC 153; HB Aperture 153, 155, 161; HB Apply Room Schedules 153; HB ConstructionSet 151; HB Hourly Plot 155; HB Intersect Solids 152; HB Label Surfaces 155; HB Model 163; HB Model to OSM 151, 152; HB Read Room Energy Result 155; HB Simulation Parameter 155; HB Solve Adjacency 152, 153; HB Visualize by Type 152; Image Sampler 98, 101, 102; ImportEPW 25; Isotrim 44, 45; Isovist 39, 76, 80–81, 122; LB Analysis Period 32, 133; LB Calculate HOY 25; LB ColRange 24; LB Directional Solar Irradiance 29; LB DirectSunHours 28; LB Direct Sun Hours 126, 128, 137; LB Download Weather 135; LB EPWMap 135; LB Hourly Plot 32; LB Incident Radiation 30; LB LegendPar 24; LB Outdoor Solar MRT 32, 36; LB Relative Humidity from Dew Point 32; LB Solar Body Parameters 32; LB Sunpath 25, 136; LB UTCI 36; LB View Percent 41, 69; LB Visibility Percent 130, 143; list item 172; Mesh

56; Mesh Brep 56, 59; Mesh Surface 63; Mesh Thicken 59; multiplication 53; orient direction 118; point 109; polyline 39, 41, 76; PtsSrfDist 92; rectangle 143; ReMap 98; repeat data 53; reverse list 24; SelClosedPolysrf 178; series 56; Simple Mesh 56; solid union 65; SrfCP 97, 102; SrfSplit 97; sweep 1 49; sweep 2 49, 51; WindRose 35
computational models of design thinking 4–5
computer-aided design (CAD) 2, 4–5, 191, 192; 3D modeling 49; preparing geometry for FDM 3D printing 178; *see also* digital fabrication; models and model making; Rhinoceros
computer numeric controlled (CNC) milling 180–183
"concept" 48
conceptual and preliminary development 48; meshes 58–60, 62–63; multipoint isovist analysis for potential retail location 63–66; NURBS 49, 51, 53, 56; *see also* Non-Uniform Rational B-Splines (NURBS); view percent analysis 67–69, 71, 73, 74
Construct Domain component 143
contemporary parametric design 11–13
convex spaces 83
critical feedback 9
Cross, N. 4
Cruz, T. 14, 16; "The Informal Algorithm Manifesto" 15
CrvCP component 97
curves 49; *see also* surface(s)
custom preview component 47
cutting operations 166; interlocking slices technique 174; laser cutting 168, 169; plasma cutting 171–172; rapid contouring 172; waterjet cutting 172

data management 194
daylight 93; autonomy 161; spatial daylight autonomy (SDA) 161; *see also* direct sun hours analysis of building components
Deamer, P. 15–17
DeBrep component 53, 92, 118
decision-making 11; empirical approaches 66; evolutionary solvers 119, 131; *see also* evolutionary solvers
Deconstruct Brep component 172
deconstruct domain component 47
Delauney Mesh component 63
design thinking 4; cognitive models 4; computational models 4–5; parametric models 5, 6; *see also* parametric design
deterritorialization of the architectural profession 16
Diamond tool 114, 115
Digital Architectural Design (DAD) 5
digital fabrication 18–19; additive operations 166; advances in 190–191; cutting operations 166, 168, 169, 171, 172, 174; interlocking slices technique 174; numbering parts 174; subtractive operations 166–167, 180–183; tools 168; *see also* additive operations; cutting operations; models and model making; subtractive operations
digital parametricism 12–13
direct sun hours analysis of building components 93–94, 128; orientation versus 126, 128; preliminary interpretations 94, 96
Disney Concert Hall 5
Dist component 97
Divide Domain 2 component 44, 45, 90, 91
domain 90
Download EPW component 160
Driscoll, M. 166
dry bulb temperature 24
DupBorder command 169

empirical approaches 189–190; data management 194; decision-making 66
energy consumption 149; architectural design and 147–148; simulation calculations 151, 152; surface area to volume ratio (SA/V) 149
energy use intensity (EUI) 148–149; basic simulation 149, 151, 152; louver system effects 157, 158; multiple building use zone simulation 152, 153, 155, 157; SA/V and 158–160
EnergyPlus 22–23
entourage 185, 186
environment-related analysis 21–22; accessing local climate data 22–23; dry bulb temperature 24; performance indicators 147, 165; psychometric chart 24; relative humidity 24; solar conditions 24–25, 28–31; *see also* solar conditions; *see also* direct sun hours analysis of building components; energy use intensity (EUI); skin systems; spatial daylight autonomy (SDA)
EvalSrf component 97
evaluate surface component 45, 130
evolutionary solvers 18, 119, 130, 187, 189–190; advantages and disadvantages 121, 122; Galapagos 120; genes 120; genome 119–121; identifying the building orientation allowing access to desired views 128–130; identifying the highest visibility point for a commercial space 130, 131; identifying the orientation of workspaces to minimize glare 126, 128; multi-objective optimization 131–133, 135–137, 139–141, 143, 146; single-object optimization 122, 124, 125; solution process 120, 121; *see also* Galapagos; Octopus
extrude component, Grasshopper 7, 8

façades 53, 87; representing 185
foot-candle 161
Fordism 13
form-driven scripting 15
form exploration: gradual rotation 53, 56; loft 49; meshes 56, 58–60, 62–63; repeating data 53; surface from points 51, 53; sweep 49, 51
Frazer, J. 11, 14
functions 10, 89; domain 90; Graph Mapper and 90, 91

fused deposition modeling (FDM) 177; in the architectural design process 180; generating supports 179, 180; preparing CAD geometry 178

Galapagos 120; annealing solver option 125, 126; direct sun hours calculation 128; Editor 122, 124; multi-objective optimization 131–133, 135; Reinstate button 125; single-object optimization 122, 124, 125; Start Solver button 124, 125
Gaudi, A. 11
Gehry, F. 5
generative parametric modeling 5
genome 121; fitness 120, 122
geographical information systems (GIS) 20–21
geometry(ies) 10, 25, 28; gradual rotation 53, 55; manipulating 7; Mesh 56, 58–60, 62–63; NURBS 48, 49, 51, 53, 56; preparing for 3D printing 178–180; *see also* Non-Uniform Rational B-Splines (NURBS)
Gero, J. 131
glare 126, 128, 161; *see also* direct sun hours analysis of building components
Google Earth 21
Google Maps 21
gradual rotation 53, 56
Graph Mapper component 53, 87, 89–91
graphs, justified permeability 84
Grasshopper 6; accessing local climate data 22–23; area component 41; Boundary Representations (Breps) 92; bounds component 47; BoxMorph component 115; Circle CNR component 96; components 7, 8; components, coordinated interrelationships 8–9; CrvCP component 97; "curve" button 53; custom preview component 47; DeBrep component 92, 118; deconstruct domain component 47; Delauney Mesh component 63; Dist component 97; Divide Domain 2 component 44, 45, 90, 91; EnergyPlus Weather File (EPW) 23; environment-related analysis 22; EPWMap component 23; EvalSrf component 97; evaluate surface component 45; "extrude" component 7, 8; Graph Mapper component 53, 87, 89–91; Image Sampler component 98, 101, 102; ImportEPW component 23, 25; Isotrim component 44, 45; Isovist component 39, 63–66, 76, 80–81; Ladybug Tools 21, 22; LB Color Range component 28–29; LB ColRange component 24; LB DirectSunHours component 28; LB LegendPar component 24; LB Psychometric Chart 24; Lunchbox plug-in 109; Mesh Brep component 56, 59; Mesh component 56; Mesh Surface component 63; mesh thicken component 59; Minkowski model 82, 83; numbering parts 174; Orient Direction component 118; Paneling Tools plug-in 92; perforated screen system design 96, 98, 101–104, 106–109; plug-ins 22; Point component 109; relationships between geometry and geometric representations 6, 7; ReMap component 98; repeat data component 53; reverse list component 24; scale component 9; series component 56; Simple Mesh component 56; solid union component 65; space syntax method 85; sphere component 8, 9; SrfCP component 97, 102; SrfSplit component 97; surface component 7; view percent analysis 67–69, 71; *see also* commands; components; digital fabrication; Honeybee; Honeybee Energy, energy simulation calculations; Ladybug Tools; models and model making
greenhouse gases (GHG) 147
Grondzik, W. T. 22

Hansen, J. 83
HB All-Air HVAC component 153
HB Aperture component 153, 155, 161
HB ConstructionSet component 151
HB Hourly Plot component 155
HB Intersect Solids component 152
HB Label Surfaces component 155
HB Model component 163
HB Model to OSM component 151, 152
HB Read Room Energy Result component 155
HB Simulation Parameter component 155
HB Solve Adjacency component 152, 153
HB Visualize by Type component 152
heating, ventilation, and air conditioning (HVAC): energy use intensity (EUI) calculation 152, 153, 155, 157
Hillier, B. 83
Honeybee 160; multiple building use zone simulation 152, 153, 155, 157; SDA analysis and calculations 161, 163; use zone 149, 151
Honeybee Energy, energy simulation calculations 151
Honeybee Radiance 161
hoys 25
HypE algorithm 132

illuminance 29
Image Sampler component 98, 101, 102
ImportEPW component 23, 25
incident radiation 29–31
Industrial Revolution 12, 87
"Informal Algorithm Manifesto" 15
information gathering 9
integration value 84–85
interiors: interspatial visibility analysis 76, 80–81; two-dimensional visibility analysis 75–76
interlocking slices 174
interspatial visibility analysis 76, 80–81
interviews 20, 21
Isotrim component 44, 45
isotropic sky model 29
isovist 36–39, 41; mean value calculation 76; multipoint analysis 63–66
Isovist component 1, 39, 122
Issa, R. 92

Jabi, W., *Parametric Design for Architecture* 10
justified permeability graph 84

knowledge-based economy 13
Kwok, A. G. 22

Ladybug Tools 21, 22, 67, 189; energy consumption, calculation and analysis 149; measuring building environmental performance 165; WindRose component 35
laser cutting 168, 169; presentation models 169, 171, 172; study models 169
LB Analysis Period component 32, 133
LB Calculate HOY component 25
LB ColRange component 24
LB Directional Solar Irradiance component 29
LB DirectSunHours component 28
LB Direct Sun Hours component 126, 128, 137
LB Download Weather component 135
LB EPWMap component 135
LB Hourly Plot component 32
LB Incident Radiation component 30
LB LegendPar component 24
LB Outdoor Solar MRT component 32, 36
LB Relative Humidity from Dew Point component 32
LB Solar Body Parameters component 32
LB Sunpath component 25, 136
LB UTCI component 36
LB View Percent component 41, 69, 71
LB Visibility Percent component 130, 143
line-drawings 192
List Item component 172
lofting 49, 62
Loop algorithm 63
louver systems 18, 96; effect on EUI values 157, 158; spatial daylight autonomy (SDA) 163
Lovelace, A. 11
Lunchbox plug-in 92, 109; Diamond tool 114, 115
lux 161

Mackey, C. 22
Makstutis, G. 9
mass production 12, 13; façades 87
materials: 3D printing 178; site model 184, 185
mathematical functions *see* functions
mean radiant temperature 32
median 73, 74
Mesh Brep component 56, 59
Mesh component 56
meshes 56, 188; multi-part 59, 60, 62–63; quadrangular 58–59; triangular 63
Mesh Surface component 63
mesh thicken component 59
Miller, N. 92
Minkowski model 81, 83
models and model making 166; entourage 185, 186; interlocking slices technique 174; numbering parts 174; parametric methods 166; presentation 166; representing the site 184; representing the structural system and slabs 184, 185; representing vertical circulation elements 185; scaling operations 167; study/sketch 166, 191; tools 167, 168
modules 87, 115
Moretti, L. 11
multi-objective optimization, evolutionary solvers 131–132; examples 135–137, 139–141, 143, 146; interpreting findings 133, 135
multi-part mesh 59, 60, 62–63
multiplication component 53
multipoint isovist analysis 63–66

naked edge 58
natural selection 120
network economy 13
Non-Uniform Rational B-Splines (NURBS) 48, 188; converting to mesh geometries 56, 58; gradual rotation 53, 56; loft 49; repeating data 53; surface from points 51, 53; sweep 1 49; sweep 2 51
numbering parts 174

Octopus 120, 132; multi-objective optimization 137, 139–141, 143, 146; optimization procedure 133
Olgyay, V. 24
Open Studio Model (OSM) 151
orientation: building 128–130, 135–137, 139, 140; workspace 126, 128
Orient Direction component 118
Otto, F. 11
outdoor mean radiant temperature (OMRT) 32
Oxman, R. 4, 5

paneling, subdividing complex geometries 114, 115
Paneling Tools plug-in 92, 188
paper-based medium, cognitive models of design thinking 4
parameters 10
parametric design 2, 4–6, 14, 16; algorithmic thinking 10; and architectural research 17–18; CAD interface 2–3; contemporary 11–13; definitions 10; developments 18–19; "fashionable" 191; Gaudi 11; generative modeling 5; parametric interface 2–3; performance-based modeling 5, 6; screen systems 96–98, 101–104, 106–109; *see also* evolutionary solvers
"Parametricism as Style-Parametricist Manifesto" 13–16
parametric methods 2, 9; architectural research and 17–18; contributions in the architectural design process 187–191; cutting operations 172, 174; direct sun hours analysis of building components 93–94; Graph Mapper 87, 89; model making 166; script 1; skin system 86
parametric thinking 1, 2, 6, 9, 11; *see also* design thinking
Pareto optimization 131–132
perforated screen system, designing: using a line as control geometry 96–98;

using number remapping and control geometries 98; using surface population 102–104, 106–109; using the Image Sampler 98, 101, 102
performance-based parametric modeling 5, 6
Piacentino, G. 58
plasma cutting 171–172
plug-ins 5, 22, 85; Galapagos 122, 124, 125; Honeybee 149; Honeybee Energy 149; Honeyee Radiance 161; Lunchbox 92, 109; Paneling Tools 92, 188; subdividing complex surfaces 92; Weaverbird 58; *see also* Galapagos; Honeybee; Ladybug Tools
Point component 109
"Politics of Parametricism, The: Digital Technologies and the Future(s) of Sociality" 14
polyline component 39, 41, 76
Poole, M. 14
populating complex surfaces, repeating modular units on complex surfaces 115, 118
post-Fordism 13, 14
presentation models 166; laser cutting 169, 171, 172
Pressman, A. 9
problem definition 9
propositions 119–120; *see also* evolutionary solvers
prototyping 18–19
psychometric chart 24
PtsSrfDist component 92

quadrangular meshes 58–59

Radford, A. 131
radiation 32
rapid contouring 172
Rasch, B. 11
Rectangle component 143
relative humidity 24, 32
ReMap component 98
Renaissance, the 12
repeating data 53
repetition approaches: repeating modular units on complex surfaces 115; subdividing complex geometries 114, 115; subdividing surfaces 109, 114
research 17; archival 20, 21
reverse list component 24
Revit 120
Rhinoceros 6, 120; command component structure 7, 8; laser cutting operations for study models 169; lofting 49, 62; Paneling Tools plug-in 92; psychometric chart 24; rapid contouring 172; relationships between geometry and geometric representations 6, 7; sweep command 49, 51; *see also* commands; components
rotation, gradual 53, 56
Roudsari, M. S. 22
Rutten, D. 120–122, 124

scale component 9
scaling operations 167, 192, 193; entourage 185, 186
schematic design 9
schizophrenia 15–16
Schön, D. A. 4
Schumacher, P. "Parametricism as Style-Parametricist Manifesto" 13–14, 16
science, strengthening connection with 193
screen system design: using a line as control geometry 96–98; using number remapping and control geometries 98; using surface population 102–104, 106–109; using the Image Sampler 98, 101, 102
scripts 1, 8, 109; form-driven 15
SelClosedPolysrf component 178
selective laser sintering (SLS) 177–178
series component 56
Shvartzberg, M. 14
Simple Mesh component 56
single-object optimization, evolutionary solvers 122, 124, 125, 135
site analysis 20; archival research 20; contextual information 21; environmental information 21–22; environment-related analysis using Grasshopper 22; geographical information systems (GIS) 20–21; interviews 20, 21; physical conditions 21; site visits 20–21; slope 41, 44, 45, 47; *see also* slope; solar conditions 24–25, 28–31; *see also* solar conditions; thermal comfort 31–32, 34–36; using findings to inform conceptual development 47; visibility analysis 36–39, 41; *see also* visibility analysis
sketchbooks 192
skin systems 109, 187; direct sun hours analysis of building components 93–94, 96–98, 101–104, 106–109; energy use intensity (EUI) 157, 158; parametric methods 86; repeating modular units on complex surfaces 115; subdividing complex geometries, repetition and paneling approaches 114, 115; subdividing complex surfaces 91–92; surface subdivision, repetition and paneling approaches 109, 110, 114; uneven subdivision of surfaces 87, 89–91
sky models, isotropic 29
slicer software 178–179
slope 41, 44; analyzing and visualizing a site's slope condition 45, 47; basic even subdivision of surfaces 44, 45
software: CNC milling 182; geographical information systems (GIS) 20–21; Grasshopper 6; plug-ins 22; Rhinoceros 6; slicer 178–179; third-party 189
solar conditions 24–25; direct sun hours and shadows analysis 25, 28–29; incident radiation 29–31; solar irradiance and illuminance 29; sun path 25
solar irradiance 29
solid union component 65
solution process, evolutionary solvers 120, 121
space syntax method: carrier 83, 84; convex spaces 83; integration value 84–85; justified permeability graph 84

spatial daylight autonomy (SDA) 161; with a louver system 163
spatial organization 75, 187; space syntax method 83–85
SPEA-2 algorithm 132
sphere component 8, 9
SrfCP component 97, 102
SrfSplit component 97
standard deviation 73, 74
stereolithography (SLA) 177–178
study/sketch models 166, 191; analog preparation 192; laser cutting 169
subdivision of surfaces 44, 45, 87; complex 91–92; repetition and paneling approaches 109, 110, 114; uneven 87, 89–91; using plug-ins 92
Subdivision Surface Modeling (SubD)-based geometries 56; *see also* meshes
subtractive operations 166–167; computer numeric controlled (CNC) milling 180–183
sun path 25
surface(s): complex, subdividing 91–92; creating from points 51, 53; loft 49; naked edge 58; population 102–104, 106–109; subdivision 44, 45
surface area to volume ratio (SA/V) 149; EUI and 158–160
surface component 7
sweep 1 component 49
sweep 2 component 49, 51
sweep command 49, 51
systems thinking 15

Tedeschi, A. 10, 59
temperature, mean radiant 32; *see also* environment-related analysis
thermal comfort 36; mean radiant temperature 32; relative humidity 32; Universal Thermal Climate Index (UTCI) 36; wind 34–35
third-party software 189
T-node 59
tools: analog 192, 193; Diamond 114, 115; digital fabrication 167, 168; Ladybug Tools 21, 22, 67; models and model making 167, 168; Zero Tool 148; *see also* commands; components; plug-ins
topography models, rapid contouring 172
triangular meshes 63
two-dimensional visibility analysis 75–76

uneven subdivision of surfaces 91
Universal Thermal Climate Index (UTCI) 36
UnrollSrf command 169
use cases, evolutionary solvers: identifying the building orientation allowing access to desired views 128–130; identifying the highest visibility point for a commercial space 130, 131; identifying the orientation of workspaces to minimize glare 126, 128; optimizing building orientation to minimize energy consumption 135–137, 139, 140; optimizing views and square footage to increase real estate value 140, 141, 143, 146
use zone: Honeybee 149, 151; multiple building 152, 153, 155, 157

Van Doesburg, T., *Towards a Plastic Architecture* 11
variables 10
Vierlinger, R. 132
view percent analysis: for commercial building location 67–69, 71; for hotel building location 71, 73, 74
visibility analysis 75; identifying highest visibility point 130, 131; interspatial 76, 80–81; isovist 36–39, 41; Minkowski model 81–83; multipoint isovist 63–66; two-dimensional 75–76; visibility percent analysis 41
visualizations: architectural concept 48–49; energy use intensity (EUI) 155; glare 126, 128; wind rose 35; *see also* models and model making
Vitruvius 11

waterjet cutting 172
weather conditions, analyzing 23; *see also* environment-related analysis
Weaverbird 58
wind 34; rose 35
WindRose component 35
Woodbury, R. 3

Yuan, P. 16

Zero Tool 148